D1437377

BRITAIN'S 500
BEST PUBS

First published in 2000 by Carlton Books Limited

10 9 8 7 6 5 4 3 2 1

A CIP catalogue record for this book is available from the British Library
ISBN 1 85868 826 4

Project editor: Martin Corteel
Project art direction: Brian Flynn
Production: Sarah Corteel
Picture manager: Lorna Ainger
Editors: Peter Arnold and David Ballheimer
Designed by Simon Mercer
Maps by Moraig Terrott

Carlton Books Limited
20 Mortimer Street
London W1N 7RD

Printed and bound in Italy

Crown Liquor Saloon, Belfast

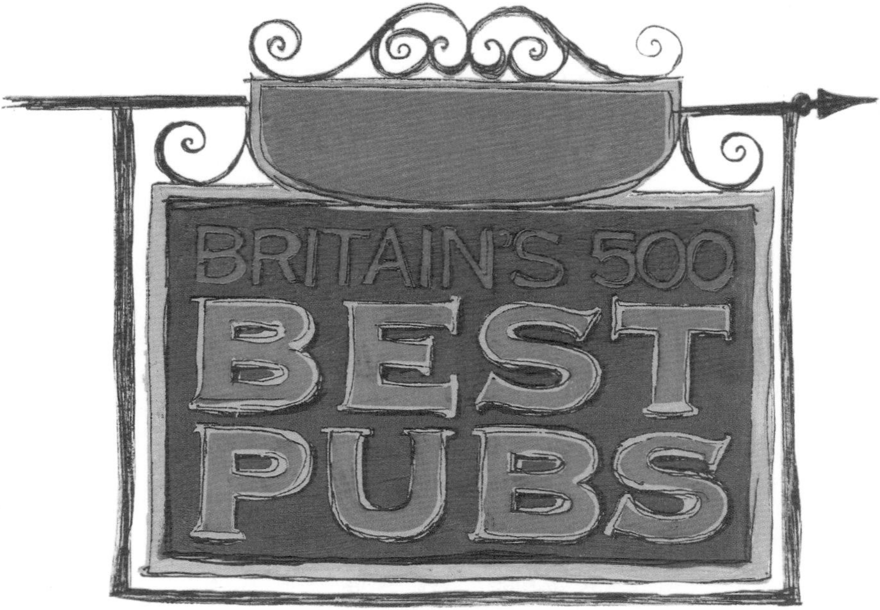

BRITAIN'S 500 BEST PUBS

Roger Protz

With illustrations by Louise Wilde

Acknowledgements

Special thanks to Andrew Purvis, my first editor at *The Observer* "*Life*" magazine, for his help and encouragement.

Thanks to Barrie and Carolyn Pepper for help with the Yorkshire pubs walk; and to Ted Bruning, who solved a small crisis near Sandy in Bedfordshire.

Extra special thanks to Colin Dexter, for his advice on the best Inspector Morse pubs, and for all the pleasure his novels have given over the years.

Sources and further reading

Good Beer Guide *(Camra Books)*
Good Pub Guide *(Ebury Press)*
Which? Guide to Country Pubs *(Which? Books)*
Good Pub Food by Susan Nowak *(Camra Books)*
Pubs for Familes by David Perrott *(Camra Books)*
Room At An Inn by Jill Adam *(Camra Books)*
Best Pubs & Inns *(AA)*
Historic Pubs of London by Ted Bruning *(Prion)*
English Country Inns by John Timpson *(Headline)*
The Village Pub by Roger Protz and Homer Sykes *(Weidenfeld & Nicolson)*
Country Ales and Breweries by Roger Protz and Steve Sharples *(Weidenfeld & Nicolson)*
Walking in Britain *(Lonely Planet)*
A Dictionary of Pub Names by Leslie Dunkling and Gordon Wright *(Routledge)*

The Campaign for Real Ale can be contacted at 230 Hatfield Road, St Albans, Herts AL1 4LW. Phone 01727 867201. E-mail: CAMRA@CAMRA.org.uk. Membership costs £14 a year.

Contents

Introduction

Writing in *The Observer*'s "Life" magazine in February 2000, Euan Ferguson described me as the "Luckiest Journalist in the World". The description is based on his assumption that I spend most of my life sitting in pubs, drinking good ale, and swiftly penning a weekly column for the same magazine. Chance, as they say, would be a fine thing.

I'm not Charles Dickens. I cannot match the size or quality of his output; neither can I consume large amounts of alcohol and remain in a fit state to put fingers to keyboard. In common with Euan Ferguson and most modern journalists, most of my working life is spent in front of a computer screen. I have devoted some 25 years to writing about good beer and good pubs. This work has been distilled into several books and the editorship of the Campaign for Real Ale's *Good Beer Guide*, where I am currently on my second stint. The Camra guide is a pub guide, with around 5,000 entries. I have, therefore, a large and regularly updated database of the country's best pubs, to which I frequently refer.

It would be a lie to claim that I never set foot in licensed premises. I frequent pubs, though neither daily nor several a day, as Mr Ferguson seems to think. I have "dry" days. But there is no greater delight than returning to a pub I haven't visited for many years and finding that it has escaped closure or a visit from a brewery "refurbishment team" who have turned it into a youth leisure experience, sans hand-pumps, sans food and deluged with raucous music that makes conversation impossible. There's a second delight: finding a pub I haven't been to before and immediately falling in love with that indefinable joy, atmosphere. The architecture is pleasing to the eye, the welcome is warm, and food and drink are impeccable. In the course of writing my column, the genesis for this book, I came across the Olde Gate Inn at Brassington, in Derbyshire's Peak District. It earns special mention in this book as the inn where I would be happy to hang my jug on a beam and settle down to happy retirement.

So this book is the result of years of research and travel. Even where I couldn't personally visit a particular pub afresh, the information here is the result of phone calls with licensees, faxes from them containing history, beer lists and menus, and wherever possible independent observations from fellow beer writers and Camra members. It is presented in a user-friendly fashion, broken down into sections that will immediately appeal to people with particular interests, be it bird watching or cycling. I have attempted a snap shot of the British pub at the start of a new Millennium, an institution buried deep in the history, culture and social life of the people, and still giving daily pleasure to millions despite intense competition from other parts of the leisure industry.

With only a few exceptions, the pubs in the book sell a style of beer unique to these islands. Brewers call it "cask conditioned", consumers prefer the term "real ale". This type of beer leaves the brewery in unfinished form and reaches maturity in casks in pub cellars and relies on the skill of publicans to know when best to tap each cask and pull the rich, flavour-filled pints. But cask ale is under intense pressure from Britain's handful of giant national brewers, who prefer the quick profits from ersatz lagers and bland, ice-cold "cream-flow" keg ales delivered to the bar by heavy gas pressure. I make no apology for dedicating this book not just to the British pub but also to the best type of beer available in it.

There is also a heavy emphasis on food. "Foodie" writers, with the honourable exception of Matthew Fort in The Guardian and Susan Nowak, editor of Camra's *Good Pub Food*, pay scant attention to what publicans put on customers' plates. But there has been an unsung revolution in the British pub. It is no longer synonymous with stale sandwiches, packet soup, instant whipped potato and vegetarian lasagne. Marvellous food is being served in pubs the length and breadth of the country, often cooked by chefs who have earned their spurs in restaurants and have accepted the challenge to prepare delicious but affordable meals for pub-goers. This book lists pubs that offer gourmet food; others may provide just excellent home-made soup or a good, honest ploughman's lunch with local cheese and a hunk of fresh bread. The imaginative way publicans and chefs cater for the rapidly-growing vegetarian market merits its own section; similarly the licensees who are meeting the demand for organic food, free from agri-chemicals. I hope the section on organic pubs may encourage brewers to produce beers with malt and hops free from farmers' sprays.

Whatever your fancy, be it an old coaching inn visited by Charles Dickens, a pub for jazz lovers, or keen horticulturists in search of roses as well as beer and food, or just an unspoilt old local peopled by ale lovers, there will be something within these pages for everyone to enjoy. And there's a bonus: in addition to Britain's best 500 pubs, I have also included some splendid bars I have encountered on my travels in Europe that offer the traditional beers of their homelands.

Good hunting. And good drinking.

Roger Protz
St Albans, February 2000

Great coaching inns

ANGEL & ROYAL

HIGH STREET, GRANTHAM, LINCOLNSHIRE (01476 565816)
Off A1

Named simply the Angel until 1866, this is one of the most important historic taverns in England. The land on which it stands was owned by the Knights Templar until they were suppressed in 1312, and there had been a hostelry on the site for at least a century before that. King John, a reluctant convert to democracy, rested there in 1209 and again in 1213 during his war with the barons. Richard III, that unfairly traduced monarch, stayed in the state room, the Chambre du Roi (now a dining room) where in 1483 he wrote to the Lord Chancellor in London, asking for the Great Seal to be sent to him so he could sign the death warrant for the treacherous Duke of Buckingham, who was leading a rebellion against him. The fact that several monarchs – Edward III and Edward VII were also visitors – stayed there suggests the inn may once have been part of a never-completed castle. In 1706, the landlord died leaving £2 a year in his will for a sermon to be preached every Christmas against drunkenness, a custom still observed (and breached) to this day. The inn was known as just the Angel until the visit in 1866 by Edward VII, then the Prince of Wales, when the "Royal" was added. A suggestion that the inn be called the Royal Angel was discreetly vetoed on the grounds that the prince might be royal but was no angel. The Angel had become a great coaching inn during the 18th century, serving the mail coaches that plied their trade between London, York and Scotland. The magnificent stone facade is covered in weather-beaten carvings and gargoyles. Above the great archway is a carving that reflects the inn's name, an angel holding a crown. To either side of the arch are carvings of Edward III and Queen Philippa, erected to mark their visit in the 14th century. The central oriel window was constructed at the same time. The Falcon Bar, to one side of the great arch, has a striking timbered ceiling, a stone fireplace and a stone-vaulted window. The Angel Bar, on the other side of the arch, has a massive inglenook, more beams and another vaulted window. On the first floor, the anglicised King's Room restaurant has a spiral staircase in one corner that leads up to a vantage point once manned by royal look-outs. It's claimed that tunnels once led from beneath the inn to the Market Square and to St Wulfram's Church, which has the sixth tallest spire in the country. There's a set of stocks in the courtyard, so don't forget to pay your bill.

The bar offers Cameron's Strongarm on hand-pump plus regular guest beers, including ales from local craft breweries. Food, lunchtime and evening, may include lobster bisque; sautéed mushrooms and prawns in garlic butter; feta and Piedmontese peppers with cherry tomatoes, Balsamic vinegar and basil leaves; soup; Lincolnshire haslet with orange marmalade; grilled lemon sole; tournedos old English with port and Stilton sauce; scampi Thermidor with mustard and cheese sauce; seafood provençale and rice; pork and pepper casserole; blackened butterfly chicken breast in Cajun spices with cream and wine; herb omelette; and ratatouille au gratin. Accommodation is available. There's a bronze statue to Sir Isaac Newton on St Peter's Hill: he was educated in Grantham. There's no statue yet to Margaret Thatcher (*née* Roberts), Grantham-born. Her family grocer's shop in the town, once a shrine for her supporters, has closed down. That's market forces for you.

GEORGE

71 ST MARTINS, STAMFORD, LINCOLNSHIRE (01780 750750)
Off A1

Lincolnshire is fertile territory for coaching inns thanks to its proximity to the Great North Way. The George, with its famous "gallows" inn sign that stretches across the road, is just one of 400 listed buildings in this breath-taking town of mellow stone where Middlemarch was filmed for television. The inn dates from 947 when monks were said to have built a hostelry on the site. The present site developed from three medieval buildings: the House of the Holy Sepulchre, a monastic hospice where the Knights of St John were entertained before starting their journey to the Holy Land; a church; and the Hospital of St John and St Thomas, founded in 1174 for the poor of Peterborough. The present site was built in1597 for the first Baron Burghley, Elizabeth I's chief minister, who ordered the execution of Mary Queen of Scots. Charles I stayed at the inn on several occasions, the last in 1645 when, disguised as a servant, he fled from Oxford and spent his last night as a free man at Stamford before joining the Scottish army at Newark. He was captured and handed over to Oliver Cromwell's forces and remained under arrest until his trial and execution. In its heyday as a coaching inn, the George serviced "20 up and 20 down" a day, a reference to the direction in

Angel & Royal, Grantham, Lincolnshire

which the coaches were travelling. At each side of the stone-flagged hall are the London and York rooms, named after the destinations of the coaches, which stopped at the inn to change horses. Among the many famous guests at the George was Daniel Lambert, who died in Stamford in 1809 aged 32 and weighing 52 stones, eleven pounds. The lobby of the George has a portrait of him and the great walking stick used to balance his enormous frame. The various rooms in the inn have some superb wood panelling, timbers, old settles, flagstones, and large fireplaces. A courtyard at the rear has flowering tubs and hanging baskets and there's also a walled monastery garden with a sunken lawn where guests can play croquet. An old mulberry bush dates from the reign of James I. Real ales in the bar include Adnams Broadside and Ruddles Best, while there's an excellent choice of Italian wines, some of which are sold by the glass. The Italian influence stems from licensee Ivo Vannocci and you will find seven pasta, risotto and gnocchi dishes on the menu along with soup with Italian bread, lamb cutlets coated in breadcrumbs on Mediterranean vegetables, and sea bream fillet on spring onions and beansprouts with Thai orange sauce. Coffee – filter, espresso or cappuccino – is excellent. Food is served lunchtime and evening, children are welcome and accommodation is available.

Ye Olde Starre Inn

40 Stonegate, York (01904 623063)
A19, off A1

Stonegate is the heart of York's medieval shopping area known as the Shambles. You can't miss the Old Starre for, like the George in Stamford, it has a gallows inn sign stretching across the narrow street, with a star perched, like a ballet dancer on points, in the dead centre. You enter the inn through a narrow alleyway (or "ginnel" in Yorkshire dialect) that opens into a forecourt with wooden tables and tremendous views of the Minster across the rooftops. The Olde Starre is the city's oldest licensed premises, dating from the 17th century, though some parts may date back as far as 900. Inside there's a rambling collection of wood-panelled rooms off a central hall. Dick Turpin and Guy Fawkes are among the famous and infamous who have visited the inn over the centuries. It has at least three ghosts, including two black cats and an old lady who was seen lying on the floor in a bedroom by a previous landlord's child. Two landlords have reported seeing their dogs knock themselves unconscious on a pillar in the bar when they supposedly hurled themselves at apparitions invisible to the human eye. The inn played an important role in the siege of York in 1644 during the Civil War. Soldiers were laid on stone slabs in the cellar to have their wounds treated. This often involved the amputation of limbs without the use of anaesthetic and the screams of the wounded could be heard for miles around. William Foster was the landlord of the Olde Starre during the siege. He was a Royalist supporter and he had to hold his tongue when the inn was used by the Parliamentary forces to celebrate their victory. The event was marked by a piece of doggerel at the time:

A bande of soldiers with boisterous dinne,
Filled up large kitchen of ye Olde Starre Inne.
Some rounde ye spacious chimney, smoking satt,
And whiled ye time in battle talk and chat.
Some at ye brown cake table gamed and swore,
While pikes and matchlocks strewed ye sanded floore.
Will Foster ye hoste, mid ye groupe was seene,
Wiht full redd face, bright eye and honest miene;
He smoked in silence in his olde inn chaire,
No jokes nor jestes disturbed his sadden'd air.

There's no sad air in the inn today, a bustling and cheery place that draws visitors from near and far. The beers on offer are John Smith's Bitter and Magnet, and Theakston's Best, XB and Old Peculier. Bar food, lunchtime and evening, includes a choice of filled rolls, Cumberland sausage, liver, sausage and onion, steak and kidney pie, or lamb with rosemary.

Bell

MARKET HILL, CLARE, SUFFOLK (01787 277741)
A1092, off A1017

The Bell started life as a 16th-century coaching inn and is set in one of the most delightful old market towns in Constable Country: Dedham Mill is a short drive away. It's also "Lovejoy" country, and both Clare and other local towns are packed with antique shops. Clare has a ruined Norman priory, a castle that stands on pre-historic earthworks, a country park and fine local walks. Close by are historic Lavenham and Long Melford while visitors can also enjoy a day at the races at Newmarket. The Bell is a striking half-timbered building, with an inn sign shaped like a church bell, and the main bar sticking out like a turret on to the pavement. Inside, the panelled and beamed bar has timbers, settles and a large open fire, while a Leggers Bar has many fascinating old prints about canal building, the Cavendish Suite is for private functions, while a spacious conservatory is used as a dining room and for afternoon tea. The excellent accommodation includes some rooms with four-poster beds. The hand-pumped beers include the full range from the local Nethergate Brewery a couple of minutes' walk away. They include Bitter and IPA and two fascinating versions of the same ale crafted by master brewer Ian Hornsey. Old Growler is a porter based on a mid-18th century London recipe for the strong dark style that created the modern commercial brewing industry and whose stronger version was known as stout. When Hornsey perfected his Old Growler (named after his dog) he did not include coriander, which was an ingredient of the original recipe. He brewed a one-off version using coriander, and the spicy ale that resulted created such interest that Hornsey now brews it on a regular commercial basis. It's called Umbel Ale, named not for supporters of Uriah Heep but from Umbelliferae, the Latin for the family of plants of which coriander is a member. In 1999 new licensees Jill and Paul Tills started a major but sensitive refurbishment of the Bell and have overhauled the menus. Bar meals may include battered cod, Cajun chicken, chilli con carne, lemon pepper chicken and Barnsley chop while the specials board always includes several vegetarian dishes. Evening meals could include a Mexican combo platter of wings, skins, nachos, chilli and salsa, tuna steak, chicken Florentine and rack of lamb. The Bell offers regular weekend breaks, including Christmas, at bargain rates.

Royal Oak Inn

Bongate, Appleby-in-Westmorland, Cumbria (01768 351463)
B6542, off A66

Close to the Lake District, the Scottish Borders and the Pennines, the Royal Oak creaks with antiquity, half-timbered walls, smoke-blackened beams, wood-panelling, open log fires, and old settles. In its heyday, the inn was a great coaching house on the routes to the North-west and Scotland, but parts are even older and date back as far as 1100. There are good, honest Cumbrian ales in the shape of Jennings Cumberland and

Yates Bitter, joined by Black Sheep and John Smith's from Yorkshire and regular guest beers: the inn is a free house and can search far and wide for its ales. There's an excellent wine list, with around 70 drawn from all parts of the vinous world, while draught cider is also available. The food is exceptional and is served in two restaurants (one smoke-free) as well as the bar. Dishes range from home-made soups, such as leek and watercress; sandwiches; filled jacket potatoes; and cod and chips; to brown shrimps "potted to Mrs Beaton's receipt"; three-bean crumble; leek and cheese sausages; roast hazelnut strudel; lentil, red pepper and mushroom lasagne; chicken with white wine and tomato sauce; roast salmon with lobster sauce; pork fillet in Madeira and cream; steaks; and steak and kidney pie cooked in stout. Desserts may include lemon tart with clotted cream. There are roast lunches on Sundays. Children are welcome in the restaurants and accommodation is available. In summer, the pleasant terrace at the front is a riot of flowers in hanging baskets and tubs. Appleby is a good base for walks and for trips on the Settle to Carlisle railway line, with its unforgettable views of the countryside.

Feathers Hotel

High Street, Ledbury, Herefordshire (01531 635266)
A417

The pub area of this black-and-white Elizabethan coaching inn is called Fuggles, underscoring the importance of hop-growing in the county: the Fuggle is one of the main traditional varieties of English hops, first propagated by a Richard Fuggle. The variety is prized by craft brewers as a result of the intense bitterness and fine aroma it gives to beer. While Kent is best-known as the major English hop-growing area, Herefordshire and Worcestershire are equally important and used almost exclusively to supply the breweries of Birmingham and the Black Country. Hop bines decorate the low-exposed beams in the inn, which also has some standing timbers, log fires, antique furnishings, and stripped brick walls. A good range of hand-pumped ales includes Draught Bass, Everards Tiger, Fuller's London Pride, Morland Old Speckled Hen and Worthington Bitter. Local country cider is also available, there's a good choice of malt whiskies and an excellent, extensive wine list. Food, lunchtime and evening, may include home-made soups; bruschetta; home-made salmon fish cakes; mixed bean and artichoke ragout; grilled pork cutlet with apple, cream and cider sauce; spiced coconut lamb cutlets; roasted Mediterranean vegetables; duck and pistachio terrine; grilled lamb cutlets with watercress and tomato sauce; and fillet of beef escalopes with wild mushrooms. Desserts could include apple and almond tarte tatin with clotted cream and Calvados. Afternoon teas are served too. There is a pleasant lawn at the back, accommodation is available, and children are welcome in designated eating areas.

Best of the Rest

White Hart
The Square, St Keverne, Cornwall (01326 280325)
B3293

Red Hart Inn
Awre, Gloucestershire (01594 510220)
Off A48 Newnham to Chepstow road

Cross Keys
Midford Road, Combe Down, near Bath, Avon (01225 832002)
B3110

Peacock Inn
School Lane, Croxton Kerrial, Leicestershire (01476 870324)
Off A607

Old Gate Inn
160 New Dover Road, Canterbury, Kent (01227 452141)
Off A2

Vine Inn
High Street, Stockbridge, Hants (01264 810652)
A30

Bell
Alderminster, Warwickshire (01789 450414)
Off A3400

Top country pubs

Royal Oak

The Square, Yattendon, Berkshire (01635 201325)
Off B4009, west of Pangbourne

In spite of the name, it was Oliver Cromwell not Charles II who stayed at the Royal Oak on the eve of the Battle of Newbury. The inn sign nevertheless shows an oak tree surmounted by a crown to underscore the legend about the fleeing monarch shinning up a trunk to escape the Roundheads. The Royal Oak in question is one of the top-rated entries in the *Which?* "Guide to Country Pubs" and is praised for maintaining a good "pubby" atmosphere in a shire county where too many hostelries have become fully fledged restaurants and have squeezed out locals who just want a pint. One of the three wood-panelled rooms in this graceful building is a bar for drinkers, a second is for bar meals while the third is a restaurant proper. The star of the show is chef Robbie Macrae, formerly a sous-chef with Marco Pierre White, and the cooking is of a high order. You may find the likes of gazpacho with pickled sardines and crème fraîche, chargrilled swordfish with crushed new potatoes and pesto, mosaic of game with redcurrant dressing and tomato compote, casserole of rabbit with roasted salsify and fondant new potatoes, tian of Cornish crab with avocado and pink grapefruit, sauté of bream with a squid risotto and bouillabaisse jus, and soup of fresh berries with vanilla ice cream. Cask ales are Fuller's London Pride and the local West Berkshire Brewery's Good Old Boy. The wine list is extensive and if your overdraft runs to it you could spend £140 on a bottle of 1985 Chateau Pichon Longueville. For those on a more modest budget there are around ten good wines by the glass. Accommodation is available.

Talbot

Knightsford Bridge, Knightwick, Worcestershire (01886 821235)
B4197, off A44

As I had the pleasurable task of officially opening the Talbot's own tiny Teme Valley Brewery, I can vouch for the fact that this splendid 14th-century coaching inn, just off the Bromyard to Worcester road, richly

Royal Oak, Yattendon, Berkshire

deserves its order of merit in the *Which?* guide. This part of Worcestershire is both Elgar country (his home is nearby and open to the public) and hop-growing land. Phillip Clift, who runs the inn with his sisters Wiz and Anne, is also a major hop farmer and his traditional English varieties, Fuggles and Goldings, are used in the house beers: This, That, T'Other, The Other T'Other, Wot and – in the picking season – Hops Nouvelle. There is a frieze of hops above the bar and the inn has a wealth of blackened beams, old coaching and sporting prints, open fires and wooden settles. The Clifts are self-sufficient in beer, hops and most food: they grow their own barley for malting, rear cattle and chickens, produce their own vegetables and pick local fungi. In the inn there are lunch-time bar meals such as stuffed filo parcels, herring roe and mushroom tart, and ploughman's. Restaurant meals, lunch-time and evening, may include crab and lobster blinis, falafel, warm beetroot salad, pork, orange and Cognac pâté, pan-fried scallops in nori seaweed, polenta with courgettes and Parmesan, and such desserts as plum compote and banana cake. As well as the house beers there is a well-chosen wine list, with some wines by the glass. Accommodation is available and brewery visits can be arranged.

ANGEL

MARKET PLACE, LAVENHAM, SUFFOLK (01787 247388)
A1141

The Angel is an ancient inn, with parts that date back to 1420. It stands on the Market Place in a town of great antiquity. Lavenham was the centre of Suffolk's medieval weaving trade where wealthy merchants built their half-timbered houses, and washed the walls in red, brown and ochre. The Wool Hall has survived, the magnificent Guildhall, a late addition in the 16th century, dominates the market place, while the church tower at 141 feet is one of the highest in the county. The inn has heavy beams, a vast inglenook, and a table in one bay window shaped like a piano. Bar or restaurant food, lunchtime and evening, may include carrot and coriander soup, warm salad of scallops and bacon, Suffolk cheese and ham pie, fresh salmon salad with new potatoes, and lamb paprika and cream. Vegetable tarts are a house speciality with such toppings as tomato and sweet potato, or tomato and mozzarella. Desserts include coffee cheesecake and sticky toffee pudding. The inn sells only Suffolk-brewed beer but with the likes of

Adnams, Mauldons and Nethergate in the vicinity your tastebuds will not be disappointed. Good wines include a local one, Shawsgate from Framlingham. Accommodation is available.

ANGEL INN

HETTON, NORTH YORKSHIRE (01756 730263)

Off B6265 north of Skipton

The Angel is 400 years old, a former farmhouse, attractively garbed in ivy outside and with wood-panelled rooms warmed by log fires and a Victorian range inside. Don't miss the "wine snob" cartoons by Ronald Searle – they're absolute mangoes. Owner Denis Watkins has built a fine reputation for his cooking and it's essential to book a table in the dining room, though customers can eat in the bar. All dishes are cooked to order and served by staff in aprons or waistcoats – there's nothing fast about the food in the Angel. Dishes may include Caesar salad, risotto of fresh basil, spinach and cherry tomatoes, seafood hors d'oeuvre, or confit of duck with cassoulet of haricot beans, Toulouse sausage and smoked bacon, followed by such desserts as sticky toffee pudding with hot butterscotch sauce or lemon tart with strawberries and clotted cream. Hand-pumped ales come from God's Own Country – Black Sheep, Tetley Bitter and Tim Taylor's Landlord. The wine list is 300 strong, with 30 half bottles and some wines by the glass. There's also a good range of malt whiskies, Armagnacs and a house Cognac.

WHEATSHEAF

MAIN STREET, SWINTON, BORDERS, SCOTLAND (01890 860257)

A6112 north of Coldstream

One enthusiastic visitor to the Wheatsheaf told the *Which*? guide it was "an oasis in a culinary desert". Alan and Julie Reid have busily improved and extended the dining side of the pub but it remains first and foremost a local for the village where ale lovers can sup Caledonian 80 Shilling and Deuchar's IPA from Edinburgh, or Broughton's Greenmantle and Bramling Cross from a Borders brewery: Bramling Cross is a "single varietal hop" beer with a superb citric aroma and flavour. The main bar has a long oak settle, wheelback chairs and a log fire. There's also a locals' bar and a conservatory. Food (lunchtime and evening) includes baked eggs Florentine and deep-fried cheese, tomato and crayfish bisque, marinated herring fillets with Madeira, chargrilled Scotch fillet with parsley butter, or suprême of halibut with a couscous crumble. The Wheatsheaf is famous for its desserts: sample the likes of iced strawberry shortcake, warm glazed chocolate tart or summer pudding in season. Accommodation is available.

Best of the Rest

ARUNDELL ARMS
LIFTON, DEVON (01566 784666)
Off A30

CAESAR'S ARMS
CARDIFF ROAD, CREIGIAU, GLAMORGAN (01222 890486)
Off M4 junction 33

SPRINGER SPANIEL
TREBURLEY, CORNWALL (01579 370424)
A388

JOLLY SPORTSMAN
CHAPEL LANE, EAST CHILTINGTON, EAST SUSSEX (01273 890400)
Off B2116

ROEBUCK
BRIMFIELD, HEREFORDSHIRE (01584 711230)
Off A49

YORKE ARMS
RAMSGILL, NORTH YORKSHIRE (01423 755243)
Off B6265

GREYHOUND
CORFE CASTLE, DORSET (01929 480205)
Off A351, directly behind Corfe Castle

Genuine Irish pubs

O'Hanlon's

8 Tysoe Street, London EC1 (020 7278 7238)

At a time when genuine Irish pubs are disappearing under a rash of fake Oirish Scruffy Murphy's, John O'Hanlon has restored faith in the breed with his bar near Exmouth Market and Sadler's Wells. He says, and who could disagree, that a proper Irish pub should be run by an Irish family not by managers stuck in by a large English brewery or pub chain. John goes one step further by brewing his own Irish stout: he has a small brewery in Vauxhall that supplies his pub and some 25 other outlets. The bar has half-a-dozen hand-pumps dispensing Dry Stout and a range of seasonal and occasional beers, such as Spring, Summer and Autumn Gold, a hazy wheat beer and an Irish Red Ale. I enjoyed a winter brew, Stout with Port, that struck me smartly behind the kneecaps and may explain why I mistook a broom cupboard for the Gents. The former Whitbread pub has scrubbed floors, benches, settles and tables, the two main bars linked by a narrow passage. It's open all day during the week and offers food lunchtime (you can book a table) and evening (6pm to 9pm): John's mother, Maeve, does the cooking and Irish stew and beef in stout are regulars along with sausage and mash, shepherd's pie, liver in red wine, poached salmon, fish pie, and such tasty soups as celery with fennel or leek and potato; there are plenty of vegetarian alternatives including a meatless roast on Mondays. Not to be missed.

Spice of Life

37-39 Romilly Street, London W1 (020 7437 7013)

"Listen to the brogue in the bar and you'd think you were in Dublin," one regular says. In fact, you're just off Cambridge Circus, Charing Cross Road and Soho, but publicans Brian and Marie McEvoy bring a warm Irish charm and welcome to this spacious pub owned by Anglo-Irish brewers McMullen of Hertford. Food is served all day and Irish stew is always available along with a wide range of other dishes. You can sup Guinness and Murphy's and the brewery's own beers – AK, Country and Gladstone – plus an Irish-style Cream Ale, along with Bushmills and Jamieson Irish whiskies. It's a theatre pub as well as an Irish one and the

O'Hanlon's, London EC1

spacious downstairs bar has a fascinating display of old theatre posters and photos of once-famous stars of the West End.

O'Conor Don

88 Marylebone Lane, London W1 (020 7935 9311)
Underground: Baker Street/Bond Street

The pub with the curious name has quickly built a large following since it opened in the mid-1990s and it's now one of the top Irish bars in London. A plaque on the right-hand side of the pub explains that a Don is the head of an Irish clan – it's got nothing to do with the Mafia. The O'Conors hail from the west coast of Ireland and the current O'Conor Don officially opened the pub. It's designed along the lines of a Dublin bar, with engraved glass windows, a marble bar and tiled floors, with masses of Guinness memorabilia on the walls. As well as Guinness, customers can also enjoy, lunchtime and evening, Irish oysters, steamed mussels, leek and potato soup, pan-fried salmon, beef in Guinness stew, and vegetable pie, with such desserts as sticky toffee pudding and treacle tart.

New Roscoe

Bristol Street, Sheepscar, Leeds (0113 246 0778)

It's called the New Roscoe because it is a faithful recreation of the Old Roscoe, bulldozed in the late 1970s to make way for a new road scheme (I was there when it closed and still remember the hangover). Landlord Noel Squire has fashioned the large pub from a former working men's club and he even has a large model of the Old Roscoe in the bar and there's a mural on the outside wall. There's a comfortable tap room and a large bar used in the evening, where live music is played four or five times a week, including Irish bands. It is first and foremost a great ale house, an institution in North Leeds. As well as the ubiquitous Tetley Bitter you can sup beer from the award-winning Rooster's craft brewery of Harrogate plus Guinness and Kilkenny. Prices are amazing: £1.30 for Tetley and no beer more than £1.50 a pint. Noel sells ten Irish whiskies, including a "legal potcheen". Legal potcheen? This *must* be a real Irish pub.

FIBBER MCGEES

HOWE STREET, EDINBURGH (0131 220 2376)

This large two storey-pub, with bars on both floors, has an imposing entrance with shuttered windows and stained-glass doors. The interior has side booths or "donkey seats" in the Irish style for both comfort and privacy – I always feel there's a touch of the confessional about them. The walls are covered with portraits of famous "Irish" stars, including Orson Welles and Alec Guinness, who happen to be American and British respectively. But then the pub is called Fibbers ... It serves Beamish Stout from Cork as well as Guinness and Kilkenny. Food ranges from filled rolls and soda bread to such well-known "Irish" dishes as haggis, Cajun chicken, lasagne and nachos.

PADDY NEESON'S

ALLISON STREET, STRATHBUNGO, GLASGOW (EX-DIRECTORY)

Irish pubs thrive in Glasgow's East End close to Celtic's football ground and the most authentic is the family-run Paddy Neeson's in the district of Strathbungo south of the Gorbals, where Irish immigrants settled when they fled the potato famine of the 1840s. The pub has an unmissable multicoloured exterior (striking or garish, according to taste) and a traditional dark brown and cream interior. It is dominated by a fine example of a Scots gantry bar that displays a good range of malt and Irish whiskies. Guinness is the big seller along with Tennent's Lager and Belhaven Best. Paddy Neeson's has regular quiz nights and is home to an extremely serious dominoes team: there is a stern warning in the bar that the team "must report for duty by 8pm on match nights".

Note: *Intense research has failed to find a genuine Irish pub left in Liverpool, of all places. Readers' sightings would be appreciated. Scruffy Murphy's, O'Neills and Beastie O'Shag's don't count.*

Pubs near London markets

Lamb Tavern

10-12 Leadenhall Market, EC3 (020 7626 2454)

Underground: Bank/Monument; train: Fenchurch Street

Elegant Leadenhall Market, with its stately curved glass roof, once vied with Smithfield as London's main meat market, but it now offers a wider range of foodstuffs with delicatessens and even oyster mongers. The Lamb dates from around 1780 but the current tavern, with a tiled picture in the lobby of Sir Christopher Wren inspecting plans for the Monument (which marks the spot in Pudding Lane where the Great Fire of London broke out in 1666), was probably built a century later. Close to Lloyd's and other City institutions, the tavern has expanded upwards from its original groundfloor stand-up bar. There's a mezzanine reached by a spiral staircase, while a top-floor bar, which was the first London bar to go no-smoking, is decorated with portraits of directors of Young's brewery in Victorian times. There's also a dive bar in the cellar with two dart boards. The tavern has gleaming tiles and masses of engraved glass, and offers full meals and snacks at lunchtime, including a carvery and a good choice of salads. The beers are Young's Bitter, Special and seasonal ales. The Lamb, which shuts at weekends, is not just a haunt of City types, for John Wayne and Robert Mitchum both filmed there.

Camden Head

Camden Passage, N1 (020 7359 0851)

Underground: Angel

Camden Passage, confusingly, is in Islington, named after the Earl of Camden, but a few miles from Camden Town. The flagstoned walkway has become a leading antiques market, joined on Wednesdays and Saturdays by the likes of military uniforms, crockery, glassware and jewellery. The Camden Head, the stallholders' local, dates from 1899, and has a pavement terrace that makes for pleasant alfresco eating and drinking in fine weather. The pink brick exterior, bedecked with hanging baskets, leads into a spacious, knocked-through bar with a central island servery. The pub was – to use the industry's dreadful term – "refurbed" in the 1960s but it was done

*Lamb Tavern,
Leadenhall
Market,
London EC3*

with rare sensitivity, with original etched glass partitions reused to form alcoves. Snacks and full meals are served at lunchtime, the pub opens for all permitted hours and the cask ales – the likes of John Smith's and Theakston's – come from the Scottish Courage range.

Spread Eagle

141 Albert Street/Parkway, NW1
(020 7267 1410)
Underground: Camden Town/Regent's Park

This is a stalwart Young's pub in Camden Town and is handy for Camden Lock (go down Parkway to the Camden Town road junction and turn left up Chalk Farm Road) with its three open yards surrounding a central market hall offering an eclectic choice of clothes, jewellery, books, food and furniture. As you walk up cosmopolitan Parkway, with Asian restaurants and Italian delis, the pub immediately appeals with seats and parasols on tables on the pavement and a hanging sign showing an eagle spreading its wings: the sign dates from Roman times when it was adopted as the national symbol. It has also been used for centuries as the insignia of several noble English families and by many countries, including Austria, France, Germany, Russia and Spain, while the bald-headed eagle with wings outspread is the symbol of the United States. The Spread Eagle has been sensitively knocked through in recent years but retains much of its early 19th-century charm, with masses of wood-panelling, old photos, and heavy brass lamps, with large plate-glass windows at the front. Hot meals are served from 11am until 3pm with such dishes as Thai green chicken, braised knuckle of lamb, chicken dijonnaise, beef bourguignon, canneloni with ricotto, spinach and goat's cheese, red Beijing duck, and smoked haddock. Sandwiches and toasted sandwiches are served at other times. The ales are Young's Bitter, Special and seasonal beers. The pub is open all day and is close to Regent's Park and London Zoo.

Windsor Castle

114 Campden Hill Road, W8 (020 7243 9551)
Underground: Holland Park/Notting Hill Gate

The pub is just a short stroll from Portobello Market, the world-famous antiques market that draws buyers from so far afield that the area is peppered with bureaux de change and the traders' guide comes in six different languages. The Windsor Castle, built in the mid-1880s, is said to have got its name from the fact that, before the area was developed into spacious squares and substantial town houses, it was possible to see the actual castle in Berkshire from the upstairs windows. The pub is an unspoilt delight, with three front bars, each with its own entrance, high-back settles, dark wood panelling, bare boards and partitions of dark wood and etched glass. Unusually for London, it has a spacious garden with wooden seats and tables on flagstones, and a secluded feel thanks to ivy-covered walls. Bar snacks and meals are served all day – filled ciabatta, steamed mussels and oysters, fish and chips, fishcakes, and bangers and mash – and children are welcome in designated areas. The hand-pumped ales are Draught Bass and Fuller's London Pride.

Blind Beggar

337 Whitechapel Road, E1 (020 7247 6195)
Underground: Whitechapel

The Blind Beggar is a good base for two markets, Spitalfields in Commercial Street, and Whitechapel street market. Spitalfields until the 1990s was London's major fruit and veg market, but today its large building is host to organic food stalls selling fruit, vegetables and bread as well as antiques and bric-a-brac. Whitechapel weekday street market is geared mainly to the Bangladeshi community, with good quality fruit and veg, and some clothes stalls. The pub is famous as a haunt of the notorious Kray gangsters in the 1960s, who terrorised East London for years. When Ronnie Kray was insulted in the pub on 8 March 1966 by George Cornell, a member of the rival Richardson gang, Kray shot Cornell: Cornell is alleged to have called Kray "a fat poof". Even without the insult, Cornell was chancing his arm drinking in an East End pub, as the Richardson gang were from South London, and mobsters leave their territory at some risk to life and limb. Twin brother Reggie, to keep up with his brother, equally infamously murdered Jack "The Hat" McVitie, an act that finally sent the brothers to prison for life. Disappointingly, the present owners have washed away not just the blood but all traces of the Krays, but it remains a fine East London boozer with one large bar, comfortable sofas and armchairs, and a modern conservatory. The name has nothing to do with its bloody 1960s history but stems from stories told about both Harold, the last Saxon king of England, and Henry, the son of Simon de Montfort, who led the barons' rebellion against Henry III in the 13th century. Both Harold and Henry died in battle and were reputed to have been "seen" years later wandering as blind beggars. Another sad sight next to the pub is the remains of the Mann Crossman & Paulin brewery, outside which General Booth, founder of the Salvation Army, preached his first sermon in 1865. In 1958 Manns became part of the Watney empire, which was to good beer what the Kray twins were to peaceful community relations: Watneys butchered the brewery. Beers in the Blind Beggar are from the Scottish Courage range, and meals and snacks are served lunchtime and evening. The pub is open all day.

Best of the Rest

Grapes

Shepherd Market, W1 (020 7629 4989)
Underground: Green Park (for Piccadilly Craft Market)

Lamb and Flag

33 Rose Street WC2 (020 7497 9504)
Underground: Covent Garden/Leicester Square (for Covent Garden Indoor Market)

Pride of Spitalfields

3 Heneage Street, E1 (020 7247 8933)
Underground: Liverpool Street (for Spitalfields, Brick Lane and Petticoat Lane Markets)

Mawbey Arms

7 Mawbey Street, SW8 (020 7622 1936)
Underground: Vauxhall (for New Covent Garden Market)

Dog & Duck

Bateman Street, London, W1 (020 7437 4447)
Underground: Tottenham Court Road (for Soho Market – could also be listed in Pubs in Miniature *section)*

Seaside pubs

OLD MILL HOUSE

MILL HILL, POLPERRO, CORNWALL (01503 272362)
A387

Close to the quayside and the coastal path, the white-painted cottage-style pub decked with hanging baskets offers an exceptionally friendly welcome, including dogs who are greeted with a biscuit. The pub-cum-hotel has been sensitively refurbished with a nautical theme: there are pictures of fishing boats on the walls while fishing tackle and netting hang from the ceiling. The floors are polished wood with some flagstones and a large log fire belts out heat on cold days. As well as the cosy bar there is a bistro for full meals, a children's room with toys, and an adult play area for darts, shove ha'penny, dominoes, cribbage and the rare game of shut-the-box. Hand-pumped ales include Draught Bass and two local brews, St Austell Trelawnys Pride and Exmoor Gold, along with farmhouse cider. Food is heavily focussed on fish fresh from the boats in the harbour: the landlady's husband is a fisherman. The "Catch of the Day" could be John Dory, red mullet, lemon sole, monkfish, sea bass, crabs and scallops in season. There are daily specials such as pasta with seafood, scallops wrapped in smoked bacon, along with home-made soup, sandwiches, vegetarian chilli, vegetarian pasta dishes, Cajun chicken, home-made humus, grilled sardines and crab. There are lunchtime roasts on Sunday. Accommodation is available.

CLIFFE TAVERN

HIGH STREET, ST MARGARET'S AT CLIFFE, KENT (01304 852400)
Off A258, four miles from Dover

There are strong Dickens connections in the area and there is something splendidly Dickensian about a pub that in the past has been a shoemaker's, corn merchant's and an "academy for young gentlemen". Don't worry: this is not Dotheboys Hall. The white-painted and weatherboarded inn dates from the 16th century and offers a splendid welcome in a pretty village on top of the cliffs. The cheery main bar is decorated with old posters and pictures, and there is a quieter lounge and dining area. In good weather you can eat and drink in a flint-walled garden with roses and sycamores. The choice of real ale is ever-changing: you may find such local beers as Harvey's and Shepherd Neame. Food in the bar and restaurant may include soup, filled baguettes, several fresh fish specials chalked on a board, such as plaice in prawn and caper sauce, or prawn and seaweed stir-fry, plus vegetable samosas, cheese bake, curry of the day and steaks, moules marinières, and such desserts as apple pie and steamed pudding. Accommodation is available.

WHITE HORSE

4 HIGH STREET, BLAKENEY, NORFOLK (01263 740574)
A149

The White Horse is a flint-faced, 17th-century coaching inn overlooking the narrow High Street and the attractive harbour, where you can hire boats to visit the National Trust's seal colony at Blakeney Point. The comfortable long bar is decorated in soft colours and has some striking watercolours by local artists of seascapes and salt marshes: these are for sale to customers. Steps take diners up to a bistro area at the back with pine tables and there's also a separate conservatory restaurant. The owners take wine seriously, stage wine tastings, and get their supplies from Adnams down the road in Southwold. Wines by the glass are chalked on a blackboard. Adnams, unsurprisingly, supplies its Best Bitter, and there are also Draught Bass and Boddingtons on handpumps. Food (bar food lunchtime and evening; restaurant, evening only, Tuesday to Saturday) may offer soup; Mediterranean vegetable and Brie flan; deep-fried herring roe with toast; cockle chowder; deep-fried whitebait; local mussels in garlic and wine; Thai green chicken curry; sweet pepper and tapenade risotto; fisherman's pie; and grilled salmon fillet with salsa verde. Desserts may include treacle tart. The inn has a no-smoking area, wheelchair access, and a courtyard. Children are welcome in one room and accommodation is available.

Saddle

24-25 Northumberland Street, Alnmouth,
Northumberland (01665 830476)
B1338, off A1

The Saddle stands on the main street of this small seaside and harbour town. The stone-built Victorian inn has a spacious main bar with a tiled fireplace and rustic wall benches and tables. There is a separate, comfortable dining area with an à la carte menu. Food is extensive, generously portioned and offers the likes of local Craster kippers, smoked mackerel with horseradish, Northumberland sausages in Yorkshire pudding, chicken or vegetarian curry, meat or vegetarian chilli, steak and kidney pie, special dishes and pies of the day, Hawaiian toast with roast ham, pineapple rings and cheese on bread, and chicken pancake. The large dessert menu includes profiteroles, knickerbocker glory, banana split and steamed suet pudding. There is an excellent cheese board, too. The 20-strong wine list has several by the glass while hand-pumped ales include Ruddles Best and Theakston's Best. As well as the surrounding beaches, you are in wonderful walking country, with Craster and its kippers, Seahouses, the Farne Islands, Holy Island, Bamburgh and Alnwick and its castle all close by. The Saddle offers such pub games as darts and dominoes. Accommodation is available.

Ship Inn

Red Wharf Bay, Isle of Anglesey (01248 852568)
Off A5025, six miles from Menai Bridge

There are tremendous sea views from this whitewashed, 16th-century inn on the beach with a backdrop of low wooded hills. The Ship has a terrace with tables and chairs for fine weather. Inside, there are roaring fires in several fireplaces on cold days, a dominating stone-built bar, a collection of Toby jugs and old hunting cartoons on the walls. A good range of hand-pumped ales from the Carlsberg-Tetley stable includes Tetley Dark Mild and Bitter, Ind Coope Burton Ale and such guest beers as Marston's Pedigree. Among the wines, six are sold by the glass. Menus change daily but you may find the likes of feta cheese and black olive salad, cream of celery and Stilton soup, hot spicy avocado, dressed crab, smoked duck with balsamic vinegar dressing, baked stuffed onions, cottage pie, and a wide choice of locally caught fish including plaice, red mullet and monkfish. Desserts include toffee crunch and rhubarb and ginger crumble. The family room and dining room are non-smoking. The whole of Anglesey, with Snowdonia glowering on the mainland, is at your feet.

Crown

9 North Crescent, Portpatrick,
Dumfries and Galloway (01776 810261)
Off A77, six miles from Stranraer

In a superb fishing village and surrounded by wonderful walking country, the Crown looks across the sea towards Ireland and inside has the air of an old fishermen's inn with a coal fire and a tobacco haze (the dining area and conservatory are non-smoking). The bar is busy with many alcoves and hidey-holes, old mirrors, paintings of local scenes, a carved settle, a bottle collection and a stag's head above the fireplace. There are separate bistro meals while the bar offers the likes of soup, sandwiches, local prawns, lobster, baked ragoût of monkfish tails, cod in beer batter, salads, and local beef. Desserts include peach Pavlova, and apple and toffee flan. There are more than 70 malt whiskies, a good wine list, draught cider and Theakston's Best and McEwan's 70 Shilling and 80 Shilling ales. There is a pleasant garden at the back and seats at the front. Accommodation is available.

Rest of the Best

Swan

Old Town Street, Dawlish, Devon (01626 863677)
A379

Highlander

Esplanade, Scarborough, North Yorkshire (01723 355627)
A171

Royal Hotel

Marine Terrace, Cromarty, Highlands, Scotland
(01381 600217)
From Inverness cross Kessock Bridge and follow signs for Cromarty

Pubs near beaches

HALZEPHRON

GUNWALLOE, CORNWALL (01326 240406)

Signposted from A3083. One-and-a-half miles south of Helston

The name means "Hell's Headland" in Cornish and storms can whip the sea over the cliff where the old smugglers' inn stands. But when the sun shines, this is a magic place, unmarked on many maps but with magnificent walks between Mullion and Porthleven, and tremendous views over Mounts Bay to Land's End. Gunwalloe Cove is a few yards away, and there is a sandy beach at Gunwalloe Church Cove. The inn is on the infamous wreckers' coast and a wall between the two bars houses a shaft to a tunnel that leads to the beach: the tunnel was once used to bring contraband from wrecked ships. Licensees Harry and Angela Thomas specialise in local ingredients for their food with fish, seafood and meat brought from St Keverne, free range eggs, and Rodda's clotted cream. Fish dishes could include fish pie, bass with fennel or salmon fishcakes. There are always several vegetarian dishes including pasta, and sauté mushrooms with herb and cream sauce, while meat eaters may find beef carbonade or steak and kidney pie. Desserts include pecan pie. There is an excellent wine list while beer drinkers can sample Sharp's Own and Doom Bar from a local small brewery at Wadebridge. Accommodation is available.

FISHERMAN'S RETURN

THE LANE, WINTERTON-ON-SEA, NORFOLK (01493 393305)

Off B1159

John and Kate Findlay's pub is a regular in the Camra "Good Beer Guide": John is a real ale fan and scours the country for beers from micro breweries. The range may vary but at present he offers Woodforde's Wherry Best Bitter and Great Eastern from Woodbastwick near Norwich, Leyland Gold from Wellingborough and Slaters Supreme from Stafford. The pub is a short stroll from the beach and handy for the Broads. It's built of brick and flint, dates from the 17th century and was originally a row of fishermen's cottages. The wood-panelled lounge has red leatherette seats, and old prints and photos of the area. There is also a spacious bar and a games room. As well as good ale, the pub offers 30 whiskies and James White's local cider. All the food is home-made and standard fare such as burgers and filled jacket potatoes is expanded by daily specials that include curries, pasta dishes, Normandy pork cooked in cider, spicy bean casserole and other vegetarian dishes, and poached salmon and plaice in watercress sauce. There is a garden with a pets corner. Accommodation is available.

LAUREL

THE BANK, ROBIN HOOD'S BAY, NORTH YORKSHIRE (01947 880400)
Off A171

The tall and narrow, red-tiled Laurel stands among fishermen's cottages on a bend halfway down the cliff to the bay and harbour. It's one of the smallest pubs in Yorkshire and the beamed bar is carved from solid rock, has an open fire, and is decorated with old photos, prints and brasses. Locals enthusiastically play cribbage, darts, dominoes, shove ha'penny and table skittles. The beers are John Smith's Bitter and Theakston's Black Bull and Old Peculier while simple bar food is confined to soup in winter and sandwiches in summer. (The Victoria, at the top of the village, offers full meals and Cameron's ales). The Laurel is decked out with hanging baskets and window boxes in summer. Below, the sea boils and crashes against the rocks and the houses at full tide; at low tide, the harbour and beach are places of tranquility. Whitby is close by. The Laurel has an apartment for two people.

FAT CAT

149 MOSTYN STREET, LLANDUDNO, CONWY, NORTH-WEST WALES (01492 871844)
Off A55

In this delightful old seaside resort with sweeping beaches and rocky headlands, the Fat Cat is a new, female-friendly bar that opened in 1997. It has a long narrow main room with bare boards and lots of reclaimed wood, including a bar made from cut-down doors. The regular beers are Boddingtons Bitter, Theakston's XB and Wadworth 6X with regular guests, possibly Cains FA from Liverpool: Llandudno is a popular holiday and work place for Liverpudlians. There's a strong emphasis on food, starting with a meat or vegetarian breakfast and a pot of Earl Grey tea; such snacks as warm baguettes with choice of fillings; pitta stuffed with prawns; tuna and melted cheese doorstep sandwich; nachos; Caesar salad; home-made char-grilled burgers; tuna steak in white wine; Thai vegetable schnitzel; and beer and vegetable stew with potatoes. Specials may include sea bass with lemon, garlic and ginger; or focaccia pizzas.

SHIP INN

THE TOFT, ELIE, FIFE, SCOTLAND (01333 330246)
A917

This is a special sort of Scottish bar, with the Sassenach game of cricket played on the beach at low tide: to even things up, impromptu rugby matches are played as well and there are live jazz and beer festivals and barbecues in the summer. The pub garden has fine views of the beach, the sweep of the bay and the pier. The Ship dates from the early 19th century and has three dining areas and a locals' bar with stone flags, beams, high-backed settles and fires in winter. Imaginative food includes seafood crêpes, grilled kippers, local fresh haddock, lentil and mushroom lasagne, vegetable curry, and ham marinaded in cider. Desserts include banoffi pie and lemon Pavlova. Belhaven 80 Shilling and Theakston Best Bitter adorn the bar and there is a good wine list, too. Children are welcome in the dining areas and accommodation is available.

SHIP INN

ST JAMES STREET, DUNWICH, SUFFOLK (01728 648219)
Off B1125

The Ship is one of the few buildings left in Dunwich, once a major medieval city and port, seat of bishops and the kings of East Anglia, with two monasteries and nine churches. But the sea silted up the river mouth and has eroded the cliffs to such an extent that most of the village now lies under the waves. Fishermen claim they sometimes hear church bells tolling out to sea. It is an atmospheric place, slightly eerie at dusk, with a fine beach, a seaside walk to Walberswick and other walks inland. Minsmere's RSPB bird sanctuary is close by. The Ship, run by Stephen and Annie Marchmain, is on the site of an ale house that dates from at least the 12th century. The present pub has Tudor cellars and a Georgian bar. The bar has a sunken flagstone floor, a fireplace with a wood-burning stove, fishermen's nets, a ship's wheel and other nautical artefacts, and prints of old Dunwich, including a map of the town in the 16th century. A large room added in Victorian times acts as an evening restaurant while a spacious conservatory at the back can also be used by diners. The pub garden has a fig tree and a vine. Excellent ale includes several hand-pumped

beers from Adnams of nearby Southwold and Greene King Abbot. The Marchmains specialise in locally caught fish that comes straight from boats on the beach. You will also find home-made soup, ploughman's, goat's cheese and tomato salad, black pudding fried with local apples, steak and mushroom pie, seafood pancakes, fishcakes, and spinach and mushroom pasta. Desserts include chocolate and Cointreau cheesecake. Accommodation is available. There is a small museum a few doors from the pub devoted to the history of Dunwich.

Ship Inn, Dunwich, Suffolk

Pubs by waterways

BOAT

GRAVEL PATH, BERKHAMSTED, HERTFORDSHIRE (01442 877152).
Off A41

The Boat, mellow red-brown brick and bestrewn with hanging baskets, stands alongside the Grand Union Canal in a small town where Graham Greene was born and which boasts a ruined castle. Perhaps it's because "Berko" is slightly snooty that London brewers Fuller's had a great battle to win planning permission to build the pub on the site of a Benskin's ale house that had been pulled down. In the typically Middle England fashion, having fought tooth and nail to stop the new Boat being built, the townspeople now flock to it and claim it's the best pub for miles around. It has a delightful terrace overlooking the canal, where you can watch boating types attempting to tie up alongside, and a spacious, open-plan interior, with comfortable seating and a long serving counter. The Fuller's range of Chiswick Bitter, London Pride, ESB and seasonal beers are on offer, while food, lunchtime and evening, may include soup, sandwiches, ploughman's, steak and ale pie, turkey escalope topped with cheese and ham, fresh fish specials, and a vegetarian dish such as penne with sun-dried tomatoes and pesto. There's no food on Fridays and Saturday evenings, which are restricted to over-21s.

BOAT INN

ASHLEWORTH QUAY, ASHLEWORTH, GLOUCESTERSHIRE.
(01452 700272)
Off A38 & A40

The Boat is a mile outside the village of Ashleworth, down a lane and past an ancient tithe barn. The Boat stands alongside the great sweep of the River Severn and, amazingly, has been in the hands of the Jelf family since the little cottage was granted a licence by Charles II. The Jelfs also plied their trade as boatmen, ferrying passengers across the river. According to local legend, the grateful king granted the licence to the family when they helped him escape his Roundhead pursuers by ferrying him across. When the present incumbent, Irene Jelf, retires, her niece Jacquie Nicholls will take over. At the front of the pub there are some benches and picnic tables alongside a building that used to be a tiny brewhouse. Going into the pub is like entering someone's parlour, with high-back settles on an undulating flag-stoned floor, a black cast-iron range with a bread oven, beamed ceilings, magazines to read, and plenty of fresh flowers. There are traditional pub games, including dominoes, quoits, shove ha'penny, and a local one called Dobbers. You can drink the full range of Westons ciders, plus such fine ales as Arkells, Bateman's, Oakhill, Smiles and Wye Valley, all tapped straight from casks. Lunchtime snacks include filled rolls and the sort of ploughman's with fresh chutney that will keep you going for several days.

CHEQUERS,

GEDNEY DYKE, LINCOLNSHIRE. (01406 362666)
Off A17

The village of Gedney is remote and close to the Wash, where King John lost his treasure. When the surrounding Fens were drained, Gedney Dyke was dug and runs past the bottom of the pub's garden. The history of the little early-18th-century inn, whitewashed, red-tiled and dormer windowed, is fascinating. Most Chequers take their names either from the coat of arms of the Fitzwarren family, who had the enviable task of licensing ale houses for Edward IV, or from the earlier Roman custom of exchanging money on a black-and-white board in a wine shop. The name here, however, derives from a drink called Chequers made from a variety of rowan berry that grows in the inn's garden. Centuries ago, the bitter berries were used in the brewing process to add bitterness before the hop plant came into universal use. Inside the pub, there's a low-beamed bar with an open fire, a conservatory used for eating as well as a small restaurant. The Chequers has a deserved reputation for its food, and was named Lincolnshire Dining Pub of the Year for 2000 by the *Good Pub Guide*. The house speciality is fresh fish and seafood, and you may find the likes of Cromer crab; sea bass; or seared monkfish with herb crumb and coriander relish. The complete range of fish dishes is chalked daily on a board. Other dishes may include Gressingham duck; guinea fowl; wood pigeon with onion marmalade and cassis jus; chestnut and vegetable roast, plus soup, sandwiches and ploughman's. A tremendous choice of beer includes Adnams Best, Draught Bass, Elgood Pageant, and Morland Old Speckled Hen, with Greene King Abbot in summer.

LITTLE DRY DOCK

WINDMILL END, NETHERTON, WARWICKSHIRE (01384 235369)

The pub is on the Birmingham Canal Navigation and the full address really needs to be read out loud in a Brummie accent: "At canalside at Windmill End, between the Bumblehole Branch and the Boshboil Arm". I'm not certain I want to know what a bumblehole is. The red, white and blue pub is genuinely eccentric, based in an old dockyard, with one bar hollowed out from the six-plank hull of a salvaged Runcorn narrowboat, with its engine room still intact. The two main rooms have ornate tiled walls, gaudy paintwork, a large model of a boat, and a vast range of canal bric-a-brac, including rudders, winches, lanterns, lifebuoys, and bargees' water jugs.

The Boat, Berkhamstead

The pub is owned by Ushers of Trowbridge and serves the brewery's Best Bitter and Founder's Ale, plus a regular guest beer. The food, lunchtime and evening, is simple and filling, and includes soup, sandwiches, faggots and peas, gammon and egg, seafood crumble, and fried herby mushrooms. There are good towpath walks, with the grand west portal of Netherton tunnel close by, and the tall tower of Cobb's Engine House, which used to pump water from the nearby coal mines to prevent flooding. They used to say in these parts that if the engine ever missed a beat, a thousand women's hearts missed one, too.

Willey Moor Lock

Whitchurch, Shropshire. (01948 663274)
Off A49

Whitchurch is indeed in Shropshire but the Willey Moor Lock is just a tad over the border in Cheshire, and, to add to the confusion, stands over a footbridge alongside the Llangollen Canal – and Llangollen is in Wales. If you can sort out the geography, this is a lovely little pub fashioned from an old lock keeper's cottage in a delightful sylvan setting. The small, interconnected and beamed rooms have log fires in winter, a sonorous longcase clock and a collection of tea pots. Outside, there's a charming terrace with tables and parasols, as well as a children's play area with swings and slides. Theakston's Best Bitter is the regular beer with such guests as Abbeydale, Coach House, Hanby and Weetwood. Bar food, lunchtime and evening, comes in generous portions and at reasonable prices. You may find sandwiches, filled jacket potatoes, ratatouille, vegetable or chicken curry, cod in batter, and minced beef and onion pie, with such desserts as spotted dick and chocolate fudge cake.

Dundas Arms

53 Station Road, Kintbury, Berkshire (01488 658263)
Off A4 between Hungerford and Newbury

Lord Dundas was the first chairman of the Kennet and Avon Canal and graciously and modestly allowed his name to endow the pub. Overlooking Kintbury lock and based by an old road bridge on a small island between the river and canal, the white-painted, late-Georgian pub is tranquil and picturesque today and is far removed from the times when roistering navvies "never drank water but whisky by the pints". In more sober times today, customers drink beers from Morland, Butts and Ringwood. There's an extensive choice of wine displayed in racks in the restaurant. In good weather there are tables by the waterside. Inside, the bar has wood panelling, rustic furniture and good views of the canal. Good quality food, cooked by landlord David Dalzell-Piper, is available lunchtime and evening (not Monday evenings) and may include ploughman's; soup; mushrooms on Italian bread; gravlax; smoked haddock risotto; monkfish with tomato and chilli sauce; steak and chips; crab au gratin; and white bean and vegetable casserole with grilled chorizo sausage. Desserts may include stricky toffee pudding. Children are welcome and accommodation is available.

Pubs on islands

Fleur du Jardin

Kings Mill Road, Castel, Guernsey (01481 57996)

This former farmhouse has been turned into a welcoming inn with the original thick stone walls and low beamed ceilings intact. The public bar has a log fire on cold days. The inn stands in two acres of fine gardens with flowering shrubs, attractive borders, hanging baskets and picnic tables. The island has two small independent breweries and you can sample the Guernsey Brewery's Sunbeam and its range of seasonal ales here. The inn also offers a good range of wines by the glass or bottle. Bar food includes soup, sandwiches, steak and ale pie, such vegetarian options as mushroom Stroganoff, and locally caught fish. Children are welcome, there's a no-smoking area in the restaurant and accommodation is available.

Star & Tipsy Toad

La Route de Beaumont, St Peter, Jersey (01534 485556)

This splendid pub has rejuvenated good beer drinking on Jersey. It has its own micro-brewery on site which can be viewed from the spacious back bar. Tours of the brewery can also be arranged. You can sample the regular brews – Tipsy Toad Ale, Jimmy's Bitter and Horny Toad – as well as seasonal ales, including a spectacular Porter in the autumn. The main bar has comfortable seating and a large polished wood counter. Bar food includes fresh cod cooked in house beer batter, ploughman's, broccoli and cream cheese bake, steak and ale pie, coq au vin and children's dishes. There is a games room, children's play areas inside and out, and regular live music shows.

Turks Head

The Quay, St Agnes, Isles of Scilly (01720 422434)

Who says real ale doesn't travel? The likes of Draught Bass, Burton Ale, Flowers Original and IPA reach the Turks Head by boat from St Austell on the mainland. It's an impressive range for a pub on an island with just 70 souls and it attracts not only day trippers but inhabitants of the main Scilly Isle, St Mary's. The pub is a small whitewashed cottage that stands above the broad sweep of a bay. You can eat and drink on the lawn or take your victuals down to the beach. The cosy wood-panelled main bar of the pub is decorated with seascapes, model ships, banknotes, flags and helmets. Bar food includes Cornish pasties, ploughman's, Cajun vegetable casserole and children's dishes. There are regular evening barbecues during the summer. Children are welcome and accommodation is available.

Wheatsheaf

Bridge Road, Yarmouth, Isle of Wight (01983 760456)

A delightful old coaching inn, handy for the ferry from the mainland, that has been sensitively opened out into bar and eating areas, with a no-smoking conservatory. It offers a generous welcome to families: children can go in the Harbour Lounge and conservatory. As well as such familiar beery names as Flowers Original and Old Speckled Hen try the local brew, Goddards Fuggle Dee Dum, a hymn of bibulous praise to the Fuggle hop. Generous portions of bar food include soup, vegetarian Kiev, trout with Stilton, pasta dishes and chicken tikka masala.

Pilchard

Burgh Island, opposite Bigbury-on-Sea, Devon (01548 810344)

The Pilchard is a wonderfully romantic old smugglers' hideout reached across the sands from Bigbury. At high tide visitors are transported in grand style by a unique vehicle on stilts called the Tractor that breasts the waves. The pub is perched high above the sands and was used by smugglers to watch for the Excisemen. It has thick stone walls and storm shutters on the windows, and the main bar has ships' lamps hanging from beams, high-back settles and a big log fire on cold days. There is a back bar where darts, shove-ha'penny and dominoes are played. When the weather is good, visitors can sit on the grass outside and watch the tide rising and cutting off the island. Food is sporadic and the licensee promised no more than soup but the Art Deco hotel on the island (same phone number) offers full meals as well as accommodation. There is also a summer-time café. The Duke of Windsor and Mrs Simpson are reputed to have visited and Agatha Christie worked there: she used the island as the setting for a mystery whose deeply offensive title was changed to *Ten Little Indians* when filmed in Hollywood.

OLDE BULL'S HEAD

CASTLE STREET, BEAUMARIS, ANGLESEY, NORTH-WEST WALES (01248 810329)

An historic coaching inn, more than 350 years old and Grade II listed, it has been visited among other luminaries by Charles Dickens and Samuel Johnson, both of whom spent so much time in the boozer it's a wonder they ever put quill to paper. The inn is wonderfully unspoilt with a comfortable bar with old settles, leather-cushioned window seats, an open fire and such fascinating local artefacts as a 17th-century water clock, a collection of cutlasses and the town's old ducking stool for miscreants. There is a separate no-smoking restaurant. The entrance to the courtyard boasts the biggest single-hinge door in Britain. There is an impressive list of nearly 200 wines while the hand-pumped beers are Draught Bass and Worthington Bitter with regular guest ales. Bar food includes soup, sandwiches, Welsh cheese ploughman's, baked cod with cheese and leeks, and poached salmon. Children are welcome and accommodation is available in rooms named after Dickens' characters. Anyone fancy a night with Bill Sykes?

TIGH OSDA EILEAN IARMAIN

ORNSAY, ISLE OF SKYE (01471 833332)
Signposted from A851

The Little Whisky Bar by the Sea has bi-lingual menus: Gaelic is the first language of some of the staff in this delightful inn overlooking the sea and with magnificent views of Skye. The main bar has panelled walls and ceiling, wall seats and an open fire topped by a large mirror. Brass lamps hang from the ceiling. As well as good bar food (sandwiches, filled jacket potatoes, local haddock and mussels in white wine, plus children's dishes) there are 34 whiskies to sample, including the inn's own blend Te Bheag, and a vatted malt Poit Dhubh. There are good wines, too, and a separate no-smoking dining room with tremendous sea views. Children are welcome and accommodation is available.

Trafalgar Hotel

West Quay, Ramsey, Isle of Man (01624 814601)
A10

This bustling little harbourside pub is on the TT motorbike course, but then most places on the Isle of Man are on the TT course. It has a genuine pub atmosphere, popular with locals but offering a warm welcome to visitors. The quality of beers can be measured by the fact that it has been named local Camra Pub of the Year in both 1997 and 1998 – and there's no shortage of good outlets on the island. It sells both Bushy's Bitter and Laxey Bosun Bitter from two local small craft breweries (there's also a bigger commercial brewery, Okell), plus Draught Bass and regular guest beers, such as Cains Bitter from Liverpool. The lunchtime food is highly recommended and is based on local Manx produce: kippers, scallops, cheese, potatoes and meat. There's usually a home-made pie of the day, a roast, and home-made lasagne. Other dishes may include gammon with egg or pineapple; ploughman's with Manx cheeses, ham, and salad; freshly-made sandwiches with such fillings as ham, corned beef and onion, bacon, lettuce and tomato, tuna and cucumber, or egg mayonaise; filled jacket potatoes; home-made soup of the day; burgers and veggie burgers; and chip and cheese butties. In spite of the name, the Trafalgar does not offer accommodation.

Highest pubs in Britain

Tan Hill Inn

Tan Hill, Keld, nr Richmond, North Yorkshire
(01833 628246)
Four miles north of Keld, off B6270

The Tan Hill in Upper Swaledale is officially England's highest pub, 1,732 feet above sea level, close to the borders with Cumbria and County Durham. (A hapless official actually moved it into County Durham during a bout of local government reorganisation but the Tyke Liberation Army promptly got it switched back to God's Own Country.) It lies below the summit of Stainmore Pass on the A66, often one of the first roads to be blocked by snow in winter. Tan Hill stands on the Pennine Way at the meeting point of tracks that predate the Roman invasion of Britain. Over the centuries the inn has been used by drovers, packhorse traders and coal miners who once worked the fell-top pits in the area. It is now used by walkers, climbers and holidaymakers in season: in winter the inn can be snowed in for weeks by giant drifts whipped up by a cruel wind. A former landlady once said the wind raged hard enough "to blow the horns off a tup"– the local word for a ram. Another landlord wished a shepherd Happy New Year on April 16 because he was the first person he'd seen that year. But in spring and summer this is a place of outstanding beauty. The inn has thick stone walls, flagged floors and wooden benches, with fascinating old photos on the walls. There is no mains electricity: even the juke box is powered by a generator. If a chill sets in, fires will be lit in the open fireplaces and a good range of malt whiskies will set the blood coursing again. Beers include the magnificent Black Sheep Bitter and Riggwelter from Masham plus a selection from the Theakston's range. Good bar food is served from noon to 2.30pm and 7pm to 9pm: dishes include giant Yorkshire puddings with a choice of fillings, home-made pies, Pennine steak, various pasta dishes, ploughman's and such vegetarian offerings as pasta bake and vegetable Stroganoff. The dining room is also used for local weddings. Children and dogs are welcome. Accommodation is available, with seven rooms sleeping 15 people.

Tan Hill Inn, Tan Hill, Keld, nr Richmond, North Yorkshire

Pack Horse

Widdop, West Yorkshire (01422 842803)

Off A646; on Hebden Bridge to Colne road; one-and-a-half miles south-east of Widdop Reservoir

The Pack Horse is several centuries old and was once on a route used by packhorse traders in this windswept yet glorious moorland more than 1,000 feet above sea level. Whether you approach from Hebden Bridge or Nelson and Colne, the road is winding and seemingly unending but the views and welcome at the inn make the effort worthwhile. The bar has thick stone walls into which windows have been cut, with splendid views of the moors. There are blazing fires on cold days. Beers include Black Sheep Bitter, Old Speckled Hen, Thwaites Bitter and Theakston's XB while there are large helpings of food: dishes include soups, sandwiches, hotpot, haddock Mornay, steak and kidney pie, ploughman's, and several vegetarian offerings. Children are welcome and accommodation is available. NB: the inn is closed weekday lunchtimes.

Wasdale Head Inn

Wasdale Head, Cumbria (01946 726229)

Off A595 between Gosforth and Holmrook

This remote inn stands in a craggy valley beneath some of Cumbria's highest peaks, Great Gable and Scafell, and is the birthplace of British rock climbing. To reach it you drive the length of eery Wastwater, where the black screes tumble down to meet the equally dark and forbidding waters of the deepest lake in the Lake District. The road then twists and dips as it makes its way up to Wasdale Head. The inn stands at the crossroads of ancient tracks used by packhorse traders and smugglers to cross over Sty Head, Black Sail and Burnmoor passes. The inn has a slate-floored bar used mainly by rock climbers with their studded boots, a wood-panelled main bar with a polished slate floor, cushioned settles, splendid photos on the walls, and a residents lounge, cheerily old-fashioned with wood-panelled walls. The main bar is called Ritson's Bar in dubious honour of the inn's first landlord, Wilf Ritson, who was both a keen mountaineer and the teller of such tall and implausible stories that he was known as the world's biggest liar. An annual liars' competition is staged in his memory. Beer needs to quench prodigious thirsts and the large range includes Jennings of Cockermouth's Cumberland Ale, Cocker Hoop and Sneck Lifter, Theakston's Best and Old Peculier and a house beer, Wast Ale. The inn serves food from 11am to 2pm and 6pm to 9pm and offers pies, chillis, soups, sandwiches, and corned beef hash. Accommodation is available in the hotel and in attached self-catering rooms.

Three Shires Inn

Little Langdale, Cumbria (015394 37215)

From A593 west of Ambleside take road signed The Langdales and Wrynose Pass

Before "local government reorganisation" destroyed so many old county names, the three shires in question were Cumberland, Westmorland and Lancashire, which met at the top of Wrynose Pass, close to the inn. As driving over the Wrynose is one of the most daunting experiences imaginable, the inn is well-placed to hand out soothing libations. The Three Shires is a 19th-century inn on the route of an old packhorse trail and has awesome views over a valley to the hills below Tilberthwaite Fells. The welcoming bar with a warming fire on cold days has old carved settles, slate flagstones, timbers, a stripped ceiling, and many old and fascinating local prints on the walls. There's a good range of hand-pumped ales that includes Black Sheep Special, Jennings Bitter and Cumberland Ale, and Theakston's XB, plus a weekly guest beer, a good wine list and several malt whiskies. There is no food in December or January; at other times you may find soups; Cumberland sausage; parnsip pie with a sage and onion salsa; strips of venison with a port and Stilton sauce; a parcel of four cheeses and spinach; beef in ale pie; and chicken, leek and wild mushroom terrine. Desserts could include bread and butter pudding. The restaurant and snug are smoke-free, children are welcome until 9pm, pub games are played, and accommodation is available.

Clachaig Inn

Glencoe, Highlands, Scotland (01855 811252)

Old riverside road; off A82, Crianlarich to Fort William road

The Clachaig doubles as inn and mountain rescue post. The slate-roofed building stands in a superb setting at the heart of Glencoe with some of Scotland's highest peaks forming a backdrop and Loch Leven close by. Rumour has it that the inn's owners, recalling the terrible massacre in

Glencoe, once put up a sign saying "Nae Campbells". But that is in the past and all are welcome today, especially walkers and climbers. The spacious public bar is designed for walkers and has a wood-burning stove in a stone fireplace. The modern lounge has cushioned wall seats and is decorated with photos of mountains and climbers. The lounge is quiet during the week but can get lively at weekends when folk music is played. The inn is a beer buffs' paradise, offering such delights as Arroll's 80 Shilling Ale, Ind Coope Burton Ale, Tetley Bitter, and Fraoch Heather Ale, plus regular guest beers. There's an enormous range of malt whiskies, too. Food is imaginative, ranging from tasty home-made soups and burgers to Quorn and salsa, haggis and vegetarian haggis, pasta dishes, hot chestnut and leek terrine, bridies, and local trout and salmon. Accommodation is available in an attached chalet.

Moulin Inn

11-13 Kirkmichael Road, Moulin, Perthshire (01796 472196)
A924, near Pitlochry on the Braemar road

This inn, with its striking whitewashed facade, is a 300-year-old coaching house at the foot of Ben Vrackie, which stands 2,757 feet above sea level, near Pitlochry, and is a giant stepping stone to the Highlands. The inn dates from the 17th century and the bar, the hub of the enterprise, is largely unspoilt. It is described by the owners as the "Original Moulin Inn". An important link with the past was restored in 1995 when, to commemorate the inn's 300th anniversary, brewing was revived in a stable block across the road. The inn sells the full range of Light, Braveheart, Ale of Athol and Old Remedial, which are also available in other outlets in the area. Ale of Athol is sold in bottle-fermented form, too. In the bar look out for a fascinating picture of Moulin when it was an important market town of greater importance than Pitlochry. The bar has open fires, exposed stone walls, small intimate booths divided by stained-glass screens, and such games as billiards, dominoes and shove-ha'penny. Bar food is available at all times, while the restaurant opens for lunch, that splendid Scottish occasion high tea, and dinner. Dishes may include soup; sandwiches; vegetable and lentil bake; sweet pepper pasta; haggis; steak and ale pie; Isle of Sky langoustines; and grilled trout. As well as the home-brewed ales, there's a good choice of wines and around 40 malt whiskies. Accommodation is in a refurbished area of the inn and all the rooms have full en-suite facilities. There are winter bargain breaks. Children are welcome, pets can be accommodated, and tours of the brewery can be arranged. The inn is in splendid walking territory.

GLAN ABER HOTEL

HOLYHEAD ROAD, BETWYS-Y-COED, CONWY, NORTH WALES
(01690 710325; FAX 01690 710700)
A5 at centre of village

The snow-topped mountains, valleys thick with pine and narrow, twisting roads of the area, with chalets by the roadside, could make you think you were in Switzerland or the Bavarian Alps. Perhaps it's this look-a-like nature of Snowdonia that made it popular with the less pecunious members of the English middle class in Victorian times who couldn't afford the Full Monty of the Continental Grand Tour. The Glan Aber meets all the required clichés: it's the perfect base for walking or climbing in the Snowdonia National Park and such attendant attractions as the Swallow Falls, the Ffestiniog Railway, Bodnant Gardens, and the dreamlike, manufactured village of Portmeirion, famously used as the base for the cult TV series *The Prisoner*. The stone-built hotel specializes in active holidays for walkers, climbers, anglers and golfers. With such visitors in mind, the Glan Aber has a drying room for guests' outdoor clothes, plus a games room, a health suite, a sauna and a solarium. A good choice of beers in the bar includes Morland Old Speckled Hen, Tetley Dark Mild and Bitter and a regular guest ale. Food in bar and restaurant is served lunchtime and evening, there's a tremendous cooked breakfast for those intent on exercise, and the accommodation is excellent, with many bargain breaks.

TAI'R BULL

LIBANUS, POWYS, WALES (01874 625849)
On A470, three miles south-west of Brecon

A homely and cheery one-bar, stone-built pub converted from two old cottages, the Bull is popular with walkers and climbers in the Brecon Beacons and has memorable views of the towering peak of Pen-y-Fan. The inn has letting rooms, and offers a good range of beers from the Whitbread stable including Boddingtons, Flowers and Wadworth 6X. Good bar food, lunchtime and evening, includes trout, cod and haddock, Cajun chicken, spinach and mushroom lasagne, Stilton and pasta bake, and steaks.

Pubs in miniature

NUTSHELL

THE TRAVERSE, BURY ST EDMUNDS, SUFFOLK (01284 705387)
Off A14

Twelve people inside and the Nutshell is packed to suffocation. There are other claimants to the title, but the Nutshell is officially (according to the *Guinness Book of Records*) Britain's smallest pub, measuring 100 square feet. The record for the greatest number of people in it at any one time stands at a mind-boggling 102, plus a dog. Curving round a corner into the Buttermarket of this glorious Georgian town, the Nutshell has a brown and cream exterior with a large inn sign, flower baskets and lamps. It's packed with such memorabilia as a miniature copy of *The Times*, the world's smallest darts board and snooker table, an elephant's tooth, a stuffed three-legged chicken, and a mummified cat and mouse. There's also a vast collection of coins and bank notes donated by visitors from around the world. In good weather there are much-needed seats on the pavement. The pub is too small to offer food but sells Greene King IPA and Abbot from the brewery in the town. The Traverse is closed on Sundays and public holidays.

NAG'S HEAD

53 KINNERTON STREET, OFF WILTON PLACE,
LONDON SW1 (020 7235 1135)
Underground: Hyde Park Corner

This is one of London's smallest pubs, tucked away down a mews in Belgravia. It's handy for Harrods, though once inside the pub you might think you were a hundred miles away from "The Smoke" due to the quietness and the warm, civilised welcome. The pub is dominated by an amazing sunken counter that connects the front room to a small basement area at the back. Adnams and Tetley's bitters are pulled by 19th-century china, brass and pewter hand-pumps. The beamed and wood-panelled front bar has an old kitchen range, while the smaller back bar has some stools and seating. Don't miss the genuine 1930s "What the Butler Saw" machine and one-armed bandit. Lunchtime and early evening there's good pub grub, such as sandwiches, chilli, ploughman's, steak and mushroom pie, and bangers and mash.

Lord Nelson

Walsingham Road, Burnham Thorpe,
near Burnham Market, Norfolk (01328 738241)
Off A149, signposted from B1155 and B1355

Admiral Lord Nelson was born in this tiny village and learnt his naval skills on the rivers, Broads and sea. The ale house named in his honour has developed from a simple farm cottage and was first named the Plough before being renamed in honour of its famous local hero; he gave a party here for the villagers when he returned to sea in 1793. It was turned into a shrine to Nelson by now-retired landlord Leslie Winter, who accumulated 60 prints or more about the life and times of the sea dog. You enter through a low door into a corridor with a bowed old brick floor. The main room has high-back settles on a polished tile floor and a fireplace with original ovens. A second, no-smoking room has flagstones and an open fire, and is mainly used by diners. There's nothing so modern as a bar: the ales are tapped straight from casks in a stillroom and brought to you in glasses or jugs. There's a splendid range of beer, including Greene King XX Mild, IPA and Abbot, plus Woodforde's Wherry and Nelson's Revenge. The pub also serves a rum-based drink called Nelson's Blood. In Leslie Winter's time "food" ran to a packet of crisps, but new landlady Lucy Stafford has developed the food side to plaudits all round. Lunchtime and evening you may find such dishes as chicken and mushroom soup, sandwiches, pan-fried garlic mushrooms, ploughman's, steak and kidney pie, fresh crab, baked cod fillet, smoked salmon with mixed leaves and red peppers, and English breakfast served all day. Desserts may include bread and butter pudding, pecan pie, apple crumble, and spicy orange cheesecake. There are occasional jazz and blues evenings. Children are welcome at lunchtime and only in the restaurant in the evening.

Royal Oak

Fritham, Hampshire (023 8081 2606)
Off B3078 and M27 junction 1

Deep in the New Forest and in superb walking country, the tiny, 17th-century, thatched Royal Oak offers a fine welcome from licensees Neil and Pauline McCulloch, who have spared no effort in restoring and refurbishing the interior and exterior of this foresters' ale house. All three rooms are small but comfortable: there's a main front bar, a back bar with an inglenook and an old brick oven, and a third room was once the landlord's living room. There are low beamed ceilings, wooden floors, wheelback chairs and tiny settles. The back room, with a low wooden ceiling and half-panelled walls, is known as the "parliament of the forest" as for centuries the people from the area have come to the pub to air their grievances. In spite of its small stature, the Royal Oak manages to sell more than 100 barrels a year of Ringwood beer, with Best, Fortyniner and True Glory tapped straight from casks behind the bar. Cribbage and dominoes are played but there are no noisy games machines to spoil the wonderful atmosphere. Lunchtime food includes soup and ploughman's; evening meals for parties in winter can be ordered in advance. Barbecues are held in the large back garden in summer.

Smith's Arms

Godmanstone, near Dorchester, Dorset (01300 341236)
Off A352 north of Dorchester

This 15th-century thatched inn closed in December 1999 due to the retirement of the landlord: he was a jockey in early life and his stature was perfectly suited to the pub. Phone from time to time to see if it has reopened, for this tiny building, just twelve metres by four, vies with the Nutshell as the smallest pub in the country. It was once a blacksmith's and, according to a local legend, was turned into an ale house by Charles II. He stopped to have his horse shod, asked for an ale, and when he was told there was nowhere to quench his thirst, promptly gave the smithy a licence: wonderful thing, the divine right of kings. There's just room inside for six tables, some small pews along the wall, and wooden stools. Let's hope this historic place can be kept going.

Best of the Rest

Travellers' Call

134 Glossop Road, Marple Bridge, Greater Manchester
(0161 427 4169)
Mellor Road

Pub walk in the Lake District

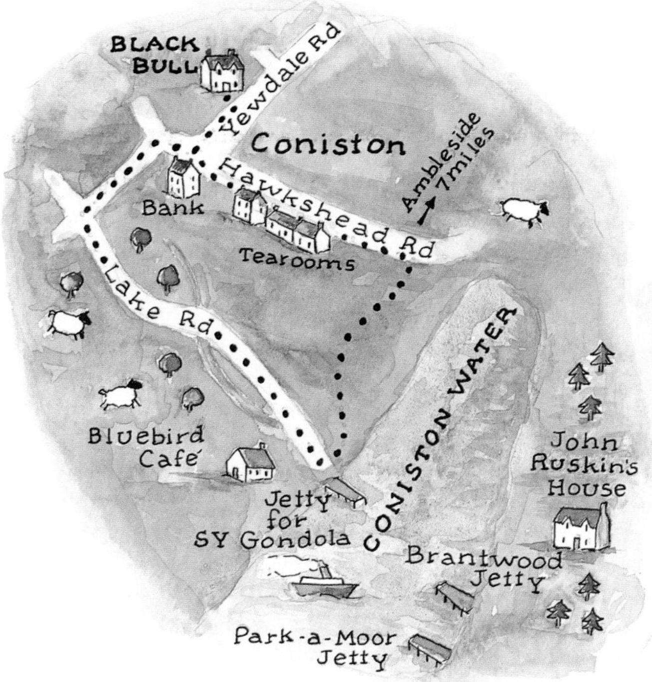

The base for this walk is the BLACK BULL INN, Yewdale Road, Coniston, Cumbria, on the A593 (015394 41335), a 400-year-old coaching inn in the heart of Coniston village, at the foot of the fells and the looming bulk of Coniston Old Man.

This is a pick-and-mix walk, as short or long as you choose, and with a delightful watery interlude, again at your discretion. Turn right outside the inn and head towards Barclays Bank immediately ahead of you. Pick up a brown road sign to the right, pointing to "Boat Landings, launches and SY Gondola".

Cross a road bridge over a beck, keep left past a petrol station and, at another brown sign, turn left into Lake Road. You walk past some pleasant stone-built houses and a school playground. The road is lined with trees and, ahead, there is a fine view of thickly wooded fells in the distance. On the right a rugby pitch appears and on the left a crescent called Beck Yeat with some new housing.

You are now in open countryside. Black-faced sheep graze in fields on either side and, over your shoulder, there is a splendid view of whitewashed and slate houses rising up the hillside beyond the village. The road bends sharply to the left by Coniston Pottery and Mill Shop (where you can book for rock climbing, abseiling and mountain biking) and crosses a stone bridge over the beck. The road narrows: on the right-hand side there is a grassy curb that allows you to walk alongside the shallow beck that runs under a canopy of trees.

The road now runs straight as an arrow but there is no indication of the delights ahead until there is a sudden glimpse of water and you are on the shores of Coniston Water by the Bluebird Cafe (hot drinks, snacks and light lunches, and lots of Donald Campbell memorabilia). To the left you can hire boats at the Coniston Boating Centre. To the right, by a jetty you can take more leisurely cruises on the Steam Yacht *Gondola*. You have a choice. You can walk alongside the lake or you can take a trip on the *Gondola*, stop off at one or two jetties on the voyage to continue your walk, or let the yacht take you the length of Coniston Water and back again.

The *Gondola* is a restored Victorian steam yacht with two plush saloons, and was the model for Captain Flint's houseboat in "Swallows and Amazons". (Further information, including "Swallows and Amazons" trips for children: 015394 41288). The yacht takes you three-quarters of the way down the lake to Peel Island and the Park-a-Moor jetty, where you can disembark and walk back along the side of the lake. The yacht then continues back along the lake to the Brantwood jetty where you can get off to visit John Ruskin's house, where the artist and champion of the Pre-Raphaelite movement lived from 1872 until his death in 1900. The imposing whitewashed buildings, set high above the lake, are open to the public and have a restaurant and tea rooms (details: 015394 41396). You can leave the yacht, visit the house and continue on foot round the head of the lake back to Coniston jetty or catch the next sailing of the *Gondola*.

Whichever way you choose to return to the main jetty, you now have to get back to the village on foot. Walk past the Coniston Boating Centre and watch for a path between trees to the left. You cross two tiny streams that flow into the lake, then the track bears left over a wooden bridge over a beck. You approach a five-barred gate where you join a wider track on the right that comes from the head of the lake. There are open fields on either side and there is a fine view ahead of the fells and Coniston Old Man rising into the clouds. The track meanders between the fields until you approach a cattle grid and another five-barred gate, where the track ends.

You now join the main Hawkshead Road but it is a pleasant walk as, on the right-hand side, a path is divided by a hedge that soon gives way to a dry-stone wall. Sheep dot the fields on either side, and the fells and mountains loom ahead. After about five minutes you are in the outskirts of Coniston village where you cross a bridge over a river. A signpost to the right says "Ambleside 7 miles". Unless you feel like a long hike to Ambleside, cross the road to get on to the pavement and enter Tilberthwaite Avenue, which takes you to the heart of the village and past several tea rooms or the Crown Hotel, if you need refreshment. Barclays Bank appears on the left and you turn right to find the Black Bull.

The inn, owned by the Bradley family, is painted barley white outside and inside has flagged floors, beamed ceilings and some bare stone walls. There are many photos of Donald Campbell and *Bluebird:* Campbell used the inn as the base for his ill-fated attempt in 1967 to break the world water speed record. A TV film about Campbell, with Anthony Hopkins playing the doomed man, also used the Black Bull and there are stills from the programme on the walls.

The inn has its own tiny brewery which in 1998 won the coveted title of Champion Beer of Britain for its Bluebird Bitter at the Campaign for Real Ale's Great British Beer Festival. The bitter plus two other beers, Old Man and Opium, are on sale in the inn. Brewery visits can be arranged. Guest beers include Theakston's Best and Timothy Taylor's Landlord, which won the championship a year after Bluebird.

Food is served all day from noon until 9pm and includes soup, jacket potatoes with choice of fillings, sandwiches, ploughman's, Cumberland sausage, fisherman's platter, scampi, fish dish of the day, roast chicken, chilli with rice and pitta bread, and a good choice of vegetarian dishes: hazelnut and mushroom pâté, aubergine bake, spinach and lentils, vegetable moussaka, wild mushroom rigatoni, leek and mushroom crumble, and spicy vegetable chilli. There are special meals for children, who are welcome in the inn. There are seats in a courtyard at the front of the inn and excellent accommodation is available (15 rooms).

Dedicated walkers who want a more demanding route should buy the Footprint Walks around Coniston (£3.50) for trips up Coniston Old Man or the disused copper mines on the fells.

The Black Bull Inn, Coniston

Pubs that brew their own beer

FARMERS BOY

134 LONDON ROAD, ST ALBANS, HERTFORDSHIRE (01727 766702)
Off A1, M1 and M25

Viv and Tina Davies have turned this small, cheery pub into a local institution with their good welcome, wholesome food and splendid home-brewed beers from the Verulam Brewery at the rear: Verulam comes from the old Roman name for the city. Viv produces Special, IPA, Farmers Joy and even a cask-conditioned VB Lager in his tiny plant. As well as English varieties, he uses American and German hops to create wonderfully aromatic and quenching brews. The IPA (short for India Pale Ale) is an outstanding beer with massive citrus fruit from the hops. Adnams Best Bitter is also a regular. The pub is dominated by a large horseshoe bar, and has a blazing fire, bare boards, benches and pews, and old photos of the area, including one of the pub early in the 20th century. An area to the right of the bar, by the tiny kitchen, is set aside for diners. Tina and her staff beaver away to provide food all day and the dishes include filled jacket potatoes, all-day breakfast, ham, egg and chips, fish and chips, sausage and chips or vegetarian sausage and chips, steak, ale and mushroom pie, and chicken, ham and mushroom pie. The Farmers Boy was named Pub of the Year by the local branch of Camra in 1998. It has a large friendly dog and a German Shepherd puppy. Brewery visits are available but must be booked in advance.

ORANGE BREWERY

37-39 PIMLICO ROAD, LONDON SW1 (020 7730 5984)
Underground: Sloane Square

This historic, 18th-century building started life as the Orange Coffee House and was dedicated to Prince William of the House of Orange who lived in Pimlico for a while, presumably without a passport in those days. The memory of the famous post-Second World War film, "Passport to Pimlico", in which the district declared independence from Britain, is commemorated in the pub with an occasional wheat beer called Passport. The pub is dominated by a long L-shaped bar, has open fires, wooden settles and tables, and scrubbed wooden floors. The tiny brewery in the cellar is an exact replica of a commercial one, with a malt mill for grinding the grain, a mash tun where malt and pure hot water are blended to turn malt starches into fermentable sugars, a copper where the sugary extract is boiled with hops, and four fermenters where yeast converts the sugars into alcohol. Tours are available for a maximum of ten people. There's a viewing area in the bar that allows customers to look down on the brewery. All the beers – SW1, SW2, Victoria Lager and such seasonal ales as Chelsea Blossom, Pimlico Porter, Sloane Danger, and Donner & Blitzen at Christmas – can be taken away in four-pint containers. Food includes sausages and mash, fish and chips and a range of pies. Children are welcome in an eating area.

Brunswick

1 Railway Terrace, Derby (01332 290677)

This remarkable, triangular ale house is just a few yards from Derby railway station and is based in an inn built for railway employees in 1842. It has been restored by the Derbyshire Railway Trust. With its flagstone floors, a warren of small, intimate rooms off a corridor, old station furnishings, coal fires, lamps, and railway memorabilia, it's an atmospheric cross between a pub, a country station and a working men's club. Licensee Trevor Harris brews some wonderfully crafted ales in his brewhouse at the far end of the corridor. They include Recession Ale, Triple Hop, Second Brew, Railway Porter, Old Accidental and many one-off and seasonal beers, all sold at remarkably keen prices. Brewery tours can be arranged in advance. Lunchtime food offers filled rolls, cobs with a choice of fillings, ploughman's, home-made chicken, leek, mushroom and celery pie, and mushroom Stroganoff. Only rolls are available on Sunday. Children are welcome in a family room and small garden. There's live jazz on Thursday evenings.

Blue Anchor

50 Coinagehall Street, Helston, Cornwall (01326 562821)
A394

This unspoilt old granite and thatch inn claims – and there are no known competitors – to be the oldest brewpub in Britain. It dates from 1400 when it was a monks' resting place. At a time when water was unsafe to drink, the inn naturally made ale for the monks and has continued to brew ever since.

The remarkable Spingo ales recall a time when ale was strong and not taxed to oblivion. The "weakest" ale is more than five per cent alcohol and there are stories about a Christmas Special of eleven per cent that extended the holiday season by several days for those who imbibed it. It has now been toned down to a more manageable 7.6 per cent. The inn has a series of small beamed rooms that are served by a central corridor. Flagstones cover the floors, tables have been fashioned from old beer casks, and one room has a large stone inglenook fireplace. There's a skittle alley, and visitors are normally welcome to visit both the ancient brewhouse across the back yard and the cellars where the finished beers are stored. The Spingo range includes Middle, Best, Special, Easter Special and Christmas Special. Lunchtime bar food includes home-made soup, rolls, sandwiches, curry, and steak and kidney pie. Children are welcome in one room and live folk and jazz are played some evenings.

Brewery Tap

80 Westgate, Peterborough, Cambridgeshire (01733 358500)
Off A1 and A47

America comes to Peterborough: most British brewpubs are tiny but Paul Hook, owner of Oakham Brewery, has fashioned a spacious pub-cum-brewery from a former Labour Exchange building that he claims is the biggest brewpub in Europe, with room for 720 customers. You don't need to book a tour, for the whole brewing process is open to view through a glass wall that shows the mash tuns, coppers, fermenters and craftsmen that produce the full range of Oakham's ales. The design of the pub is inspirational, using the original architecture to great effect, with iron pillars supporting a mezzanine, light bulbs in the rim of a suspended steel ring, and a long bar of pale wood backed by a display of wine bottles held in a wall of wooden cubes. The orange walls are decorated by blow-ups of newspaper clippings. There are always three Oakham ales on tap, usually the award-winning Jeffrey Hudson Bitter (JHB), with Bishop's Farewell, Old Tosspot and a range of seasonal brews that includes Helterskelter, Mompesson's Gold, and Black Hole Porter. Thai and Oriental food are the specialities of the house (food is served all day until 10pm), with such dishes as wan ton, dim sum, tempura vegetables, spring rolls, stir-fried noodles with sweet radish, tamarind sauce, bean sprouts, spring onions, peanuts, chillies, egg and tiger prawns, and curries. The bar also offers such guest beers as Draught Bass and Fuller's London Pride. Children are not admitted.

Beacon Hotel

129 Bilston Street, Sedgley, West Midlands (01902 883380)
A463, off A4123

If you want to know what mild ale tasted like in its heyday then the Beacon, with its Sarah Hughes' Brewery, can supply the answer. The tiny brewery behind the Victorian hotel was opened in the 1860s and was bought by Sarah Hughes in 1921, where she brewed a Dark Ruby Ale. After her death, the plant lay unused until 1987 when her grandson, John Hughes, found her brewing recipe in a cigar box among her effects. Most of the brewing plant had rotted away and was replaced by new vessels bought from other breweries, including Ansells in Birmingham. The brewhouse is designed along Victorian "tower" lines, with the stages of the brewing process flowing by gravity from floor to floor. Brewed from pale and crystal malts and hopped with Fuggles and Goldings varieties, Sarah Hughes Dark Ruby Mild is an astonishing six per cent alcohol, proving that genuine milds were not weak but simply less hoppy and bitter than pale ales. Pale Amber and Surprise beers have been added and all are sold in the meticulously preserved Victorian pub from a central bar that supplies, through a hatch, a room with a piano, carpeted floor, marble fireplace, velvet curtains and mahogany tables. A tap room across the corridor has a black-leaded fireplace topped by a mantlepiece with an embroidered protector, a sort of antimacassar for fireplaces. There's a large conservatory packed with flowers and plants. The only food is cheese and onion cobs. Children are welcome in a family room and there's a play area in the garden. As the 21st century dawns, go and marvel at this wonderful example of Victorian ale and design. Brewery tours can be arranged.

Best of the Rest

Bitter End

15 Kirkgate, Cockermouth, Cumbria (01900 828993)
A66

Wine Vaults

Albert Road, Southsea, Hampshire (023 9286 4712)
Off A3

Brewery taps

Flower Pots Inn

Cheriton, Hampshire (01962 771318)

B3046, four miles south of New Alresford, off B3046 and A272

The Flower Pots is the "brewery tap" for the on-site Cheriton Brewhouse: historically, a tap is the nearest pub to a brewery, where the first casks of a new brew are tapped or broached. Cheriton was built in 1993 to supply the Flower Pots, and the ten-barrel plant, in a wood-slatted building with a steeply pitched roof, now supplies 40 other pubs in the area. The Mid-Hants Steam Railway – the Watercress Line – runs close by at Alresford, and Cheriton beers are sometimes available on the trains. In its short life, the brewery has won two major prizes from Camra in the annual Champion Beer of Britain competition. The splendid aromas of warm malt and boiling hops seep across the car park and the large gardens into the pub, which once belonged to the retired head gardener of Avington Park, who gave it its name. The brick-built former farmhouse dates from the 1820s and has two unspoilt bars with quarry tiled floors and old farming implements on the walls. Children are welcome in one room where paper and coloured pencils are on hand. Food is served lunchtime and evening (not Sunday evening) and may include filled baps, sandwiches, ploughman's, hot-pot, chilli, curry, lamb and apricot casserole, and beef and ale stew. The ales from the other side of the car park include Pots Ale, Best Bitter, Diggers Gold, Flower Pots and seasonal specials. Morris men perform in the large, raised back garden in summer and Cheriton is close to the site of a major battle in the Civil War. Accommodation is available in the pub.

Castle Inn

Chiddingstone, Kent (01892 870247)

Off B2027, east of Edenbridge

This superb mellow brick inn dates from 1730 and takes its name from Hever Castle, the former home of Anne Boleyn. It has ancient beams, a tiled roof and porch, settles that form booths round tables, and latticed and mullioned windows. It's just down the lane from Larkins Brewery, which is based on a hop farm. The brewery is run by the Dockerty family who started brewing in 1986 in Tunbridge Wells before they moved to the farm, where they turned an old barn into a brewhouse. Additional fermenters and a new copper have been installed to cope with demand for the succulent ales that are available in some 60 pubs in the South-east. The beers use only Kentish hops, including the prized Fuggles and East Kent Goldings, some of which are grown on the farm and dried in a conventional oast house. In the Castle, bar food may include home-made soup, filled baguettes, ploughman's, vegetable curry, extremely hot chilli (be warned) and children's meals. Evening meals could include braised lamb with garlic, pork fillet with cider, and poached salmon. The beers on offer are Larkins Traditional Ale and Chiddingstone Bitter as well as Harvey's Best from Sussex and Young's Bitter from London. If Larkins Porter is on, don't miss one of the finest of the revivalist examples of the style. The surrounding village has some magnificent Tudor buildings.

GEORGE

4 SOUTH STREET, BRIDPORT, DORSET (01308 423187)
A35

Publican John Mander has been running this Georgian hotel, opposite the Guildhall, for more than 20 years and offers good food, accommodation and tasty ales from Palmer's brewery in the town. The brewery is based in lovely stone buildings close to the sea and the Dorset chalk cliffs. One part of the brewery is thatched and at the rear there is a large waterwheel alongside the river: the wheel used to provide the power for the brewing operations. The site dates from 1794 and was bought by John Cleeves and Robert Henry Palmer a century later: it is still run by two Palmer brothers. The beautifully crafted ales use English, American and Slovenian hops. The beer called Bridport Bitter, just 3.2 per cent alcohol, is one of the last surviving West Country ales known as "boy's bitters" that were designed to refresh agricultural workers and keep them relatively sober. In the George, Bridport Bitter is joined by IPA and 200, the last named brewed to celebrate Palmer's 200th anniversary. The two cheerful bars, divided by a corridor, have tiled floors with big rugs, ancient dining tables and wheelback chairs. There's a log fire in winter. Coffee and croissants are served in the morning while bar meals may include fresh fish from West Bay, home-made fishcakes with tomato sauce, smoked mackerel pâté, kedgeree, Welsh rarebit, lamb's kidneys in Madeira, and a range of pies with such fillings as lamb and turnip, and chicken and mushroom. There's a good wine list and a range of malt whiskies. Children are welcome in eating areas and accommodation is available.

Pear Tree

Hook Norton, Oxfordshire (01608 737482)
Off A361 near Banbury

The Pear Tree is just 100 yards down a lane from the Hook Norton Brewery, which looms incongruously over this small and pleasant Oxfordshire village. The brown stone brewery is one of the finest in England and is a splendid example of a Victorian "tower brewery", in which each stage of the production process flows by gravity from floor to floor, removing the need for pumps. It was designed by William Bradford, who also designed Harvey's of Lewes and Tolly Cobbold of Ipswich: all the breweries bear his signature of a pagoda tower at the top. Hook Norton was built in 1850 by John Harris on the site of a maltings and the company is still run by his family. Much of the original equipment is still in use, including a 25-horsepower steam engine that draws Cotswold well water to the surface. The Pear Tree offers the full Hook Norton range of Best Mild, Best Bitter, Generation and Old Hooky. The bar has rustic furniture on the wooden floor and open fires in cold weather. It offers such dishes as home-made soups, sandwiches, beef in ale casserole, sweet and sour chicken or Thai chicken curry. Children are welcome, there's a large garden, traditional pub games are played, and accommodation is available.

Nelson & Railway

Station Road, Kimberley, Nottinghamshire (0115 938 2177)
Off A610, three miles from M1 junction 26

This is the story of two pubs that served two railway stations in a former mining village with two breweries. Everything has been merged or, in the case of the pits, closed. The Lord Nelson and the Railway Hotel were long ago knocked into one while Hardy's and Hanson's breweries, founded in 1832 and 1847, amalgamated in 1931. The company is still controlled by members of the ruling families and the double-chimneyed, red-brick buildings dominate the village. For decades Hardys & Hansons brewed easy-drinking mild and bitter ("good slutching ales", they say in these parts) for miners' pubs and clubs. But in recent years a new and more demandingly bitter Classic has been added along with several seasonal beers. The Nelson & Railway offers the full range of Kimberley ales in the attractive beamed bars with wood panelling, a rare etched glass door, and old railway and brewery memorabilia. The home-cooked food, with specials chalked on a board, may include soup, such pies as chicken and mushroom, steak and kidney or rabbit, battered cod, deep-fried vegetables with cheese and garlic sauce, lasagne, ploughman's, and chicken tikka masala. There's a children's menu, a large garden with swings, pub games – including darts, alley and table skittles, dominoes and cribbage – and accommodation. D. H. Lawrence's home is close by in Eastwood.

Flower Pots Inn, Cheriton, Hants

SUN INN

MAIN STREET, DENT, CUMBRIA (015396 25208)

Off A683; signposted from Sedbergh

Dent is disputed territory, officially in Cumbria but claimed by Yorkists to be part of God's Own Country. Whichever way you slice it, it's a breathtakingly lovely Dales village, home to Dent Brewery and its pub the Sun (it also owns the George & Dragon, almost next door). The brewery was set up in 1990 in a barn behind the Sun to supply just the pub, but it now serves 20 other outlets in the area and has its own distribution company, Flying Firkin, to wholesale beers nationwide. Local spring water is blended with English malt and Kent, Worcestershire and Slovenian hops to create rich aromas and flavours for the uncompromisingly bitter beers. The white-

washed Sun has beams and old photos, and a coal fire for cold days. It serves Dent's Bitter, Kamikaze and T'owd Tup, which means an old ram. Simple, sustaining bar food may include home-made soup, sandwiches, ploughman's, lasagne, home-made steak and kidney pie, Cumberland sausage, Brie and courgette crumble, and ham and eggs, with children's portions. Accommodation is available.

Brewery Tap

Colston Street, Bristol, Avon (0117 921 3668)

The brewery in question is Smiles, which is next door to the pub. Smiles was founded in 1977 and is one of the longest-surviving small craft breweries in the country. The Tap won Camra's Best New Pub Design award in 1991 for its simple layout with a small wood-panelled bar and a horseshoe serving counter. A no-smoking extension has been added and children are welcome there. The pub sells Smiles BA, Golden Best and Heritage as well as a vast range of seasonal and occasional brews. Food starts with a celebrated breakfast at 8am known as the Blowout. From lunchtime until 8pm, food may include home-made soups, often suitable for vegetarians, plus bean-burgers; lentil bake; lamb chops in red wine; chicken in garlic cream sauce; beef braised in Bristol Stout with herb dumplings; and pasta dishes. There are no evening meals on Sundays. The tap is just five minutes' walk from Bristol city centre.

Best of the Rest

Tally Ho

Market Street, Hatherleigh, Devon (01837 810306)
A386

Farmers Arms

Lower Apperley, near Apperley, Gloucestershire (01452 780307)
B4213, off A38

Railway Tavern

Reedham, Norfolk (01493 700340)
Off B1140 Acle to Beccles road

Pubs that serve traditional cider

Cider House

Dunkerton's Cider Mill, Hays Head, Luntley,
near Pembridge, Herefordshire (01544 388161)
A44 from Leominster; in Pembridge turn left at New Inn, Dunkerton's is one mile

This is the "cider tap" for one of the most determinedly traditional yet far-sighted of England's small band of cider and perry makers. Dunkerton's has ploughed a different furrow from the giant producers of fizzed-up alcoholic drinks made mainly from apple concentrate rather than whole fruit. Both cider mill and bar-cum-restaurant are run with enormous enthusiasm by Susie and Ivor Dunkerton who gave up the London high-life (where Ivor was a television producer) to grow apples and pears free from agribusiness chemicals to make fine-tasting natural drinks. They have a Soil Association certificate, and grow such apple varieties as Binet Rouge, Breakwells Seedling, Brown Snout, Cider Ladies Finger, Tremletts Bitter, Roi de Pomme, and Yarlington Mill, and have planted orchards for such rare varieties as Bloody Turk, Kingston Black and Sheeps Nose. They have also planted pear trees, with such varieties as Barland, Blakeney Red, Butt, Moorcroft and Red Horse, in a bid to save perry from extinction. The Cider House is based in two 400-year-old converted timber-frame barns with flagstone floors and an open log fire. The ciders include traditional dry (no sugar added), medium dry, medium sweet or sweet; single varietal ciders when available; and perry. Sparkling cider is served in bottles. There are two organic beers available, Golden Promise from Caledonian of Edinburgh and Bucher Pilsner from Germany. There's a good choice of wine as well. Bar lunches include sandwiches with home-made bread and a choice of cheese, salad or egg mayonnaise, Cider Maker's Delight with bread and three British cheeses, or cold meat salad. A full lunch or dinner could include mildly spiced Mulligatawny soup or field and forest mushroom soup; beetroot and red pepper bavois with piquant raspberry and orange; lightly chilled Stilton and Caerphilly cheesecake with gooseberry and apple crème fraîche; warm salad of beef fillet, bacon and sweetbreads in port and redcurrant sauce; followed by roast butternut squash with caraway and carrot ratatouille; cauliflower, courgette and banana crumble with mustard and Breakwells Seedling cider sauce; duck leg and pear flaky pastry pasty with vanilla and almond cream; slowly braised rabbit cooked and served in its own sweet cider and damson wine sauce; grilled breasts of pigeon with oregano, potatoes and rich onion gravy; and pan-fried chicken breast with lemon, ginger and spring onion and minted sour cream. Desserts could include bitter chocolate rum and raisin parfait with almond ice cream. Organic ingredients are used wherever possible and a bigger herb and vegetable garden was planned for 2000 to supply the restaurant. Draught and bottled ciders and perries are available from a shop on the site, and the mill and orchards can be visited (01544 388653). Cider House opening hours: Monday to Saturday 10am to 5pm or dusk in winter; dinner Thursday, Friday and Saturday from 7pm; Sunday lunch from 11.45am. Booking essential for dinner. Closed January and February.

CHURCH HOUSE INN

HARBERTON, DEVON (01803 863707)

Off A381 near Totnes

Churchward's cider is the speciality of the house: the cider comes from Yalberton Farm (near Paignton Zoo) which is open for sales of sweet, medium and dry ciders and tours during the summer (01803 558157). The

Wenlock Arms, London N1

Church House is an ancient, one-bar inn in a small village on a steep, winding hill. The pub gets its name from the fact that it was the chantry house for monks from the local church. Parts of the pub date from the 12th century and there are 17th and 18th century pews, settles, an inglenook with a wood-burning stove, and latticed windows. There's a no-smoking family room hidden behind a medieval oak screen. As well as local cider, the pub serves Bass and Courage beers plus several guest ales. The food menu changes daily (there's a board for Specials) but you will always find home-made soup, sandwiches and a ploughman's, along with such dishes as crêpes Florentine au gratin, mustard and herb sausages with onion gravy, roasted red pepper and aubergine parmigiana, curries, baltis, chicken supreme, scallops, prawn and monkfish kebabs, and a separate children's menu. Occasional summer-time entertainment comes from Morris Men and folk groups. Accommodation is available.

Rugglestone Inn

WIDECOMBE IN THE MOOR, DEVON (01364 621327)
B3387

Widecombe, with its Uncle Tom Cobleigh associations, nestles in a valley betwen high tors. The inn is a few hundred yards outside the village, past the church, converted in 1832 from a farm cottage. It's a tiny stone-built pub with a main bar that has a few settles and tables while a second room has a stone fireplace and some benches and tables: darts, shove-ha'penny, cribbage, dominoes and West Country euchre are played here. Dry cider comes from Lower Whiddon Farm at Ashburton 3½ miles away, where Gerry Vallance makes just 100 gallons a year, using local apples and their natural yeasts, and matured in oak casks. (You must phone in advance if you wish to visit: 01364 652840.) The inn also serves Butcombe Bitter, Dartmoor Best and a third beer in summer, all served straight from casks behind the bar. Food is simple and homely fare: home-made soup, pasties (either meat or vegetarian), ploughman's, stew and dumplings, rabbit casserole, cheese, leek and potato bake, roast Mediterranean vegetable bake, and steak and kidney pie, with such desserts as treacle and walnut tart or apple pudding. The inn has friendly cats and dogs, and there are seats in a field outside. Mind you don't fall in the passing stream on the way to the outside toilets. Children under 14 are not admitted but they can take shelter in bad weather.

Wenlock Arms

26 Wenlock Road, Hoxton, London N1 (020 7608 3406)
Underground: Old Street

The Wenlock has been transformed from a run-down backstreet boozer into one of the finest ale and cider houses in London, run by devoted members of the Campaign for Real Ale. It's a simple but homely and welcoming one-bar pub with a wide and ever-changing range of ales plus Biddenden's Bushell Cider, a powerful 6 per cent alcohol and made by Biddenden Vineyards of Little Whatmans, Biddenden, Ashford, Kent. It is the biggest independent cider maker in the South-east, producing more than 30,000 gallons a year (tours by arrangement: 01580 291726). The Wenlock also occasionally sells perry. The pub is handy for the Regent's Canal, offers simple snacks at lunchtime and has traditional jazz on Friday and Saturday nights and a ragtime pianist on Sunday afternoons.

Lytton Arms

Park Lane, Old Knebworth, Hertfordshire (01438 812312)
Three miles from A1M junction 7

A spacious, Victorian building designed in the late 19th century by Sir Edward Lutyens, brother-in-law of Lord Lytton (whose family still live on the adjacent Knebworth Park), the pub has several comfortable and carpeted rooms, each one with a photographic theme, such as steam railways and Old Knebworth itself. Alongside the wide range of ales (more than 3,000 served in a decade), you'll find four traditional ciders, including Weston's Old Rosie. Weston's of Herefordshire is one of the major independent cider makers that has refused to tamper with tradition and quality. It matures its splendid products in ancient wooden casks called Pip, Squeak and Wilfred that began life as porter vats in 19th-century London. (Details of visits: 01531 660233.) The Lytton Arms has a couple of no-smoking areas for diners and food may include grilled butterfly chicken breast, vegetable chicken masala, king prawns, minted lamb steak, steak and kidney pie, mushroom Stroganoff, sausages made specially for the pub, and such desserts as spotted dick or chocolate pudding. The back garden has a play area, there are regular summer barbecues, and traditional pub games – dominoes, shove-ha'penny and table skittles – are played, plus giant chess on a terrace at the front.

Falkland Arms

Great Tew, Oxfordshire (01608 683653)

Off B4022, five miles from Chipping Norton

A wonderful creeper-clad, 15th-century inn built of mellow Cotswold stone in a village of thatched cottages, the bar has an inglenook fireplace, a stone-flagged floor worn smooth over the centuries, high-back settles, oak panels and beams, and mullioned lattice windows. The inn is named after Viscount Falkland, secretary to Charles I, who lived nearby. The tiny bar area dispenses Wadworth's ales from Devizes on antique handpumps, guest beers, and Weston's ciders from small casks. There's a no-smoking dining room and a large back garden with a dovecote. Bar food may include soup, sandwiches, filled baguettes and jacket potatoes, while in the evening you may find mushrooms cooked in double cream with port and Stilton, beef and ale pie, pork in cider, ploughman's, and lamb and rosemary casserole. Children are welcome in the dining room and parts of the bar are set aside for eating. Accommodation is available.

New Inn

Dowlish Wake, Somerset (01460 52413)

Off old A303 and A3037, south of Ilminster

The New Inn is, in fact, a delightful 350-year-old inn with old beams decorated with hops, wood-burning stoves, an inglenook, and high-back settles. As well as such hand-pumped ales as Butcombe Bitter, Theakston's Old Peculier and Wadworth 6X, there's Perry's medium and dry draught cider, made in the village, with a 16th-century cider mill in a thatched barn; tours available and free tastings (01460 52681): many of the traditional cider apples used are organic. The inn has a vast range of traditional pub games, including bar billiards, darts, dominoes, shove ha'penny, and both alley and table skittles. The family room is no-smoking. Bar food (not Sunday evening in winter) may include soup, sandwiches, ploughman's, omelettes, nut and lentil roast, liver and onions, and such Swiss dishes as raclette and charbonnade. There are tubs of flowers at the front of the inn and a pleasant back garden with a children's climbing frame.

Note: *For information about Camra's cider and perry group, APPLE, phone 01727 867201.*

Pubs with good wine

Nobody Inn

Doddiscombsleigh Village, Devon (01647 252394)

Signposted from B3193; off A38

Good wine and pubs sounds like an oxymoron but times are changing. *The Good Pub Guide* remarks that it had no awards for wine back in 1990 but now singles out more than a dozen pubs for praise, while the *Which? Guide to Country Pubs* devotes two whole pages to a list of pubs with "better-than-average" wine. Both include the Nobody Inn, which is the GPG's Wine Pub of the Year for 2000.

Licensee Nick Borst-Smith has around 850 wines in his cellar from just about every wine-producing country in the world. There are always around 20 wines available by the glass and they are chalked on a board. The range changes regularly but could include the likes of Frascati, Chilean Chardonnay, German Riesling, and Greek and Australian Muscats among the whites, two clarets and a Merlot from France, a Cabernet from Chile, and a Californian Zinfandel. There's also an English house white produced by Three Choirs in Gloucestershire. Mr Borst-Smith is also a wine merchant and you can buy wines from him: he provides a list with detailed tasting notes. He also serves 250 whiskies, farm cider, real ales that include a house beer brewed by Branscombe Vale, and 50 cheeses from the West Country. The 15th-century pub has original beams and old settles, excellent food and offers accommodation, but isn't suitable for children.

Trengilly Wartha

Constantine, Nancenoy, Cornwall (01326 340332)
Off A394, signposted Constantine

The name means "Place Above the Trees" and the inn of that name clings to the side of a wooded valley. It's remote and hard to find but worth the effort for the wine and the food (it's another GPG Dining Pub of the Year). One end of the main beamed bar has shelves of wines with different prices for drinking there or to take away. Licensees Nigel Logan and Michael Maguire also run their own retail business called Cochonnet Wines: the name is an elaborate joke, cochonnet being the small target ball in boules, which also means piglet, so you can make a pig of yourself on the wines. The range is awesome and includes half-bottles and between 15 and 20 by the glass. There's also a good choice of Armagnacs, malt whiskies and such cask ales as Cotleigh, Keltek, Skinners and Sharps. Food in the bar or conservatory dining room may include smoked mackerel and cheese pot; wild mushroom pasta gratin; meat or vegetarian pasties; ploughman's; Thai chicken in tomato sauce; and cod on boulangère potatoes. Children are welcome and accommodation is available.

Opposite: Trengilly Wartha, Constantine, Nancenoy, Cornwall

Pheasant Inn

Keyston, Cambridgeshire (01832 710241)
B663

The Pheasant is part of the small Huntsbridge Group of pubs in the county, with wines chosen by Master of Wine John Hoskins. There are 14 wines available by the glass, including Laurent Perrier Champagne, plus pudding wines and ports. The wines in general cover most regions and range from good-value affordable bottles to expensive vintages. Chef Martin Lee also offers food of the highest quality (it's the GPG's Cambridgeshire Dining Pub of the Year) in the thatched and beamed old inn: you may find tomato and basil soup with olive oil; stir-fried vegetables; fillets of brill with aubergine purée; spinach and ricotta ravioli with sage butter; char-grilled tuna with confit of peppers; and fresh tagliatelle with sun-dried tomatoes, roast red peppers, Parmesan and olive oil. If ale is your preferred tipple, the Pheasant offers Adnams Bitter and a regular guest beer. Children are welcome. (Other pubs in the group are the White Hart at Great Yeldham, Old Bridge in Huntingdon, Three Horseshoes at Madingley (*see page 86*), and the Falcon at Fotheringhay.)

General Tarleton

Harrogate Road, Ferrensby, North Yorkshire (01423 340284)
Off A6065

The General Tarleton, an 18th-century coaching inn, is run by Denis Watkins and John Topham, who also own the Angel at Hetton (*see page 20*). The wine list here is quite short, around 25 in total, but carefully chosen, with 18 by the glass, several in half-bottles and three pudding wines. In 1998 the owners spent £250,000, to use the horrible jargon of the times, a "makeover" that developed a covered courtyard for additional dining space. Nothing has been done to spoil the atmosphere of an inn named in honour of Sir Banastre Tarleton, MP for Liverpool, and a general under Wellington: that was in the days when MPs didn't have pagers. There's a low-beamed bar with open fires, brick pillars, exposed brickwork and comfortable rustic seats. Beyond the bar there's a pleasant, tree-lined garden. Business must be good at both the pubs owned by Messrs Watkins and Topham, as the signature dish at both places is called

Little Money Bags, which is seafood baked in a filo pastry. Other dishes, in bar and restaurant, lunchtime and evening, may include fish soup; baked tomato tart drizzled with pesto; taglioni with smoked salmon and avocado; char-grilled spring lamb leg steak; rib-eye steak; sausage and mash with roasted shallots and red wine sauce; a deli platter of chicken liver and foie gras parfait, Cheddar, Somerset Brie, pastrami, salami, roast ham and goose rillettes; and confit of duck. Desserts may offer "Hetton Mess", a punny pudding with meringue, yoghurt and raspberry coulis; summer pudding and brandy snap basket. Ales are strictly Yorkshire kosher: Black Sheep, Tetley and Tim Taylor. Children are welcome and accommodation is available.

LAMB AT HINDON

HIGH STREET, HINDON, WILTSHIRE (01747 820573)
B3089

This stone-built hotel, with dormers in the steeply-pitched roof, creeper-clad and with attractive flower beds adding to the welcome, was a 17th-century coaching inn but parts date back to the 13th century and the inn had a reputation as a haunt of smugglers at one time. There's a large painting of Salisbury Plain in the beamed bar, underscoring the time when mail coaches thundered across the plain, past the eerie and ancient edifice of Stonehenge, and stopped to refresh both horses and passengers at the Lamb. The spacious bar has a large inglenook with a log-burning fire, old settles, sonorously ticking clocks and a slate floor. The well-chosen wine list has a good selection of New World varieties, several vintages, and around a dozen wines by the glass. The beers are equally well chosen: as well as the ubiquitous Wadworth 6X, which hails from nearby Devizes, there are ales from such craft breweries as Ash Vine, Butcombe, Exmoor, Otter, Slaters and Tisbury.If you want to eat, lunchtime or evening, the bar and restaurant offer excellent food, and dishes may include soup; ploughman's; deep-fried squid; Greek salad; a choice of pasta dishes; vegetable and cheese bake; spinach and cottage cheese lasagne; venison and mushroom casserole; Dover sole; seared scallops with smoked chicken; and glazed lamb chops with hawthorn jelly. Desserts could include treacle tart and bread-and-butter pudding. Children are welcome, accommodation is available, and Fonthill Park is close by.

Pub walk in Upper Wharfedale, North Yorkshire

The starting point for this circular, seven-mile ramble is the **FOX & HOUNDS** at Starbotton, Upper Wharfedale Road, near Kettlewell (01756 760269). It has been an inn for 160 years but the building is 400 years old. It's in a charming hamlet surrounded by hills, has a bar with high beams from which whisky jugs hang, a flagstone floor and a vast stone fireplace. The dining room is non-smoking. James and Hilary McFadyen divide their roles as hosts: James looks after the cellar while Hilary is in charge of cooking. The popular menu includes Yorkshire puddings with such fillings as mince or ratatouille, tomato and basil soup with home-made granary bread, blue cheese soufflé with tomato and onion salad, baked salmon with a herb crust, peppered venison steak, parnsip and chestnut crumble, and such home-made desserts as brown sugar chestnut meringues and rhubarb

The Fox and Hounds, Starbotton, nr Kettlewell, Yorkshire

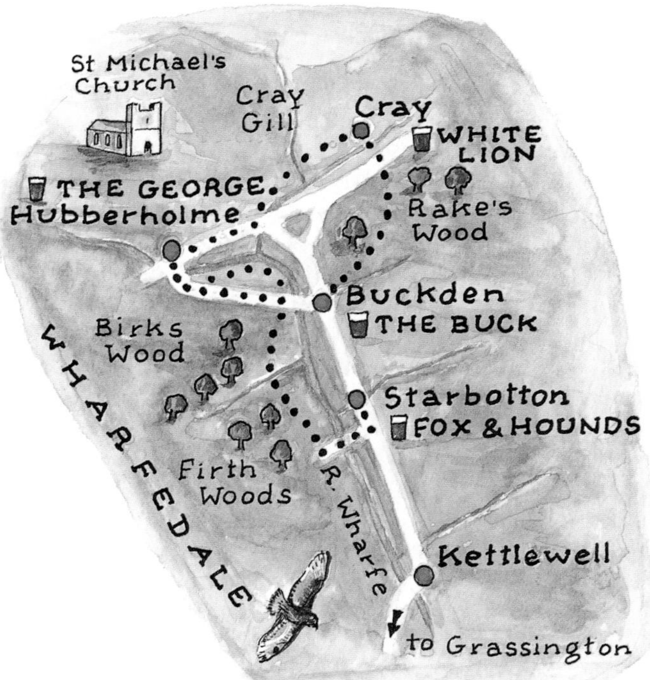

and ginger. Local ales include Black Sheep Best Bitter, Timothy Taylor's Landlord and Theakston's Best and Black Bull. There is a good choice of malt whiskies. The Fox & Hounds offers accommodation and closes in the afternoon. It's also closed on Mondays between January and mid-February except for bank holiday lunchtimes.

From the pub, turn left on the road towards Kettlewell. Three hundred yards on the right there is a footpath sign to Buckden. Go down a disused cart track and cross the River Wharfe by a footbridge. Turn right and follow the river bank for 500 yards. The path turns away from the river and goes through meadows and alongside Firth Woods: this is a fine area for spotting such birds as buzzards, curlews, dippers, mallards and shovellers.

At Birks Wood the path rejoins the river and leads to the bridge at Buckden. At this point you have a choice: you can turn left and take the road, or continue along the footpath by the river. Both routes lead to Hubberholme where you can stop for a well-earned drink or meal at the GEORGE (01756 760223), which nestles at the foot of the hills by the bridge. The 18th-century whitewashed inn started life as a farmhouse and later became the vicarage for St Michael's church. Pub, church and bridge form Yorkshire's smallest conservation area. The pub has two comfortable rooms with heavy beams supporting the ceiling, bare stone walls decorated with old plates and photos, flagstone floors and mullioned windows. Bar food, chalked on a board, includes sandwiches, home-made soups, goat's cheese lasagne, gammon and eggs, Cumberland sausage, and steak and kidney pie, and such puddings as sticky toffee and rum and raisin cheesecake. Beers include Black Sheep Special and Tetley Mild and Bitter, plus good wines and malt whiskies. The pub has letting rooms and is closed in the afternoon. Find time to visit the Norman church with a memorial to J. B. Priestley, whose ashes were scattered in the churchyard.

From the George, follow the road on the north side of the river and, just before a road junction, take the footpath and the stiff climb up Cray Gill with superb views of the waterfalls to your left. You soon arrive in Cray and the 17th-century WHITE LION (01756 760262), the highest pub in Wharfedale. The former packhorse and drovers' inn is in a breathtaking setting, with a stream running alongside, picnic tables overlooking a lane and the hills all around. Inside, the pub has flagstones, open fires, walls decorated with old farming tools and a beamed ceiling. You can play the ancient pub game of ring the bull, relish Moorhouse's Pendle Witches Brew and regular guest ales such as Black Sheep and Roosters, and enjoy such bar food as home-made soup, sandwiches, vegetable lasagne, steak and mushroom pie, venison casserole, and toffee nut cheesecake and hot chocolate fudge cake. The White Lion has bed and breakfast accommodation and opens all day in summer.

From the pub, cross the road and the stream by stepping stones and follow the footpath signs for Buckden. There is a short, sharp climb to join the ridge path, which has magnificent views over Upper Wharfedale. Turn right to follow the well-defined track that drops through Rakes Wood to Buckden car park. Cross the car park to the **BUCK** (01756 760228), a stone-faced and creeper-clad inn that faces the sloping village green: Denis and Edna Healey spent their honeymoon here in 1945. There are fine moorland views from the terrace. Inside, the open-plan bar has flagstones in one area, bare stone walls, a log fire, local pictures and a collection of willow-pattern plates. Food includes home-made soup, sandwiches, Mediterranean vegetables with a spicy tomato sauce, terrine of pressed bass, home-made salmon fishcakes, roasted escalope of salmon with a sorrel and Vermouth veloute, followed by sticky toffee pudding or chocolate truffle cheesecake. The dining area and restaurant are non-smoking. Beers include the full Theakston's range of Best, Black Bull, XB and Old Peculier. There are occasional guest ales, plus good wines and malt whiskies. There are bedrooms for hire and the pub opens all day.

From the pub the road takes you back to Starbotton, a distance of two miles.

Pubs with outstanding food

Three Horseshoes

High Street, Madingley, Cambridgeshire (01954 210221)
Off A1303, near junction 13 of M11

Richard Stokes is landlord and chef at this old thatched and white-washed pub on the village high street with a spacious bar and restaurant inside, bare boards, an open fire and pastel green walls. You can eat in the bar as well as the flower-decked, no-smoking restaurant based in a conservatory with waiter service. There's a daily set lunch or you can choose from the same menu in bar and restaurant. The emphasis is Italian/Mediterranean, backed by a superb wine list compiled by Master of Wine John Hoskins, which includes more than a dozen sold by the glass. The food may include a mixed tapas starter of radishes with butter, gazpacho, chorizo, almonds and manchego cheese with raisins and honey; soup of borlotti beans, barley and spring greens; wild rocket, dandelion, raddichio and herb salad with cherry tomatoes, feta, aubergine toasts, olives and basil aioli; char-grilled scallops; char-grilled leg of lamb with new potatoes, salsa verde, green and yellow beans; seared salmon fillet with green papaya salad and fish sauce; char-grilled chicken breast with wasabi mashed potato, stir-fry of shi-itake mushrooms, sugar snap, sesame and salsa; roast halibut with beetroot, horseradish and parsley and tumeric oil; and peppered veal with a salad of baby vegetables and truffle mayonnaise. Vegetarians can choose larger portions of the meat-free starters. Desserts may include fruit salad of blueberries, nectarines and mango with star anise and chilli syrup or toffee and brioche pudding with hot chocolate sauce and Jersey cream, accompanied by a pudding wine such as Jurançon Clos Uroulat. In good weather you can eat on the lawn with its shrubs, rose bushes and trees. Hand-pumped ales always include Adnams Best Bitter with an ever-changing range of guests that may include Batemans XXXB, Elgoods Cambridge Bitter, Everards Tiger, Fuller's London Pride, Morland Old Speckled Hen and Shepherd Neame Spitfire. Food is served lunchtime and evening every day and children are welcome.

Angel Inn

Polstead Street, Stoke-by-Nayland, Suffolk (01206 263245)
On B1068/A134

The 16th-century Angel is in a medieval village of timber-framed buildings where the 120-feet tower of St Mary's Church dominates the landscape. Stoke-by-Nayland is in the Dedham Vale conservation area, good walking country with Constable connections. The inn's main bar has massive beams, standing timbers, stripped brick walls, and a large log fire. There's also a no-smoking room with sofas, a wood-burning stove and handsome Victorian paintings on the walls, while a cheery bar for beer drinkers offers Adnams Best and Greene King IPA and Abbot with a guest, which could be Nethergate's Umble Ale from nearby Clare. The Well Room, with rough brick walls and a 52-feet deep well, acts as the dining room, where it's advisable to book a table. The menu, used throughout the pub, changes daily and is chalked on a blackboard; owner Peter Smith and head chef Mark Johnson concentrate on local produce, including fish and seafood from the Essex and Suffolk ports. You could settle for a ploughman's lunch or choose from the likes of deep-fried Cambozola; home-made soup; griddled fresh sardines in oregano; freshly dressed crab with home-made mayonnaise; supreme of chicken filled with Brie and coated with crushed hazelnuts; griddled haddock, skate wing or plaice; vegetable filo parcels with fresh tomato coulis; steak and kidney pudding; honey-glazed rack of lamb; or ballotine of duckling with cassis sauce. Desserts may include brown bread ice-cream, or steamed apple pudding with vanilla sauce. There's a carefully chosen wine list with some half-bottles and house wines by the glass. Food is available lunchtime and evening and accommodation is available.

Froize Inn

Chillesford, Suffolk (01394 450282)
Three miles from Orford on B1084

The curious name of the pub comes from an ancient dialect word for friary: it once stood between two friaries and sold savoury pancakes called "froise" to passing pilgrims. Orford Friary on the coast still stands and is about 40 minutes away on foot. The old inn dates from the late 15th century, is built of red Chillesford brick, has exposed beams, a stove in a big brick fireplace, and offers several traditional pub games including darts, dominoes, and shove ha'penny. Chef

Alistair Shaw and his wife Joy won the coveted Seafood Pub of the Year award in 1998 and their culinary skills are backed by fresh fish supplied by local fishermen as well as trawlermen at Lowestoft. You may find deep-fried cod; plaice and haddock in fresh batter; pan-fried sardines; fresh scallops; skate with brown butter; whole grilled mackerel with Parmesan; and fish pie. For a snack you may choose from Cheddar, crab or beef cobblers. Full restaurant meals could include king prawn in rice paper; wild mushrooms with Madeira under pastry; oysters; and home-made soups followed by whole steamed bass for two; local crab baked with spinach, bacon and nutmeg; scallop-filled pancakes with mango and lime; whole poached red gurnard; fish bubble and squeak with sea cabbage; and Kenyan-style kingfish with coconut sauce. There are several vegetarian options, such as filled pancakes or fried wild mushrooms in Madeira and cream sauce with a pastry topping. Desserts could include toffee and pistachio ice-cream. The tremendous range of real ales concentrates on East Anglian brewers and as well as such familiar names as Adnams and Greene King you can sample the likes of Mauldons (who brew the house beers), Earl Soham, Green Dragon, Iceni, Nethergate, St Peter's, and Tolly Cobbold. The pub lays down a cask of strong winter ale to mature for a year, a splendidly traditional, old country touch. There's a good wine list, too, with several by the glass. Food is served lunchtime and evening until 9pm but the pub is closed on Mondays. The main bar of the inn has beams, chairs and pews, and an open stove in a brick fireplace; the dining room is no-smoking. Accommodation is available and there are facilities for camping and caravanning in the large grounds.

Bishops Finger

9-10 West Smithfield, London EC1 (020 7248 2341)
Underground/train: Farringdon

The Bishops Finger was chosen as one of the star entries in the new edition of Camra's *Good Pub Food*, published in 1999. Edited for the fifth time by Susan Nowak, her guide has been at the heart of the food revival in Britain's pubs: when she started her gastronomic *tour de force* of the nation's hostelries in the mid-1980s, pub food all too often was a packet of pork scratchings, a dog-eared sandwich or a "perfect portion" of something inedible prepared in a big brewer's factory and reheated in a microwave. Today you can eat well from eclectic menus in pubs and at a fraction of restaurant prices, so let's raise a glass of Shepherd Neame's Kentish ale in the Bishops Finger and toast Susan Nowak's remarkable achievement. While it's close to Smithfield Market, the pub, with its big windows, polished wood floors and walls decorated with old prints, stands in a pleasant square with a grassy centre. The tremendous improvements in pub food quality and the ability of chefs to dare to break out of the steak-and-kidney mould are underscored by a menu that offers, as snacks or starters, home-made Japanese food and sushi, including chilled miso soup, raw salmon sushi, chicken kara-age, which is fried chicken with ginger and dressed salad leaves, or barbecued spare ribs with Oriental apple marinade. Main courses may include tonkatsu of pork with orange and cabbage in fruity sauce; yakisoba (stir-fried chicken, pork or vegetables with noodles); or oyakodonburi (chicken cooked with eggs and peas in soy and mirin sauce on rice). European-influenced dishes include a special ciabatta menu of rolls filled with smoked chicken and avocado; rare roast beef with horseradish and beetroot relish; beef tomato with goat's cheese and basil pesto; or rib-eye steak with mustard. You may also find fresh haddock in beer batter with pesto mayonnaise; seared salmon with garlic mash; or char-grilled lamb chump with mustard glaze. A good range of vegetarian dishes could include mushroom and spinach tartlets or roast peppers with sun-dried tomatoes and artichoke hearts. There's a good choice of wines, including several by the glass, and the range of Shepherd Neame ales includes Master Brew Bitter, Spitfire, Original Porter in the autumn, and Bishops Finger, the beer that gave the pub its name and which in turn comes from an ancient form of road sign in Kent shaped like a finger. Food is available lunchtime and evening, until 9pm, but the pub is closed at weekends.

Maltsters Arms

Bow Creek, Tuckenhay, Devon (01803 732350)

From Totnes take A381 to Kingsbridge and watch for Tuckenhay sign

Keith Floyd is a hard if not hard-drinking act to follow but Denis and Quentine Thwaites, formerly award-winning licensees of the White Cross on the Thames at London, have transferred with aplomb to another waterside inn, known for a few years as Floyd's Inn under his rumbustious ownership. The pub is in a lovely location by a wooded creek with tables by the water and moorings for boats. The long main bar is linked to a snug and a third room with kitchen chairs on a wooden floor. The pub is a haven for games players, offering shove ha'penny, cribbage, dominoes, chess and backgammon. Cook Denise changes her menu daily and makes great use of local ingredients. She is renowned for her home-made soups and you may find the likes of samphire and leek; curried sweet potato; or Chinese leaf and Thai herb. Other starters could be fresh fig and physalis with orange and dill sour cream or grilled sardines piri-piri. Main courses may offer cucumber barrels in white wine and lavender; celeriac, asparagus and tomato bread-and-butter pudding; venison casseroled in Blackawton ale; partridge, pheasant and teal on "slider sauce" (the sauce is made from steeping sloes in cider); crofter's haggis pie; roe deer ragoût; wild boar; juniper and cranberry pie; cod in coconut cream with roasted garlic; or whole red mullet with lime juice, ginger and chilli. There's a good children's menu, too. Real ales include local Blackawton 44 Special and Princetown Dartmoor IPA. There's also local farm cider and a good choice of wines, with several by the glass. Food is available lunchtime and evening until 9.30pm. Excellent accommodation is available.

Sir Charles Napier Inn

Sprigg's Alley, near Chinnor, Oxfordshire (01494 483011)

Off B4009; turn right at Chinnor roundabout; junction 6 of M40

Almost lost in the Chiltern Hills and surrounded by beech woods and fields below Bledlow Ridge, the farmhouse inn is an eccentric, iconoclastic pub-restaurant run with enormous flair by Julie Griffiths and her family. The inn is packed with an eclectic choice of statues and there's a welcome log fire in winter, while in warm weather you can play croquet or boules on the lawn or stroll by the paddocks by lovely beech woods that merge into the Chiltern Hills. Bar and restaurant meals always come with a surprise, such as baked sardines with piccalilli, or pan-fried calf's liver with balsamic crème fraîche; or char-grilled Mediterranean vegetable salad. Other dishes could include seared tuna with lentil salsa; baked sea bream with aubergine, peppers and tapenade; saddle of lamb with couscous and rosemary jus; whole steamed Cornish crab with basil and chilli oil; or crispy Cressingham duck. Desserts may include raspberry brûlée while the English cheeseboard includes Bonchester, Cotherstone and Wainbody varieties. Two-course lunches or dinners for around £15.50 might include cauliflower and Stilton soup, or Caesar salad to start, with char-grilled Mexican chicken salad with guacamole, or salmon fish-cake with sorrel sauce. There's a vast range of well-chosen wines and Champagne by the glass. Ales come from Wadworth of Devizes and include IPA, 6X and seasonal brews. There are also chilled vodkas and eaux-de-vie. Sunday lunch is a special attraction at the inn and in summer can be eaten in a courtyard at the back with crazy paving and an attractive arbour of vines and wisteria, which is lit at night by candles. Children over seven are welcome in the evening. The inn is closed Sunday evening and all day Monday.

Griffin Inn

Fletching, near Uckfield, East Sussex (01825 722890)
Off A272

The inn, with twin porches to welcome you and dormer windows in the eaves, is more than 400 years old and is the focal point of an attractive village close to Sheffield Park Garden, Glyndebourne, the Bluebell Steam Railway, Rudyard Kipling's home at Batemans, and Bodiam Castle. Inside there are heavily beamed ceilings, panelled walls, old photos, and blazing log fires, one fronted by two snarling iron griffins. A small snug has pub games, comfortable sofas and newspapers. The inn is run with a sense of fun, panache and dedication by Bridget Pullan, her family and their partner, John Gatti. They use locally sourced ingredients, including organic meat and vegetables, whenever possible for menus that change daily. The bar menu could offer fresh asparagus and herb soup; confit of pork and mungbean terrine with plum chutney; deep-fried crab wontons with chilli sauce; avocado and black olive mousse with organic tomato salad; or Ashdown Forest ewes' cheese and parsley mousse terrine with sun-dried tomato dressing. Main courses may include ham, chicken and leek pie with sauté potatoes and green beans; Griffin fish cakes of salmon, smoked haddock and coriander with lemon mayo; bouillabaisse; spicy lamb meatballs with minted yoghurt on tagliatelle; spaghetti vongole; penne with piperade and mozzarella, basil and Parmesan; home-made sweet potato gnocchi, roasted plum tomato and basil; leek and potato pie with Wensleydale and spring vegetables; char-grilled Fletching sausage, grain mustard mash and onion gravy; grilled local sardines marinated in garlic, rosemary and olive; and tart of smoked mackerel and melted red onions with Jersey royals. There are also hot ciabatta sandwiches with a choice of fillings and such desserts as bread and butter pudding, rhubarb and ginger crumble, and upside-down pear and polenta cake with custard. The à la carte menu might offer leek and potato soup; game terrine stuffed with chorizo sausage; swordfish and courgette char-grilled brochette; spicy salmon, vegetable and mussel broth; and deep-fried crab fritters, hoisin and plum dressing; followed by char-grilled Scottish fillet steak with sauté Lyonnaise, herb and garlic butter; roast rack of Sussex lamb with a roasted hazelnut hollandaise sauce; pan-fried breast of duck marinated in ginger, garlic and soy on stir-fried vegetables with crispy fried noodles; and pan-fried cod fillet with warm pesto potatoes, leaves and crispy red anchovies. Desserts may include spiced kumquats and figs mulled in port with vanilla ice-cream; tarte au citron, and a selection of English cheeses. There's a fish night every Thursday that could include mussels, sardines, crab, sea bass, roast cod, red bream, marlin steak, whole grilled lemon sole, and, for vegetarians, roasted squash filled with Provençal ratatouille, goat's cheese and summer leaves. There's an imaginative wine list of more than 70, including Barkham Manor from a vineyard one mile from Fletching, with Champagne and port bottled for the inn. Cask ales include such locals as Ballard's Best and Harvey's Best along with Badger Tanglefoot and a regular guest, such as Thomas Hardy Royal Oak. In good weather customers can eat and drink in the back garden with fine views of the countryside; spit roasts are held here in summer. A converted coach house offers excellent accommodation. Children are welcome and get special menus. Food is served lunchtime and evening; the restaurant is closed for Sunday dinner in winter.

Riverside Inn

Aymestrey, Herefordshire (01568 708440)

Off A4110 near Leominster

A 16th-century, half-timbered inn standing alongside the River Lugg and against a backdrop of wooded hills, the black and white timbered Riverside has a series of linked rooms decked with flowers and hops. The large dining area has glass walls and overlooks the river while the comfortable bar has a log fire, beams, oak tables and chairs, and an eye-catching Librairie Romantique poster advertising Victor Hugo's poems, perhaps placed there to make the French chef, André Cluzeau, feel at home. Monsieur Cluzeau draws on fresh local produce, including some home-grown vegetables, salads and herbs, as well as locally reared lamb and beef, and makes good use of beers from the Woodhampton craft brewery in the village. For lunch or dinner, in bar and restaurant, you may find home-made soup including bouillabaisse; risotto with a sun-dried tomato and Cheddar wafer; mushrooms with Madeira; spinach and mushroom roulade with a fresh tomato coulis; local duck marinated in coriander and honey; supreme of brill with a salmon mousse and citrus cream sauce; Hereford rump with a scoundrel's sauce; rack of Marches lamb with red and green peppers; or nut roast with chestnut stuffing and red wine sauce. Desserts could include apricot and Amaretto ice-cream or lime and grape cheesecake. If you are confronted with steak, kidney and kingfisher pie don't turn pale: the Kingfisher in question is one of Woodhampton's ales: others on draught include Red Kite, Jack Snipe and Ravens Head Stout. There's a good range of wines, including some bin ends and wines by the glass; local farm ciders are also available. Children over seven are welcome in the dining areas and accommodation is available. The inn can arrange fishing on the River Lugg while the 25-mile Mortimer Trail between Ludlow and Knighton is close by. The inn is also a good base for visiting Croft Castle, Croft Ambrey iron-age fort and Berrington Hall with gardens landscaped by Capability Brown.

Fox and Hounds

Great Wolford, Warwickshire (01608 67422)
Off A44 3 miles north-east of Moreton-in-Marsh

The Fox and Hounds gets plaudits all round, featured in the *Which? Guide to Country Pubs*, the AA's *Best Pubs and Inns*, and the *Good Pub Guide*, where it has been awarded the title of Warwickshire Dining Pub of the Year. The stone inn dates from 1540, so it has a bit of history on its side, which befits a hostelry close to the even older, pre-historic Rollright stone circle. The bar has low beams garlanded with hops and drinkers' mugs, tables lit by candles on a flagstone floor, and a large inglenook that includes both a log fire and an ancient bread oven. The beers are served from a small tap room and the selection is strong on regional producers with such delights as Adnams Best, Black Sheep Bitter, Hook Norton Best, Fuller's London Pride, Jennings Cumberland, and Shepherd Neame Spitfire, with perhaps a small craft brewer represented by the likes of Wychwood. The wine list offers half-a-dozen by the glass, while the pub boasts just about every malt whisky known to drinking kind. Graham and Ann Seddon cook up some delights for bar and dining room, with such straightforward pub fare as soup, sandwiches and ploughman's backed by daily specials that could include fresh sardines stuffed with onions and basil with Provençal sauce; salmon and crab fish cake with a saffron and leek sauce; Scottish salmon on scented couscous; game terrine with quail eggs; roasted breast of guinea fowl with port and juniper; pork fillet wrapped in bacon and spinach with green peppercorn sauce; roasted lamb noisettes with a herb crust and served with risotto; smoked goose breast on potato salad; Dover sole with Napolitana sauce; lamb kleftiko; and grilled red snapper with Provençal butter. Desserts may include stricky pudding with ice-cream, chocolate terrine, and coconut parfait. A pleasant terrace has a well and the inn, which offers accommodation, is close to the border with Gloucestershire and Moreton-in-Marsh's antique shops. Food is served lunchtime and evening.

OLD BOAT

KINGS BROMLEY ROAD, ALREWAS, STAFFORDSHIRE (01283 791468)

Off A38 between Lichfield and Burton-on-Trent

The Old Boat comes with plaudits from Susan Nowak's *Good Pub Food* where she found chef Stephen Sander in fine form with a constantly changing menu and a daily specials board that lay great stress on fresh fish and seafood brought from a market in Birmingham. Stephen, who worked in multi-starred hotels before taking up the pub challenge, may offer an outstanding lobster, crab and mussel bisque; sea bass on red pepper sauce; and a giant seafood platter with crabs and lobsters for two people. Vegetarians are not ignored and could be offered four-cheese and basil souffle with asparagus garnish and a special of the day. Main menu starters could be pan-fried fish cakes with chive and white wine sauce, or warm goat's cheese and sun-dried tomato vinaigrette followed perhaps by Thai chicken with coconut and coriander; roast cod with

Nantyffin Cider Mill, near Crickhowell, Powys

pancetta and wild mushrooms; pigeon breasts with smoked bacon, savoy cabbage and Burgundy; and Cumberland sausage with apple and potato rosti. There's a tempting range of desserts while the beers come from Ushers of Trowbridge and include Best Bitter, Founder's Ale and seasonal brews. The large pub has a nautical theme as befits its name and a large garden leads down to a canal. Food is served lunchtime and evening and the pub has a children's certificate.

Blue Lion

East Witton, North Yorkshire (01969 624273)
On A6108

The former 18th-century coaching inn in the Yorkshire Dales is close to the famous brewing town of Masham, home to both Black Sheep and Theakston, both of whose beers feature in the Blue Lion. The main bar has ham hooks suspended from the ceiling, a soothing log fire in winter, old prints on the walls, and some fine settles on the flagstone floor. Chef John Dalby's bar and restaurant meals are impressive and make the pub one of the most sought-out eating places in the Dales. Starters might include smoked wild boar sausage with bubble and squeak; onion and blue Wensleydale tart with tomato chutney; or crab Thai fish cake with chilli jam. Main courses may offer cassoulet of pork rib; cherry tomato and tapenade tart; peppered duck breast with port and blackberry sauce; fresh tagliatelle tossed with leeks and oyster mushrooms and toasted with Parmesan; steamed steak and kidney suet pudding; roast fillet of cod with spring onion mash and a chive and tomato butter sauce; char-grilled chicken and pancetta; or trio of fish with fricassée of leeks and oyster mushrooms. Desserts might include pear tarte tatin with honey ice-cream or dark chocolate pudding with a white chocolate centre. The wine list is enormous – more than 120 bins – concentrating on France and with some grand cru clarets. Children are welcome in the dining room and accommodation is available.

Star Inn

Weaverthorpe, North Yorkshire (01944 738273)
Off A64

A friendly, welcoming Wolds inn where cook Susan Richardson rewards customers with a free pint of beer if they supply her with local crab apples. She turns the apples into apple jelly, which she uses in several dishes such as fresh pheasant supplied by local farmers. Other dishes may include hare with red wine and bacon; pigeon breasts with garlic and Stilton; rabbit casserole with sage dumplings; and game pie. Fish dishes could include red snapper with tomato and garlic salsa; tuna with Mojo sauce; whole plaice on the bone, or sea bass with prawn sauce. Susan is a vegetarian and her meatless dishes include herb pudding with savoury gravy as a starter. The Sunday roast naturally comes with splendid Yorkshire puddings. The hand-pumped ales include Banks's Bitter, Cameron's Bitter and Hambleton Stallion from a local craft brewery. Food is served lunchtime and evening except Tuesdays, with lunch only at weekends and bank holidays. Accommodation is available.

O'Hara's

41-43 West High Street, Forfar, Tayside (01307 464350)
A90

This is a newish outlet, opened just five years ago by old school friends Mary Wilson and Dawn Darling, and comprises a first-floor bar and a downstairs restaurant with a striking hand-painted South American mural. All the food is prepared on the premises and there's a set menu and a daily specials board. Ingredients come from the "wee fish shop down the road" and other local suppliers of meat, bread and vegetables. Beer is matched with food, with Harviestoun's raspberry ale with desserts in summer and dark, stronger brews in winter with venison sausages or roast beef and Yorkshire pudding. At lunchtime you may find baguettes with such fillings as banana in peanut sauce or blackened Cajun chicken with jalapeno salsa, or toasted buns with local venison burgers topped with grilled Cheddar and bacon with chips and salad. More substantial meals could include fresh tandoori haddock in prawn, ginger and coriander sauce or chicken breast stuffed with ham and Italian cheese. Specials could include Arbroath haddock pan-fried in oatmeal or Italian aubergine layer with char-grilled peppers and feta. Dishes that make use of beer include mushrooms in Guinness batter; cheese and ale soup; and pumpkin, apple and ale chutney. The real ales change constantly but you may find such local craft brews as Harviestoun of Dollar. Food is served lunchtime and evening Monday to Saturday.

Nantyffin Cider Mill

Brecon Road, near Crickhowell, Powys (01873 810775)
Near junction of A40 and A479

This 16th-century drovers' inn at the foot of the Black Mountains has fine views along the valley of the Usk towards the Brecon Beacons. Until the 1960s, the building was a working cider mill with its own orchard and press. The restaurant area was once the apple store, and it houses the original cider press and wheel. A family farm supplies organic meat and vegetables, and chef Sean Gerrard makes every effort to buy local ingredients: cockle and laver bread from Swansea in spring, and mackerel and crabs from Pembrokeshire. Food is available in the raftered restaurant or in the bar and may include such starters as Moroccan filo parcels filled with fresh spinach, soft cheese and merguez sausage served with toasted sesame dressing; baked field mushrooms with a butter, Stilton and spring onion crumb topping; or deep-fried spicy Thai fish cakes with noodles and coriander coconut broth. Main courses could be spiced potato cakes with a chilli, tomato and coriander chick pea casserole; lamb with a chorizo and herb crust; grilled lobster with oregano butter; spinach and ricotta tart with a herb crumb topping; oak-smoked salmon; or venison with smoked pear and game sauce. Superb desserts may include tart au citron or whimberry ice-cream. There's a constantly rotating range of real ales that might include Brains SA and Tomos Watkin from Wales plus Marston's Pedigree, Old Spot or Old Speckled Hen from England, plus an almost exclusively New World wine list, and such craft ciders as Dunkertons, Mendip and Thatchers.

Best of the Rest

Kings Arms

Church Street, Cleobury Mortimer, Shropshire
(01299 270252)
A4117

Victoria

6 Union Road,Lincoln, Lincolnshire (01522 536048)
Off A57 and A15

Pubs for curries

BHURTPORE INN

WRENBURY ROAD, ASTON, CHESHIRE (01270 780917)

Off A530, five miles south of Nantwich

It's fitting that this inn specialises in curries, for it takes its name from the Siege of Bhurtpore in India in 1825, a campaign led by Lord Combermere, the first British commander to use Ghurka troops. The inn is owned by Simon and Nicky George, who bought it from a brewer and restored it to the George family after a break of 90 years. The lounge bar has a large number of artefacts with an Indian theme. The public bar is set aside for people who want to sup without eating: cask ale enthusiast Mr George caters for them with an impressive range that includes Hanby Drawell and nine constantly changing guest beers, mainly from small independents such as Backdykes, Whim and Snowdonia. There are also Belgian and Czech beers in bottle and on draught with wines and malt whiskies as well. Food, in bar and no-smoking restaurant, is served lunchtime and evening, and includes spicy lamb samosa with a cool yoghurt and mint dip, lamb rogan josh, mushroom balti, chicken jal frezi, Quorn or vegetable balti, and vegetable korma. There's plenty of food to please those who don't like curries and baltis, with an excellent choice for vegetarians, while the tempting desserts include blueberry roulade, apple and blackberry crumble, and banana pancake with toffee sauce. Children are welcome until 8pm and live folk music is played on the third Tuesday of the month.

BULL'S HEAD

102 CHURCH STREET, OLD GLOSSOP, DERBYSHIRE (01457 853291)

Off A57

The Bull's Head is known to locals as the "ale and curry house", such is the emphasis on Asian food and good beer. The menus have been created with the help of chefs from one of Manchester's top Indian restaurants. There are 20 starters including shami kebab and fish tikka, while main courses include a wide range of vegetarian dishes such as peas with panir, and potato, cauliflower and vegetable rogan josh. Other dishes may include chicken dansak with pineapple and coconut cream, kofta sag chanay, Karahi chicken and gosht, lamb bhindi methi, Sabzi gosht, mincemeat with peas, king prawn or chicken with hot spicy lentils, and makhani dishes prepared with crushed tomatoes, cream and almonds. You can wash these delicious dishes down with Robinson's Old Stockport, Best Bitter, and Old Tom in winter. The Bull's Head is a 16th-century listed building at the foot of the Pennines with a traditional northern tap room and a no-smoking front lounge. Food is available in the evenings from 6.30 to 10.30 (4–10pm on Sunday). Children are welcome.

Old Crown

56 Sandwell Road, West Bromwich, West Midlands
(0121 525 4600)

Off A41/A4031

Wonderfully good value, authentic curries are the order of the day at this small, one-room, side-street pub run by Manjula and Chania Patel, who produce celebrated baltis, bhunas, and tikka masalas. Vegetarians are well catered for with a wide range of vegetable curries served with rice and nan bread, such as potato bhuna, mushroom curry and vegetable masala. Other dishes include lamb, prawn, chicken and keema, chicken tikka balti, and chicken tikka masala. Food is served lunchtime and evening, and there are always three rotating guest beers. Children are welcome.

Vine

Roebuck Street, West Bromwich, West Midlands (0121 553 2866)
Off A41 near M5 junction 1

West Bromwich is curry paradise for pubgoers. Don't ask for the Vine: it's known as "Suki's", for this is where chefs/landlords Suki and Bhanu Patel work their daily miracle of producing a vast range of home-made curry dishes at astonishingly reasonable prices. You can eat for as little as £2.95. The Patels offer around 30 dishes cooked in a large dining room over ranges under smoke extractors. You may find chicken and mushroom balti, lamb, mushroom and potato balti; prawns with mushroom, tomatoes and potato curry, and keema curry, all served with rice or potatoes, chapatis and nan bread. There's also a nightly barbecue that offers chicken tikka, lamb tikka, tandoori drumsticks, and shish kebab. Vegetarians can choose from a wide choice of meatless curries and baltis. The Vine is a small Victorian street-corner pub with several small bars opening off a corridor. There's an ever-changing range of cask beers from independent breweries.

RED LION

24 HIGH STREET, KEGWORTH, LEICESTERSHIRE (01509 672466)
A6, off M1

This cheery, unspoilt local is the former headquarters of the Tynemill pub group, a small but imaginative company with pubs in the East Midlands that was launched by Chris Holmes, a chairman of Camra in its early days, who believes that such traditional values as good ale, good food and pleasant surroundings will see off the flash-and-fancy theme bars. He proves the point here and in such other splendid hostelries as the Lincolnshire Poacher in Nottingham, the Swan in the Rushes in Loughborough, and the Victoria at Beeston (now also the head office of the group). The Red Lion has a wide-ranging menu but there are usually a couple of Indian-inspired dishes on the menu, such as chicken tikka masala or the popular beef Madras. There are also vegetable curries for non-meat eaters, plus home-made pakoras and samosas. The pub has two small front bars for serious drinkers with two at the back set aside for dining. Food is served lunchtime and evening, children are welcome, and there's a large garden with a play area. The ales, of course, are excellent and constantly changing but you may find Bateman's Mild and XB, Castle Rock Hemlock, and Marston's Pedigree.

WASHINGTON

50 ENGLANDS LANE, BELSIZE PARK, LONDON NW3 (020 7722 6118)
Underground: Belsize Park; Chalk Farm

This magnificent pub, built in 1830, has original tiling, etched glass and mirrors, and is home to several sports teams and the Hampstead Comedy Club. It also stages occasional beer festivals. The Washington opens at 10am for breakfast with a vast fry-up and tea or coffee for £3.95, and then carries on serving food until 10 at night. Until 2.30pm the emphasis is on snacks of the filled jacket potato and burger variety, but then a different chef takes over and the spices and herbs start to sizzle as Thai green chicken curry, chicken cooked either Penang, Caribbean or Tobago style, vegetable tikka masala, and beef Madras are prepared, all served with rice for around £5.45. The beers are supplied by Carlsberg-Tetley and usually include Ind Coope Burton Ale, Marston's Pedigree, Tetley Bitter, Young's Bitter and Wadworth 6X. As well as good ale and food, marvel at the glasswork and partitions introduced in the early 1890s by the firm of Walter Gibbs. The Washington has mercifully been saved from a modern "knock-through" and a partition separates lounge from public bar. The etched glasswork includes a panel depicting George Washington (who has no known connection with North London). Unusually, the Washington has clear-glass sashed windows, making the interior exceptionally light and airy. Externally, the white upper storey rests on a black-painted ground floor with marble pilasters at the entrance, above which a sign in gold lettering announces "The Washington – a splendid traditional public house", a claim that cannot be gainsaid.

Best of the Rest

Walter de Cantelupe Inn

Main Road, Kempsey, Worcestershire (01905 820572)
A38

Eastcote Arms

6 Gayton Road, Eastcote, Northamptonshire (01327 830731)
Just off A5

Bell

21 High Street, Standlake, Oxfordshire (01865 300784)
Off A415

Black Horse

29 Main Street, Caythorpe, Nottinghamshire (0115 966 3520)
Off A612

Bread and Roses

68 Clapham Manor Street, London SW4 (020 7498 1779)
Underground: Clapham Common

Pubs for cheese

LONE TREE

THORNBOROUGH, BUCKINGHAMSHIRE (01280 812334)
Off A421 between Bletchley and Buckingham

The Lone Tree specialises in seeking out rare English cheeses and matching them with an equally eclectic choice of traditional draught beers. The inn, built in 1695 on an old Roman road, has an accreditation from the British Cheese Board and has at least a dozen cheeses available every day: a description of each cheese is written on a special blackboard. The range could include organic Ashdown Foresters, Cotherstone, Single Gloucester, Somerset Rambler made from ewes' milk, Ticklemore (a Devon goat's cheese), and Terrick Truckle beer mustard cheese made by the Chiltern Brewery near Aylesbury. The inn has served close to 1,000 real ales to date: the range is ever-changing but could include the likes of Black Sheep Bitter, Chiltern Beechwood, Hook Norton Best Mild, Rebellion Smuggler and York Stonewall. There's often a farm cider, too, and a good range of bottled beers. The bar has beams, wood panels and a blazing log fire. Such pub games as cribbage, dominoes, shove-ha'penny and shut-the-box are played. Children are welcome in eating areas and a thatched barn next door, which has been both a brewhouse and stables over the years, now houses a working Victorian post box. The one thing you won't find is the lone tree that gave the pub its name: it was knocked down by a lorry as long ago as 1918.

BELL

HIGH STREET, STILTON, CAMBRIDGESHIRE (01733 241066)
Just off A1 south of Peterborough

I couldn't leave out the Bell as it has played such a significant role in the development of the King of English Cheese. The cheese isn't made in the village – it comes from Melton Mowbray and other parts of Leicestershire – but was first sold at the Bell to travellers on the Great North Road in the 1720s and became so popular that it took on the name of the village. The bar menu always features Stilton and celery soup: the inn uses Long Clawson Stilton and the variety is used in such dishes as Stilton cheese pizza on ciabatta; mushrooms with Stilton cheese rarebit and

Colcannon potatoes; chicken in Stilton, cider and cream sauce; Stilton sausages and mash; or ripe Stilton served with plum bread. The 16th-century stone-built coaching inn has a courtyard with seats for fine weather, while inside the bars have flagstones, bow windows, and a log fire in a stone fireplace. Food is available lunchtime and evening in the bar or a separate restaurant. A good range of ales includes Oakham Jeffrey Hudson's Bitter from Peterborough, Greene King Abbot, Marston's Pedigree and ever-changing guests such as Dent Bitter, Iceni Fine Soft Day or Wychwood Special. Dick Turpin, Lord Byron, Clark Gable and Joe Louis have stayed at the Bell over the centuries: it still offers accommodation and children are welcome in eating areas at lunchtime. Don't miss the magnificent inn sign, a faithful recreation of the 16th-century original, that hangs over the street and weighs three tons.

Maltsters Arms

Chapel Amble, Cornwall (01208 812473)

B3314, off A39 Wadebridge road

Alastair and Mary Gray prove that ale and cheese are fine companions. At the Malsters they offer Cornish Coaster from Sharp's, a local craft brewery, which also supplies a house beer named after the inn. You will also find Draught Bass (which retains a big following in the West Country), Fuller's London Pride, Greene King Abbot and Young's Bitter. Cheeses on offer include Cornish feta, St Endellion, Ticklemore goat's cheese and Village Green. The whitewashed, 16th-century inn has a thatched porch and inside there are old beams, stripped back stone walls, flagstones and a big fireplace. Delicious bar food, lunchtime and evening, may include fresh fish dishes such as pan-fried sardines in garlic butter; fillet of John Dory with Chinese-style dressing; wild trout with a saffron, wine and cream sauce; and brill with roasted peppers. Vegetarians may find broccoli and Stilton bake, roasted sweet pepper with Cornish feta cheese or wild mushroom tart. Starters could be ciabatta bread with choice of fillings or avocado and prawns. The ploughman's naturally comes with a good choice of the local cheeses. Desserts could be bread and butter pudding or a choices of sponges and tarts. There's an excellent wine list, with a heavy emphasis on French varieties and several by the glass. The Grays may suggest a glass of port with your cheese, the perfect end to a meal.

Masons Arms

Knowstone, Devon (01398 341231)
Off A361 and B3227

The Masons Arms is a venerable old inn that began life as farm cottages and has been a licensed hostelry since the 13th century. The white-washed and thatched exterior leads, through perilously low doors, into a main bar with head-cracking black beams, a stone floor, old bucolic furnishings, a fireplace with a bread oven, a collection of ancient farm tools, and a vast range of bottles from all over the world. Light at night comes from oil lamps and candles. David and Elizabeth Todd, among a fine range of food, offer a wide range of West Country cheeses with names as esoteric and even similar to rare apples and pears used in cider and perry production. Look out for Tower Farm Cheddar, Curworthy, Nancarrow, Sharpham Rustic, Yarg and a goat's cheese called Vulscombe that wouldn't be out of place on the Starship Enterprise. Not surprisingly, cheese features in such dishes as cheese and leek pie, and a splendid ploughman's with fresh crusty bread and real chutney. Other dishes may include smoked mackerel and cider pâté; game pie with rabbit and pheasant; Devon cassoulet; spaghetti with tomato sauce; roast cod with puy lentils; plus chicken tikka masala or vegetable korma for curry lovers. Tempting desserts may include chocolate and nougat ice-cream, banana in rum, and gooseberry crumble. The inn often has home-made marmalades, fruit bread and chutneys for sale. West Country ales include Cotleigh Tawny from Wiveliscombe and Otter, a local Devon craft brewery. Children are welcome in designated areas, there's a good choice of traditional pub games, including cribbage, darts, dominoes, and shove-ha'penny, and accommodation is available. Knowstone is in a conservation area and the National Trust's Arlington Court and Knightshayes are close by, along with the Royal Horticultural Society's gardens at Roseover.

Strathmore Arms

Holwick, Co. Durham (01533 640362)
Off B6277, west of Middleton in Teesdale

The Strathmore has its own smokehouse where publican Alwyn Hawdon produces smoked cheese – Blue Stilton, Blue Wensleydale and White Wensleydale – plus bacon, trout and salmon. Smoked cheese naturally features on the menu in its own right or in such dishes as chicken breast stuffed with salmon and smoked cheese sauce. You can buy all the smoked food in the pub shop called the Smoking Poacher. Beers include Black Bull Bitter, Ruddles Best and Theakstons Best. The 17th-century, stone-built inn lies under Holwick Scars near the Pennine Way and is in ideal walking country. There's a warm and welcoming bar on the ground floor, such traditional pub games as darts, dominoes, skittles and shove-ha'penny, live music upstairs at the weekend, and two bedrooms.

SHIP INN

WHITES HILL, OWSLEBURY, HAMPSHIRE (01962 777358)
Off B2177, a mile north of Marwell Zoo

The Ship has a wide and tempting range of cheese dishes, including warm goat's cheese salad. A special lunchtime ploughman's offers a choice of Brie, Blue or White Stilton, Red Leicester, Port Salut, or oak-smoked Cheddar served with home-made chutney, salad and fresh bread. For £1 more, you can can have soft blue Cambazola. The17th-century inn has wall timbers, beams, and a large fireplace. There's a nautical theme in the Mess Deck eating area and cricketing memorabilia in the main bar. The ales are from Greene King: XX Mild, IPA and Abbot, plus a regular guest beer. There's excellent walking country all around and good views of the Solent and the Isle of Wight from the garden, which has animals and a children's play area.

Best of the Rest

BRADFORD ARMS

LLANYMYNECH, SHROPSHIRE (01691 830582)
A483

SUN INN

WINFORTON, HEREFORDSHIRE (01544 327677)
A438

Pubs for Thai food

Black Horse

Main Street, Walcote, Leicestershire (01455 552684)

A427; One mile from M1 junction 20

Whatever the Thai term is for the Real McCoy, this is it. Saovanee Tinker has been cooking genuine Thai meals for a decade or more

Harpenden Arms, Harpenden, Hertfordshire

in this small and unpretentious pub in a pleasant village of mellow stone buildings. Mrs Tinker offers a Thai mixed grill of meats and livers served with sweet and sour sauce; mixed vegetable stir-fry; beef, pork, chicken or prawn with a choice of garlic and chilli sauce, oyster sauce or stir-fried with ginger and onion. She adds for good measure Thai curries (Kaeng Phed) with spices, herbs and coconut cream with either chicken, fish or prawns; searingly hot Khao Phat Prik of fried rice, fresh chillis and garlic with chicken, topped with a beaten fried egg; and Khao Mu Deang, marinated leg of pork with boiled rice and a chilli and ginger side sauce. Fried rice can be eaten as a dish on its own with meat, sliced omelette and peas, flavoured with nampla sauce and topped with a fried egg. In the welcoming bar with a fire on cold days you will find a good choice of ales such as Greene King Triumph and Abbot Ale, Hoskins & Oldfield HOB Bitter and guest beers.

Harpenden Arms

188 High Street, Harpenden, Hertfordshire (01582 712095)
Off A1081

Thai food, prepared by a Thai chef, is available seven days a week in this spacious pub overlooking a common and close to a golf course and cricket green. The long main bar, with scrubbed wooden tables and benches on a thick pile carpet, with attractive low-slung light shades above the counter, leads into a spacious dining area at the rear. The lengthy menu offers stuffed spring rolls; crispy fried wuntun with minced chicken; and deep-fried squid among the starters or such soups as the classic Thai Tom Yam Kung of hot and sour prawns flavoured with lemon grass; and Tom Yum Hed, mushrooms in spicy soup. Fried dishes include a choice of meats or prawns with chilli and basil leaves; stir-fried chicken with cashew nut, dried chillis and mushrooms; or roast duck with bamboo shoots in chilli and basil leaves. There are several searing curries, noodle or rice dishes and a welcome range of vegetarian alternatives including special salad with fresh vegetables and peanut sauce and egg with crispy wanton; rice stick noodles stir fried with bean sprouts; vegetable curry; spicy fried aubergines and mushrooms; and fried rice noodles with green cabbage and egg in soya sauce. The pub is run by Fullers which means you accompany the food with Chiswick Bitter, London Pride, ESB or such seasonal ales as organic Honey Dew. The pub offers a take-away food service and you can also buy four pints of beer in a special pitcher to take home with your food.

Churchill Arms

119 Kensington Church Street, London W8 (020 7727 4242)
Near Notting Hill and Kensington High Street Underground stations

It sounds like an elaborate joke: an Irish-run pub dedicated to Winston Churchill and serving Thai food. But landlord Jerry O'Brien not only celebrates Churchill's birthday but serves splendid Thai food in an attractive conservatory area decked out with plants. Dishes include chicken and cashew nuts; Thai noodles; and roast duck or beef curries. It is a Fuller's pub offering the full range of Chiswick Bitter, London Pride, ESB and seasonal ales. The bar is decorated with miners' lamps and horse brasses, photos of United States presidents, books about butterflies (Mr O'Brien collects them) and, of course, masses of Churchill memorabilia. No food Sunday evening.

Wrestlers

337 Newmarket Road, Cambridge (01223 566554)

A busy, boisterous pub on the eastern side of Cambridge towards Newmarket, with live music twice a week, open fires in winter and a fine reputation for its Thai cuisine, which can be ordered as take-aways as well as eaten on the premises. Cooking is done by Thai chefs led by Kalaya Goode, wife of landlord Tom Goode. You can choose from seafood chilli; prawn Tom Yum; hot Thai special; green chicken curry; crab fried rice; beef with ginger or oyster sauce; chicken chow mein; or fried rice with pork and bean sprouts. Vegetarian options include vegetables in oyster sauce; vegetables with egg; and egg fried rice. There is a daily Thai special and a good range of Thai desserts. A tremendous range of real ales includes Adnams Best, Badger Tanglefoot, Morland Old Speckled Hen, Wells Eagle and Bombardier plus a regular guest beer. There's often a genuine farm cider as well. Food is not served on Sundays.

Nag's Head

Pickhill, North Yorkshire (01845 567391)
From A1 take turn for Masham; village signposted off B6267

Search for the Thai dishes among the eclectic offerings in this fine old coaching inn run for nearly 30 years by the Boynton brothers: you may find a sizzling hot curried green chicken or a brochette of Thai-style king prawns. There are also Indian and Italian dishes on the menu: you can eat in the bar or in the separate restaurant; the restaurant is closed Sunday evenings. The bars are decorated with coaching horns, yards of ale, and local paintings for sale. There are smoke-darkened beams and open fires, and such pub games as shove-ha'penny, darts, dominoes and cribbage. One table is inset with a chess board. In summer there's a pleasant verandah at the front and there are also pitches for boules and quoits. Good beers come from local craft breweries: Black Sheep Best or Special and Hambleton Bitter along with Theakston's Black Bull. Accommodation, with much-praised breakfasts, is available.

BLACK BULL

CHURCH STREET, CLIFFE, KENT (01634 220893)
B2000 north of Rochester; off A2 and M2

Landlady Soh Pek Berry hails from Brunei and cooks mainly Malaysian dishes in the Nonya tradition of her ancestors but she has also added some delicious Thai meals as well. You may find Thai beef or chicken green curries, or Thai noodles and pineapple rice. Lunchtime specials may include coconut rice with prawn sambal, boiled egg, fried anchovies and peanuts with Soh Pek's fiery Malaysian vegetable pickle Achar Awak. She also provides chicken braised with potato and carrot in a spicy bean sauce, Mee Goreng, and Hokkien braised pork with Chinese mushrooms (Hokkien Mee), which won her the Guinness Pub Food award in the mid-1990s. There's a separate restaurant in the cellar with a full Malaysian menu. Don't miss the 50-feet deep Roman well in the cellar, one of many fascinating features of this Victorian free house near the Thames Estuary. There's a tremendous range of real ales that includes Courage Directors, Harvey's Best, Morland Old Speckled Hen, Young's Special and a wide range of guest beers. Food is served lunchtime and evening Tuesday to Saturday and children are welcome in eating areas.

King William IV, Heydon, Cambridgeshire

Pubs for vegetarian food

KING WILLIAM IV

HEYDON, CAMBRIDGESHIRE (01763 838773)

Off A505 and M11 junction 10

Elizabeth Nicholls' inn was crowned Vegetarian Pub of the Year in the 2000 edition of the *Good Pub Guide*. It was a major achievement, for Mrs Nicholls was up against stiff competition. Many publicans and their chefs now recognise the needs of the growing number of sensitive souls who eschew meat and fish on ethical, political or health grounds. You'll find ten vegetarian dishes every day in this spacious yet intimate old inn that I first got to know when it was run by an eccentric horse-riding Austrian named Josey whose many attributes did not include being *gemütlich* to non-meat eaters. The King William has rambling, interconnected and heavily-beamed rooms with standing timbers, log fires and masses of such eclectic decorations as beer steins and horse harness (probably left by Josey), ploughshares, cowbells, blacksmith's bellows, samovars and decorative plates. The menu changes frequently but you may find such vegetarian dishes as spinach and cream cheese crispy pancakes with a tomato and chive sauce, mushrooms and Mediterranean fruits with Swiss Gruyère, fettucine with artichokes, mushrooms and roasted pine kernels and Italian tomato sauce, or nuts and date curry with Basmati wild rice and poppadoms. Bar lunches may include sandwiches, filled baguettes, and deep-fried Brie with cranberry chutney. Desserts might be spotted dick, and fresh berries and fruit in a chocolate shell. Hand-pumped ales include Adnams Best with Regatta in summer, Boddingtons, and Greene King IPA and Abbot.

THREE ELMS

NORTH WOOTTON, DORSET (01935 812881)
Off A3030

A country pub that was first built as a cider house to serve the neighbouring farms, it shows its roots by still serving farm cider, usually from Burrow Hill. The Three Elms is also famous for a vast range of model cars and other vehicles, numbering around a thousand, and displayed in glass cases. Other collections include, bizarrely, milk bottles and, more prosaically, beer pump clips. There's a tremendous choice of vegetarian and vegan dishes in the bar and restaurant that may include oat and walnut crumble; vegetable beans and peppers in cider sauce topped with sliced potato, cheese, nut and spinach strudel, apricot and cashew nut bake, cauliflower korma with tarka dahl and spicy tomato and chick pea on rice and popadums, and layered French terrine of carrot, coriander, sweet potato, nutmeg, spinach and mushroom. Hot ciabatta includes a filling of cheese and mushrooms. Ales include a house beer from the craft Otter Brewery plus Fuller's London Pride and Shepherd Neame Spitfire. Children are welcome and accommodation is available.

Axe & Compasses

Wicken Road, Arkesden, Essex (01799 550272)
Off B1038

This partly-thatched, 17th-century inn stands at the heart of a charming village where a stream runs alongside the road and is punctuated by small footbridges. Outside the inn, there are little dormer windows peeping from beneath the thatch, leaded main windows, and a vast array of hanging baskets and flowers in tubs. Inside, there's a bar with bare boards and settles, and a carpeted lounge with polished wood seats, a fire, and a plethora of brasses decorating the walls. There's also a separate restaurant and a patio. Bar food and full meals are served lunchtime and evening (not Sunday evening in winter) and the Greek influence of landlord Themis Christou can be seen in such dishes as home-made taramasalata and Greek salad. Other vegetarian dishes could include mushroom pancake with cheesy cream sauce, stir-fry vegetables in a pastry case with mustard sauce and vegetarian cannelloni, or deep-fried mushrooms with garlic dip. Desserts include tiramisu, and hazelnut meringue. The pub is owned by Greene King and sells the brewery's IPA and Abbot Ale plus seasonal beers.

Masons Arms

Strawberry Bank, Cartmel Fell, Cumbria (015395 68486)
Off A5074; watch for sign for Bowland Bridge, one mile up hill

This remote old inn was once a secret meeting place for Kendal Freemasons, while Arthur Ransome lived in a cottage up the lane alongside when he was writing some of his "Swallows and Amazons" children's novels. Today the Masons Arms is renowned for both its food and the Damson Ale brewed in the tiny Strawberry Bank Brewery behind the whitewashed and timbered inn. Damsons from the surrounding Lyth Valley are picked and added to the ale, giving it a tart, fruity and quenching character similar to that of a Belgian cherry beer. Other ales from the brewery and on sale on draught in the inn include Ned's Tipple, Blackbeck and Rulbuts. Owner Helen Stevenson has won legions of admirers for the quality of her food, which has a powerful emphasis on vegetarian and vegan dishes. In rooms with beams, flagstones, Jacobean panelling, miners' lamps, pews, settles, log fires and a kitchen range, you can sample such delights as roast pepper and ricotta strudel, courgette and gruyère pie, home-made chickpea humus and vegetable burritos, lentil and hazelnut pâté, stuffed vine leaves, wild mushroom strudel, spinach and Puy lentil moussaka, red onion and Wensleydale quiche, vegetable tikka, or Mediterranean roasted vegetable lasagne. Desserts may include apple, raspberry and scrumpy crumble, profiteroles and chocolate sauce, and hazelnut crumble. As well as the house beers you will find such guests as Bateman's, Barnsley, Blackpool, Brains, Jennings, and Marston's on tap, plus a stunning choice of beers from around the world including Belgian Trappist and fruit ales, German Bocks and such American classics as Anchor Steam Beer. A terrace with rustic seats is a fine vantage point for views over the Winster Valley to Whitbarrow Scar. Self-catering accommodation is available; children are welcome until 9pm and there's a family room. To avoid my mistake of almost driving into a small tarn, Cartmel Fell should not be confused with Cartmel.

Druid Inn

Main Street, Birchover, Derbyshire (01629 650302)
Off A6 and B5056

This 200-year-old, creeper-clad inn claims to have druidical connections with the Rowtar rocking stones that loom over the area. Inside the inn there's a Tap Room, Garden Room, and a two-storey, candlelit restaurant, and a warming coal fire in winter – and it can get decidedly chilly in the Peak District. Landlord Brian Bunce looks after vegetarians well with the likes of deep-fried Buxton blue cheese with an apricot dip, aubergine filled with rice, mushrooms and peppers in a peanut and garlic sauce, casseroles and curries, fruit and vegetable lasagne, peppers, cheese and mushrooms in a peanut and garlic sauce, Mexican mole, and lentil, carrot and nut rissoles. Desserts include Bakewell pudding, apple and marzipan torte, or sherry trifle. Children are welcome in the dining room until 8pm and they get half-price menus. Hand-pumped ales include Druid, a house beer brewed by the Leatherbritches craft brewery in Ashbourne, Mansfield Bitter, Marston's Pedigree, and Morland Old Speckled Hen. There are picnic tables at the front of the inn, which is in ideal walking country.

Victoria

Dovecote Lane, Beeston, Nottinghamshire (0115 925 4049)
Off A52

Lovers of good ale and trains must think they've died and gone to heaven when they visit the Victoria; it not only serves a tremendous range of traditional draught ales but also backs on to Beeston railway station. You can sit in the small back patio and sup your ale as the trains go by. You can also leave the car at home and visit the red-brick Victorian commercial hotel by rail. The pub stands opposite Beeston Maltings, owned by Scottish Courage, where barley is transformed into malt for the brewing industry. The Victoria has four unspoilt bars with stripped woodwork and bare floorboards, some stained glass, and comfortable wooden furnishings. There's a genuine public bar while the dining room is no-smoking. There's a strong emphasis on vegetarian food, with such dishes as stuffed vine leaves with buffalo Mozzarella and peppers, goat's cheese salad with ruby grapefruit and mange-tout, pasta with herb, tomato and fresh rocket pesto, baked field mushrooms with garlic, Parmesan and fresh herbs, or asparagus, taleggio and chive tart. Menus change daily so be prepared to be surprised, astonished and delighted. Desserts may include hot bananas with dark rum and ice cream or apple crumble. You'll also find more than 100 malt whiskies and Irish whiskeys, good wine, traditional cider, and a good choice of tea and coffee.

White Swan

Market Place, Pickering, North Yorkshire (01751 472288)
A169; off A64

The White Swan is a 16th-century coaching inn and the stone-built hostelry stands at the heart of this small Yorkshire market town. The inn was once used by salt smugglers *en route* to and from Whitby. There's a wood-panelled bar with an open fire and a comfortable lounge. The Buchanans have run the inn for 15 years and have built a deserved reputation for their food, which includes a splendid range of vegetarian dishes. Menus for bar and restaurant change daily and are chalked on a board, but you may find the likes of beetroot fritters with caramelised onion, mustard cream and herb rice, char-grilled vegetables with polenta, root vegetables with balsamic vinegar, nut oil syrup and capsicum risotto, and tagliatelle bound with coconut cream and fresh garden mint, served with apple crisps. Desserts include blood orange burnt cream and chocolate marquise with coffee bean sauce. Good Yorkshire ales come in the shape of Black Sheep Best and Special, and Hambleton's from Thirsk. The vast wine list includes around 70 from the St Emilion region. Children are welcome in the bar eating area and accommodation is available.

FAT CAT

23 ALMA STREET, SHEFFIELD, SOUTH YORKSHIRE (0114 249 4801)
Tram: Shalesmoor

The Fat Cat and the tiny Kelham Island Brewery to the side are the realization of a dream by owner Dave Wickett that small is beautiful. A lecturer at the local university, Dave developed a theory that big brewers had got too big and too removed from their customers. His pub is a genuine, no-nonsense, old-fashioned local that serves fresh and fine-tasting ales from the adjacent brewery, plus superb food based on Dave's own strong vegetarian predilections. His ales are "fined" (cleared) with Irish moss rather than isinglass made from fish bladders, and he will even provide beers free from any finings if customers so wish and order in advance. The Camra *Good Beer Guide* describes the Fat Cat as "an urban legend" as a result of serving more than 3,000 guest beers from independent breweries since the pub opened: following the closure of the city's three big commercial breweries, Stones, Ward's, and Whitbread Exchange, the pub and its brewery are vital beacons of choice. The Fat Cat has two delightful, unspoilt rooms downstairs supplied by a hatched, central servery: the rooms have coal fires, wooden tables, cushioned wall seats and old advertising mirrors. There's also a first-floor room that can be used by families unless it's been booked for a function. Lunchtime food is based around a constantly changing menu but you may find the likes of lentil soup, nutty parsnip crunch with salad and granary bread, spinach and red bean casserole with rice, Stilton pasta with salad and granary bread, ploughman's, cheese and onion quiche, and such desserts as apple crumble and jam roly-poly with cream or custard. The brewery's own Bitter, Pale Rider and seasonal beers are complemented by Timothy Taylor's Landlord and a vast number of guest beers that may include Iceni, Maypole,

Roosters, and Rudgate. There's a new visitor centre in the backyard with fascinating brewery memorabilia and beer served by gravity straight from casks. For visits to the centre and the brewery, phone 0114 249 4805. This is an institution, a celebration of good ale and food, and not to be missed.

Bryn Tyrch

Capel Curig, Conwy, North-west Wales (01690 720223)

A5 near Betws-y-coed

Bryn Tyrch means "Boar's Hill" and there's a boar motif in the inn, a bit off-putting for dedicated vegetarians. But this welcoming walkers' hostelry in Snowdonia offers some splendid vegetarian and vegan dishes, which come in large portions for those who've spent hours hiking in the spectacular mountainous countryside. The two bars are comfortable and relaxing, with open fires, wooden furnishings, and newspapers and magazines to read. Bar food is served lunchtime and evening until 9.30pm and may include such tempting dishes as zucchini [courgette] dippers with spicy tomato sauce, Mexican fajitas and beer-battered mushrooms in teriyaki sauce, bara brith [Welsh fruit loaf], Caerphilly Welsh rarebit, filled ciabatta sandwiches, butterbean and vegetable curry, carrot, courgette and lentil cottage pie, and broccoli, cauliflower and Stilton crumble. Desserts include vegan chocolate sponge, or scrunchy syrup tart, plus rhubarb crumble. There's a tremendous range of ground coffees, or tea accompanied by vegan fruit cake. At breakfast, you can choose the usual fry-up or a vegetarian alternative. Draught beers include Castle Eden Ale, Flowers IPA, and Wadworth 6X with a summer guest ale. There's a good wine list, too. Children are welcome and accommodation is available.

Pear Tree

Hildersham, Cambridgeshire (01223 891680)

Off A604

As the phone number indicates, Hildersham is close to Cambridge (eight miles) but it's a remote, attractive village where the Pear Tree, as the only pub, is the hub of the community. There's just one comfortable bar with wooden settles round the walls but plenty of space for those who just drop in for a pint and a chat. Don't the miss the memorabilia concerning the 1933 Hildersham football team that was famous for never winning. A good range of vegetarian dishes might include leek roulade with a cream cheese filling, vegetable nuggets or spicy blackeye beans with rice and salad. The menu makes it clear that only vegetarian cheeses are used in the ploughman's lunch as well as sauces. Non-vegetarians are not ignored, with the likes of halibut Provençal; gammon and pineapple; chicken supreme with a white wine and tarragon sauce; crispy crab pancakes with sweet and sour sauce; and butterfish fillet with mango sauce. Delicious desserts may include chocolate fudge cake and treacle tart or lemon layer pudding. The pub is owned by Greene King, which supplies its IPA, Abbot ale and seasonal brews, along with a guest ale. There's a good choice of wines, including some New World bottles, with several served by the glass.

Snowdrop

South Street, Lewes, East Sussex (01273 471018)

Off Cliffe Street and A26

Cliffe Street is home to Harvey's, one of the best-loved, family-owned and fiercely traditional breweries in the country. It's in a lovely setting alongside the river and the brewhouse ia splendid example of a Victorian "tower" construction, where the brewing process flows by gravity from floor to floor. The Snowdrop could hardly be more different and less traditional. It breaks all the rules of what a pub should look and feel like. It's more like an antique shop (did someone say junk shop?) than a conventional pub, with bric-a-brac everywhere, old ships' figureheads, plank walls, and, upstairs, a large mural of the sea. The pub is not exactly quiet, with a juke box belting out jazz, blues and folk. The beers are good, with Harvey's Best Bitter joined by Fuller's ESB, Hop Back Summer Lightning and an ever-changing number of guest ales. The menu shows that the owners, Tim and Sue May, wear their hearts on their sleeves. They serve no red meat at all and the emphasis is on vegetarian and vegan dishes, including pizzas (the margheritas are highly praised by satisfied customers); soups; humus in pitta; sandwiches and burritos; and spicy stuffed peppers. Fish is offered and comes in the shape of fresh catch of the day or Mexican seafood. Children are welcome and get their own helpings. The coffees are good. In spite of the decor, it's not a young people's bar but welcomes a wide cross-section of customers. There's live jazz on Monday evenings.

Organic pubs

Duke of Cambridge

30 St Peter's Street, Islington, London N1 (020 7359 3066)
Underground: Angel

This is the only known pub in Britain totally dedicated to organic food and drink and, on the strength of its offerings, the management is seeking a Soil Association certificate. It is run by partners Geetie Singh and Esther Boulton, while the chef, Caroline Hamlin, is an experienced "gastro pub" cook who worked previously at the Lansdowne in Primrose Hill. The Duke of Cambridge was built in 1851 and has been carefully restored with wood floors, and some exposed beams and brickwork. The re-design involved the use of reclaimed building materials and all the furniture is second-hand. Singh and Boulton describe the pub design as "junkshop minimalist". The only noise in the pub is conversation, as there's no music, TV, juke box or games machines. There is a spacious bar at the front with smaller and more intimate areas at the back reached by a corridor. Caroline Hamlin uses as many as 40 small suppliers for her ingredients and this means the daily blackboard menu changes frequently depending on what is available. You may find white bean and chilli soup with greens; chicken liver pâté with pickles, relish and toast; scallops with sautéed potatoes, bacon and spinach; roasted pheasant with olive oil mash, prunes and red wine; char-grilled whole grey mullet with sweetened red cabbage and couscous; roasted loin of lamb stuffed with tapenade with peperonata and polenta chips; potato and mushroom pie with mixed leaves; and conchiglie with butter nut squash, sage butter and Parmesan. Desserts may include fig, raspberry and almond tart with cream; chocolate, prune and praline cake with crème fraîche; plum and apple crumble with custard; and Roquefort, pear and oatcakes. The wine list is 40-strong while the draught beers include Caledonian Golden Promise, Freedom Organic Lager (an organic version of Freedom Pilsner from Putney, brewed specially for the pub), Eco Warrior and Pitfield organic lager from the small Pitfield craft brewery in Hoxton and a house beer, Singhboulton, also brewed by Pitfield and named after the pub's partners, plus Adnams Broadside, which is free of additives. All the bottled beers, including German wheat beers, are organic. Even the cigarettes in the fag machine are organic: is this a plus point? Food is served lunchtime and evening (no food Monday lunchtime).

Duke of Cambridge, Islington, London N1

Castle

115 Battersea High Street, London SW11 (020 7228 8181)
Train: Clapham Junction

This is a Young's pub with a real touch of chemical-free class – the organic meats include lamb raised on Prince Charles's Highgrove estate in Wiltshire. Landlady Gill Markwell doubles as chef and her fast-changing menu may include parsnip soup; chicken breast wrapped in bacon stuffed with Mozzarella, basil and roast peppers; herb pancakes stuffed with spinach, leeks and Stilton; warm goat's cheese salad with roast peppers; smoked chicken, crispy bacon and avocado salad; fresh salmon fillet on buttered leeks with Hollandaise; gammon in Madeira with parsnip mash; or spiced Moroccan lamb with apricots and couscous. Desserts may include chocolate pudding, spiced apple crumble or coconut ice cream with cherry compote. Food is available lunchtime and evening (not Sunday evening). Mrs Markwell will cook vegan dishes to order where possible. The impeccable, though inorganic, hand-pumped ales are Young's Bitter, Special and seasonal brews. The spacious pub, with the air of a French farmhouse and a garden for spring and summer drinking, stages live jazz on Wednesday nights.

Swan Inn

Craven Road, Lower Inkpen, Berkshire (01488 668326)
Off A4, on Hungerford–Combe road

The beers in the Swan aren't organic but there's a strong emphasis on naturally produced food here as the owners, Mary and Bernard Harris, have their own organic farm that supplies the pub with beef and vegetables. The 16th-century inn has exposed beams, three open fires in winter and a games room, and is close to Combe Gibbet. As well as bar meals, there's an organic restaurant while a galleried farm shop sells more than 150 items including wines, ciders, fruit juices, eggs, cheese, cream, butter, chickens, lamb, and dried fruit, all from organic producers. Food in the pub is based around ten dishes a day using organic meat, vegetables and fruit, and may include soup; freshly made sandwiches; ploughman's with organic cheese; beef in beer with Yorkshire pudding and fresh vegetables; cottage pie made from organic minced beef; leek and mushroom crumble; beef Stroganoff with rice and salad; beef curry with chutney, rice and poppadom; Boston bean bake with salad; and leak and bacon gratin with chips and salad. Draught beers include Butts Bitter and Blackguard from a small craft brewery in Hungerford, and Hook Norton Mild and Best, with guest ales and Lambourn Valley cider. Food is available lunchtime and evening and there are cream teas in summer. The Swan offers accommodation and is based in excellent walking country.

Blacksmith's Arms

Ricknall Lane, Preston-le-Skerne, Co. Durham (01325 314873)

One mile east of A167, on Aycliff-Great Stainton road

Owner Pat Cook and her daughter are dedicated vegetarians and are keen to use as much organic produce as possible. As supplies are variable and sometimes unreliable, they are converting five acres of land next to the pub to grow their own vegetables, salad vegetables and fruit, though these will take a year or two to come on stream. For the time being they buy vegetables from organic suppliers and meat from a local butcher. The duck, chicken, guinea fowl and peacock cheerfully roaming the pub grounds will definitely not appear on an eclectic menu that may include Caribbean scampi with coconut and fruit; beer rarebit; layered hot roast beef toasted sandwich with mushrooms, onion and fried egg; lamb braised in real ale with rosemary; Cajun spiced cod; lemon and coriander chicken; mushroom tart with potato scallops; steak and ale pie; curries; pasta dishes; and mixed plates for two including dimsum, Tex Mex and vegetarian. There is something quite out of the ordinary: a good, thoughtful children's menu offering a dozen dishes with the likes of fishcakes, pizza, pasta in cheese sauce and chicken dippers. Food is available lunchtime and evening (Sunday roast lunch; no food Sunday evening). Pat Cook is a passionate supporter of small craft breweries in the North-east. The beers change every week but you may find the likes of Castle Eden Nimmos XXXX, Hambleton Nightmare and White Boar along with Black Sheep Bitter, John Smith's Magnet and guest beers. There are organic wines, too, and Mrs Cook holds free wine and ale tastings every Friday night, including rare bottled beers. The pub is known locally as The Hammers but I'm assured it has no connection with my football club in East London.

Vine

Vine Road, Skegness, Lincolnshire (01754 763018)
One mile south of town centre off Drummond Road

Chef Stephen Coggins uses pork and bacon from pigs raised on a local farm on organic home-grown maize. With the North Sea knocking on the door, he also makes good use of fresh fish and you will find cod, Dover sole, brill and flounder on the menu. Bar meals may include home-made soup; onion bhajis with curried cucumber dip; and cheese and beer fritters. As the pub-cum-hotel is owned by renowned family brewers Batemans of neighbouring Wainfleet, chef Coggins makes generous use of their beers in several of his dishes. Main courses may include game pie; catch of the day; grilled lamb cutlets with minted brandy and cream sauce; steak and Bateman's pie with garlic crust; celery, leek and cashew au gratin; and Thai vegetable stir-fry. In the restaurant you may find moules bonne femme; crostini selection; goat's cheese lasagne; duck's breast on couscous; pan-roasted pigeon supremes; or chicken with wild mushrooms. The hotel is on the edge of the seaside resort and vegetables, herbs and fruit are grown in the grounds. The hand-pumped ales include Bateman's Mild, XB, Valiant, XXXB and seasonal beers. Food is available lunchtime and evening. Excellent accommodation is available.

Wenlock Edge Inn

Hilltop, Wenlock Edge, Shropshire (01746 785678)
B4371

Stephen and Di Waring are introducing as much organic material as possible for their lovely old inn that was fashioned from quarrymen's cottages at the turn of the 18th century. It has its own well, 190 feet deep, a wood-burning stove in an inglenook, an oak bar, and pews from a Methodist chapel in Liverpool. Bread is baked on the premises from organic flour while both Double Gloucester and Shropshire Blue cheeses are organic, as are the sirloin steaks. Food in the bar and no-smoking dining room may include for starters carrot and celeriac, and tomato with sweet pepper soups, and Loch Fyne hot smoked salmon. Main courses could be organic beef and mushroom pie; Shrewsbury lamb casseroled with vegetables, redcurrant jelly and Worcestershire sauce; South Shropshire venison, beef and red wine pie; and cheese, leek and tomato flan; and such home-made desserts as apricot and almond sponge, treacle tart, and chocolate and orange mousse cake. Hand-pumped ales are from Hobsons, a small craft brewery in Cleobury Mortimer, which supplies Best Bitter, Town Crier and Old Henry. There are good wines by glass and bottle, malt whiskies and proper ginger beer and lemonade. The inn has a herb garden and a wildlife pond and is based in wonderful walking country. Children are welcome in eating areas and accommodation is available.

Riverside Inn

CANONBIE, DUMFRIES & GALLOWAY (01387 371512)
Village signposted from A7

Overlooking the River Esk in delightful Borders country, this small, comfortable inn run by Robert Phillips offers organic ingredients whenever possible. The vegetables and bread are organic and bought daily while the cheeses are unpasteurised and fresh fish is delivered three times a week. There is local game in winter. Bar food and restaurant meals (lunchtime and evening) may offer Guinness and treacle loaf; home-made carrot and sage soup; fresh fish and shellfish soup; duck liver pâté; pigeon terrine; Morecambe Bay shrimps; vegetarian homity pie; mushroom-stuffed aubergines; cod fillet roasted with red onion and cheese crust; poached cod with mussels and parsley sauce; fresh haddock in beer batter; roast ham; lamb rogan ghosh; or guinea fowl braised with paprika, cream and tomatoes. Desserts may include apricot crumble; Scottish raspberries with cream; toffee apple bake; and ginger syllabub. There's a three-course Sunday lunch. The hand-pumped ale comes from Yates over the border in Cumbria and there are such regular guests as Caledonian Deuchar's IPA and an organic lager. There's a good wine list, with several by the glass, as well as several malt whiskies. The dining room and parts of the bar are non-smoking. Accommodation is available and the inn can arrange fishing permits on the river.

Bottle Inn

MARSHWOOD, DORSET (01297 678254)
B3165 between Crewkerne and Lyme Regis

The pub and village sit on the Dorset/Devon border but choose to be firmly in Dorset (just as the man who lived on the Polish/Russian border who chose the Polish side because he couldn't stand Russian winters). The pub is ancient, with the date 1585 cut above the door of the thatched exterior. Inside there's an impressive inglenook with a cheering log fire in winter, a high-back settle and other wooden furnishings. Landlords Sim Pym and Chloe Fox-Lambert specialize in organic and vegetarian food along with organic beers, wines and ciders. They will do their best to cater for people with special needs and food allergies. Dishes of the day (lunchtime and evening; closed on Mondays November to Easter) are chalked on two boards, one for flesh eaters, one for vegetarians and vegans. Dishes could include butter-bean, garlic and parsley pate; filled baguettes; ploughman's; pumpkin and coconut curry with rice, poppadom and chutney; homity pie; stuffed aubergines with spicy tomato coulis; Matar Paneer, an Indian dish made from tofu, peas, tomatoes and warm spices served with aloo sag and pilau rice; and mushroom Stroganoff. Meat eaters can choose from leg of lamb stuffed with rosemary and garlic; wild boar casserole; and chicken balti. Desserts include organic ice-creams, frozen organic yoghurts, and Dorset apple cake with Calvados. Hand-pumped ales feature Branscombe Vale Branoc and Otter Head from Devon plus Fuller's London Pride, Morland Old Speckled Hen, Wadworth 6X and other guest beers. Draught beers are not organic, though Fuller's turned its Honey Dew into an organic ale in February 2000 and may feature at the Bottle. Mr Pym can offer you a wide choice of organic bottled beers. Children are welcome and the pub has a beer garden and a skittle alley.

White Hart

Dartington Hall, Dartington, Devon (01803 866051)

Off A384, signposted Dartington

The White Hart is part of the Dartington Hall complex where a bold experiment in switching to organic farming is under way: the complex includes three dairy farms and an organic market garden. The entire estate covers 1,000 acres, with 28 acres of landscaped gardens alongside the River Dart. The inn, heralded by beer casks at the entrance, is part of the 14th-century courtyard of the hall that was built for John Holand, a half-brother of the ill-fated Richard II. Inside, there's an L-shaped room with a bar, log fires, stone floors and oak tables. Bar food is available at lunchtime and evening and menu is backed by a blackboard listing daily specials. You may find filled baguettes; generous thick-cut sandwiches; gravadlax; pan-fired pigeon breasts with mustard dressing; red snapper in white wine sauce; organic Cornish lamb steak; or local game casserole. Desserts could include organic raspberries with cream. There are also local cheeses. The beers come from the West Country and include Blackawton Bitter, Butcombe Bitter and Dartmoor IPA. The hall is based in wonderful walking territory and there's a full programme of literary and artistic events. Children are welcome in the restaurant and accommodation is available.

Quick bites

LIVE AND LET LIVE

40 MAWSON ROAD, OFF MILL ROAD, CAMBRIDGE
(01223 460261)

This is a good example of a pub that is geared to busy people who need a quick but wholesome snack or those on low incomes, such as students, who can't afford a three-course meal. The Live and Let Live, close to the city centre, is popular with students and tourists, and is famed for sandwiches described by Susan Nowak, editor of Camra's *Good Pub Food*, as "not for the fainthearted". The small, unpretentious backstreet local, with timber-and-brick bars, offers granary or white bread with such fillings as sausage, bacon and egg, Brie and cranberry, and cheese with celery and apple, plus filled Yorkshire puddings, baguettes filled with hot beef and horseradish, or black pudding with onion and mango chutney. Beers include Adnams Best and Everards Tiger with regular guest ales that always include a dark mild. The pub closes in the afternoon. Well-behaved children are welcome in the eating areas.

ROSE & CROWN

ST MICHAEL'S VILLAGE, ST ALBANS, HERTFORDSHIRE (01727 851903)
Off A1, M1 and M25; from city centre go down George Street and into Fishpool street to St Michael's

Landlord Neil Dekker is an American and is famous for his American-style deli sandwiches made with a sense of humour as well as white and granary bread and baps baked fresh for him every day. The sandwiches are named after stars of stage and screen: look out for a Clark Gable with roast beef, American cheese, onions, cucumber, tomato and horseradish; a Judy Garland for vegetarians with peppers, mushrooms, tomato, cucumber, lettuce and French dressing; a Benny Hill with ham (who says Americans don't have a sense of irony?), peanuts, American cheese, tomato and mayonnaise; and a Baloo for *Jungle Book* addicts with peanuts, watercress, bananas and honey. For Thanksgiving Neil produces a Gobble-Gobble with turkey, Swiss cheese, bacon, watercress and mayonnaise, while at

Christmas there's a Kriss Kringle with turkey, cranberry sauce and peppers. Neil stopped doing a Frank Sinatra out of respect when Ol' Blue Eyes passed on, but he may bring it back after a decent interval (will it have new Jersey potatoes?). There are also more basic sandwiches and a few hot dishes such as soup, vegetable Stroganoff, chilli and moussaka. Food is served lunchtime only (not Sunday) and children are welcome in designated eating areas. The old pub has rough cast walls, a vast fireplace in one bar, timbers, beams, and traditional pub games. Cask ales include Adnams Best, Tetley and Wadworth 6X plus a regular guest beer. The Rose & Crown is a good base for visiting Roman St Albans, including Verulamium Park with its excellent Roman Museum.

Yellow Lion

45 High Street, Apperknowle, Derbyshire (01246 41381)
Near M1 junction 30

This sounds like a pub you'd find the Wizard of Oz frequenting. Although less prevalent than the Red Lion, the Yellow Lion has similar heraldic origins and was used by aristocratic families to indicate power and strength. Unlike red lions, the term yellow is an attempt to indicate the natural colour of the animal. The Apperknowle Yellow Lion is a 19th-century stone-built inn with a welcoming saloon bar with an old organ and brass lamps, plus a no-smoking dining room where children are welcome until 9pm. Full meals are served but the pub is famous for its sandwiches and toasties. Sandwiches include vegetarian burger and cheese; grilled liver and onions; bacon and egg; roast pork with stuffing; and rump steak, while toasties weigh in with a range from Red Leicester to boiled ham and pickle. Small main meals, such as grilled meat and chips or rainbow trout and chips, cost just over a fiver. The regular beers are Greene King Abbot and Stones plus four weekly guest ales. The Yellow Lion closes in the afternoon. There's a garden with a safe children's play area and the pub offers probably the best-value B&B in the country at £10 a head. The pub has been run by the same family for 30 years and has been listed in the *Good Beer Guide* every year since 1977.

Opposite: The Rose and Crown, St Michael's Village, St Albans

Exeter Arms

Main Street, Wakerley, Northants (01572 747817)
Off A43 between Stamford and Corby

Publican Dave Docherty cooks daily specials that augment a menu of such simple fare as home-made steak, kidney and mushroom pie at £5.25 or a mixed grill for £8.95. Specials may include curry, cottage pie, fisherman's pie or burritos and chilli. Most meals cost around a fiver. A good range of ales includes Adnams Best, Marston's Pedigree and Tim Taylor's Landlord. The inn is a 17th-century stone-built free house with a wood-burning stove in a cheery lounge and a large garden with a fish pond and swings. It's close to Wakerley Woods and pleasant walks in the Welland Valley. Accommodation is available. The pub closes in the afternoon and there's no food on Monday.

Jolly Fisherman

Haven Hill, Craster, Northumberland (01665 576461)
Off B1339

The pub is well-named, for Craster is famous as the Northumbrian seaside home of smoke-cured kippers. The pub has superb views over the sea and its snug is popular with workers from the harbour and the kipper smokeries. The ground-floor lounge has open fires, there's a second lounge on the first floor and a small garden. The pub is celebrated for its home-made crab meat soup with fresh cream and whisky, along with home-made Craster kipper pâté with salad and Melba toast, and stottie cake pizza topped by tomato, ham, mushroom and cheese. Made-to-order sandwiches include fresh salmon, crab, cheese, and home-cooked honey roast ham. All the food is tremendous value at between £1.60 and £2.25. The regular beers are Tetley Bitter and Marston's Pedigree. Children are welcome in the eating area of the bar until 9pm. The pub is open all day in summer but closes winter afternoons. You can walk from Craster along the cliff tops to Dunstanburgh Castle.

HALFWAY HOUSE

PITNEY, SOMERSET (01458 2552513)
Off B3153 two miles from Langport

If you're 24 hours from a good meal, Pitney is the place to stop where the Halfway House has a tremendous range of ales, three bars with log fires, flagstone floors, large wooden tables, newspapers and books to read, and a cheery garden with tables. At lunchtime you will find thick home-made soups, a generous ploughman's with Cheddar or Stilton, two hefty slices of granary or white bread, locally made chutney, a pickled onion, gherkin, tomato, raw onion and a Cox's apple, plus filled jacket potatoes, bangers and mash, smoked salmon bagels, or bubble and squeak. At night the Halfway House serves its revered home-made curries. The beers include Butcombe Bitter, Cotleigh Tawny, Hop Back Summer Lightning, Otter Bright and Teignworthy Reel Ale, all from West Country small craft breweries. There's also a selection of bottled Belgian beers and Wilkins farm cider. No wonder the pub was chosen as Camra's national pub of the year in 1996. It closes in the afternoon and there's no food on Sunday. Well-behaved children are welcome.

Best of the Rest

RISING SUN

116 HORSLEY ROAD, TIPTON, WEST MIDLANDS (0121 5309780)
Off A461

TIVIOT

8 TIVIOT DALE, STOCKPORT, GREATER MANCHESTER
(0161 480 4109)
Off A560/B6167 junction

GOLDEN FLEECE

LINDLEY ROAD, BLACKLEY, WEST YORKSHIRE (01422 372704)
1 mile south of Elland near M62 junction 24

Pubs with barbecues

Ship

41 Jew's Row, London SW18 (020 8870 9667)
Near Wandsworth Town railway station

The Ship is a hidden delight, a London gem. You turn off the busy Warple Way, skirt a bus garage and, just before you fall into the Thames, you find the pub. A Thames barge is moored alongside and can be hired for trips on the river. The Ship has a two-tiered terrace and patio, a delightful spot in summer with hanging baskets, flowerbeds, tubs, flowers climbing up trellis work and cobbles under foot. To the left, facing the river, is a large barbecue area where food is cooked to order every lunchtime and evening in summer. You can choose from fish steaks, king prawns, vegetable or meat kebabs, special giant burgers and cheeseburgers, and a daily rotating choice of other dishes. You can eat at picnic tables on the terrace or sit on the wall overlooking the river. Don't miss the pub interior. There is an old-fashioned and now rare public bar with bare boards, half-panelled walls, an old kitchen range and a large photograph of a sea-going clipper. In sharp contrast, the saloon has been extended into a light and airy conservatory and has leather sofas, a large clock, a harmonium and jugs of flowers dotted around the place. The fine ales come from Young's Brewery a short walk away. There is an extensive wine list, with several served by the glass, and you can also have tea and coffee. If inclement weather closes the barbie you can eat equally well inside the Ship, where the emphasis is on free-range products for such dishes as rabbit terrine with sweet pepper and ginger pickle, home-made pork sausages with chive mash, lamb and spinach curry, roast cod with clams, and daily specials. Special celebrations at the pub include a Bonfire Night party and a boozy musical evening to coincide with the Last Night of the Proms.

Ship, Wandsworth, London SW18

THE SHIP

Beer Engine

Station Road, Newton St Cyres, Devon (01392 851282)
Off A377; follow signs for station

This cheery, beamed pub was built in 1850, at the same time as the Barnstaple railway line was being laid: it's now only an occasional service, which gives you the chance to get a few pints in. It's a brewpub, with the Beer Engine Brewery attached, which shares the same phone number as the inn. The brewery was built in 1983 and now has two other regular outlets, while the beers are distributed further afield by wholesalers. The regular brews are Rail Ale (straw-coloured and fruity), Piston Bitter (light brown in colour and bitter-sweet) and Sleeper Heavy (reddish and fruity). Tours of the brewery are available. The high-spot of the pub in summer are the regular barbecues in the spacious, sun-filled garden. The interior of the white-painted "station hotel", to give it its proper title (though accommodation is not provided) has alcoves, comfortable chairs and banquettes while the dining area is smoke-free. Food, lunchtime and evening, is based on fresh fish from Brixham and even more local produce, such as gammon and steaks from the nearby butcher. The home-made soup is always suitable for vegetarians and starters may include garlic bread, mushrooms and prawns. Main courses could be chicken in barbecue sauce; steak and ale pie; casseroles; curries; and grilled pork chops. The ploughman's is recommended by the British Cheese Board for the use of local Devon cheeses, while the ham for the meat ploughman's is cooked in cider. Vegetarian dishes could include spinach lasagne; aubergine, tomato and Mozarella bake; or bean and pepper bake. Whatever happened to the British Rail sandwich?

Bear

Leatherhead Road, Oxshott, Surrey (01372 842747)
A244

The Bear has a superb, multi-award winning garden where you can eat at benches and tables. Weather permitting, there is a barbecue every lunchtime that offers more than the usual burgers and steaks, though they come in various shapes and sizes and include lamb burgers and veggie burgers. You can also try Cajun chicken, pork chops and sausages and a vast dish called The Works made up of two burgers with bacon and cheese. All the dishes come with chips or jacket potatoes. Beers are from Young's of Wandsworth and there is also a good selection of wines. The handsome old pub has some original beams in the single bar, which is decorated with hops and a collection of Teddy bears. There is a restaurant in a conservatory area.

Bull & Butcher

Turville, Buckinghamshire (01491 638283)

Off A4155, between B480 and B482, five miles north of Henley

This small pub with black and white timbers is in a delightful Chilterns village with a green and a church. The spacious garden has tables on the lawn, fruit trees and a hawthorn. The barbecue operates on Saturday and Sunday lunchtimes and offers fresh fish and various cuts of meat all served with jacket potatoes. Inside, the two small bars have beams from Spanish ships captured during the Armada, a high-back settle and cushioned wall seats. Food inside the pub is imaginative and eclectic, including Balti curries, such vegetarian dishes as vegetable hotch-potch, and Stilton soufflé on pears poached in red wine and spices, plus home-smoked pastrami on rye and chicken Dijon, pan-fried halibut steak with lemon and capers, with cheese-cake and ice-cream among the desserts. The full range of Brakspear's ales from Henley is available along with good house wines. If you drive an MG enquire about the monthly meetings of the MG Club.

White Lion

Barthomley, Cheshire (01270 882242)

M6 junction 16, take Alsager Road and watch for Barthomley signpost

The White Lion is a peerless pub with homely bars and beamed ceilings, panelled walls, latticed windows and settles, close to a 15th-century sandstone church. The barbecue area on a rear terrace serves food on Sundays from 4pm to 9pm and on Wednesdays from 7pm to 9pm. Burgers come *au naturel* or with lemon or mint, there are vegetable kebabs for non-meat eaters and giant pork sausages for dedicated carnivores. Lunchtime food in the bar includes cheese and onion oatcakes, home-made hotpot, ploughman's, pie and peas, and lamb with redcurrant jelly and mint sauce. The local Burtonwood brewery supplies succulent ales, there is live folk music some Sundays and accommodation is provided in a converted grain store.

Red Hart Inn

Blaisdon, Gloucestershire (01452 830477)

Off junction of A40 & A48

Barbecues are staged in the attractive garden at the back of the Red Hart, which is also home to some pot-bellied pigs and ponies: if you bring a dog, please keep it on a lead. The handsome old inn has flagstones in the main bar, walls seats and a log fire topped by a large painting of a sailing ship. There's a separate dining room and an overspill room for diners, such is the clamour for food, lunchtime and evening. The menu may include sandwiches; ploughman's; excellent home-made curries; ham and egg with bubble and squeak; salmon and coriander fish cakes with hollandaise sauce; roast monkfish; lamb with port and cranberry sauce; or smoked salmon and avocado salad. there is a separate children's menu and a roast lunch on Sundays. A splendid choice of hand-pumped cask beers includes Cottage, Exe Valley, Hook Norton, Tim Taylor, the local Uley craft brewery (which celebrates its 15th birthday in 2000) and Wychwood. There's also a good choice of wines. The Red Hart, which welcomes children, stands in the centre of a delightful village and has twice won the award of Gloucestershire CAMRA Pub of the Year.

Fleur de Lys

Pilley Street, Pilley, Hampshire (01590 672158)

Off A337, north-west of Lymington

History a-plenty here in the oldest pub in the New Forest. It dates from 1096, when it was fashioned from two forest workers' thatched cottages. The stone-flagged entrance lists all the landlords from as far back as the 15th century, and inside there are heavy oak beams and a large inglenook fireplace that still has the implement on which hams were roasted: a cauldron on the fire is still used to prepare lamb stew and rabbit broth in winter. The garden boasts a medieval wishing well and a dovecote. The Sunday barbecue in the garden offers vegetable kebabs, venison, pheasant, fish, lobster and spare ribs. Food inside the pub includes steamed pudding of the day with mash and mushy peas, venison sausages, fish and chips, and such specials as lamb cutlets marinated in oyster sauce, or pan-fried bream with garlic roast peppers. Beer from the pumps or straight from casks includes Ringwood's Best and Old Thumper from a large craft brewery in the New Forest plus Flowers Original, Marston's Pedigree and Wadworth's 6X. There is a good selection of wines and farm ciders. Make a point of visiting nearby Boldre church with its Fleur-de-Lys window.

DARBY'S

SWANTON MORLEY, NORFOLK (01362 637647)
B1147 near Dereham

This is another conversion from two farm labourers' cottages: the work is detailed in a portfolio of photographs on the wall at one end of the bar. The conversion is recent: when one of the pubs in the village closed in 1988, farmer John Carrick knocked the two deserted cottages into one and fashioned a brilliant new pub that manages to look several hundred years old. Its success prompted the closed pub in the village to reopen. The garden at Darbys has a children's play area and a barbecue that operates on Thursday, Friday and Saturday evenings and both lunchtime and evening on Sundays. Food includes steaks, kebabs and vegetable kebabs and burgers. Inside the comfortable beamed pub decked out with old farming tools you will find splendid lunchtime and evening meals that include home-made soups, Brancaster mussels (from water off the North Norfolk coast that has been designated some of the cleanest in Europe), Cromer crab, fresh cod in beer batter, clear Thai Tom Yum soup with spiced chicken and mushroom, mushroom and cheese bake, jacket potatoes with choice of fillings, vegetable curry, steak and kidney pudding, Darby's mushrooms deep-fried and served with a garlic dip, and such desserts as summer pudding and lime and lemon crunch. There's a strong emphasis on local produce. A tremendous range of ales includes such locals as Adnams Bitter and Broadside, Badger Tanglefoot, and Woodforde's Wherry, but be prepared for a changing range, as hundreds of small brewers' beers have been served since Darby's opened. Accommodation is available and the surrounding estate offers golf, fishing, nature walks and clay pigeon shooting.

Pubs for bed and breakfast

Cap and Feathers

8 South Street, Tillingham, Essex (01621 779212)

B1021; off A12; from Chelmsford take A414 and follow signs for Burnham-on-Crouch and then signs for Tillingham

This fine example of an Essex weather-boarded inn is in the heart of the Dengie Marshes and is an ideal base for walking, sailing or visiting St Peter's on the Wall, England's oldest church. The listed, 15th-century building, with flower tubs and hanging baskets in season, has beams, open fires, and a wealth of traditional pub games. The pub is reputed to be haunted by the ghost of an old seaman who is so devoted to real ale that he turns off the gas supplies to the keg beers in the cellar. Food is served lunchtime and evening (including all day on Christmas Day, a rare event). The menu changes constantly, but you may find the likes of Stilton and celery soup; ploughman's with a choice of Cheddar, local goat's cheese, Brie, Camembert or Stilton; filled jacket potatoes; sandwiches; deep-fried Brie with redcurrant; smoked mackerel with horseradish; Tillingham pie marinated in Crouch Vale ale with herbs in a shortcrust pastry; pork loin with mustard and cream sauce; chicken tikka masala with Basmati rice and mango chutney; minted lamb kebabs; mushroom Stroganoff; and vegetable curry. Desserts may include summer pudding; gooseberry crumble; or German apple cake. The Cap and Feathers was the first tied house owned by the Crouch Vale craft brewery in South Woodham Ferrers (it now has a second, the Queen's Head in Chelmsford) and sells its full range of cask ales, including Woodham IPA, Best Bitter, Millennium Gold, SAS and Essex Porter. Children are welcome, dogs can be accommodated by arrangement, and there are vast breakfasts for guests. The comfortable four bedrooms share a bathroom. Demand for B&B is brisk and it's advisable to book well in advance.

Marquis of Lorne

Nettlecombe, Dorset (01308 485236)

Three miles east of A3066 Bridport-Beaminster road

You'll need a stiff drink, a good meal and a bed for the night when you've managed to find this remote old inn on a hill that overlooks the village of Powerstock. I've found it, which, given my legendary ability to get lost, suggests that most of the rest of Christendom should be able to get there, too. The flower-bedecked and stone-built inn dates from the 16th century and nestles under Eggardon Hill Iron Age earthworks. The inn has four bars and dining areas, one of which is no-smoking. There are wooden floors, mahogany panelling, log fires, and old prints and photos on the walls. In good weather customers can spill out into a large garden to eat, and there's a play area there, as well. The inn is owned by Palmer's, a family-owned and uniquely thatched brewery in Bridport, and sells its Bridport Bitter, IPA and 200: the last-named celebrated the company's 200th anniversary in 1994. There are good wines, too, with several available by the glass. Food, lunchtime and evening, may include a good choice of such soups as tomato and asparagus, curried parsnip, or carrot and orange, smoked mackerel supplied by a local smokery, deep-fried Mozzarella with pear and ginger chutney, avocado with curried chicken, fresh cod in homemade batter, mussels, fresh Portland crab with salad, lamb Valentine on a redcurrant sauce, cold leek, Stilton and walnut pie, spinach and walnut lasagne, and lentil and mushroom cannelloni. Desserts may include summer pudding, almond and apricot strudel, and profiteroles. Accommodation is excellent, with *en suite* bedrooms and additional rooms in a nearby thatched cottage. The Marquis of Lorne was a general who fought with the Duke of Marlborough.

Cavendish Arms

off Main Square, Cartmel, Cumbria (015395 36240)

From M6 junction 36 take A590 and follow signs for Cartmel. In village take first left

This 450-year-old coaching inn, run by the Murray family, is the oldest pub in Cartmel and built within the original village walls. Its age can be measured – sometimes painfully – by the low beams. The main bar has an open fire, and comfortable chairs, stools and tables. There's a separate restaurant, plus seats at the front and the back of the inn, with a stream running past. The regular hand-pumped beers are Jennings Cumberland Ale from Cockermouth, Draught Bass, Tetley Bitter plus a regular guest ale that changes every week. There are good wines, as well, with several by the glass. Splendid food in bar and restaurant, lunchtime and evening, may include sandwiches, soup, spinach and ricotta cheese cannelloni, smoked fish platter, steak and ale pie, Cumberland sausage and mash, vegetable and cheese crumble, and stuffed baked cod with a tomato and fresh basil sauce. The restaurant is no-smoking

Cap and Feathers, Tillingham, Essex

and children are welcome. The Murrays are renowned for the warmth of their welcome and the quality of their accommodation.

New Inn

Cropton, North Yorkshire (01751 417330)

Take Rosedale turn from A170

Sandra and Michael Lee offer not only good food and accommodation, but the added pleasure of home-brewed ales from their Cropton

Brewery on the site. This is North Yorkshire and it can get extremely cold in winter: try phoning the boss and telling him you can't get back to work because you're snowed up in a brewpub. It was the threat of winter weather that encouraged the Lees to launch their brewery in 1984. Cropton has been so successful that the original tiny brewery in the cellar has been abandoned for a new purpose-built plant behind the pub that also serves many other outlets. The lounge bar has beams, Victorian church panels, and an open fire. The charming no-smoking restaurant has genuine Victorian and Edwardian furnishings, while the family room in a conservatory has fascinating historical posters painted by a local artist. The full range of Cropton ales are on offer, including Two Pints, King Billy, Scoresby Stout, Uncle Sams, Backwoods Bitter and Monkmans Slaughter. All the beers are also available to take away in bottle-fermented form. Delicious food, lunchtime and evening, often makes use of the beers, as in steak and mushroom pie with Scoresby Stout in the gravy, New Inn dippers in beer batter, or cod in beer batter. Other dishes may be lamb with minted gravy, home-made broccoli and mushroom cream pasta, celery and Stilton pot, salmon cakes, and salmon fillet served with fromage frais and tarragon. Desserts include a delectable Champagne sorbet. The pub has a garden with a pond, and all around is the North Yorkshire Moors National Park, splendid walking country. The inn has six double rooms with additional accommodation in an adjoining cottage. If you wonder why one of the beers is called Two Pints, Michael Lee will explain that you surely won't be satisfied with just one …

Elsted Inn

Elsted Marsh, West Sussex (01730 813662)

Off A272

The trains don't stop here any more, but the inn was built in Victorian times to serve a station that stood next door, and the age of steam is commemorated in many old pictures on the walls of the two bars which have open log fires, wooden floors, rustic furniture, and original shutters. The charming restaurant is candlelit at night and has patchwork curtains and an old oak dresser. Both the beer and the food are exceptional. The pub was the original home of Ballards Brewery, which has since moved to new premises. The cooking is in the tender care of Barry Horton, a former brewer, and his partner Tweazle Jones, who was once an Egon Ronay inspector. Food, lunchtime and evening, may include locally made sausages with mash, Barry's revered Sussex bacon roly-poly, steak and kidney pudding, chicken gibbo with cream, wine and capers, Spanish paella, roulades, bakes and roast vegetables with couscous for vegetarians, fish pie, and as bar snacks, creamy onion soup, filled jacket potatoes, ploughman's or macaroni cheese. Desserts may include fresh rhubarb crumble, dark chocolate mousse, or apple and cinnamon crumble. Wednesday nights are theme nights with such specialities as curries or smorgasbord. Sunday lunch is so popular it must be booked. The splendid ales include Ballards's Trotton, Best Bitter, Wassail and seasonal brews, plus other independents, such as Arundel and Cheriton. Excellent wines are supplied by the neighbouring Midhurst Wine Shippers. There's a spacious garden where boules is played. Accommodation (four rooms) is in the former brewery building.

NEUADD ARMS HOTEL

THE SQUARE, LLANWRTYD WELLS, MID WALES (01591 610236)
A483

This is not so much a hotel as an institution, where landlord Gordon Green organises two real ale festivals, Saturnalia in January and a second in November. The Neuadd Arms is home to the annual World Bog-Snorkelling Championships and Gordon also organises rambles, guided walks and mountain bike holidays called Real Ale Wobbles, and still finds time to run the hotel with his wife Diana and pull the odd pint of Felinfoel Double Dragon and Hancock's HB. The hotel has Georgian origins and was extended in Victorian times when the English middle classes flocked to Wales for touring holidays. The cheerful bar and lounge have log fires. Food, served lunchtime and evening, may include lamb Peking with shrimp crackers, lamb rogan josh, Kashmiri lamb, Thai green beef curry, chicken tikka masala, grilled Welsh lamb cutlets, cod in batter, gammon and fried egg, freshly made omelettes, and shepherd's pie with mushy peas. Simple snacks include plain and toasted sandwiches and home-made soups. Most of the 20 guest rooms are en suite and most have colour TVs. There's also a TV lounge and games room. Pets are welcome by arrangement.

Pub walk on the Peddars Way, Norfolk

Little Cressingham to Castle Acre

The Peddars Way passes by the WHITE HORSE at Little Cressingham (Watton Road, off B1108: tel 01953 883434) and the pub is the ideal watering and refuelling point for the walk. The White Horse is a small 17th-century inn with a white and shuttered exterior, and one bar inside with beams and log fires. There's a games room while the dining area off the bar has comfortable sofas with old tin trunks used for tables. Landlord Paul Hickman offers an eclectic choice of meals lunchtime and evening. He is famous for his balti

Ostrich Inn, Stocks Green, Castle Acre

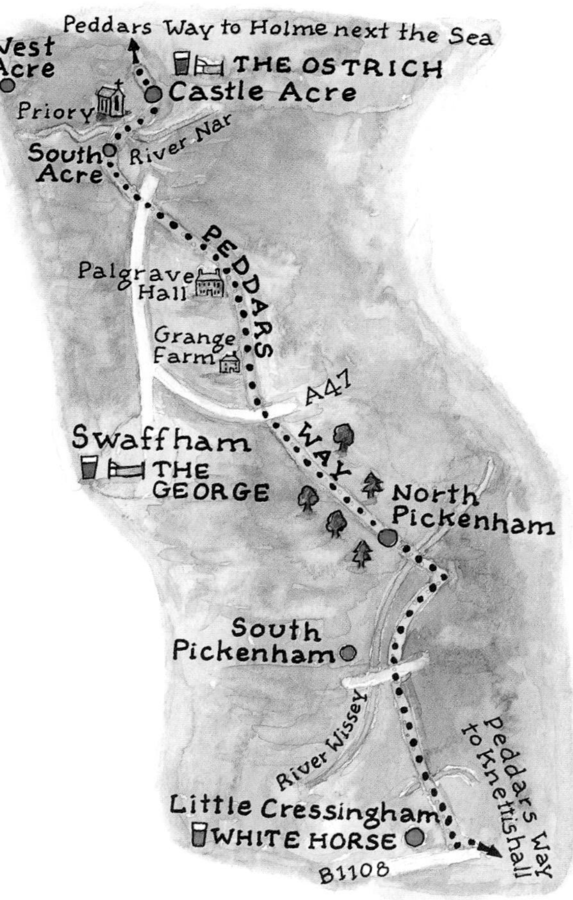

dishes, which are cooked to order: you choose the main ingredients, either meat or vegetable, and decide whether you want it mild, medium or hot. Other food includes "jaw breakers" – baguettes with a choice of fillings – steaks, beef or mushroom Stroganoff, ship's pie, vegetable and cheese bake, vegetable Kiev, cod and chips, and creamy chicken. The real ales include Flowers Original – "because that's what I drink," Paul says reasonably – and such guest beers as Wadworth 6X and Mauldon's of Suffolk.

From the pub, head north along the route known here as Pilgrims' Way: the walk to Castle Acre is 12 miles. The Peddars Way is an old Roman road, built around 60 AD, that originally stretched from Colchester to Holme Next the Sea on the Norfolk coast, from where troops were ferried over the Wash to Lincolnshire. Today, the Peddars Way starts at Knettishall on the Suffolk border to Holme, a distance of 46 miles that takes you through the Brecklands and, near Thompson, pools formed during the Ice Age and known by the delightful dialect word of pingos. The name of the Peddars Way came after the Romans and is thought to derive from an ancient word for path or a corruption of the Latin pedester, from which comes pedestrian.

The Roman road was built following the bloody suppression of the Iceni led by Queen Boudicca. The route is now a pleasant path across undemanding flat country but originally was garrisoned with watch towers and forts: the Romans had been badly shaken by Boudicca's victories at Camulodunum (Colchester) and Verulamium (St Albans).

Walk along the lane for about three miles into the valley of the River Wissey. The Peddars Way now follows a path that leads to the village of North Pickenham. North of the village the path becomes a green track known as Procession Way, with beech trees, conifers and fields on either side.

The pleasure of the walk is interrupted briefly by the need to cross the A47 Norwich-King's Lynn road, where a yellow "M" announces a McDonald's – but you wouldn't, would you? If you are in need of sustenance at this point, leave the route, go into Swaffham to the **GEORGE**, Station Street (01760 721238), with recommended bar meals, Greene King beers and accommodation if you need to billet your bunions.

Once across the A47, the path follows a narrow road that leads past Palgrave Hall and Grange Farm and has a junction with the Swaffham-Castle Acre road. Cross the road and walk towards West Acre and then approach Castle Acre via a picturesque ford across the River Nar, with superb views of the village, which you enter through the 13th-century bailey gate. The village, a mystical, medieval place often shrouded in mist, and surrounded by the remains of its Norman castle, was an important trading post long before the Normans, when the Nar was navigable. The village was controlled for several centuries by the Warennes family, the earls of Surrey, who founded the castle as a manor house and developed it into a fortress.

The village, where the centre – Stocks Green – is surrounded by brick and flint houses, also has the imposing ruins of an 11th-century Cluniac priory. It was established by William de Warenne and was an off-shoot of the Benedictines who took their orders from the Abbot of Cluny in France: the monks were persecuted for several centuries as "aliens". The remains of the priory often appear eerily through the mist: the inner walls, and the west front, south tower and prior's house still stand.

Our resting place is a marvellous coaching inn, the **OSTRICH** (Stocks Green: tel 01760 755398). There are several Ostrich pubs in Norfolk and the origins of the name are contentious. Some claim it comes from the coat of arms of Sir Edward Coke (1552-1633), an eminent lawyer and landowner in East Anglia. Coke (pronounced "Cook"), became Speaker of the House of Commons. A contrary view is that Ostrich is a corruption of "hospice", a resting place run by monks, and that is certainly how the Castle Acre Ostrich began life in the 16th century. It was rebuilt in the 18th century and has the air of a large country house rather than an inn. The main bar is on two levels and has two vast inglenooks. The front area has a mantelbeam with hooks above the fire, used in winter to cook soups and ham. There's a low ceiling, comfortable country chairs and many old photos of the village. The back area has a high pitched ceiling with oak beams and trusses, with the end wall built of exposed 16th-century masonry. The serving bar rests on old wooden beer casks. The exterior of the inn is built of red brick with a steeply tiled roof and three small dormer windows. There's an archway leading to the inn through a courtyard with a beamed entrance. A sign in the wall for the "ostler's bell" shows that the entrance was used for horses during the inn's coaching days. Hand-pumped ales come from the Greene King range. Landlord Ray Wakelin is a celebrated pub chef and always has a good range of vegetarian dishes on his menu. He makes his own granary rolls and pizza bases. Imaginative ploughman's lunches include Cheddar, Stilton, pickled herring and the Continental with garlic sausage and salami. There is even a cockles and mussels ploughman's: well, it's hard work ploughing the ocean. Hot dishes include steaks, salmon, pizzas with a choice of toppings and omelettes to order. Daily specials may include the likes of chilli Quorn taco, vege mince burritos, aromatically coconutted chickpeas with pilau rice and popadom, Mex-chili cheese combi with Cajun tomato dip, smoked chicken, pastrami of beef in pitta bread, salmon crumble pie, roast Kashmiri lamb in pitta, and chicken, sausage and red cabbage bake. Desserts include baclava, galatabourica, rum baba, apple strudel and treacle roly-poly. Accommodation is available and is probably essential if you finish dinner with treacle roly-poly.

Ancient pubs

Royal Standard of England

Forty Green, Buckinghamshire (01494 673382)

Three-and-a-half miles from M40 junction 2; A40 to Beaconsfield then B474; follow signs to Forty Green

The Royal Standard lays claim to being one of England's oldest inns. It's at least 900 years old and has an air of great antiquity with its canopied entrance and mullioned windows. Inside there are heavy, blackened beams, oak panelling, ships' settles – one curved to fit the transom of an Elizabethan ship – powder flasks, warming pans, bugles, swords, muskets and pewter tankards. The present name of the inn was the result of Charles II presenting his royal standard to the innkeeper when he allowed the king to hide in the rafters as the parliamentary forces were searching for him after the battle of Worcester in 1651. Among the warren of small, candle-lit rooms there is inevitably one named after King Charles. In winter the inn is warmed by great open fires; in summer and early autumn visitors can sit on the terrace at the front. Two rooms are non-smoking. Bar food includes several vegetarian specials, soup, local sausages, pork escalope, and lamb brochettes. Excellent ales include Brakspears from Henley and Adnams from Suffolk.

George

off 77 Borough High Street, London SE1 (020 7407 2056)

Underground: London Bridge or Borough

The George is a brilliant replica of a galleried Elizabethan coaching inn and even the replica is extremely ancient. The original inn was destroyed in the Great Fire of Southwark in 1676. It was rebuilt in 1677 and once occupied three sides of the courtyard. But in the great railway boom of the last century, Guy's Hospital, then the owners of the inn, sold it to the London and North Eastern Railway Company and the railway barons, in an act of appalling vandalism, tore down part of the site to make way for engine sheds. The ground floor bars of the George are small and low-ceilinged, with lattice windows, beams, bare-board floors and wooden settles. The back bar, the nearest to the main road, has an old Parliamentary Clock, recalling that parliament in 1797, in one of its periodic mad moods, imposed taxes on timepieces. The serving area, seen through a low hatch, has a fine example of a Victorian "cash register" beer engine, with the small pump handles that deliver beer sliding up and down grooves in a wooden frame. A narrow corridor leads to a long central bar and then into a more spacious area used for eating. Outside, a cobbled courtyard is overlooked by the galleried upper storeys. Morris Men perform in good weather in the courtyard and occasionally strolling players perform extracts from Shakespeare's plays. The inn today is owned by the National Trust and leased to Whitbread so expect to find beers from the group's stable, with guests such as Fuller's London Pride. Bar food is fairly basic: soup, sandwiches, vegetarian lasagne, and steak and mushroom pie. An impressive stairway leads up to first-floor dining rooms.

Prospect of Whitby

57 Wapping Wall, London E1 (020 7481 1095)

Underground: Wapping

This creakingly ancient riverside alehouse was built in 1520 and takes its name from one of the great sailing ships that plied their trade between the North of England and the Thames, though it was known for years as the "Devil's Tavern" when it was a haunt of smugglers and thieves. Samuel Pepys was a regular when he was Secretary to the Admiralty: a coastal chart presented to the diarist in 1686 is on display in the Pepys Room upstairs. A less welcome visitor was "Hanging Judge" Jeffreys, who brutally despatched the Monmouth rebels after their failure to remove James II from the throne in 1685. When Jeffreys lived in the suitably named Butcher Row he would dine at the Prospect of Whitby in order to gloat at the sight of men he had ordered to be executed hanging from gallows across the river at Execution Dock. When James was overthrown in 1688 Jeffreys attempted to follow the king into exile disguised as a coal heaver but was spotted in the coal hole of the pub and carted off to the Tower of London, where he soon died. The bar has a stone-flag floor with a long and unusual counter made from pewter that is 400 years old. There are beams, pillars and open fires and, surprisingly for this part of London, a beer garden with a willow tree. There is an upstairs dining room and wherever you sit at the back of the inn you will find stupendous views of the Thames flowing past. Bar food is basic fodder: roasts, sausages and chips, and salads with more elaborate meals upstairs. Ales include Courage Best, Theakston's XB and Young's Special.

Ye Olde Fighting Cocks

16 Abbey Mill Lane, St Albans, Hertfordshire. (01727 865830)
Off A1 and M25

The setting is magnificent, with the great Abbey Cathedral of St Alban, England's first Christian martyr, looming up the hill above the inn, and beyond the broad sweep of Verulamium Park, with a lake and Roman remains, including a hypercaust. The inn claims to be one of England's oldest licensed premises, though the licence was granted in Stuart times for cock fighting, not for drinking. There has been a building on the site since 795, when the abbey was founded by King Offa, and it served as a gatehouse to the abbey in Norman times. The current inn is almost circular in design and was known as the Round House when it first opened to serve ale in 1600. Inside there are low beamed ceilings, wooden partitions, plenty of nooks and crannies, and an impressively vast inglenook with a log fire in winter. To the left of the bar, steps take you down to a sunken area that was the original cock-fighting pit. Tetley Bitter is always on tap, with a rotating list of guest beers that may include Old Speckled Hen, Young's Bitter and Maclays from Scotland. Food includes chilli, chicken Kiev, plaice and chips, Fighting Cocks pie and several vegetarian options. There is a large back garden with trestle tables and benches, with more seats at the front overlooking the park and the River Ver. To find the inn from the city centre, go down George Street, turn left into Romeland, through the Abbey Gateway and then down Abbey Mill Lane until you reach the park: the inn is on the left. As well as the abbey, the splendid museum at the entrance to the park is packed with fascinating information about life in Roman Verulamium.

Ye Olde Trip to Jerusalem

Brewhouse Yard, Castle Road, Nottingham (0115 947 3171)

This is claimed to be England's oldest inn, carved from the sandstone rock below Nottingham Castle. The date 1189AD decorates the whitewashed exterior and this is used to suggest that the Trip was a meeting place for crusaders having a last glass of ale before leaving for the Holy Land, where alcohol was in short supply. The problem is that the word trip did not exist in the English language until the 14th century and means a short journey or stagger, not a long hike to the Holy Land. The

Ye Olde Trip to Jerusalem

most likely explanation is that a brewhouse once stood on the site to supply ale to the castle, and crusaders may have been given a farewell drink by the lord up the hill. The present inn is 17th or 18th century and developed out of the brewhouse. Whatever the exact origins, this is a fascinating building, with caves open to the public, cramped but comfortable small rooms on the ground floor served by a hatch, and an upstairs cavern bar with its panelled walls disappearing into the dark of a rock funnel above; this room is thought to be the site of the earlier castle brewhouse. The inn is owned by local brewers Hardy and Hanson of Kimberley and it sells their Mild, Bitter and Classic ales plus Marston's Pedigree. Good value bar food includes soup, sandwiches, cobs, filled jacket potatoes, giant Yorkshire puddings with a choice of fillings, pork and apple cider bake, and cheese and onion hot-pot. Next door, don't miss the fascinating museum of Nottingham life.

Bingley Arms

Bardsey, Church Lane, West Yorkshire (01937 572462)
off A58

Whatever Nottingham's claims, the Bingley Arms has an equally powerful hold on the title of England's oldest inn. It was mentioned in the Domesday Book and dates from 953AD. It was first known as the Priests' Inn; a brewhouse stood alongside the inn and members of the same family ran it from the time of Samson Ellis, the first recorded innkeeper, until 1780 when Baron Bingley changed the name. The central area of the inn is the original building. The ceilings were raised in the 17th century from the original height of 5 feet 11 inches. The lounge has a massive inglenook: if you peer upwards you will see a priest's hole. The north remained loyal to Catholicism at the time of the Tudors and many old buildings had hidey-holes where priests could escape the monarch's men; it must have been a bit dicey if someone lit the fire. There is a small public bar downstairs where pub games are played. Upstairs, the restaurant is dominated by the stone chimney breast of the inglenook below. There is a pleasant terraced garden at the back where barbecues in good weather sensitively offer vegetarian dishes as well as meaty ones. Inside, bar food inclues soup, sandwiches, lasagne, Thai spiced chicken, cucumber and red onion salad, wild mushroom ragoût, fish dishes and steak and kidney pudding. Beers include the excellent Black Sheep Best Bitter plus Tetley Bitter and guest ales. You can also visit the local village church with its Saxon tower. Bardsey was the birthplace of the dramatist William Congreve.

Best of the Rest

Cott Inn

Dartington, Devon (01803 863777)
Off A385

Three Horseshoes

Bridge Street, Warham All Saints, Norfolk (01328 710547)
Off A149 and B1105

Heritage Pubs

Prince Alfred

5a Formosa Street, Maida Vale, London W9 (020 7286 3027)
Underground: Maida Vale

The Prince Alfred, built in 1863, is one of the treasure trove of classic pubs listed in *Heritage Pubs of Great Britain*, by Mark Bolton and James Belsey. It has five bars, each with its own entrance. The four smaller bars, or snugs, can be reached only by passing through tiny, waist-high doors that were originally designed to be used by cleaners. The building is an incredible piece of design: the front is open, the entire weight of the upper floors supported by lintels held up by slim iron columns. The windows bear no loads and are in effect screens inside sculpted mahogany frames that form arches around the etched glass. Even the standard lamps on the pavement were erected by the pub's owner to both light the street and advertise the pub. The bars are grouped around an ornate serving counter. One bar was originally set aside for women and still retains its "snob screens", pivoting small etched partitions that can be turned to stop people from looking in. The pub is named after Queen Victoria's second son who was installed as Duke of Edinburgh in 1862 and who turned down an offer from Greece to become King of the Hellenes. Bar snacks are served lunchtime and the beers include Tetley Bitter, a house beer called (presumably ironically) Prince Alfred Bitter, and a guest ale such as Young's Bitter. The pub is handy for the Little Venice canalside area.

Barley Mow

Main Street, Kirk Ireton, Derbyshire (01335 370306)
Off B5023 south of Wirksworth

A sundial on the front wall bears the date of 1683, and records show that the tall, gabled, Jacobean building, on a hilltop in the Derbyshire Dales, has been an inn for at least 200 years. Ales are tapped straight from casks behind a counter or brought in jugs from the cellar, and include Hook Norton Best and Old Hooky plus a regular guest beer such as Black Sheep, Burton Bridge, Cottage or Leatherbritches. Farm ciders are also available. The interior is a warren of small rooms, with beams, standing timbers, stoves, ancient settles, woodwork, tiled floors, and slate tables made from an old snooker table. There are bar snacks at lunchtime and full meals in the evening for residents using the guest rooms. Children are welcome at lunchtime. The pub has a good-sized garden and benches at the front, and is in fine walking country.

Three Stags Head

Wardlow Mires, near Tideswell, Derbyshire (01298 872268)
Junction of A623 and B6465

This homely old pub is a traditional Peak District long house built between 1680 and 1700. It had living accommodation for the family at one end and covered pens for farm animals at the other. Two rooms were added in early Victorian times. Today it's a thriving country pub with many original features such as flagstone floors, a working step grate and side oven, ladder-back chairs and old tables. Geoff and Pat Fuller bought the pub in 1988 in order to combine running the place and restoring the interior with their skills as working potters. They use an adjacent outhouse as a pottery. As well as the main bar, the small dining room has been renamed the Music Room and local folk musicians play there regularly. Traditional pub games such as backgammon, cribbage, darts and nine men's morris are played. The hand-pumped cask beers are supplied by the Abbeydale craft brewery in Sheffield and include Matins, Absolution and Black Lurcher. A second craft brewery, Springhead, supplies its Bitter and there's a regular guest ale plus genuine European bottled lagers. Geoff Fuller only permits one pressurised beer in the pub in the shape of Guinness. Pat Fuller weighs in with brilliant food, including several vegetarian offerings and always one vegan dish. Look out for home-made soups; steak and kidney pie; beef stew with dumplings; Derbyshire lamb stew; chicken kebabs; leek and Stilton hot-pot; vegetable and bean stew; chick pea and apricot couscous; and spinach and cheese lasagne. The pub is in marvellous walking countryside and often fills up with tired, wet and hungry customers.

Case is Altered

Case Lane, Five Ways, Haseley Knob, Warwickshire (01926 484206)
Off junction of A4177 and A4241

The licensees of the Case is Altered are such sticklers for tradition that they still adhere to old-fashioned opening hours: 11.30am to 2.30pm and 6pm to 11pm during the week; 12 noon to 2pm and 7pm to 10.30pm on Sunday.

Afternoons are sacrosanct, like the "holy hour" once observed by Irish pubs. The pub's pre-decimal till registers sales in pounds, shillings and pence (though you have to pay in modern pounds and "pees"), and a splendid old billiards table only accepts old-fashioned tanners as payment. The curious name of the pub stems from a comedy of that name by Ben Jonson concerning a court case in which new evidence is introduced: where pubs are concerned, the name was adopted when a licensee ran into problems with the local bench. In this particular case, a 19th-century landlady named Mercedes Griffiths won a legal battle to sell spirits as well as beer, and celebrated by changing the name of the

Drewe Arms, Drewsteignton, Devon

pub to its present one. The Case is Altered is a whitewashed cottage standing in a narrow lane. You reach the entrance through a wrought-iron gate and a small paved yard. The main bar has a few leather-covered settles on a tiled floor and some tables. An old poster shows the long defunct Lucas, Blackwell & Arkwright brewery, while a clock spells out the name of Thornleys, another defunct brewery. A beamed lounge, with carved oak furniture, copper jugs, and a glowing log fire, is used only at weekends. A third room houses the old billiards table. Beer — Ansells Mild, Flowers Original, Greene King IPA and a regular guest ale — are served by small pumps attached to casks mounted behind a counter. There's no food, children, dogs, machines or canned music.

Drewe Arms

Drewsteignton, Devon (01647 281224)
Off A30

The thatched and barley-white old inn is better known as "Auntie Mabel's" in honour of Mabel Mudge, who died just a few years ago aged 101. Mabel and her husband Ernest took over the pub in 1919. He died in 1951 but Mabel just went on running the simple old alehouse until she became too infirm and moved to a nursing home. Rumours that the owner, Whitbread, planned to modernise the inn or even close it sent shock waves through the community. A Save the Drewe Arms campaign was launched and the inn has remained unchanged and unaltered save for the introduction of a wider range of food. There are two rooms, served from a hatch, with rustic furniture, and log fires. Flowers IPA, Wadworth 6X and such guests as Marston's Pedigree are drawn straight from casks in a tap room, along with Gray's cider. The one major change since the departure of Mabel has been the addition of a dining room at the back that offers sandwiches, excellent ploughman's, crab and mushroom bake, duck breast, and sausages with bubble and squeak.

Wines are served by the glass. There's a skittle alley and darts and dominoes are played. Accommodation is available. Nearby is the remarkable Castle Drogo, a "medieval" castle built in the early part of the 20th century for Julius Drewe, who had made his fortune from the Home and Colonial Stores, a forerunner of today's supermarkets. He got Sir Edward Lutyens to design the castle, which took 20 years to build. Drewe died just two months after it was completed. It was called Drogo after a Norman noble of that name whom Drewe claimed as an ancestor. Drewe had the electricity cables in the village buried beneath ground to improve the view and changed the name of the inn from the Druid's Arms to the Drewe Arms. Amazing the power of grocers.

CROWN LIQUOR SALOON

44 GREAT VICTORIA STREET, BELFAST (028 902 79901)
Rail and bus stations: Victoria Street

This is a classic pub that is Grade I listed, a magnificent example of high Victorian art and design. It was created by Michael Flanaghan in the late 1800s as the ultimate architectural fantasy of its time. The spectacular porticoed and marble exterior leads into a shrine of Victoriana with a tiled floor, tinted glass mirrors, moulded plaster ceiling, and a porticoed back bar. Beer and spirits are served across a unique granite-topped bar counter while a surprisingly intimate air is provided by the ornately partitioned side alcoves, separated from each other by carved wood and painted glasswork, and known irreverently as "donkey boxes". Lunches, with waiter service in the alcoves, include Irish stew and Strangford Lough oyster in season. As well as the ubiquitous Irish stouts, the saloon serves Whitewater Belfast Bitter from a small craft brewery. It stands opposite the much-bombed Europa Hotel, has had windows blown out on several occasions but, miraculously, has survived. Go and marvel.

Note: *All the pubs in this section appear in the book* Heritage Pubs of Great Britain, *by Mark Bolton and James Belsey, published by Camra, £16.99.*

Award-winning pubs

THE WHARF

WHARF 10, WALSALL, WEST MIDLANDS (01922 613100)
Off A34 and M6

The Wharf has won a rare award – top in the 1998 "New Build" category in the annual Pub Design Awards run by English Heritage and the Campaign for Real Ale. The award is rare, for it's the first time in 14 years that a prize for a new pub design has been made. As one of the judges, Dr Steven Parissien of the Paul Mellon Centre, said in his citation: "Most new pubs were either couched as veneered bunkers or heritage horrors. This past year, however, some pub owners appear to have summoned the courage and foresight to combine the familiar virtues of the public house with the best of modern design." The pub is owned by the local Highgate and Walsall Brewing Company, run on a shoe-string following a management buy-out from mighty Bass, and the new owners richly deserve the award. For those steeped in mock-Tudor and fake beams, the Wharf will come as something of a shock. It stands in the revitalised waterside Wharf area of Walsall and is alongside the new Lottery-funded Art Gallery. The pub is single storey with a large pitched roof, tiled gable ends and plain windows giving good views of the waterfront. Dr Parissien says the interior is "defined by a Scandinavian-style use of pale wood and by a back-to-basics approach to fixtures and fittings. There are no heritage blackboards, only graphics painted directly on to wood, brick or glass, while the seating is simple, honest and functional". It's an open-plan pub and landlord Kevin Cryan says it was designed to be multi-functional, with a mobile stage for live music at weekends and intimate areas during the week. "We wanted to break down the barriers that exist in most pubs," he said. "It's female-friendly for a start and it's popular with students who drop in to do their homework over a coffee. Others play chess." The Wharf opens at 10am for late breakfast and there is bistro-style food during the rest of the day with such dishes as lamb cutlets in a silver onion sauce, pan-fried cod on potato cake, and whole baked peppers with mushroom risotto. The Highgate Brewery beers include its famous Dark Mild, plus Saddlers Bitter and such seasonal beers as Breacais, a beer brewed with whisky malt.

Station Buffet

Platform One, Stalybridge Station, Market Street, Stalybridge, Greater Manchester (0161 303 0007)

Stalybridge Station bar is one of the last-surviving Victorian buffets in the country and it won the Best Refurbishment category in the English Heritage/Camra awards. In the 1970s and 1980s it managed to avoid the dreaded Traveller's Fare revamp but was closed by British Rail in the early 1990s. It has re-opened with Railtrack's support, has two additional rooms and much-needed inside toilets (as the citation notes: "In the old days, after

the station toilet had been locked at 5pm, desperate customers had no choice but to utilise the adjacent track bed while nervously scanning the horizon for approaching expresses"). The original old bar is cramped but comfortable and has a welcoming fire in winter. The new rooms are based in the station-master's house and ladies' waiting room. Beers include Boddingtons, Wadworth 6X and Flowers IPA with guest ales from small craft breweries. There are also farm ciders and bottled Belgian beers. Food includes ploughman's, liver and bacon, and pasta bake. Close your eyes and imagine Celia Johnson and Trevor Howard sitting in the corner. The station is on the Manchester to Huddersfield line.

Stalybridge Station Buffet, Stalybridge, Greater Manchester

Brown's

Earl Street, Coventry, West Midlands (01203 221100)
Off A45 and M6

The Midlands has scored well in the awards, with Brown's winning a Highly Commended in the New Build category. The family-run pub led by owner Ken Brown has been designed to pay homage to the 1950s architectural style known as the Golden Age of Coventry. The English Heritage/Camra citation applauds "the reinterpretation of a 1950s ethos in a thoroughly contemporary manner." The design incorporates strong, curving forms in warm wood and steel with bold wall colours of maroon and pale green. Outside, the copper roof curves up to cradle and frame the glazed front. Inside, laminated wooden arches support the ceiling, which is boarded in the manner of the local railway station in the 1960s, and a glazed gallery. The citation says that "the randomly pigmented floor of polished concrete, the steel balustrades, the marvellously pendant lamps and the spare but sophisticated seat furniture are light years away from the tired, pseudo-historical catalogue horrors we have become used to in new pubs." Brown's opens at 10am for breakfast and food is available all day long. There are always at least 12 vegetarian dishes such as spinach roulade in cream and tomato sauce; a daily roast; fish dishes; steak and kidney pie; and lamb bourguignon, with a wide choice of fresh vegetables. The only disappointment is the poor choice of real ales: just Ruddles County and Webster's Yorkshire Bitter, but there is a good wine list that focuses on New World varieties.

Fat Cat

49 West End Street, Norwich, Norfolk (01603 624364)
Off Dereham Road

The Fat Cat, named Camra Pub of the Year for 1999, and owned by Colin and Marjorie Keatley, is a community pub that straddles two streets in down-town Norwich. The long, narrow bar, with scrubbed pine tables, bric-a-brac and stained glass, is decked out with brewing memorabilia from around the world. Mr Keatley is a beer buff *sui generis*: he scours the world for the finest beers and always has at least 20 on tap. As well as such home-brewed cask ales as Adnams Best, Greene King Abbot, Iceni,

Reepham, and Woodforde's Nelson Revenge and Wherry (all East Anglian beers) he also offers genuine lagers from Germany and the Czech Republic, and Belgian fruit and wheat beers. Some beers are served by hand-pumps on the bar, others are drawn from casks in a cooled ground-floor cellar, seen through windows behind the bar. Country wines and Norfolk cider are also available. Lunchtime food is restricted to filled rolls. Colin Keatley said of his award: "Tradition is the cornerstone of our business. We have worked hard to build a good reputation for a wide selection of quality beers at reasonable prices." The Camra citation added: "The Fat Cat is a traditional pub serving an excellent range of good quality real ales. It is extremely encouraging to see that community pubs continue to thrive despite moves from certain sectors of the brewing industry to replace them with bland theme pubs."

Plough and Harrow

Monknash, South Glamorgan, Wales (01656 890209)
Off B4265 between Llantwit Major and Wick

The Plough and Harrow, highly commended in Camra's Pub of the Year competition, stands in the grounds of a 12th-century monastic grange and is close to the coast at Nash Point with fine walks along the coastal path. The inn has massive stone walls. There's a log fire in a fireplace with a side oven in the main bar, which used to be the monks' scripture room and mortuary. Settles stand on the flagstone floor while old ham hooks hang from the heavy ceiling beams. Licensee Andrew Davies, known to all and sundry as "Pugsley", said: "People drive from miles around to come here because they know they will receive a warm welcome, a good pint and value for money." Ales include Draught Bass, Brains, Buckleys, Felinfoel, Greene King Abbot, Shepherd Neame Spitfire, and Worthington Best plus regular guest beers. Food lunchtime and evening includes filled rolls, faggots and chips, ploughman's, pasta dishes, and steak and ale pie. Booking is advised for evening meals. The pub is quiet during the week but busy and lively at the weekend.

Pubs in unusual buildings

TRAM DEPOT

5 DOVER STREET, OFF EAST ROAD, CAMBRIDGE (01223 324553)

The city's horse-drawn tram system closed down in 1914 but part of the buildings – the stables that housed the horses – have been saved and turned into a brilliant example of a modern, atmospheric pub. The bare brick walls and stone floor are saved from looking too spartan by a glazed

Tram Depot, Cambridge

mezzanine that offsets the high ceiling. It is light and airy thanks to a skylight that runs the length of the building. Imaginative use has been made of reclaimed materials: panelling from an old school, timbers from a former maltings, cast-iron radiators and a fine miscellany of tables and chairs. The pub is owned by Everards of Leicester and sells its full range of Mild, Beacon, Tiger, Old Original and its autumn special Equinox. Food is served lunchtime and evening until 9pm, with a strong emphasis on vegetarian meals including pasta dishes, macaroni cheese, and veggie burgers, plus home-made soups, sandwiches with salad and crisps, corned beef hash, bangers and mash and daily specials based on one meat dish and one vegetarian.

Fantail & Firkin

87 Muswell Hill Broadway, London N10 (020 8883 1183)

This member of the ever-expanding Firkin chain is housed in a former church. You enter through the old church doors into an open-plan interior where the bar has been fashioned out of the altar. Above is the bell tower and an arched ceiling: stairs lead up to a balcony with a second bar. The original pillars and stained-glass windows remain, though the chandeliers add a distinctly un-churchy touch. To the left of the entrance is the house brewery that produced the likes of Golden Glory, Fantail, Broadway and Dogbolter until new owners Punch Taverns unceremoniously closed all the Firkin breweries in September 1999. You will now find Tetley Bitter with Ind Coope Burton Ale and such guests as Adnams Bitter. Food is served from 12 noon until 8pm and includes sandwiches with salad, tagliatelle, lasagne, salmon fishcakes and chicken in white wine sauce.

Lord Moon of the Mall

16 Whitehall, London SW1 (020 7839 7701)

The name is an elaborate pun on the first pubs in the Wetherspoon's chain, which were called the Moon Under Water, based on an *Evening Standard* essay in 1946 by George Orwell, who gave the title to his favourite but mythical pub. The pun encompasses a large painting in the main room of a 19th century gentleman who is actually Wetherspoon's founder, Tim Martin. The building was opened in 1872 as a bank owned by Cork, Biddulph & Co, who numbered members of the Royal Family in

Buckingham Palace as their customers; the royals had their own secret entrance to the bank. The company was taken over by Barclays: members of the banking family were also London brewers Barclay Perkins. The main high-ceilinged room leads through an arch to a second room with a long bar, bookshelves and monochrome prints of Whitehall and its environs. There is a no-smoking area. Food is served from 11am to 10pm (9.30pm Sunday) and includes filled baguettes, Somerset Pie, half a roast chicken, and several pasta dishes including vegetarian ones. Hand-pumped beers are Fuller's London Pride, Theakston's Best and two rotating guest ales, plus Courage Directors, another neat touch as Courage took over Barclay Perkins.

COUNTING HOUSE

24 GEORGE SQUARE, GLASGOW (0141-248 9568)

Another converted bank, another Wetherspoon's: this one was formely owned by the Royal Bank of Scotland. The Counting House is sumptuous, in the heart of the Merchant City. Customers enter up a wide staircase (manned by courteous bouncers at weekends) into an elegant and vast main room with a high and decorated ceiling topped by a central dome, and caryatids (pillars in the form of nymph-like women) playing a supporting role. The pub is always busy but the sheer size of the place means there is plenty of standing and seating room. The great, polished wood island bar is manned by staff who serve at lightning speed, offering the sublime Deuchar's IPA from neighbouring Edinburgh with Courage Directors, Theakston's Best and several guest ales, often from small Scottish independents. There is a good choice of malt whiskies and wines, too. Food, served 11am to 10pm (9.30pm Sunday) includes soup, pasta, including vegetable lasagne, steaks, chicken and leek pie, and bridies. There are several well-furnished side rooms: I was surprised in the "no-smoking" room to be asked by another customer "Can you gie us a fag, Jimmy?" – but that's Glasgow.

FLEECE

THE CROSS, BRETFORTON, WORCESTERSHIRE (01386 831173)

Signed from B4035 Evesham road

In the heart of the Vale of Evesham is one of England's most remarkable inns. While there premises are officially licensed, the Fleece is actually a medieval farmhouse that was converted to an inn in 1848 by Henry Byrd and remains almost completely unchanged since then. The farm and, later, the inn were in his family's hands for close on 500 years. Byrd's great-granddaughter, Lola Taplin, ran the Fleece for 30 years and when she died in 1977 at the age of 83 she left it to the National Trust on the clear understanding that its interior, exterior and gardens should be left intact. Lola was one of that breed of indomitable pub landladies who ran the place with a rod of iron, made it abundantly clear to her customers that they were privilged to enter her home, and if they blasphemed they would be flung out. The most famous artefact in the Fleece is an enormous oak dresser that holds a magnificent and priceless set of 48 pieces of Stuart pewter. According to a legend, the pewter was left at the farm by Oliver Cromwell in return for gold and silver plate taken to pay the parliamentary army during the Civil War. The interior and ornaments date back to the 19th century. The farm's dairy became a brewhouse that produced beer and cider for the inn and the vessels can still be seen in a room known as the Brewhouse, though beer has not been produced for more than 50 years. Off this room is the Dugout, once the farmhouse pantry, and it still contains the rare table in which dough was left to "prove" before being baked. Throughout the inn there are great oak beams, standing timbers, flagstones, grandfather clocks, high-back settles, a rocking chair and utensils in an inglenook that were once used for spit-roasting. In the main room and the Brewhouse you can see "witch marks", charms and circles drawn to ward off evil spirits. Outside there's a wonderful garden and orchard with a thatched barn, an adventure playground and animals in an enclosure. The regular beer is M&B Brew XI, one of the least interesting real ales it's possible to find, but the link is important for this Bass subsidiary in Birmingham has supplied the Fleece for generations. Fortunately there is a splendid range of guest beers, including Hook Norton Best, Uley Old Spot and Wyre Piddle, plus country wines and cider. Bar food, lunchtime and evening, is not extensive but may include such simple fare as ploughman's; chilli; broccoli and cheese quiche; mixed grill; chicken and leek pie; and such desserts as apple pie or lemon meringue. If you need to ask the way, Bretforton is pronounced "Breffurton". The Fleece was run for the National Trust for a period by the Campaign for Real Ale and it remains on the Campaign's national inventory of pubs of historic interest.

Pub walk in Suffolk

Southwold and Walberswick sit either side of the mouth of the River Blyth. Town and village were important ports in the Middle Ages but they declined as the river silted up. Regency Southwold, with its flint-faced church, in-shore lighthouse, Adnams brewery, a clutch of good restaurants and famous, brightly painted beach huts, is one of the most popular seaside resorts in East Anglia. George Orwell, when he was still Eric Blair, lived there for a while. Walberswick, a haunt of Fabian socialists in the 1930s, and home to actors, retired politicians, artists and potters, has a quiet and unspoilt charm. Both are off the A12 – Southwold via the A1095, Walberswick by the B1387. To start the walk, you can have a snifter in any of Adnams' dozen or so pubs in Southwold. Good hostelries include the **LORD NELSON** in East Street, with a warm welcome and high-back settles, and, close to the beach, the **RED LION** on East Green (long, comfortable main bar with a separate dining room, and benches and seats on the pavement) and the **SOLE BAY INN** between the brewery and the lighthouse (a charming, old-fashioned local). The jewel is Adnams' **CROWN** (01502 722275) in the High Street, a fine hotel with a spacious front bar with beams, settles, scrubbed tables and an impressive fireplace; the restaurant is through an arch on the right-hand side. The back bar has a good pubby feel, with oak panelling and benches. The bar menu changes daily, but always includes fresh, locally caught fish. There's a choice of around 300 wines: Adnams is a leading wine merchant as well as brewer.

From the Crown, walk up the High Street away from the town centre. As the road divides, take the smaller fork to the left and follow this road until you come to a large green with football and rugby pitches. Across the green to the right you'll see a tall water tower. Head for the tower and you will find yourself on the narrow road that leads down to the river; it cuts across a golf course, so watch out for balls whistling past your head. Once clear of the tower and the golf course, the road runs ruler-straight down to the river, with marshes on either side criss-crossed by streams where wildfowl swim.

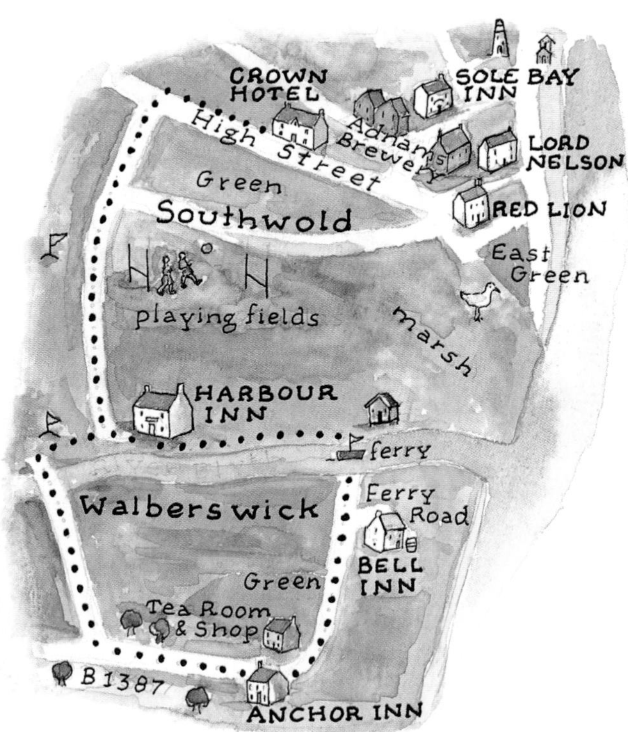

The harbour area, known as Blackshore Quay, is a gem, a small piece of forgotten, untouched rural England, where fishermen ply their trade. Their boats are tied up alongside huts and you can buy fresh fish here at remarkably low prices. The 300-year-old **HARBOUR INN** (01502 722381) serves this tiny community of cottages and bungalows set back from the water's edge. First and foremost, this beamed Adnams' pub is a working fishermen's local, with a ship-to-shore radio and wind-speed indicator in the main bar. The brewery's Mild, Bitter, Broadside and seasonal specials are available. The next-door shed, which used to store nets, has been converted into a restaurant. Chef/landlord Rob Dawson's menu focuses on fresh fish and lobsters caught locally or up the coast at Lowestoft: Mediterranean fish soup; smoked mackerel and horseradish pâté; whole plaice on the bone with chips. At lunchtime you can get large baps filled with char-grilled chicken; smoked bacon; Adnams pork sausages with ale; and farmhouse Cheddar with celery and apple. Friday night and Saturday lunchtimes are a feast for lovers of traditional fish and chips with a choice of cod, haddock, plaice, rock and skate. The restaurant is open for lunch from Wednesday to Saturday and for Sunday lunch, and offers fish cakes with cucumber dip; scallops with smoked bacon and black pudding as starters and such main courses as Harbour Inn fish pie; roast cod and scallops on saffron risotto; or brill with clams and Chardonnay. There's usually one meat dish, such as medallions of pork, and a couple of vegetarian dishes, such as vegetable tart or stir-fried vegetables in sweet and sour sauce. Desserts include home-made ice-creams and hot coconut pudding. There's also a British farmhouse cheeseboard. You can sit outside the inn in pleasant weather: there are tables and chairs overlooking the river at the front; at the back, an area of marshland has been turned into an attractive garden.

If you turn right outside the Harbour Inn and walk along a track by the river, you reach a metal bridge that takes you over the River Blyth. Once across, the straight track crosses marshland and then heath: to the left you will glimpse Walberswick. After a 15-minute walk, the track brings you to some houses and then joins the B1387. Turn left and follow the road, lined with trees and covered in a canopy of branches: you walk down a green tunnel into the village. There are fine houses on either side, including a half-timbered cottage decorated in traditional Suffolk pink. As you pass the ANCHOR INN on the right, the road bears sharp left and on the left there are a few shops, including a craft shop with a tearoom serving light lunches. Ahead, a large green has swings and other children's play equipment. A few

yards on, the road becomes a track leading down to the river. Don't head for the water. Turn right into Ferry Road where, on a slight rise, you will find the BELL INN (*see page 235*) with a fine view of Southwold across the river.

The brick-faced inn is 600 years old and has a flagstone floor bowed with age, oak beams, settles and a vast fireplace with a wood-burning stove. Like the Harbour Inn, the Bell was built for fishermen and they still occupy most of the seats by the bar: the inn is said to be haunted by a long-dead fisherman. The main bar has old photos and other memorabilia of the village. Adnams has added a conservatory dining area at the back of the building where food, lunchtime and evening, includes soup; sandwiches; ploughman's; fish and chips; and daily specials such as pasta with lentils and fresh herbs; fish cakes; steak and kidney pie; and Thai crab cakes with a chilli dip. There's the full range of Adnams' ales and a good choice of wine. The large back garden has a boules pitch. Accommodation is available.

To return to Southwold you can either retrace your steps or, if the ferryman is on duty, ask to be rowed from Walberswick jetty to the Southwold side of the river. Pick up the road at Blackshore Quay and follow it back into Southwold.

Pubs near places of historic interest

Waggon & Horses

Beckhampton, Wiltshire (01672 539418)

Junction of A4 and A361

The shingle walls of this ancient waggoners' inn are built from smashed stones from the nearby Avebury Ring, Europe's biggest Neolithic stone circle: the inn makes the perfect spot for visiting the ring and enjoying a meal and good ale. Avebury has some 200 stones, made up of broad stones called female and upright ones called male. The entire site consists of two small circles within a larger one and is surrounded by high earthworks and connected to a temple – the Sanctuary – by an avenue of standing stones. The Sanctuary has been demolished but its position is marked by posts. The site dates from around 2500 BC and is thought to have taken several centuries to complete. The 400-year-old thatched inn, with its mellow stone walls, mullioned windows and heavy oak doors, has a cobbled entrance over which great waggons were pulled centuries ago. To get up the Old Bath Road, the waggons had eight wheels and were drawn by teams of carthorses with more horses at the back to push and act as a brake, the forerunner of the 125 InterCity train. Later the Waggon & Horses became an important coach stop on the London to Bath route and was used by Charles Dickens as the inn in "The Bagman's Tale" in *Pickwick Papers*. The beamed bar has a great curved settle and Windsor chairs. In good weather you can sit outside on the front cobbles with tables set amid troughs of flowers. The pub is owned by Wadworth of Devizes, which delivers by horse-drawn drays. The beers include IPA, 6X, Farmers Glory, Old Timer in winter and Summersault when the sun shines. Food is available lunchtime and evening and includes soup, sandwiches, Cajun shrimps, beef and Stilton pie, pasta and fish dishes, and such home-made desserts as fruit pie. As well as the Avebury Ring, the inn is handy for Silbury Hill prehistoric mound near Marlborough and the West Kennet long barrow. This is an area bursting with history, with Stonehenge just a short drive away.

Royal Oak

23 Long Street, Cerne Abbas, Dorset (01300 341797)
A352

This thatched and creeper-clad 16th-century hostelry was once a coaching inn with a blacksmith's on the site. It stands in a lovely village, with houses built of Purbeck stone, and overlooked by the amazing figure of the Cerne Giant. The giant is a chalk outline cut from the turf. Opinions vary on his origins. Some say he is a god – possibly Hercules – from the Roman period, others argue that he dates from much earlier times and is connected with fertility rights. As well as a club in one hand, the 60-metre high figure is mightily well endowed. The local legend says the giant came to destroy the settlement that is now Cerne Abbas, stopped for a nap, and was killed by a shepherd boy. The grateful villagers carved an outline in the turf round the giant's body. Even today young couples anxious to have children stand on the giant's outline by his powerful organ. With this rude pagan image on the hillside, it seems curious that Benedictines built an abbey in its shadow. The giant outlived the abbey, which was dissolved by the Tudors. The Royal Oak was built at this time and used some of the stones from the abbey. There are seats at the front as well as in a small beer garden while inside the flagstoned rooms have oak beams, panelled walls, log fires and an inglenook with an oven. The walls and ceilings are decked out with horse brasses, agricultural tools, old china and ancient photos of the village. There is a good range of ever-changing hand-pumped beers: you may find Bass, Old Speckled Hen, Flowers Original and such local brews as Palmer's of Bridport and Otter from Devon. Excellent home-made food includes rough Dorset pâté, ploughman's, country pie, game, whitebait, steak and Stilton, and moussaka. There's a good range of wines and malt whiskies.

All Nations

20 Coalport Road, Madeley, near Telford, Shropshire
(01952 585747)
A442

The All Nations is a place of historic interest in its own right, and old brewpub that existed long before the present "nouvelle vogue" of brewpubs arrived on these shores. It has brewed its own beer for around 200 years and has been run by the Lewis family since 1934. It's still known locally as

"Mrs Lewis's", after the formidable landlady who was the mother of current licensee Keith Lewis. The pub is set in that curious part of Shropshire that is a blend of delightful countryside and the remains of the Industrial Revolution. All Nations is just off the Ironbridge to Coalport road, names synonymous with the growth of heavy industry in the 19th century. Ironbridge and its gorge played a pivotal role in the development of Britain as an industrial power and can be visited before or after a swift beer in this pub. It was built for workers on the adjacent railway line that took coal from Coalport to nearby depots. The All Nations is a listed building and Keith Lewis makes few concessions to the modern world, though he has added lunchtime sandwiches in recent years. The one homely bar has lino on the floor and formica on the tables where locals play darts and cribbage. Behind the pub, amid a huddle of outbuildings and a hencoop, the tiny brewery produces just one beer called Pale Ale. With a modest strength of just 3 per cent alcohol, it's more a light mild than a bitter, and was fashioned to slake the thirsts of workers who were looking for refreshment after long hours of hard, sweaty work.

MILECASTLE INN

HALTWHISTLE, MILITARY ROAD, NORTHUMBERLAND
(01434 321372/320682)
B6318, off A69

This slate-roofed, 17th-century inn stands on wild moorside alongside Hadrian's Wall. The wall was built by the edict of Emperor Hadrian between 120 and 123 AD as a defence against the North British tribes who constantly raided over the border into England. The wall links the Solway Firth in the west with the mouth of the River Tyne in the east and marks the northernmost frontier of Ancient Rome. Most of the wall remains, 117 kilometres across the narrowest point of England. More than four metres high and one metre wide, the wall is built of stone with earth and clay acting as "cement". Mile castles, which explains the name of the inn, were placed at every Roman mile (1,480 metres) to allow soldiers to watch for marauders from the north. A World Heritage Site plaque on the wall is close to the inn. Despite its remote location, the Milecastle is often busy with walkers (no rucksacks allowed inside) and agricultural workers who sup the local brews Castle Eden Banner and Northumberland Castles, plus Tetley Bitter in the beamed bar decorated with horse brasses and prints of local beauty spots. There is a good wine list and a choice of malt whiskies. Bar food and restaurant meals, lunchtime and evening, are famous for their generous portions and come in the shape of local game and sausages, beef or vegetable curry, steak and kidney pie, duck, soups, ploughman's, and home-made desserts.

Abbey Hotel

Llanthony, Gwent (01873 890487)

Signposted from A465 Abergavenny to Hereford Road

The Abbey was once the prior's house in the now ruined complex that was a 12th-century Augustinian priory. Against a backdrop of the Black Mountains, this is one of the most peaceful and inspiring places in the British Isles. According to legend, St David, the patron saint of Wales, built a wattle and daub cell on the site of the parish church that bears his name. The cell fell into ruins and in 1108 the priory was established on the spot and took around 100 years to complete. Looters and brigands repeatedly attacked the priory and it had lost most of its religious importance even before Henry VIII dissolved the monasteries. In the 18th century it became a shooting lodge before becoming a hotel. The bar is reached down steps into a vaulted crypt, originally the undercroft of the prior's quarters. There is a stone-flagged floor with wooden settles while the superb dining room has a curved high-back oak settle. There is accommodation available, the rooms reached by a stone spiral staircase. In good weather you can drink in the view of the ruins and the mountains from benches at the front. Bass is the regular beer and there is always at least one other ale from the likes of Brakspear, Shepherd Neame or Ushers. There's often a local farm cider, too. Lunchtime food is confined to generous bar snacks such as home-made burgers and nut burgers, bean goulash and sandwiches. In the evening there are daily specials – you may find lamb in garlic and wine; chicken and mushrooms; beef in red wine; nut roast and bean goulash. The hotel is open every day from the end of March but only at weekends in winter.

Traquair Arms Hotel

Traquair Road, Borders (01896 830229)

B709, off A72, six miles from Peebles

Bear Ale in the bar of this stone-built hotel is brewed round the corner at Traquair House, Scotland's oldest inhabited stately home. "Quair" is a

Scottish term for a winding burn or stream: the stream here runs into the River Tweed, which marks the border between Scotland and England. Parts of the imposing, white-faced and turreted house date from the 12th century. It was rebuilt in the 17th century and a copper was added to the ancient brewhouse in 1738. In common with most aristocratic houses, the brewhouse was an important part of the construction, providing healthy ale for the family, their retainers and guests. Mary Queen of Scots stayed at Traquair and her room, with its basic toilet facilities (a hole in the wall leading down to the grounds) is one of the many rooms open to the public (Easter–September: 01896 830323). Bonnie Prince Charlie, who no doubt enjoyed a tankard or two, also visited Traquair to raise support for the Jacobite cause. The house is owned by the Maxwell Stuart family, devout members of the Stuart clan. They keep the main Bear Gates locked, more in hope than expectation, until a Stuart returns to the throne. In 1965 the laird of Traquair, Peter Maxwell Stuart, found the disused brewhouse behind piles of jumble. He cleaned out the buildings and started to brew again, turning the bottled Traquair House Ale into an international cult beer. Since his death in 1990, the estate, including the brewery, has been run by his daughter, Lady Catherine. As well as the house beer and the draught Bear Ale, she produces a Jacobite Ale and occasional brews such as the Wedding Ale that celebrated her own nuptials. The bottled beers as well as Bear Ale are available in the hotel, along with another Scottish Borders brew, Broughton's Greenmantle. Owner Hugh Anderson is a renowned chef: bar food and restaurant offer such delights as Teviot salmon with tarragon mayonnaise, local lamb and venison, chicken stuffed with haggis, mussels with potato and spiced sausage, and a good choice of vegetarian dishes including oat and bulgar loaf, spinach and filo parcels, and stir-fried noodles with soy, honey and spices. There is a good wine list with several half bottles. Cider is often available, too.

Lord Crewe Arms

Blanchland, Northumberland (01434 675251)
B6306; off B6278 and A68

Blanchland Moor and the village of Blanchland take their names from the "white monks" who occupied the local abbey, which now stands in ruins. The abbey was established in 1165 and flourished until the dissolution of the monasteries ordered by Henry VIII. Earlier, in 1296, the abbey was sacked by Scots in an incident celebrated in a ballad called "The Blanchland Bells". The Scots, as was their habit at the time, were raiding and marauding over the border but they failed to see the abbey as they passed by one moonlit night as a result of the extremely pale stone from which it is built. In the morning the monks rather unwisely rang the abbey bells to give thanks to God for their deliverance. Unfortunately, the Scots were still within earshot and returned to destroy the abbey and its bells. The abbey was rebuilt and survived until Fat Hal. In the 18th century the village was restored and laid out as a model village. On his death, Lord Crewe, the Bishop of Durham, left the village to a trust to ensure it remained untouched and so it has been ever since. The pub, named in his honour, was originally the 13th-century abbot's guest house while its walled garden was part of the cloisters. The main entrance to the Lord Crewe leads into what was once the kitchen, with a massive stone fireplace once used to roast oxen. The Derwent Room has beams and old settles while the barrel-vaulted Crypt Bar is stone-flagged and has benches set in walls that are eight feet thick in places. The centrepiece of the Hilyard Room is a 13th-century stone fireplace that acted as the hiding place for the Jacobite general Tom Forster in 1715, a member of the family that owned the buildings before they passed to Lord Crewe. Forster surrendered somewhat ignobly to the government forces without a fight, but he escaped from London's Newgate Prison before he could stand trial for treason, thanks to the fighting spirit of his sister, Dorothy. She rode to London disguised as a servant and managed to obtain duplicate keys to the prison. Tom Forster made good his escape and fled to France. The ghost of Dorothy is said to haunt the Bamburgh Room of the inn, pacing the floor while she waits to hear news of her brother. In the inn today bar food and restaurant meals are served lunchtime and evening and may include sandwiches; soup; filled rolls; ploughman's; Brie and broccoli bake; wild boar and pheasant pie salad; pork and apple burgers; grilled fillet of cod; grilled lamb cutlets; and sautéed breast of chicken with tarragon sauce. There are special children's dishes and tempting desserts. The inn used to sell beers from the Vaux Group's breweries but in 1999, following in Henry VIII's large footsteps, the group dissolved the breweries, so you can no longer enjoy the likes of Vaux Samson and Ward's Best Bitter. The beers are now supplied by national brewers. Accommodation is available and there is magnificent scenery and walking country all around. This pub should not be confused with the Lord Crewe Arms in Bamburgh (*see page 178*).

Pubs associated with famous people

Constable Country

MARLBOROUGH HEAD

DEDHAM, ESSEX (01206 323250)
Off A12

This timbered medieval inn is opposite John Constable's old school: the artist lived just over the River Stour in East Bergholt, which is in Suffolk, as is Flatford Mill, one of his most famous paintings, though the present mill is Victorian. The inn started life as a wool hall and provided a home for wool merchants from the 15th to the 17th centuries. It became an ale house in 1704 and was named in honour of the Duke of Marlborough, who had defeated the French at the battle of Blenheim. It has some magnificent stripped beams, vine and grape carvings on a mantelbeam above a fireplace in the lounge, and partitioned alcoves in the Constable Bar at the back. The Marlborough is owned by the Old English Pub Company, a group that has a good track record for maintaining the style and tradition of many fine old inns (it also owns the Tudor Sun in the village). Food is served lunchtime and evening and dishes may include soup; sandwiches; chicken with lobster sauce; mushroom pasta bake; lasagne; roast duck; deep-fried Brie; and herring fillets. The hand-pumped ales are East Anglian and come from Adnams and Greene King. Accommodation is available and children are welcome in a family room. As well as visiting East Bergholt and Flatford Mill, don't miss Dedham church, one of the finest flint-faced churches in the area, rebuilt by wealthy cloth merchants when Dedham was part of the wool trade. Constable summed up the charm of the area as follows: "I love every stile and stump and lane in the village; as long as I am able to hold a brush I shall never cease to paint them." Castle House has a collection of the paintings of another artist, Sir Alfred Munnings.

Chartwell and Winston Churchill

Fox & Hounds

Toys Hill, Kent (01732 750328)
Off A25

It is fitting that a pub near Churchill's home should have a "We'll fight 'em on the beaches" air about it. Back in 1986 the brewery that owned the pub wanted to do what is known in the trade as "a tart up". This was fought bravely by the Pelling family, who have been licensees for more than 30 years. The present incumbent, Hazel Pelling, will be glad to tell visitors the story, and there are press clippings and letters of support decorating the walls. The Fox & Hounds is splendidly old fashioned and unspoilt, and looks like a pub from the 1960s, with two rooms which the brewery (not the current owner) wanted to knock through. There are old sofas and armchairs, magazines such as *Country Life* to read, occasional sing-songs, and darts, dominoes, cribbage and shove-ha'penny are played. Greene King supplies IPA and Abbot Ale while lunchtime snacks run to filled rolls, ploughman's, cauliflower cheese, and sausage and tomato pie. There's a delightful garden at the back and magnificent views of Kent from the village. Switch off mobile phones in the pub or Mrs Pelling will show you the door. It's good walking country and Chartwell (owned by the National Trust) has a collection of Churchill's paintings in his studio.

William Henry Fox Talbot

George

4 West Street, Lacock, Wiltshire (01249 730263)
Off A350 near Chippenham

Lacock, with its abbey and mellow stone buildings, draws not only tourists but film and TV crews like magnets: it's a popular place for shooting such period dramas as *Emma*, *Moll Flanders*, and *Pride and Prejudice*. It also houses the Fox Talbot Museum of photography, run by the National Trust. Fox Talbot (1800-77) was a physicist and a pioneer of photography, and the museum has a fascinating collection of early photographic equipment and photos. The George is one of three inns in the village and is almost certainly the oldest. It dates from 1361 and has been licensed since the time of Oliver Cromwell's republic in the 17th century. It proudly displays its age, with a heavily beamed low ceiling, upright timbers and antique furniture. The centrepiece of the inn is the enormous fireplace with a roasting spit and a dog wheel. This unpleasant Tudor contraption, which gave rise to the expression "it's a dog's life", was a canine version of a treadmill and was just big enough to house a dog that had to run inside, turning a spit that roasted meat by the fire. A special breed of dog, called a turnspit, was developed to carry out this dreadful task: the hapless animals were described as "long-bodied, crooked-legged and ugly dogs, with a suspicious, unhappy look about them." Ungrateful creatures: why didn't they look cheerful? The practice stopped in Victorian times, not because of public pity for the dogs but as a result of the invention of a mechanical roasting spit. Three dogs that survived the cages were taken to Windsor Castle as pets for Queen Victoria. The inn today belongs to Wadworth of Devizes and sells the brewery's IPA, 6X, Farmer's Glory and seasonal ales, plus a good selection of wines. Bar food is served lunchtime and evening and there's a separate restaurant. Dishes may include home-made soup; sandwiches and baguettes with a choice of fillings; ploughman's; spinach, mushroom, nut and blue cheese crumble; red snapper fillet with creamy lemon sauce; nut roast Italienne; chicken and apricot pie; goat's cheese salad; and Scotch salmon fillet with hollandaise sauce. Desserts include raspberry and hazelnut crumble and bread and butter pudding. There's a large garden with a children's play area. The host, John Glass, offers first-class accommodation in his farmhouse, with free lifts between inn and farm.

Grace Darling

Lord Crewe Arms

Bamburgh, Northumberland (01668 214243)
B1340, off A1

Bamburgh and the Farne Islands are linked to the heroic activities of Grace Darling who in 1838 rescued some shipwrecked sailors with the help of her lighthouse-keeper father. There is a Grace Darling Museum in Bamburgh run by the National Trust. The pub, like everything else in Bamburgh, stands in the shadow of the great Norman castle that overlooks the sea and the great sweep of the sandy beach. (The castle is still lived in and has a fascinating collection of armour.) The back bar of the pub has a bar top covered by a collection of pre-decimal copper coins and the beams are covered with fishing implements. There's a second, more modern bar to the side. Food includes lunchtime snacks and full evening meals in a restaurant: dishes may include ploughman's; soup and sandwiches; or local fish and locally smoked kippers; steak in ale pie; vegetarian pasta bake; lamb casserole; and poached salmon. The beers come from the Bass stable and include Draught Bass and Stones. Accommodation is available and children are welcome in eating areas of the pub. From nearby Seahouses there are frequent boat trips to the Farne Islands with their collection of sea birds.

Rudyard Kipling

Bell

BURWASH, EAST SUSSEX (01435 882304)
A265 near Heathfield

The Bell is a quintessential English village local opposite the church and a blaze of colour in season with hanging baskets and tubs full of flowers. Rudyard Kipling's last home, Bateman's, is close by, a name with a pleasing bibulous ring, for Batemans is a renowned family-owned brewery in Lincolnshire. Kipling (1865-1936), who was born in India, has recovered in recent years from a reputation of being either a cheap jingoist or a writer of whimsical stories for children. After all, he was awarded the Nobel Prize for Literature in 1907. Bateman's, run by the National Trust, is open to the public. With a nice feel for the name of the house, the Bell's hosts, Colin and Gillian Barrett, include Bateman's XB among their beers, along with the local Arundel Footslogger, Greene King IPA, and Harvey's Best; they also offer a good choice of wines and malt whiskies. The cheery main bar has high-backed stools and pews, and a vast range of bells, barometers and metal work decorating the dark ceiling and walls. There's a welcoming log fire for cold days. It's a real locals' pub with a tremendous range of traditional games, including bar billiards, shove-ha'penny and dominoes. Bar food (lunchtime and evenings; not Sunday evening) and a no-smoking restaurant offer sandwiches; ploughman's; spinach and ricotta cannelloni; smoked salmon and smoked mackerel platter; sweet and sour chicken; cod and chips; duck with plum sauce; and good old egg and chips. Children are welcome and accommodation is available.

Turner Collection

BADGERS

COULTERSHAW BRIDGE, PETWORTH, WEST SUSSEX (01798 342651)
Off A285

A delightful and elegant country pub, Badgers has a deserved reputation for its food but it's also the kind of place where locals can just pop in for a pint. The beers, naturally, include Badger Best Bitter from Hall & Woodhouse of Blandford along with the superb Hop Back Summer Lightning pale ale from Salisbury and the more travelled Theakston's Best. The main room, with large shuttered windows, is served by an island bar and has several charming and intimate areas with an eclectic choice of furniture. Bar food may include tapas; fish stew; grilled salmon with sun-dried tomato sauce and roast vegetables; pheasant with rosti; or pasta with scallops and basil. A pleasant terrace has additional seating and don't miss the old monk's chair just inside the entrance to the pub. There is a separate restaurant and children over five are welcome by arrangement in designated areas. Petworth House (NT) has J.M.W. Turner's paintings of the area as well as Old Masters by Bosch, Claude and Teniers, and portraits by Van Dyck.

Robert Baden-Powell

BREWHOUSE

68 HIGH STREET, POOLE, DORSET (01202 685288)

The Brewhouse, as the name suggests, is a brewpub, a busy, lively local in the town centre that serves Best Bitter and Bosun Bitter and seasonal and occasional beers from the attached brewery. It was set up in 1980 by David Rawlins who added the pub three years later. The brewery now has a capacity to brew 1,000 barrels a year and serves 15 other outlets direct and many more through wholesalers. The pub is handy for Brownsea Island in Poole Harbour where Robert Baden-Powell developed the ideas for his Boy Scout movement and trained young recruits. There are regular boats to the large island: you need to go down to the harbour area by the car ferry to Studland: the boats are on the right. The island is fine for walking, with many pine trees, peacocks, peahens and England's last known breed of red squirrels. The bigger grey variety hasn't worked out a way to get across the harbour and wipe them out. According to a story on the island, one lone grey squirrel did once swim to the island, but it was caught and "despatched" before it could harm its red cousins. A palatial house on the island, administered by the National Trust, stages regular concerts and operas in summer.

The Rothschilds

FIVE ARROWS

HIGH STREET, WADDESDON, BUCKINGHAMSHIRE (01296 651727)
A41 between Aylesbury and Bicester

This Grade II listed building, with imposing chimneys, a half-timbered façade with wrought ironwork, was built by Baron Ferdinand de Rothschild in 1887 as part of the family Waddesdon estate. In the style of the time, the inn was constructed for the workers employed to build the manor house: rarely can artisans have been given such oppulent B&B. The five arrows, carved into the bar counter, are the family crest and refer to the five sons of Meyer Amschel Rothschild, founder of the dynasty, who dispersed his sons across Europe to set up great banking houses. Wine, beer and food are of the highest order, as you would expect, but the inn is not at all snooty and prices are surprisingly reasonable. The bar has a good pub feel to it, dominated by the carved counter, with portraits of both the family and estate workers on the walls, and cushioned settles as seating. There are delightful gardens and a terrace outside, ideal for summer eating and drinking, and of course you can go from the inn to visit Waddesdon Manor, with a collection of Sevres porcelain, and its grounds, which include an aviary. Bar food is available lunchtime only (there's a separate no-smoking restaurant) and dishes may include soup; sandwiches, ploughman's; deep-fried artichoke hearts on a bed of rocket; field mushrooms with sun-dried tomatoes and Dolcellate; aubergine stuffed with feta and sun-dried tomato; Cajun blackened salmon with smoked potato wedges; char-grilled breast of chicken with a tomato and herb mayonnaise butter; and lamb cutlets with a red wine jus in season. Home-made desserts feature strongly on the menu and may include hazelnut meringue with hot chocolate sauce, treacle tart, or apricot and orange trifle. The beers include Adnams Best and Fuller's London Pride. The wine list is extensive but not over-priced, but a 1984 Chateau Mouton Rothschild will set you back £80. There are several first-growth Rothschild clarets. Accommodation is available.

Note: *For information about opening times and admission prices for National Trust properties, phone 020 8315 1111, 9am-5.30pm Monday to Friday.*

Pubs with royal connections

King's Head

Gorams Mill Lane, Laxfield, Suffolk (01986 798395)

Off B1117

This is a rural classic and ardent republicans can happily sup here as it's universally known as the Low House on the grounds that it's in a dip below the churchyard and Laxfield's other pub. The free-standing inn sign is slightly schizophrenic, with Henry VIII adorning one side and Charles I the other. The thatched Tudor pub has a simple parlour at the front dominated by a large three-sided, high-backed settle that faces an open fire. Other small rooms have scrubbed tables, pews and old prints on the walls while a passageway has some built-in wall seats. There's no bar: beer is poured straight into glasses from casks tapped in a room at the back. And splendid Suffolk ale it is, too, with Adnams Best Bitter, Broadside and Extra from Southwold and such guests as Greene King IPA. James White's local cider is also available in summer. Bar food may include ploughman's; bangers and mash; bamboo shoots; chicken fillets; Norfolk dumplings filled with pork and thyme; parsnip and apple soup; lamb casserole; grilled plaice; and tagliatelle with roast peppers and pesto sauce. Desserts include sticky toffee pudding or rice pudding. There are seats outside the pub and a small garden at the back. Laxfield, a medieval wool town, has a half-timbered guildhall while the church has a memorial to William "Smasher" Downing, a Puritan destroyer of church ornaments.

Prince of Wales

11 Cross Road, Oatlands, Surrey (01932 852082)

Off A3050 via Anderson Road; near Weybridge

As brewers and publicans are ever anxious to tug a forelock in the direction of the monarchy, it's surprising that, among a plethora of Kings and Queens Heads and an astonishing number of William IVs (surely some mistake) there are relatively few Prince of Waleses. Given the farming inclinations of the present incumbent, this Prince of Wales pub has a grainy, organic ring to its location. The small, bustling local with welcoming log fires has a splendid array of ales, including Adnams Best, Draught Bass,

Boddingtons, Fuller's London Pride and Tetley Bitter, while landlady Pat Ford cooks up some splendid tucker lunchtime and evening. Pat is renowned for her steamed steak and kidney or sausage and bacon puddings; chicken with ham and broccoli pie; tuna and sweetcorn bake; bubble and squeak; freshly made omelettes; and cod or plaice in batter. In the evening, you may find sweetcorn and bacon soup or French onion soup; garlic mushrooms; mussels; king prawns and avocado with warm bacon; and such main courses as salmon or trout with almonds; Italian chicken breast in Parma ham; or caramelized pork tenderloin. Desserts include steamed treacle or fruit pudding, or raspberry pie. Sunday lunch draws the crowds with a choice of four roasts with Yorkshire puddings; curried meat balls; or corned beef fritters. The restaurant is open in the evening from Tuesday to Saturday.

Duke of York

Iddesleigh, Devon (01837 810253)
B3217

This remote village pub on a hill is as old as they come, dating from the 12th century; it was Camra's North Devon Pub of the Year for 1999. The white-painted and thatched exterior leads into a comfortable bar with rocking chairs and scrubbed oak tables in front of a log fire. A good choice of ales tapped straight from casks includes Cotleigh Tawny, Sharp's Doom Bar and Smiles Golden from the West Country along with Adnams Broadside, Thatcher's Farmers Tipple cider, Stowford Press cider and English country wines including Down St Mary. The food menu is written on cards pinned to the wall and may include the likes of home-made celery and watercress soup; vegetable korma; port and Stilton pâté; salmon fish cakes; steak and kidney pudding; and turkey and mushroom pie; there's a three-course menu in a separate restaurant where you can sample a diet-busting selection of ten desserts, such as brown sugar meringues with raspberries and whipped cream; Caribbean rum bananas; and walnut and butterscotch sponge pudding. It's good walking country (and needs to be to walk off the pub's puddings) and the pub offers accommodation.

Queen's Head

Main Street, Hawkshead, Cumbria (015394 36271)

B5285

This is a strikingly handsome black and white building with a beamed and panelled bar decorated with Toby jugs, brass and china, and warmed by a log fire. There's a separate restaurant as well. Vegetarians are well catered for with the likes of goat's cheese crostini or sweet potato casserole, while carnivores can tuck into roast quail with grapes; mushrooms and bacon; or Moroccan chicken. Desserts include chocolate and banana pudding and sticky toffee pudding. There are simple dishes at lunchtime, such as filled baguettes and jacket potatoes with a choice of fillings. Hartleys XB comes straight from the cask while Robinson's Frederics is via the handpump. Accommodation is available and Hawkshead is the ideal base for visiting Lakeland and the Beatrix Potter Museum. As well as the Queen's Head, the village also boasts a King's Arms with the local award-winning Coniston Bluebird ale.

Queen's Head

Market Square, Stow-on-the-Wold, Gloucestershire (01451 830563)

Junction A429, A436 and A424, near Chipping Norton

The inn is worth a visit if for no other reason than supping the local Donnington ales, XX, BB and SBA. Owned by Claude Arkell, the brewery is in an idyllic setting down a lane near Stow, with a 13th-century watermill and a large lake with weeping willows and swans. The inn has heavy beams, flagstones, high-back settles, some exposed stonework and log fires. Bar food, lunchtime and evening, has a daily specials board and such dishes as soup, sandwiches, jacket potatoes, omelettes, lasagne, steak and kidney pie, cottage pie, macaroni cheese, pork and chive sausage, and chicken and leek pie, with chocolate pudding and fruit crumble as desserts. There's a small courtyard garden at the back.

Pubs near acclaimed gardens

Crown Inn

St Ewe, near Mevagissey, Cornwall (01726 843322)
Off B3273 at Tregiskey crossroads

This 16th-century whitewashed cottage inn is close to the Lost Gardens of Heligan. The Crown is in a village named after a local saint and the exterior, with its porch entrance topped by a lucky horseshoe, blazes with flowers in tubs and hanging baskets in summer. The inn has been run by the Jeffery family for close on 40 years and is cared for with a great feel for its history. The centrepiece of the flagstone-floored bar is a 400-year-old curved high-back settle while the fireplace has an equally ancient roasting spit. There are low beams and a fascinating collection of fine pewter. The pub is owned by the local brewery, St Austell, and sells its Tinners and HSD ales plus seasonal beers. HSD stands for Hicks Special Draught and is named after the brewery's founder, but it's known throughout Cornwall as "High Speed Diesel". There are good wines and several malt whiskies, too. Locally caught fresh crab is a major feature of bar snacks and restaurant meals and comes in the shape of sandwiches, salads and filled jacket potatoes. Other dishes range from soups and pasties, to lemon sole and gammon. There are daily specials. Watch out for such tempting desserts as mincemeat and brandy pie.

Note: *The Lost Gardens of Heligan, 4 miles south of St Austell, off B3273 (01726 844157) are open all year, daily, 10am to 6pm.*

Anchor

Lock Lane, Pyrford Lock, Surrey (01932 342507)
Off A3

This large and spacious 1930s pub is in an idyllic location alongside a busy lock on the River Wey Navigation. It is also close to the Royal Horticultural Society's gardens at Wisley: to reach pub and canal you have to turn off the A3 at the signs for Wisley, go past the gardens and follow the narrow road until it reaches a hump-backed bridge over the canal. The Anchor has a large waterside terrace with trestle tables and benches, ideal for eating, drinking and watching the narrowboats go by. Inside, the pub has natural pine in abundance with walls festooned with canal memorabilia while large picture windows give further views of the canal. A family room upstairs has more canal artefacts and is used as a family room. Food is served lunchtimes and ranges from steak and kidney pie to vegetarian dishes and children's portions. Beers are from the Scottish Courage range and include Courage Best, Directors, John Smith's and Theakston's. The pub can get extremely busy at weekends. There are excellent walks along the canal towpath where many boats are moored: one is named Simpkiss after a much-loved and long-closed Black Country brewery.

Note: *RHS Garden, Wisley, Woking. 240 acres. Open every day, 10am to sunset; members only on Sundays (01483 224234).*

Chelsea Ram

32 Burnaby Street, London SW10 (020 7351 4008)

Underground: Earls Court

The Ram takes its name from the Young's Brewery mascot and was bought by the Wandsworth family-owned company in the 1980s. It is a renovated, Victorian corner pub with a large L-shaped bar with arched windows and an extension with a glass roof, and is a good fuel stop for Chelsea Physic Garden. As well as Young's Bitter, special and seasonal brews, it serves some of the best pub grub in London and has earned a star in Susan Nowak's *Good Pub Food*. Food is served lunchtime and evening until 9.45pm and there's always a fresh fish dish of the day, such as salmon and cod duo with red wine and saffron sauces; mullet with potato and artichoke salad; or crab risotto cakes with poached claws. Other dishes may include Chelsea Ram salad of chicken, bacon, avocado and sour cream; sausage cakes with horseradish mash and roast banana shallots; saffron chicken with almonds and sultanas; and rump of lamb with herb crust and mushroom ragout. Desserts include pudding of the day or there is a daily cheese selection with walnut bread and green tomato chutney. There's a roast lunch on Sundays.

Note: *Chelsea Physic Garden, 66 Royal Hospital Road, SW3. Entrance in Swan Walk. Open Wednesdays 2pm to 5pm and Sundays 2pm to 6pm. There are additional opening times in May and June: information phone 020 7352 5646.*

Old Bull & Butcher

Oxford Road, Ryton-on-Dunsmore, Warwickshire
(01203 301400)
A423, off A45

Dating from 1835, this spacious roadside pub started life as a simple alehouse with brewing on the premises. It is a good base for visiting Ryton Organic Gardens. The white, cream and green exterior of the pub leads into a comfortable bar with carpets, benches and stools, with a large cartwheel decorating one wall. A pleasant conservatory has been added to the back of the pub. The hand-pumped ales include the classic West Midland dark mild from Ansells, plus Tetley Bitter and Ind Coope Burton Ale, arguably the finest premium real ale produced by a giant brewer and the only national brand ever to win Camra's prestigious Champion Beer of Britain accolade. Bar meals and restaurant meals are served at both lunchtime and evening and include a large range of steaks, mixed grills, chicken, omelettes, courgette and mushroom lasagne, and mushroom Stroganoff. There are children's portions while four-course senior citizen's meals are served Monday to Friday for £4.25.

Note: *Ryton Organic Gardens/Henry Doubleday Research Association. B4029. Open all year. Restaurant serves organic beer and wine (01203 303517).*

FEATHERS

MARKET SQUARE, HELMSLEY, NORTH YORKSHIRE (01439 770275)
A170

A handsome stone-built inn, handy for Helmsley Walled Garden, it has a magnificent and unspoilt locals' bar with ancient beams and dark panelled walls, a log fire in a stone inglenook, and cast-iron tables topped by slabs of wood. The centrepiece is a fascinating wall carving of a bird with a dragon-like face surrounded by a grape vine. The hotel area (accommodation is available) has a smart and comfortable lounge. Hand-pumped ales include John Smith's Bitter and Theakston's Old Peculier. Bar meals and restaurant meals include sandwiches and soup, ploughman's, steaks, locally caught fish such as Whitby haddock, steak pie, chicken stuffed with mozzarella, Stilton and walnut pâté, broccoli and Stilton quiche, and a good range of desserts. There are seats and tables in a back garden and the awesome ruins of Rievaulx Abbey are close by.

Note: *Helmsley Walled Garden, Cleveland Way, Helmsley. Off A170 by Helmsley Castle. Open daily March to October 10.30am to 5pm (01439 771427).*

Note: *The Three Chimneys near Biddenden, Kent, featured in the section on pubs with gardens, is also close to Sissinghurst Gardens.*

Best of the Rest

Westonbirt Arboretum

GUMSTOOL

PART OF CALCOT MANOR HOTEL, TETBURY, GLOS (01666 890391)
A4135, off A46

Pubs near bluebell woods or gardens

White Cross

Water Lane, Richmond, Surrey (020 8940 6844)
Train/Underground: Richmond

Handy for Kew Gardens (which has a magnificent display of bluebells around the cottage built by George III for Queen Charlotte), this is one of London's most popular Thames-side pubs. It has superb views of the river from the paved garden at the front, which is open – river levels and weather permitting – in the summer and even in winter. Tables on the terrace are sheltered by a large tree, classified by Kew Gardens as a rare Greek whitebeam. Boats leave from the pub to Hampton Court and Kingston. There are two main bars served by a wooden island servery, curved seats in big bay windows, old prints and photos on the walls, and three log fires: the White Cross has the air of a country hotel, which it once was. There's also a spacious first-floor room where children are welcome. In good weather there's an outside bar on the terrace. Lunchtime bar food includes sandwiches; sweet potato and cream cheese bake; home-made sausages; game pie; and other daily specials. The pub is owned by Young's of Wandsworth and offers the brewery's Bitter, Special and seasonal brews, with a good choice of wines as well. There is occasional live music.

Red Lion

High Street, East Haddon, Northamptonshire (01604 770223)
Ten miles north-west of Northampton, off A428 and A5199, formerly A50

An imposing stone-built and thatched inn with oak settles, oak and mahogany tables, and low beams, the Red Lion is a good base and watering hole for visitors to Coton Manor Gardens, which has a brilliant bluebell display in spring, as well as Althorp House (which, of course, you will pronounce "Althrop" to avoid incurring the wrath of Earl Spencer) and Guilsborough Grange Wildife Park. The Red Lion is no slouch when it comes to gardens: it has two, with flowerbeds, roses and fruit trees. Children can eat in the restaurant and designated bar areas. Food is served lunchtime and evening, and meals (with a good vegetarian choice) may include carrot and coriander soup; sandwiches; ploughman's; goat's cheese toasted sandwich; almond and sweet potato cakes with tomato and basil sauce topped with Parmesan; steak and mushroom pie in Guinness sauce; Loch Fyne kippers with scrambled eggs; chicken chasseur; lemon-crusted deep-fried Brie and halloumi with Cumberland sauce; Lincolnshire sausage; and cashew nut roast with tomato sauce, plus such old-fashioned desserts as Bakewell tart, syrup sponge and sherry trifle. There are both Old and New World wines on the list along with Charles Wells Eagle and Bombardier hand-pumped ales (it's a Wells' pub) and such guests as Adnams Broadside or Morland Old Speckled Hen. Coton Manor Gardens (01604 740219) is two miles away and has five acres of bluebells.

CROWN

GANGSDOWN HILL, NUFFIELD, OXFORDSHIRE (01491 641335)
Off A4130

The Crown is an atmospheric old brick-and-flint waggoners' inn, rebuilt in 1715, with low beams and two large inglenooks. It's at the heart of an attractive village on the edge of the Chilterns and is on the Ridgeway Path, making it an ideal base for walkers as well as bluebell lovers, who can visit the display in Oaken Copse. Home-made food, with bread from a local baker, may include deep-fried Brie with hot cranberry sauce; roast pork hobbler with apple gravy; catch of the day fresh fish; or vegetarian Kiev. Brakspear's fine ales from nearby Henley include Bitter and Special plus seasonal beers. There's a good wine list, too. Well-behaved dogs and children are welcome. From the pub follow the Ridgeway Path into Oaken Copse.

Rose and Crown, Sandridge, Hertfordshire

Bull

Dunster Mill Lane, Three Legged Cross, near Ticehurst, East Sussex (01580 200586)

Off B2099 at Ticehurst

A delightful old brick and tile pub covered with clematis and roses, the Bull dates from the 14th century when it started life as a Wealden hall. It's a handy base for Bewl Water and the gardens of Pashley Manor. The pub has several small, black-beamed rooms with flagstoned or brick floors, a blazing log fire on cold days and plenty of comfortable seats and heavy oak tables. It has pub games (including a round pool table) with two pétanque

pitches in the charming garden, which has a weekend bouncy castle. Food is served in the bar and restaurant (not Sunday or Monday evenings) and children are welcome. Food may include barbecued spare ribs; rogan josh with onion bhaji and nan bread; soup; ploughman's; filled baguettes; fresh whole plaice; estoufadde de boeuf; liver and bacon and steak and kidney pie; with such desserts as chocolate marquise and sticky toffee pudding. Good local ales come from Harveys of Lewes (Best and Sussex Pale Ale) and there are regular guest beers. Bewl Water (owned by Southern Water, 01892 890 661) has a 13-mile walk around the perimeter and there is a blaze of bluebells in the wood.

ROSE & CROWN

24 HIGH STREET, SANDRIDGE, HERTFORDSHIRE (01727 856462)
B651

A splendid old wayside inn near St Albans, with low ceilings, beams, rambling rooms at different levels, a large fireplace in the main bar, separate dining area, and a small beer garden, the Rose & Crown is thought to date back to the 15th century and is in a charming village with a fascinating Saxon church. It's a Whitbread pub but it's leased to the Old English Pub Company, and the beer range includes Fuller's London Pride, Courage Directors and a regular guest, such as John Smith's Bitter. Food is served lunchtime and evening, seven days a week, and includes such bar meals as filled jacket potatoes and baguettes, curry, home-made soups, pasta dishes and steaks, while the restaurant offers pork loin with whisky and cream sauce; half a roast duck in Grand Marnier; spinach and pepper tart; or asparagus and cream tortellini. Specials are chalked on a board and there are always several vegetarian dishes. From the pub, cross the road and walk up Sandridgebury Lane. When it forks left, take the path to the right and turn left after the Scouts Hut. You can walk in the woods here and enjoy the bluebells and the rabbits. There are splendid views over the barley fields to the village and its church.

Note: *Bluebells flower for only a short period, usually in early May (and should not be picked), but the pubs are worth visiting at any time.*

Pubs for Greenwich and the Dome

PLUME OF FEATHERS

19 PARK VISTA, GREENWICH SE10 (020 8858 0533)

This is a Tardis-like pub, its small, green-tiled exterior, with two benches for warm weather, belying the spacious character of the interior. As the address suggests, it's opposite Greenwich Park and just a few yards from the entrance to the National Maritime Museum. The pub dates from 1691 and, given its position, has a plethora of naval and maritime artefacts. It's also bang on the Meridian and you can work out pub opening times in the rest of the world as you sup your pints of Adnams Best, Old Speckled Hen, Webster's Yorkshire or a guest ale such as Boddingtons. The single room is dominated by its polished wooden bar topped by a glass-holding gantry: the bar doubles as a food servery at the back where the room opens up into an area set aside for serious diners, with tables and chairs. Beyond, through French windows with an Art Nouveau floral motif, there's a garden for summer eating and drinking. The front area of the pub offers comfortably plush red wall banquettes with a fire in a brick fireplace. Lunchtime food includes the likes of filled jacket potatoes, scampi, ploughman's, sausage and mash, and vegetable or meat curry, while in the evening the restaurant offers soup, pâté, Chinese chicken, roast beef and halibut steaks. The Plume also has early Beatles on tape, a reminder of what the group sounded like before it was prettified by George Martin.

TRAFALGAR TAVERN

PARK ROW, GREENWICH SE10 (020 8858 2437)

The Trafalgar is enormous, a vast eating and drinking emporium by the Thames, with large bowed windows and balconies giving stunning views of the river and the London skyline, with the Dome to the right. Built in the mid-1770s, it was known first as the George and then the Old George until it was rebuilt in the 1830s to accommodate day trippers to Greenwich who came by river or the new train service. Famous and infamous people who have frequented the Trafalgar include Dick Turpin, Dr Johnson, wife murderer Dr Crippen and Charles Dickens, who used the tavern in *Our Mutual Friend*. The Trafalgar was

named in honour of Admiral Lord Nelson, whose portrait hangs in several places, notably in a first-floor ballroom that can accommodate more than 200 people: don't miss the tiny Hawk and Howe bar on this floor, designed fetchingly like a sailing ship's deck. Downstairs, the entrance leads into a hotel-like reception with a snug bar to the right. The main bar, dominated on one side by its enormous windows and on the other by a long serving counter and gantry, has marble-topped tables, wooden chairs, moulded ceilings, mirrors, two pianos, and a stove in a large fireplace. Beyond the bar there's a large restaurant with photos of celebrities who have visited the Trafalgar plus more naval heroes. Food is served every lunchtime and evening except Sunday and Monday evenings. Starters include organic soup and fish soup, roasted vegetables and sun-dried tomato tartlet; grilled organic goat's cheese and whitebait (the Trafalgar is famous for its whitebait dinners, attended in the last century by cabinet ministers and Prime Minister William Gladstone, who journeyed by boat from Westminster). Main courses may include shepherd's pie; steak and mushroom pie; tuna niçoise; mixed leaf salad; sea bass; Scottish salmon;

lobster; red snapper; grilled lamb cutlets; baked chicken; a choice of steaks, various pasta dishes (with several suitable for vegetarians), and for dessert tarte tatin, chocolate truffle cake and lemon chiffon pie. The wine list embraces France, Spain, Australia and Chile while hand-pumped ales include Courage Best and Directors and a regular guest, such as Futtock from the Flagship micro-brewery in Chatham Dockyard, a nice naval touch.

The Trafalgar Tavern, Greenwich

Cutty Sark

Ballast Quay, off Lassell Street, SE10 (020 8858 3146)

Despite its name, the Cutty Sark is a fair haul from the great tea clipper marooned in the heart of Greenwich. You reach it along the waterfront and the Royal Naval College: it's a logical pub to visit after the Trafalgar. The pub was first built in 1695 and was known as the Union before the name was changed to commemorate the exploits of the ship. The pub is a listed building and has a striking black and white facade dominated by a first-floor bowed window that juts out over the pavement and gives dramatic views of the Thames and the Dome. Inside, the two storeys have heavy beams and old ships' lamps, flagstones, settles, bare brick walls and, on the ground floor, a vast fireplace surmounted by a large ship's timber acting as the mantelpiece, with a ship's wheel above it. Children are welcome in the upstairs area until 9pm. Real ales include Fuller's London Pride, Morland Old Speckled Hen and Young's Special, with a good choice of wines and whiskies. Bar food includes filled baguettes, roast vegetable lasagne, cod or plaice, Cajun chicken, and steak and ale pie.

Gipsy Moth

60 Greenwich Church Street, SE10 (020 8858 0786)

The Gypsy Moth is a just a few yards from the *Cutty Sark*, the boat that is. It's another pub that has changed its name – from the Wheatsheaf, built in 1795, and recast in 1975 – to mark the round-the-world voyage by Francis Chichester in his boat, the *Gipsy Moth*, which nestles in the dry dock next to the *Cutty Sark*. The pub is open-plan but is divided by pillars and arches into several smaller areas, opening out into a spacious dining room at the back, with a large and attractive garden beyond. As you enter, there's a long serving counter to the right, supported by heavy polished wooden timbers; to the left there's a pleasant raised area with wood-panelled walls. The exterior is imposing with three storeys, a black-painted fascia and gold-lettered name, hanging baskets, small leaded windows, and large carriage lamps hanging from the first floor. The beers include Adnams Best and Broadside plus Tetley Bitter, with a good choice of international wines.

Food includes deep-fried Jalapeno peppers filled with cream cheese, potato skins with bacon and melted cheese, sandwiches, fish and chips, steak and kidney pie, ploughman's, meat or vegetable lasagne, tagliatelle with goat's cheese and spinach cream sauce, and, for dessert, apple pie, treacle sponge, and apple and blackberry crumble. Special children's meals are cooked to order.

Admiral Hardy

7 College Approach, SE10 (020 8858 6452)

The Admiral Hardy is a tremendous, no-nonsense boozer, a few yards from the imposing bulk of the Naval College and next to Greenwich covered market. It has an inn sign bearing the portly figure of "Kiss Me" Hardy and inside there's a single spacious bar with a central drink and food servery. The fireplace at the rear has a ship's anchor between the grate and the log fire. There are comfortable red leather banquettes and wooden tables, half-panelled walls, pebbled and leaded windows and, in a snug to the left, some old settles and tables. Although not owned by Shepherd Neame, the Hardy serves the Kent brewery's Bitter, Spitfire and Bishop's Finger plus such guests as Bateman's XB and O'Hanlon's Union Bitter, all in splendid nick. A Scottish manager also offers a great range of single malts, chalked on a blackboard: Balvenie, Macallan, Aberlour, Glenkinchie, Auchentoshan, Knockandoo, Highland Park and Laphroaig. Lunchtime food includes filled jacket potatoes, haggis, tatties and neaps, lasagne, quiche and salad, ploughman's, tomato and carrot soup, and filled rolls. The back door of the pub takes you into the market.

Note: *You can get to Greenwich by rail from London Bridge to Maze Hill and Greenwich stations, by boat from Westminster or by a new extension to the DLR (Docklands Light Railway), stopping at Greenwich and Cutty Sark. The Jubilee Line (Underground) stops at North Greenwich on its way from Central London to Stratford.*

Pub walk in the Cotswolds

The Cotswold Way runs past the **OLD SPOT INN** in Dursley (May Lane/Hill Road: 01453 542870), making it the ideal starting point for the walk. The inn is run by Ric Sainty, a great Cotswold character and famed lover of good ale. His inn started life as a farmhouse in the 18th century, became a school – which explains the high ceilings – and ended up a Whitbread pub. "A *failed* Whitbread pub," Ric stresses. "It sold 55 barrels of beer a year. I do 500 barrels." The inn has several rooms (one no-smoking), two open fires, bare boards, and masses of pictures and memorabilia devoted to pigs. The inn is named after a breed called the Gloucester Old Spot, and it has a close relationship with Uley Brewery, which produces Old Spot, Hogshead and Pigor Mortis ales, plus a house beer called Old Ric, in the nearby village of Uley.

The Old Spot also takes beer from Marston's and guest ales from such small craft breweries as Hampshire and Otter. Ric is at pains to point out that he does not serve chips with meals. Instead, he offers Old Ric sausages and doorstep sandwiches with local cheese. The inn

Old Spot Inn, Dursley, Gloucestershire

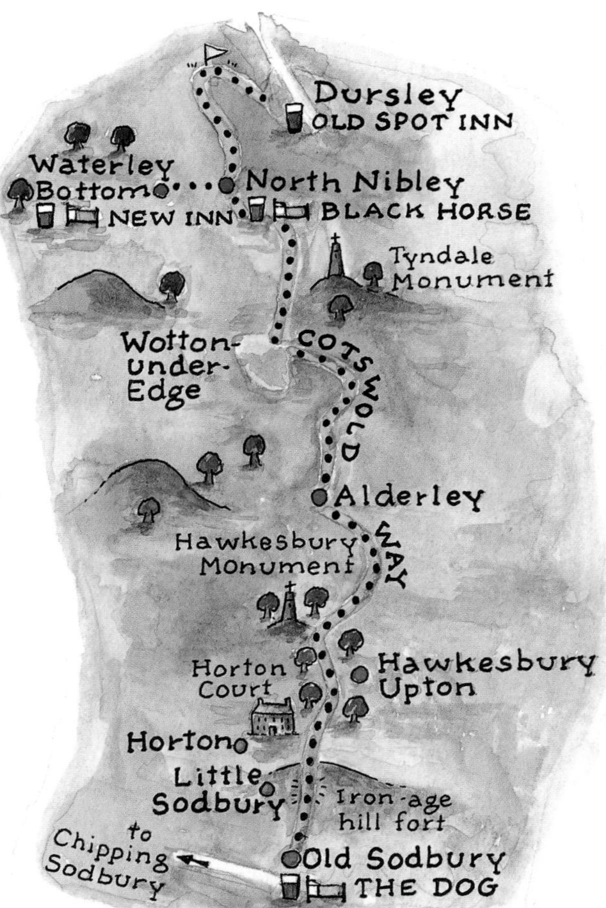

has a small garden, and there's a large car park across the road if you want to leave your car in Dursley while you enjoy the walk. The complete walk to Old Sodbury is 20 miles, and I've included several drop-out points for those who want a shorter itinerary or overnight accommodation to break up the journey.

From the Old Spot, the road climbs steeply to the golf course. The Cotswold Way skirts the edge of the course and then climbs to the top of Stinchcombe Hill before dropping down to North Nibley. There's a good choice of bed and breakfast accommodation in the village, including the **BLACK HORSE** (01453 546841). The pub has old beams, standing timbers, stone walls and log fires. The beers include Flowers Original and guest ales. The bar meals are home made and a restaurant is open Tuesday to Saturday.

You can finish this stage of the walk in North Nibley, but it's worth going a little further to one of the Cotswolds' most remote yet fascinating pubs, the **NEW INN** at Waterley Bottom (OS map reference ST758964; phone 01453 543659). Set in a lovely wooded valley, the New Inn was run for years by a great local character named Ruby Sainty (Ric's former wife). Ruby retired in 1999 and new hosts took over. Jackie and Jacky Cartigny arrived from France: he's French, she's British but lived in France for 20 years so there are some Gallic treats on the menu, such as chicken chasseur, coq au vin, duck confit, Brie crumble and filled baguettes. There are also soup, sandwiches and ploughman's and at least two vegetarian options, such as the Brie crumble already listed and spinach and mushroom crumble. There's no hot food on Mondays. Parts of the pub started life more than 200 years ago as a rustic cider house, and the old cider press is still on view. The lounge has some high-back settles and bare stone walls. Both bars have splendid antique beer engines, including one called the Barmaid's Delight: if you wonder why, observe the shape of the pump handle. Another ancient engine was rescued from the New Cut street market in London, where it was being used to dispense paraffin. The ales include Berkeley Dicky Pearce from a local craft brewery, Cotleigh Tawny, Greene King Abbot and Smiles Best. There's a house beer, WB, brewed by Cotleigh. Inch's cider is also available. Berkeley Castle is four miles away.

If you press on to Old Sodbury, the road climbs out of North Nibley to the Tyndale Monument, built in 1866 to commemorate William Tyndale. He was born in North Nibley and wrote the first translation of the Bible in English in the 16th century. For his pains, he was burned at the stake for heresy in 1536. He missed out on a solid wad of royalties, since just two years later, Henry VIII declared that every church in the land must have a Bible written in English.

The Cotswold Way now runs along a path through Westridge Woods that comes out at the Jubilee Clump, a walled enclosure of trees planted in 1815 to commemorate Wellington's victory at the Battle of Waterloo. The route drops down to Wotton-under-Edge, a former wool town where the church of St Mary the Virgin dates from the 13th century. There are almshouses as well as the birthplace of Isaac Pitman, the inventor of shorthand, in Orchard Street. From Wotton, the road climbs to the splendidly named Nanny Farmer's Bottom. Now the route drops down to Alderley and turns into a lane with old houses standing beside a stream, before climbing again through woods and fields. It joins a road close to the soaring memorial known as the Somerset or Hawkesbury Monument, which marks the heroic efforts of one of the commanders at the Battle of Waterloo. Just before the village of Hawkesbury Upton, the route swings away, runs alongside fields and dives into woods, passing close to Horton Court. A path becomes a lane to the village of Horton and continues to Little Sodbury, where it climbs to the ramparts of the Sodbury Iron Age hill fort, which also has Roman and Saxon connections. A few minutes later, the intrepid walker is in Old Sodbury, where food, drink and, if necessary, a warm bed await at the DOG (01454 312006). The Dog is a splendid old country inn with open fires, bare stone walls and beams. There's a no smoking bar and a large lounge. Beers include Marston's Pedigree, Flowers, Boddingtons, Wadworth 6X and Wickwar BOB. Food is served all day and every day and may include sandwiches, ploughman's, cheese and onion flan, ravioli, vegetarian moussaka, sweet and sour chicken, curry, barbecued spare ribs, a children's menu, and such desserts as rhubarb crumble or jam roly-poly.

Pubs for cyclists

Cumbria

MILL INN

MUNGRISDALE, CUMBRIA (017687 79632)

Off A66 Keswick to Penrith road. On Coast-to-Coast cycle route

The 16th-century coaching inn is in a secluded village location in a valley at the foot of Blencathra, with Ullswater close by. The Mill is on the Coast-to-Coast cycle route that runs from Whitehaven in the west to Newcastle-on-Tyne and Sunderland in the east. Part of the building was once the village mill and the original millstone stands in the bar which also has ancient beams and a stone fireplace. The inn has been visited by the likes of Charles Dickens, Wilkie Collins and the John Peel commemorated in the hunting song "D'you ken John Peel", who is buried nearby. There is a strong emphasis on sport in the inn, with a games room that has paragliding photos and where darts, cribbage and carpet bowls are played. The food is based on local ingredients and there is a good choice of vegetarian and vegan dishes including mushrooms in a cream sauce; spinach and feta cheese pie; and burgers made of vegetables, pulses, fruit and nuts. Ploughman's include a choice of 14 cheeses with home-made chutney. Other dishes include soups; sandwiches; potted trout; Cumberland sausage; black pudding and bacon with mustard sauce; tuna steak; chicken or duck pies; and such home-made desserts as Mill Inn sticky toffee pudding and chocolate parfaît. The restaurant is non-smoking and offers a children's menu. Local Jennings Bitter and Cumberland Ale from Cockermouth are on hand-pumps while a sensible wine list offers several by the glass. In good weather customers can sit in a pleasant garden by a small river. Accommodation is available.

OLD CROWN

HESKET NEWMARKET, CUMBRIA (01697 478288)

One mile south-east of Caldbeck; village signposted from B5299. Coast-to-Coast cycle route

The Old Crown is a splendid stop for food, drink and recuperation. Kim and Lyn Matthews have taken over the pub while former landlord Jim

Fearnley brews his ales in a converted barn at the rear. Jim is keen to retire and villagers are putting together the finance to run the brewery as a co-operative. There is a strong emphasis on community involvement in the pub as well: all ingredients for food are grown or reared locally and villagers come in to cook some of the dishes, such as Ann's steak in ale pie and Audrey's Solway fish pancakes. The Old Crown is famous for its real curries in the evening: they include chicken korma; lamb dhansak; blackeye bean curry; and sweet potato curry. All the ingredients, including spices, are grown or supplied locally – "We do genuine Cumbrian curries," says Lynn. Lunchtime meals include a wide range of soups, sandwiches, and Cumbrian sausage, egg and chips. There is a strong emphasis on vegetarian food. The pub is part of a terrace of stone cottages with the Caldbeck Fells providing a superb backdrop. The cheerful and welcoming bar has old church pews for

seats and a coal fire. There's a small separate dining area where children are welcome. Jim Fearnley's succulent ales include Great Cockup, Blencathra, Skiddaw Special, Doris's 90th Birthday Ale, Catbells Pale Ale, Old Carrock, and Pigs Might Fly. As the names of the beers suggest, this is no ordinary pub. There are no meals Sunday or Monday evenings except at Bank Holidays.

Shepherds Inn

Melmerby, Cumbria (01768 881217)

A686 Penrith to Alston road. Coast-to-Coast cycle route

There are old beams and mantelbeams in this 18th-century sandstone pub that has developed from a tiny ale house into bigger premises by swallowing up a row of adjacent terraced cottages. It's in a village at the foot of the Pennines near Hartside Pass, with fields and fells all around. The pub is divided into a series of small rooms, some with carpets, others with flagstones, open fires and a wood-burning stove; pub games are played in one room. There is a good and constantly changing range of cask beers: Jennings Cumberland Ale is a regular and guest ales may include Black Sheep, Hesket Newmarket, Holts, and Wychwood. Beers from abroad may include the Belgian Trappist Orval or a German wheat beer. There's also a good range of whiskies. Food naturally includes Shepherd's pie, plus Cumberland sausage hot-pot; marinated herrings; vegetable soup; vegetable couscous; haddock and broccoli pancakes; roast duckling; barbecued spare ribs; and "build your own" ploughman's with a choice of 17 cheeses including mature Allerdale goat, Cotherstone, Lancashire, Redesdale, Swaledale and oak-smoked Westmorland. Desserts include blackcurrant and hazelnut roulade, and rhubarb and strawberry compote. Children are welcome and smaller portions are available for them. Accommodation is available in cottages in the village, which is also home to the Village Bakery with its renowned breads, ranging from French baguettes to Russian rye, pasties, biscuits and breakfasts, lunches and teas, with everything made from organic ingredients.

West Country

Black Horse

Clevedon Lane, Clapton in Gordano, Somerset (01275 842105)
Off A369 and B3124

This whitewashed, 14th-century cottage pub is tucked away down a remote lane in the Gordano Valley and is a good stop on a cycle route from the Avon Gorge and Clifton Suspension Bridge, through country lanes to Portbury, Portishead, Clevedon, Kenn Moor, Brockley Combe, Long Ashton and back to the suspension bridge. The main bar of the Black Horse has flagstones, winged settles and built-in wall benches, photos and cartoons of the pub, and a log fire on cold days in a large inglenook, with horse stirrups and old flintlock guns on the mantelbeam. A window in the snug remains barred, recalling the days in the 19th century when the room was a local magistrate's lock-up. Mugs hang from the beams and the room contains some superb settles, one donated by the Motor Racing Club of North Somerset, another with an Art Nouveau inset with the oddly Scottish sentiment "East, West, Hame's Best". A third room is set aside for families; there's a children's play area outside, too. Lunchtime meals and snacks (not available on Sunday) include ploughman's, filled baguettes, chilli and lasagne. Real ales are stillaged behind the bar and include the local Bristol brew Smiles Best plus Courage Best and a regular guest beer.

East Anglia

Beehive

The Street, Horringer, Suffolk (01284 735260)
On A143

Horringer is a pleasant stop on a gentle cycle ride through flat Suffolk countryside starting and ending in Newmarket, and taking in Moulton, Gazeley, Barrow, Little Saxham, Rede, Hawkedon, Wickhambrook and Kirtling: be prepared to give way to horses and jockeys out training. The Beehive is a small, 19th-century thatched and flintstone cottage pub with no inn sign but with a large beehive at the front. The small rooms inside off a central bar have low beams, flagstones, wall settles, a wood-burning stove, stripped-back brickwork and some ancient settles. This is a Greene King pub and offers the brewery's IPA, Triumph and Abbot ales along with a regular guest beer such as Old Speckled Hen, which is now brewed by Greene King. Snacks and meals include grilled plaice; paella; tiger prawns on tagliatelle; steak sandwich; avocado with prawns; ploughman's; ham, cheese and onion hash; mushroom risotto; salad niçoise; and soups. Children are welcome and the pub is a good stop for Ickworth Park.

Near London

WALNUT TREE

FAWLEY, BUCKINGHAMSHIRE (01491 638360)
Off A4155 Henley to Marlow road and B480

Fawley features on a delightful cycle ride through the Chiltern beech woods starting at Henley-on-Thames and taking in Turville Heath, Christmas Common, Ewelme, Sonning Common and back to Henley. The pub is owned by local brewer Brakspear and offers Ordinary Bitter, Special Bitter and seasonal beers. The 1950s-built Walnut Tree has tremendous views some 400 feet above Henley. There are tables at the front, a large garden at the rear, and the pub welcomes not just cyclists but horse-riders, with a hitching rail provided for their mounts. Inside, the pub has two conservatories with non-smoking dining rooms, and two bars, one with a log fire. Children are welcome in areas set aside for eating. Food may include salmon and quails' eggs; calamari with chilli; baked stuffed aubergine; home-made pies and ravioli; chicken with Stilton and walnuts; grilled lemon sole; ploughman's; Oriental vegetable stir-fry; and such desserts as sticky toffee pudding, treacle tart, home-made cheesecake and spiced apple torte. There is accommodation available.

Note: *For information about cycle routes contact Sustrans, 35 King Street, Bristol BS1 4DZ (0117 926 8893). Highly recommended: the Hamlyn/Ordnance Survey series* Cycle Tours.

Oxfordshire

Plough

Kelmscot (01367 253543)

Off A417/A4095 north-west of Faringdon

The Plough is close to the Thames Path, with its splendid walks, and the Oxfordshire Cycleway runs almost alongside. With fishing and boating to hand, the inn is a fine base for all active visitors and cyclists can potter cheerfully around the countryside with its many small towns and villages built of mellow Cotswold stone. If you build up a thirst, the Plough can slake it with the likes of Draught Bass, Flowers Original, Morland Original and Wadworth 6X in a bar with old flagstones underfoot and bare stone walls. There are two lounges as well, so there is plenty of space to enjoy a drink, a meal or watch a major sporting event on a satellite screen. Cribbage, darts, dominoes and shove-ha'penny are played. Bar food, lunchtime and evening, may include soup; sandwiches and toasted sandwiches; baguettes and baked potatoes; and garlic mushrooms; followed by vegetable bake; filled pancakes; spicy chicken; pork in prune and Calvados sauce; grilled trout; and steaks. Desserts could include such good old traditional nursery puddings as apple crumble or bread-and-butter pudding. The Plough provides moorings for boats, it has a pleasant, flowery garden, and children are welcome in eating areas until 9pm. Accommodation is available.

Best of the Rest

Chequers

The Street, Doddington, Kent (ex-directory)

North Downs cycle route

Stag and Huntsman

Hambleden, Buckinghamshire (01491 571227)

Off A4155; Chilterns cycle route

Red Lion

Chalton, Hampshire (023 9259 2246)

South Downs cycle route

Pubs for bird-watchers

STAR INN

FORE STREET, ST JUST-IN-PENWITH, CORNWALL (01736 788767)
Off A3071

Locals call the Star "the last proper pub in Cornwall". Close to Land's End and Cape Cornwall, it's a good base for walking the coastal path to spot birds in the St Just area: this is not a formal bird reserve, but the granite cliffs, moorland and rough grazing fields provide a home for a wide variety of birdlife. In winter, gannets and divers can be seen offshore, while there are harriers and other raptors on the moorland, and chiff-chaffs and firecrests in the valleys. Resident species in the area include buzzards, little owls, peregrines, sparrowhawks, green woodpeckers, rock pipits and ravens. A tremendous range of traditional pub games in the Star includes table skittles, bar billiards, shut the box and euchre. The beamed inn is owned by St Austell Brewery and offers its full range of ales, including XXXX Mild, Tinners, HSD and Trelawny's Pride. There's mulled ale in winter, local cider and mead. Food includes home-made soup, vegetable curry and fishcakes. Children are welcome in a small snug and accommodation is available.

GEORGE AND DRAGON

HIGH STREET CLEY NEXT THE SEA, NORFOLK (01263 740652)
On A149

This imposing inn, built in the 17th century and rebuilt in the 19th, is dedicated to bird-watching: it has its own hide in the lounge where twitchers can watch for rare species on Cley Marshes Nature Reserve (Cley is pronounced "Cly"). A "Bird Bible" stands on a lectern in the bar, and the inn even has its own "scrape" or shallow lake to invite birds. As well as resident bitterns, grebes, hawks, herons, gulls, wagtails and woodpeckers, the reserve attracts winter buzzards, divers, cormorants, eiders, geese, guillemots, puffins and razorbills. The inn, with a terracotta George and dragon over the entrance, has masses of G&D memorabilia inside, including a stained-glass window depicting the saint slaying the mythical beast. Food (lunchtime and evening) is strong on fresh fish and seafood, and may include local crab stuffed into mushrooms and deep fried; cider-pickled herring; seafood and melon salad with ginger and lime dressing; herring roes on toast; lemon sole fillet with crabmeat; and pan-fried slip soles or dabs. There are usually curries available and several vegetarian options. Delicious desserts could include strawberry and pear filo tart, or marmalade sponge with citrus sauce. Beer is supplied by Greene King and includes IPA, Abbot Ale and seasonal brews, while a good wine list has bottles from the New World. Children and dogs are welcome and accommodation is available.

FEATHERS

MARKET SQUARE, WOODSTOCK, OXFORDSHIRE (01993 812291)
Off A44

The Feathers is a fine old Cotswold stone hotel fashioned from four separate houses. It's a popular starting point for visiting Blenheim Palace and park, built by a grateful nation for the Duke of Marlborough in 1704 following the Battle of Blenheim. With an area of 2,400 acres, the grounds offer a variety of habitats for birds and flora. High Park is the most important area for breeding birds and resident species include coots, finches, ducks, grebes, kestrels, mallards and woodpeckers. December sees the arrival of winter ducks, bitterns and lapwings. The elegant Feathers is decorated with antiques, oil paintings and water-colours, and in winter the flagstoned bar is warmed by an open fire fuelled by gas flames. A triangular garden bar at the back has a good pubby atmosphere and it opens on to a sun-filled courtyard. The single cask ale is Wadworth 6X while the long wine list has several half-bottles and a few by the glass. Food in the bar and no-smoking restaurant is imaginative and may include red pepper soup with basil; risotto of rocket, rouille and olive salsa; confit of tomato and fresh Parmesan crostini; duck terrine with toasted brioche; smoked haddock with poached egg and hollandaise; sausage and mash, thyme and deep-fried cabbage; or salmon fish cakes with a mustard hollandaise. Desserts could include apple and cinnamon fritters, or apricot delice. Children are welcome in eating areas and accommodation is available.

Crown

Westleton, Suffolk (01728 648777)
B1125, off A12 near Saxmundham

The Crown is an old coaching inn that is a good base for the RSPB reserve at Minsmere and Dunwich Heath Nature Reserve, homes to such resident breeds as grebes, cormorants, bitterns, teals, lapwings and woodcocks. December sees the arrival of divers, buzzards, eiders, harriers, gulls and shags. The inn is also handy for Snape Maltings, the world-famous concert hall founded by Benjamin Britten, who was born in Lowestoft: both Britten and his companion, Peter Pears, are buried in Aldeburgh churchyard. The Crown is cheery, welcoming and unspoilt, its walls decorated with old farm tools, prints and photos. There are old beams and log fires, and locals play shove-ha'penny and skittles in the bar. There's a separate restaurant, and an attractive garden (landscaped by gold medal winners from Chelsea Flower Show) with an aviary and a floodlit terrace. Six cask beers are always on tap: Adnams Best from Southwold is a regular and the other five rotate constantly. The wine list numbers 80 with several half-bottles and six wines by the glass. There's also a good range of whiskies. Bar food and restaurant meals are available lunchtime and evening and may include home-made soups; locally-caught fish such as grilled oak-smoked haddock in garlic butter; sea-fish Thermidor; and steamed fillet of turbot. The house speciality is "knaves on horseback", mushrooms stuffed with pâté and bacon. There's a good choice of vegetarian dishes plus home-made ice-creams such as chocolate, orange and Cointreau. Children are welcome in the dining room and accommodation is available.

Olde Ship

7 Main Street, Seahouses, Northumberland (01665 720200)
On B1340, off A1

The Olde Ship, built in 1745, has a powerful nautical atmosphere, with its saloon and cabin bars decked out with ships' figureheads and wheels, brass lamps and lifeboat oars. There's a ship's museum upstairs, too. From Seahouses you can catch boats to the Farne Islands, with their colonies of birds and seals: birds on the islands include puffins, kittiwakes, gulls, cormorants, shags, fulmars and terns. Lindisfarne, or Holy Island, reached by a causeway covered at high tide, has the largest flock of wintering geese in Britain. In winter, red-throated divers and Slavonian grebes can be seen, along with cormorants, shags, greylag geese, sandpipers, gulls, harriers and whooper swans. Back at the inn, fish and seafood feature strongly on the menu, with crab soup; bosun's fish stew of prawns; squid and cod with onions; tomatoes and bacon; or smoked fish chowder. Other dishes might include curried egg mayonnaise; spicy lamb stew; vegetarian dish of the day; and liver and onion casserole. Desserts might be chocolate trifle or coconut ice cream. There's a tremendous choice of beers including Draught Bass, Marston's Pedigree, Ruddles Best, John Smith's Bitter and Theakston's Best. Children are welcome in a family room and accommodation is available.

Craw Inn

Auchencrow, Borders, Scotland. (01890 761253)
B6437

A pub called the craw (dialect for crow) is clearly a good base for visiting St Abbs Head on the coast, a rocky headland where the sheer cliffs, some 100 metres high, plunge into the boiling North Sea. The cliffs are home to around 60,000 seabirds. Inland from the cliff top, grazed grassland, trees, scrubland, and a man-made loch provide further habitats. The area is a national Nature Reserve managed by the National Trust for Scotland and the Scottish Wildlife Trust. Around the cliffs, you can see fulmars, shags, kittiwakes, guillemots, razorbills and puffins. The trees around Mire Loch attract chats, flycatchers and warblers. In winter, wildfowl such as goldeneyes and widgeon are seen on the loch, while divers can be spotted off the coast. The Craw Inn, which dates from 1680, has a wood-beamed bar and a log fire. Witches used to be hanged in the garden, a practice that ended some years ago. After appearing in the newspaper column that spawned this book, the Craw closed in 1999 but reopened when it was bought by Trevor Wilson. He's a real ale enthusiast and chooses such a wide range of ales from craft breweries that it's impossible to list regulars, though he is devoted to beers from the Orkney Brewery and you may find its brews on offer. Trevor is also partial to a drop of Tomintoul from the Highlands while beers from as far afield as Jennings in the Lake District and Stonehenge in Wiltshire have also graced the bar. Fresh fish bought daily from Eyemouth is the main feature on the menu, along with meat supplied by local farmers. There's always at least one vegetarian dish for non-meat eaters. Children are welcome in designated areas and accommodation is available.

Rose and Crown

12 Market Square, Potton, Bedfordshire (01767 260221)
A603

Sandy Lodge, the grand Victorian mansion and extensive grounds that form the headquarters of the Royal Society for the Protection of Birds, is just two miles from Potton, with its handsome, early-Georgian main square. The Rose and Crown hotel, a tall, red-brick, neo-classical building, dominates the square but inside there is none of the formality suggested by the exterior. A large but cosy bar stocks Adnams Best and, from Bedford, Charles Wells Eagle Bitter and it always offers at least one beer from the new Potton Brewery in Shannon Place (01767 261042). The small craft brewery is run by Clive Towner and Robert Hearson, brewer and manager at the Greene King plant in Biggleswade, which closed in the late 1990s. They resurrected the Potton Brewery name, which disappeared in 1922 as the result of a takeover. As well as the Rose and Crown they supply 100 outlets with a range of ales that includes Pheonix Bitter, Shambles Bitter and Pride of Potton. Food in the Rose and Crown includes steak and ale pie and chicken and Stilton pie and there are always several vegetarian dishes such as mushroom Stroganoff and filo vegetable parcels. The hotels has 15 *en suite* rooms and promises that, unlike the address of the RSPB, it will not have Sandy Beds. (The Locomotive in Sandy is also recommended for its railway memorabilia, excellent food and Charles Wells' beers.)

Pubs for rail travellers

Hamilton Hall

Bishopsgate/Liverpool Street Station, London EC2
(020 7247 3579)
Underground: Liverpool Street

This pub, on the concourse of Liverpool Street rail and Underground station, must be the busiest in the J.D. Wetherspoon's chain. Based in the old ballroom of the Great Eastern Hotel, it's a sumptuous shrine to *la belle époque*, with great chandeliers, Louis XIV mirrors, plaster nudes, moulded fruit ceilings, and a magnificent sweeping staircase that leads to an upper mezzanine and no-smoking area, the whole named in honour of Lady Hamilton, Admiral Lord Nelson's mistress. There are monitors showing train departures and arrivals. Being city-based, Hamilton Hall sells a lot of wine and Champagne to well-heeled commuters. Real ales include Ridley's ESX, Fuller's London Pride, Theakston's Best, Courage Directors and a guest beer twice a week. Food, served all day, includes steak and ale pie; chicken casserole; mozzarella and tomato penne; and filled baguettes. Unlike most city pubs, this one is open until late every day. It's worth missing a few trains for, and you can use the toilets for free, whereas Railtrack charge you "to spend a penny" on the main concourse, one of the many benefits of privatization.

Head of Steam

1 Eversholt Street, Euston Square, London NW1
(020 7388 2221)
Just off A40; Underground: Euston Square, Warren Street or Euston

One of a growing chain run by real ale enthusiast Tony Brookes, this pub is tucked between the station concourse and the bus terminus. The bar is designed like a traditional station buffet, with masses of railway memorabilia. There's a plethora of real ales, such as B&T, Black Sheep, Brakspear, Cottage, Hop Back, O'Hanlon, Shepherd Neame, and at least one dark mild, such as Highgate from Walsall. Biddenden traditional cider is available on tap, plus a good range of whiskies. Food includes soup, sandwiches and several vegetarian dishes, plus a children's menu. There's a raised no-smoking area.

Head of Steam

St George's Square, Huddersfield, West Yorkshire
(01484 454533)

Based in the Grade I-listed Huddersfield Railway Station, with an entrance on St George's Square, this branch of Head of Steam is dedicated to the great age of the railway. It's stuffed with locomotive nameplates and number plates, old railway posters, maps, and staff uniforms. The pub is open all permitted hours and always has several real ales on tap: Black Sheep Bitter is a regular, with rotating beers from independents and craft breweries. There are frequent beer festivals, such as an Irish festival with rare real ales brought from the Republic. Home-cooked food includes spare ribs; giant Yorkshire pudding with onion gravy; Stilton-and-potato croquettes; and vegetable Balti.

Philharmonic Dining Rooms

36 Hope Street, corner of Hardman Street, Liverpool
(0151 709 1163)

Opposite the Philharmonic Hall and handy for Liverpool's stations, this remarkable pub is a veritable romp of Art Nouveau and neo-Renaissance styles. Even the gents' is decked in marble and mosaic, with 1890s stalls built by Twyfords. As well as the large public bar, there's a succession of small rooms and snugs. The heartbeat of the pub is a serving counter with polished mahogany partitions. The main hall has stained-glass windows with portraits of such Boer War "heroes" as Robert Baden-Powell. Wherever you turn there's more etched glass, mahogany and copper panels. An etched stained-glass window in one snug announces "Music is the universal language of mankind", and has illustrations of musical instruments. It's an early example of the Mersey beat. Food includes soup, gammon, fish pie, and steak and kidney pie. Children can eat in a designated area. Real ales include Marston's Pedigree, Old Speckled Hen and Tetley Bitter.

MANNINGTREE STATION BUFFET

PLATFORM ONE, MANNINGTREE STATION, STATION ROAD, LAWFORD, ESSEX (01206 391114)
Off A137

This splendid traditional buffet is in a listed Victorian railway station on the Liverpool Street to East Anglia line. There are five hand-pumps on a solid marble bar, and a tiny hidden no-smoking dining room entered via the kitchen. Managers Richard and Debbie Rowley serve up a tempting range of real ales, such as Adnams Best, Crouch Vale Millennium Gold, Fuller's London Pride, and Shepherd Neame Spitfire. Food includes a full breakfast for commuters, all-day snacks, lunchtime main courses such as braised lamb chops; steak and kidney pie; liver and bacon casserole; sausage and onion pie; and steak braised with mushrooms in white wine. In the evening there could be roast leg of lamb with garlic, or fresh cod or haddock fish cakes for children. Vegetarian dishes may include spinach gnocchi with roast pepper and blue cheese sauce; or cheesy choux with blue cheese and apple filling. Desserts might be apple stuffed pancakes, or sticky toffee pudding. There's even a Railway Pudding. Commuters can order from the train on mobile phones.

Best of the Rest

SPRING BANK TAVERN

SPRING BANK, HULL, EAST YORKSHIRE (01482 581879)

VAT & FIDDLE

12-14 QUEENSBRIDGE ROAD, NOTTINGHAM (0115 985 0611)
Near Nottingham Station

OLD JOINT STOCK

4 TEMPLE ROW WEST, BIRMINGHAM (0121 200 1892)
Opposite Birmingham Cathedral

Note: *See also Station Buffet, Stalybridge, Greater Manchester (*page 158*)*

George

Market Place, Castle Cary, Somerset (01963 350761)
Off A371

Castle Cary, deep in rural Somerset, may seem an unlikely place to have a good hostelry for rail travellers but not only is there a station but also InterCity trains stop there. On a visit to the Cottage Brewery, I found, on my return to the station, that the London train had been severely delayed and I was glad of the chance for a soothing glass of beer in the George. If the train had been much later, I could availed myself of the hotel's bedrooms. The George is a stone and thatch, 15th-century inn with Grade II listed status. The beamed front bar has an impressive black elm mantelbeam above the fireplace that is claimed to be more than 1,000 years' old. The bar also has a seat in a bowed window and a high-backed settle by the fire. A glazed partition separates the entrance from a second bar that is for non-smokers and is nicely decorated with some large landscapes and smaller pictures on the walls. Hand-pumped ales include Otter Bitter from Devon and Morland Old Speckled Hen, with a good choice of wines, with several by the glass, and malt whiskies. Bar and restaurant food, lunchtime and evening, could include home-made soup; pâté and toast; omelette and chips; duck terrine with pistachio nuts and sweet peppers; lamb casserole; steak and kidney pie; chicken en croute; chicken layered with potato pancake, bacon and tomatoes and a sweet basil dressing; and fillet of salmon with samphire and lemon sauce butter. Desserts could include steamed sponge pudding, sticky toffee pudding or hot chocolate pudding with vanilla ice-cream. Cribbage and dominoes are played in the bar and accommodation is available. Children are welcome in designated eating areas.

Burton Bridge Inn

24 Bridge Street, Burton-on-Trent, Staffordshire
(01283 536596)
A50

This pub could grace either the home-brew or brewery tap sections as well as this one. It's one of the finest brewpubs in the land and keeps aloft the proud craft brewing flag in what was once England's capital of brewing. But Burton has been sadly reduced as a result of takeovers, mergers, closures and the general rapaciousness, madness and lack of concern for drinkers that are the hallmarks of too many big brewing corporations. The Burton Bridge Brewery, fronted by the inn, was set up in 1982 by Geoff Mumford and Bruce Wilkinson who had worked for various satraps of the Allied Breweries empire and who finally decided that there must be more to life than working the night shift at Ind Coope's brewery in Romford, Essex (they were right, for the Romford brewery was closed and the brewing equipment was flogged to China). They returned to the East Midlands, set up a small brewing plant and produced such delectable beers for the inn that their fame spread and they now supply some 250 other outlets. The inn is everything a good, homely town boozer should be, comfortable, friendly and welcoming, with an oak-panelled bar with wooden pews, and a slightly more cosy lounge. The walls are decorated with posters advertising local events but principally with all the awards the brewery has won for its beers – and it has won more awards than you can shake a mashing fork at. Wonderful beers they are too, fruity, hoppy and with that special whiff of sulphur that is the tasteprint of Burton, with its Trent Valley wells rich in gyspum and magnesium. The range is constantly changing with occasional and seasonal brews but the regulars are likely to be XL, Bridge Bitter, Porter and Festival Ale. Several of the beers are also available in bottle-fermented form: the Porter is a magnificent example of the style and comes in a plain, embossed bottle. Don't miss the Empire Pale Ale, only available in bottles, which was the 1997 Camra/*Guardian* bottle-fermented beer of the year. It replicates the famous Burton India Pale Ales by being matured in wooden casks for three months before being bottled: three months was the time it took for supplies of IPA to go from Burton to Calcutta by sailing ship in the 19th century when thirsty colonial Brits were demanding refreshing ale from the home country. Lunchtime food is simple but nourishing: filled cobs; oatcakes; faggots and mushy peas; and filled Yorkshire puddings. The inn has an upstairs room for meetings and a skittle alley. Visits to the brewery must be booked long in advance (01283 510573/fax 515594). If you never visit the Burton Bridge Inn your life will be the poorer for it.

Crocker's, near Lord's cricket ground, London NW8

Pubs near cricket grounds

Crocker's Folly

24 Aberdeen Place, London NW8. (020 7286 6608)
Underground: Warwick Avenue/St John's Wood

Crocker's is more than just a handy watering-hole a few minutes from Lord's, it's one of the most amazingly ornate pubs in London. Once through the doors you could be sailing in a sumptuous 1930s Cunard liner, with state rooms, moulded ceilings and revolving ceiling fans. It has a sad yet funny history, built at the height of the great Victorian railway boom by a speculator, Frank Crocker, who was advised (no doubt by the Victorian equivalent of Arthur Daley) that Marylebone Station was due to be built on the very spot where he was keen to build a hotel. With a fortune almost within his grasp, Crocker spared no effort or money in rushing up a rococo masterpiece called the Crown, with bars and restaurants on the ground floor, and guest rooms reached by sweeping marble staircases. When it was finished, Crocker stepped back to admire his handiwork only to have the dread news that the planned station had been moved a mile down the road. Alas, poor Crocker went bankrupt, though it's pure myth that he committed suicide: he lived to a ripe old age. Londoners, with their morbid sense of humour, nicknamed the Crown "Crocker's Folly", and the name was eventually changed in the 1980s to commemorate this *folie de grandeur*. The main bar is a riot of marble: marble pillars, marble bar counter, marble fireplace and even marble walls. The ceiling is a marvellous piece of intricate purple and gold relief moulding, and the windows have engraved glass. Through an archway, the Music Room is spacious and elegant, with ceiling fans, yet another marble fireplace, and plush sofas. The public bar is almost plain by comparison to all this splendour but is tasteful and elegant, with green leaded windows and gilt cherubs. Food is available lunchtime and evening, with all-day roasts on Sundays. The menu changes daily, all the food is home-cooked and you may find the likes of fish and chips, a range of pies, steaks, braised lamb, mixed grill, stuffed chicken breasts and always at least one vegetarian dish. The hand-pumped ales include Adnams Bitter, Draught Bass,

Brakspear's Bitter and Busy Bee, and Gale's HSB and GB. The pub is said to be haunted by poor, sad Frank Crocker, a man with ideas above his station.

Stratford Haven

Stratford Road, West Bridgeford, Nottinghamshire (0115 982 5981)

This is a new pub, opened in 1999, and run by the Tynemill Group that also owns the splendid Lincolnshire Poacher on Mansfield Road, Nottingham, as well as other pubs in the East Midlands. The Stratford Haven, with a punny pub sign alluding to William Shakespeare, is a former pet shop that adheres to the Tynemill formula of providing pubs for all-comers, not just the youth-and-student market. There are several small rooms, nooks, snugs and crannies, all served by a central bar. There's a tremendous range of hand-pumped ales that include Bateman's XB, Belvoir Star Bitter, Castle Rock Hemlock and Marston's Pedigree. There's always a dark mild available, and a popular version of the style is Whim Brewery's Magic Mushroom. There are always three guest beers that may include the likes of Adnams Best, Brain's SA from Cardiff, or Caledonian Deuchar's IPA. Food is served from 12 noon until 8pm and includes such "light bites" as sandwiches and filled baguettes, plus full meals such as fillet of monkfish; breast of chicken; and Lincolnshire sausage and mash; with vegetarian lasagne and harvester pie for herbivores. Most of the food is cooked on the premises. Stratford Road is a short walk from the pavilion end at Trent Bridge.

Alexandra Hotel

203 Siddals Road, Derby (01332 293993)

This is another Tynemill outlet, a comfortable, no-frills Victorian pub-cum-hotel (accommodation is available) with two rooms, masses of fascinating old railway memorabilia, dark wood floors and chunky pub furniture. It's handy for both the Racecourse Ground, home to Derbyshire CCC, and the railway station. As well as a good selection of beers, including Bateman's XB, Castle Rock Hemlock and Marston's Pedigree, plus regular guest ales, there's a good selection of malt whiskies, bottled Belgian beers and genuine European lagers on draught. Food is simple, filling and remarkably good value: look for ploughman's, filled rolls, pie and peas or a daily roast.

Peveril of the Peak

127 Great Bridgwater Street, Manchester (0161 236 6364)
Oxford Road station/St Peter's Square tram

Popular with both Manchester United football and Lancashire cricket supporters and worth the short trip back on the brilliant tram system from Old Trafford, "the Pev" is named after a famous 19th-century stage-coach on the London to Manchester run. Sir Walter Scott commemorated the coach in the title of a novel. The stagecoach was built in 1825 by James Grundy who made so much money from his trade that he was able to buy land and build a pub that he named after the source of his wealth. The wedge-shaped pub has a fine green-tiled exterior with an imposing Art Nouveau tiled frieze. Inside there is a central bar with a great deal of polished wood and stained glass. The cheerful public bar has a curved serving counter carved out of a wood, a table football machine, and a darts board with a net below it to catch badly aimed arrows. A long, narrow lounge has a Victorian fireplace with inset tiles. Simple pub snacks are served lunchtime. Hand-pumped ales include Theakston's Best and Wilson's Bitter with regular guest beers. "The Pev" is closed lunchtimes Saturday and Sunday but usually opens for Saturday lunch when Manchester United are playing at home, and may do so for major cricket matches: phone to check.

Queen's Head

30 Lower Anchor Street, Chelmsford, Essex (01245 265181)
Off B1007

Vibrant, welcoming local just 100 yards or a hefty straight drive from the cricket ground, it had its original 1895 name restored in 1999 after some years trading as Partners. A two-sided new pub sign shows Queen Victoria against different cricketing backdrops. The pub has a large car park and, in good weather, there is a large patio at the back with benches and tubs of flowers. The exterior is cream painted and the first thing you see as you enter the bar are the hand-pumps offering a constantly changing range of real ales: the local craft brewery Crouch Vale is the only regular with its Bitter and Woodham IPA. Guest ales, which always include a dark beer, mild, stout or porter, are chalked on a noticeboard by the bar. They may include such delights as RCH Slug Porter and Hop Back's Summer Lightning,

Thunderstorm wheat beer and Entire Stout. The beams in the bar are decorated with the pump clips of all the ales the pub has served – it sells 300 barrels of cask beer a year. Lunchtime food is all home-cooked and includes steak and ale pie; sausages with Crouch Vale beer; chicken and mushroom pie; vegetarian stir-fry; ratatouille; and omelettes cooked to order. There's no canned music, the art of conversation – cricket and beer predominating – flourishes, and darts, bar billiards, shove-ha'penny and cribbage are played with enthusiasm. A great boozer.

Old Moseley Arms

53 Tindal Street, Moseley, Birmingham (0121 440 1954)

This traditional late-Victorian ale house is about half a mile from Edgbaston cricket ground, home to Warwickshire CCC and a major Test match venue. It has two small rooms with 1930s wood panelling, plus a pool room. As well as cricket supporters in season, the pub attracts local workers and students and offers a superb view of the city centre skyline. There are simple bar snacks only but there are regular curry nights. The regular hand-pumped beers include Ansells Bitter, Enville Ale and Marston's Pedigree, plus a regular guest ale.

Wellington Arms

56 Park Road, Freemantle, Southampton (01703 227356)

This busy and welcoming back-street pub, the best local for Hampshire CCC, is dedicated to the Iron Duke: memorabilia about him and his campaigns are the dominant theme. It's a free house with a vast range of cask ales and features Ringwood Best, Fortyniner, XXXX Porter and Old Thumper from a New Forest small craft brewery that is celebrating 21 years of brewing this year. Other beers include Courage Directors, Fuller's London Pride and Wadworth 6X. There are no games machines. Good lunchtime pub food includes renowned real ale sausages and mash. Also try the Waterloo Arms, 101 Waterloo Road, Freemantle, dedicated to the Salisbury craft brewery Hop Back: its GFB, Crop Circle, Entire Stout, Thunderstorm and Summer Lightning are sold and the walls are festooned with awards the brewery has won for its beers. Sausages with beer are a special treat.

Pub walks in Dorset

Swanage to Studland across Ballard Down

Limber up for the walk with a pint in the **RED LION**, 63 High Street, Swanage (01929 423533), open all day, serving lunches and Flowers Original and Ringwood Fortyniner ales. It's a cheery two-bar pub with beams decorated with mugs and keys. The lounge bar leads to a garden with a children's room.

From the High Street turn left for Shore Road and pick up a map of Swanage from the Tourist Information Centre opposite the beach. You will need this to find the small side streets that lead to Ballard Down. Park, if you are driving, in Ballard Road, Parsons Close, Hill Road or Redcliffe Road and then follow the footpath to the down. A stile by a farm leads on to Ballard Down, which is administered by the

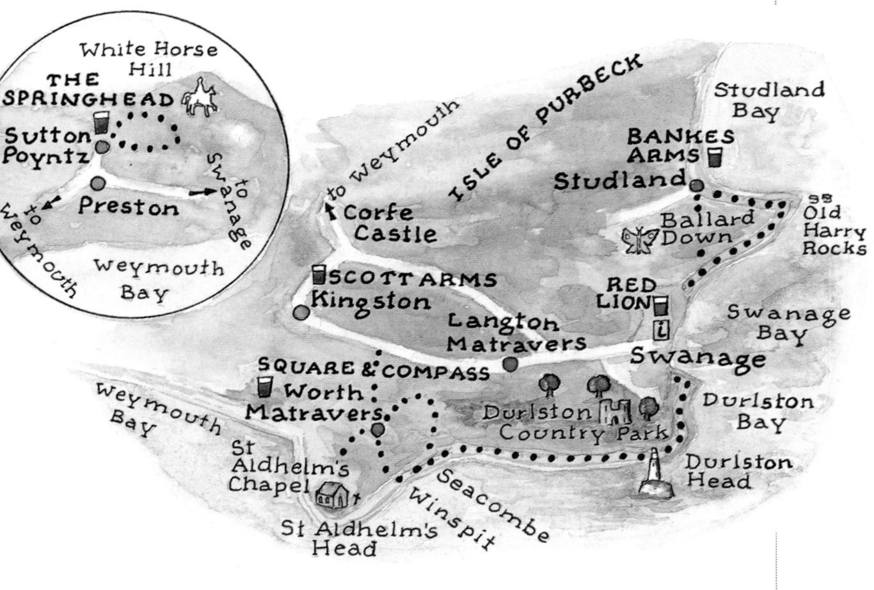

National Trust and is home to many rare species of birds and butterflies: the first stretch of the walk is along a narrow track between trees at the end of which a large board beyond a five-bar gate gives detailed information about the flora and fauna to be seen.

The path now rises gently, with the down falling away to the right and giving a fine view over Swanage Bay. Ahead, the Isle of Wight breasts the sea, often floating eerily in the mist or haze according to the weather. As Swanage Bay begins to disappear and is replaced by views of Studland Bay you will reach a signpost that offers a choice of going direct to the village of Studland or round the headland via Old Harry Rocks. If you choose the former you start to descend towards a gate, a cluster of houses and a narrow road that leads down to Manor Farm (simple lunches and teas available) and then right up Manor Road to the Bankes Arms.

If you take the longer route you will see at close hand the chalk stacks of Old Harry that have become separated from the mainland by centuries of erosion. The rocks are named after a 15th century Poole privateer named Harry Paye. The broad path now leads down towards Studland, with spectacular views over Poole Bay to Bournemouth. The track eventually brings you to Manor Road where you turn right for the pub.

THE BANKES ARMS (01929 450225) is a stone-built, ivy-covered pub with a large bar and separate restaurant. There are tables and benches outside the pub and many more tables on a grassy headland across the road, with fine sea views. The pub is open all day and serves lunches: there's a strong emphasis on locally caught fish, plus the likes of vegetable lasagne, mushroom Stroganoff, curried pork, smoked trout or mackerel, ploughman's and filled baguettes. Cream teas are served in summer. The pub has a policy of selling beers from craft breweries only: the list is ever-changing but you may find the local Poole Brewery plus Cottage, Hampshire, Hop Back, Smiles and Wychwood. There's also Old Rosie Cider all year round with three or four other farm ciders in summer. Accommodation is available. Don't miss the Norman church close to the pub and Manor Farm.

Swanage to Worth Matravers

From Swanage High Street bear right and walk along the harbour and past the coastguard station to the headland called Peveril Point. Here you pick up a coastal path with tremendous views of the sea to one side and the Isle of Purbeck inland. The path runs along the top of Durlston Bay with to the right Durlston Country Park, with its famous giant outdoor globe of the world set amid splendid gardens. If you need to pause for refreshment you can have tea, coffee, snacks, or a full lunch with a licensed bar in Durlston Castle.

Once past Durlston Head the grass land rises steeply to the right up to the villages of Langton Matravers and then Worth Matravers. To reach Worth you can take a path either at Seacombe or, a short walk further, at Winspit. The village is full of lovely mellow Purbeck stone cottages and is home to one of the classic, unspoilt ale houses in the whole of England, the SQUARE AND COMPASS (01929 439229), named after tools used by workmen digging and fashioning the local stone. The pub has been run by the Newman family for more than 90 years. It has flag-stone floors, beer served straight from casks behind a hatch (Badger Tanglefoot, Ringwood Fortyniner, Quay Old Rott, rotating guest beers and farm cider). There is a large room with drawings, paintings and cartoons of local characters on the walls. At the back of the pub, landlord Charlie Newman has created a small museum (entry is free) with local fossils, old tools and weapons. Children will be fascinated by the dinosaur exhibits: the creatures were active in the area. There are more benches outside the entrance where you can eat a choice of pasties, pork and chilli, or cheese and onion pie. The pub is open all day on Saturday and closes weekday afternoons.

If you continue through the village the road peters out and a path takes you to St Aldhelm's Chapel and then on to the great outcrop of St Aldhelm's Head (named St Alban's Head on some maps). If you need a pub with a greater choice of food, take the path from Worth to Kingston for the creeper-clad SCOTT ARMS (01929 480270), which is open all day, specialises in locally caught fish dishes, has a children's menu and serves Ringwood Best Bitter among a good clutch of ales. There are splendid views of Corfe Castle from the garden.

Sutton Poyntz near Weymouth

In Preston, on the A353 Warmwell to Weymouth road, turn north on Sutton Road and bear right into Sutton Poyntz. The **SPRINGHEAD** pub (01305 832117) is signposted on the right. Leave you car and either have a refresher in the charming Purbeck stone pub or start the walk. You go past a mill pond, then turn right and go along a track marked "private farm road". Go through two gates and you will soon see White Horse Hill to your left with the figure of a mounted horseman cut from the chalk. The horseman is George III and the figure was cut in 1815 to mark his patronage of Weymouth.

Bankes Arms, Studland

The path bears to the right. You have to clamber over a stile into a meadow. Head for a gate in the hedgerow on the far side, cross the next field and look for a double stile on the other side. Keep straight on, looking for a gap to the right of a tree that stands taller than the hedgerow. Once through the gap, bear right and follow the path until a metal gate takes you on to a paved track. The next track on the right is signposted Sutton Poyntz. Follow the track to a metal gate and shortly after this take the right or lower path. The White Horse comes into view again.

Go through two gates and head towards a gap in the bottom right-hand corner of the field. Cross a stile in a clump of trees and follow

the edge of two fields, with a hedgerow to your right. At the end of the second field you join a path with the houses of Sutton Poyntz in front of you.

Back at the Springhead you will find bar snacks and full meals available lunchtime and evening, with special dishes such as coq au vin on a board and some vegetarian options, with barbecues some summer evenings. There is a children's farm play area in the large garden. The beamed pub is open all day and serves Wadworth 6X, Draught Bass, Flowers IPA and several guest ales, plus 12 malt whiskies and a good range of wine. There is often live music on Sundays.

In nearby Weymouth you can eat at BREWERS QUAY, a development based in the former Devenish Brewery, which also houses The Quay micro-brewery, with a wide range of cask and bottle-conditioned ales (01305 777515).

Pubs with live jazz and blues

Bull's Head

373 Lonsdale Road, Barnes, London SW13 (020 8876 5241)
Train: Barnes Bridge

Always called "the Bull's Head at Barnes" to distinguish it from other bovine hosteleries, this is Britain's premier jazz pub and vies with Ronnie Scott's as the leading London jazz venue. Landlord Dan Fleming says that by the end of 1999 the pub, which started featuring jazz in 1959, had staged 16,000 concerts. There is jazz every day, including Sunday: two sets on Sunday between 2pm and 4.30pm and two sets every evening between 8.30pm and 11pm. Top American musicians often appear and regulars include Kevin O'Brien, the Hertford Jazz Orchestra, the London Blues Band, Run For Home and the Odyssey Blues Band. The concerts are in a large hall at the back of the pub and there's a small charge, ranging from £3.50 to £7: leading British saxophonist Pete King costs just £6. The Bull's Head is a stately pub in its own right. It overlooks the Thames and in good weather drinkers take their pints of Young's ale and sit on the embankment wall. The three-storey exterior has a pillared entrance, iron-work balconies between the first and top floors, and a dormered steeple that is reminiscent of a Kentish oast house. Inside the large counter serves the main bar and several side alcoves. The walls are lined with photos of jazz stars who have performed at the pub. Food is served lunchtime and evening and includes a highly recommended bistro. All the food, including ice cream, is home-cooked and ranges from soup and sandwiches to pasta and meat dishes. Unlike jazz clubs, where you pay an arm and a leg for a bottle of lager, you can sup Young's divine Bitter, Special Bitter and seasonal beers at sensible prices.

Wild Goose

Combeinteignhead, Devon (01626 872241)
Off A380, between Newton Abbot and Shaldon on unclassified road

Rowland and Thelma Honeywill have run this 17th-century inn near the coast and the mouth of the River Teign for 14 years and have featured live jazz on Monday nights throughout that period. While the Bull's Head is strictly modern, the Wild Goose concentrates on the stomping, uncomplicated rhythms of traditional jazz, using half a dozen groups from the West Country plus any visiting bands that happen to be in the area. There's no charge for the music: drinkers just mingle and move around in the bar, tapping their feet on the flagstone floors. It's a marvellous old inn with thick stone walls, beams and standing timbers, and a large fireplace with a wood-burning stove. Rowland Honeywill is a devoted supporter of small craft breweries, especially those in the West Country. He has six hand-pumps on the bar with some 30 rotating beers. You may find the likes of Teignworthy Spring Tide, Exe Valley Devon Glory, Jail Ale and Dartmoor

The Bull's Head at Barnes

IPA from the Princetown Brewery, and Otter Bright. Meals and snacks include locally caught fish, home-made steak and kidney pudding, and such vegetarian dishes as vegetable moussaka and vegetable stir-fry. Thelma Honeywill is famous for her desserts, including spotted dick and treacle tart. The Wild Goose is a real country local with such pub games as darts, cribbage and shove-ha'penny and is the base for the local cricket club in summer. There's an annual jazz festival in September.

ALBERT

1 WEST STREET, BEDMINSTER, BRISTOL (0117 966 1968)

The Albert is a shrine to modern jazz, from bebop to contemporary, with concerts every Sunday. The 19th-century pub has been staging jazz concerts for 15 years (there's also folk on Wednesdays) and the walls of the pub are decorated with photos of musicians and old record sleeves. The lounge bar has recently been redecorated and is now called the Blue Note after the leading American jazz recording company: its sleeves decorate the walls. Landlord Ian Storror has a special stage with lighting and microphones: "We stage proper gigs – people aren't allowed to chat during the performances," he says. There's a charge that depends on the group: prices start at £3.50 and could be as high as £15 for a top American group. The pub can accommodate 65 people seating and 20 more standing. The food is excellent, too, with a strong emphasis on vegetarian dishes such as pasta and pesto, cauliflower cheese and veggie burgers, with rice preferred to chips. There are also fish dishes including salmon steaks, plus home-made soups and omelettes. Real ales are locally brewed: Bath Gem and Smiles Best Bitter.

FUGGLE & FIRKIN

14 GLOUCESTER STREET, OXFORD (01865 727265)

Near Gloucester Green car park and central bus station

This is a top of the range Firkin, the national chain of fun pubs several of which used to brew their own beer on the premises. It is still better known under its old name of the Oxford Bakery & Brewhouse and its stone flagged floors, beams, old beer casks, wood-burning stove, rough brick and pine walls and a mezzanine that allows customers to find quieter places to drink, chat and eat marks it out from the usual din of an open-plan Firkin.

Monday nights feature big names in the world of blues: "We can't afford the very top American bands when they're on tour but we do attract the best of the second division of American and British groups," says manager Jonathan Lee. There's no charge to listen to the music. Since Punch Taverns bought the Firkins and stopped brewing activities, cask ales are brought in and usually include the likes of Adnams Bitter, Tetley Bitter, Ind Coope Burton Ale. Food lunchtime and evening includes pasta bowls, salads and burgers. The pub has a large beer garden and inside there are plenty of nooks and crannies "where lecturers can get away from their students," says Mr Lee.

WHITE HORSE INN (NELLIE'S)

22 HENGATE, BEVERLEY, EAST YORKSHIRE (01482 861973)

By bus station

It has to be traditional jazz at Nellie's: modern jazz would be too sudden for such an ancient inn known universally by the name of the revered and feared landlady who ran it until 1976. With its bulging brick walls, this is an inn of great antiquity, possibly built to accommodate the builders of Beverley's great minster or smaller churches: the White Horse is close to St Mary's Church. There's nothing so modern as electricity: the maze of tiny rooms are lit by gas, including a magnificent chandelier operated by a pulley. The central bar has an old-fashioned cash register, bare boards and an open fire with an attractive tiled surround. All the smaller rooms and annexes have open fires, too, and wags say it used to take the entire production of the local coal fields to keep them going. The walls and ceiling are nicotine-coloured and there are many old cartoons and prints. An upstairs room is used for jazz on Wednesday nights – there are also folk and poetry evenings. Jazz is performed by a regular group of local semi-pros who play New Orleans-style music. There's a charge of £1 to listen to them. Downstairs you can sup Samuel Smith's Old Brewery Bitter and eat such home-cooked food as sandwiches, toasted sandwiches, Yorkshire puddings with gravy, steak pie or vegetarian lasagne. As for Nellie, she is long gone but her memory haunts the place. Locals say that if the fruit machine paid out too much money for her liking she would switch it off, telling the hapless winner that it was out of order. Her long-time live-in lover was known as "Suitcase Johnny" as a result of the number of times she threw his belongings out of the window. She probably hired the jazz group to drown their rows.

JENNY WATTS

41 HIGH STREET, BANGOR, NORTHERN IRELAND (028 9127 0401)

The tradition in this seaside pub on the marina is the Sunday jazz lunch. The local Murray Wilson Band plays – as it has done for many years – between 1pm and 3pm while customers tuck into a traditional Sunday roast or generous snacks. There are always vegetarian choices and if nothing suits you then the chef will attempt to cook something to order. At other times food may include champ, the Irish dish of mashed potato and spring onions, Irish stew, a large range of soups, mushroom bake, vegetable chow mein and ice cream specials. The pub dates from 1740 and has stone walls, a large "island" bar, two open fires and masses of mirrors. Real ale is Theakston's Best Bitter. As for Jenny Watts, there are several theories about who she was, ranging from an Irish chieftain's lover to a Victorian smuggler: the theories are spelt out in the bar.

Best of the rest

CROWN AND ANCHOR

COTS LANE, LUGWARDINE, HEREFORDSHIRE (01432 851303)
Off A438

BELL

CASTLE HEDINGHAM, ESSEX (01787 460350)
B1058

CROWN

LANLIVERY, CORNWALL (01208 872707)
Off A390

Haunted pubs

OLDE FERRY BOAT INN

HOLYWELL, NEAR ST IVES, CAMBRIDGESHIRE (01480 463227)
Signposted from A1123 in Needingworth

The Ferry Boat is one of England's oldest inns – it may even be the oldest. It dates back more than a thousand years and has been recorded as selling ale as long ago as 1068. In the centre of the heavily beamed bar there's a stone that marks the 900-year-old grave of Juliette Tewsley or Tousley who hanged herself from a nearby willow tree when she was rejected by the local woodcutter. Her ghost now returns to weep, wail and point at the grave on 17 March, the date of her death. The lovely old thatched inn stands on the banks of the River Ouse in a remote part of the Fens: you have to keep your eyes peeled for the signpost at Needingworth. The breathtakingly ancient building has a mix of timbered and panelled walls, four open fires, settles, rush seats, fascinating old carved mouldings, and fine views of the river from a rear window. There's a splendid range of cask ales, including Fuller's London Pride, Greene King Abbot, Marston's Pedigree, Morland Old Speckled Hen and Tim Taylor's Landlord. Food (lunchtime, evening and often all day in summer) includes a welcome number of dishes for vegetarians: there are at least four dishes every day, which could include Thai vegetable curry, char-grilled aubergine filled with Mediterranean vegetables, mushroom and walnut Stroganoff, or leek and goat's cheese lasagne, plus several pasta dishes. Other courses may include tomato and basil soup, garlic and herb mussels, smoked salmon wrapped round Atlantic prawns, Cajun potato wedges with salsa, Caribbean chicken curry with coconut, steak and kidney pudding, pasta with smoked chicken, mixed grill, poached salmon, and such snacks as filled jacket potatoes, baguettes, and ploughman's. In good weather there are seats on a front terrace and on an attractive back lawn. There are moorings for boats and accommodation is available.

Bell

Walberswick, Suffolk (01502 723109)
Off B1387

The Bell is also featured in our Suffolk Walk but deserves mention here as it stands in possibly the most haunted village in the country. You have to take the sightings seriously when none other than George Orwell was a witness. One ghost is that of a large black dog that runs across the marshes at low tide, a sort of East Anglian Hound of the Baskervilles. As long ago as 1577, a pamphlet warned of: "the Devil incarnate in the form of a Black Dog." In the 1970s a local author found that the beast was still about and was described by one witness as "a phantom dog the size of a calf" that haunts the road between the Bell and the vicarage. Other people have heard invisible horses galloping across the green in broad daylight while apparitions have been seen on the common, the green, in the church, on the ferry to Southwold, and in a local farmhouse. In July 1931, George Orwell, aged 28, and still known by his real name of Eric Blair, was sitting outside the church when he noticed a "small and stooping" man dressed in brown entering the churchyard. Orwell, struck by the fact that the man had made no noise, followed the figure into the churchyard but it had disappeared. As for the pub, a customer named Brenda Marshall noticed one evening a man in old-fashioned fisherman's clothes sitting on an oak bench by the window and staring at her. She turned to catch her husband's attention, but when she looked back the fisherman had disappeared. Her husband also saw the figure and both were convinced it was a ghost. The 600-year-old inn is owned by Adnams of Southwold and sells the full range of the brewery's beers. Accommodation is available.

Grenadier

18 Wilton Row, London SW1 (020 7235 3074)
Underground: Knightsbridge

A Guards officer haunts this Belgravia pub, which was once the mess for the Duke of Wellington's officers: the duke's portrait hangs above the fireplace, and there are other paintings and prints in the pub showing guardsmen of many periods. The ghost in question, whose exploits are described in detail in newspaper cuttings in several languages framed on the walls, is as famous as the pub itself, which is painted a patriotic red, white and blue and stands in a mews that is sealed by a sentry box, bollards and the odd parked Rolls-Royce. The officer was caught cheating at cards in an upstairs room and was given a sound hiding, subsequently falling (or being pushed) downstairs to his death. An investigator of ghosts spoke in the 1950s to the then landlord, Roy Griggs, and his family, who all attested to seeing shapes, shadows and transient blobs, some of which looked like the figure of a man. Later investigators were told by a barman, Tom Westwood, that he was pulling a pint one day when the beer supply was suddenly cut off. He went down to the cellar, where he found the tap in the cask had been turned to cut off the beer. The barman was the only person in the pub at the time who had access to the cellar. Tom Westwood and the landlord's wife described seeing one day a "wisp of smoke" in mid-air in the bar: the ashtrays had all been emptied, nothing was on fire, and there was nobody else in the bar. A few days later, a brewery inspector (a retired CID officer) was standing near the site of the wisp of smoke when he felt a sudden burning sensation on his wrist, on which there appeared a mark as if he had been burnt with a cigarette. Expert ghost and poltergeist investigators believe that what they call "hot spots" are caused by a ghost attempting to materialise by means of ectoplasm. If you need to steady your nerves after this eerie information, the Grenadier serves the best Bloody Mary in London as well as soothing pints of Courage Best and Directors, Marston's Pedigree and Morland Old Speckled Hen from hand-pumps on a pewter-topped bar. There are stools in the tiny bar, a single table outside in the mews, and an intimate restaurant at the back. Bar food, lunchtime and evening, includes nachos, ploughman's, sandwiches, sausage and mash, and fishcakes. There's sometimes a roast lunch on Sundays.

Haunch of Venison

1 Minster Street, Salisbury, Wiltshire (01722 322024)

The Haunch is another ancient inn, one of England's oldest, built in 1320 to offer victuals to the workers constructing St Thomas' Church that stands behind it. The black-beamed and white-painted three-storey inn is opposite the equally ancient Poultry Cross, site of an old chicken market. From the street, you enter the smallest bar in Salisbury: it's more of a lobby, welcoming you into the inner sanctum. It has panelled walls and a large fireplace as well as the serving area with a pewter counter and four hand-pumps for ale, and a bank of taps that dispense fortified wines and spirits by gravity from casks above. The dispense system was installed at the turn of the 20th century by a local plumber for the then owner, the splendidly Dickensian-sounding Bradbeer, a wine and spirit merchant. To the side of the lobby there's a tiny snug that was once a ladies' room. A few steps lead up to a quiet back room with leather settles, a curved oak chair that's nearly 300 years old, a heavily beamed ceiling and another fireplace. The room is known as the House of Lords as it was once used exclusively by bishops. As well as a cabinet containing old clay pipes you can see behind glass the mummified hand of an unfortunate card player who was caught cheating in the 18th century and had his offending limb hacked off: as the London Guards officer in the Grenadier found, cheats do not prosper. The upstairs rooms are quite breathaking in their antiquity. One was formerly owned by an Elizabethan merchant and has an imposing fireplace. The room to the right, now the main restaurant, has some original panelling, a fire certificate from 1836, and a fine view of Poultry Cross. The entire floor has timbered walls and beamed ceilings. This floor is where the ghost is active. She's known as the Lady in White. Landlady Victoria Leroy told me that the ghost has never been seen in her time in the pub, but there are older reports of the woman, wearing a white shawl, being observed from St Thomas' churchyard below. Mrs Leroy and customers are aware of her presence and a pleasant fresh smell "like newly dug earth or washing-up liquid". Fair gives you the shivers. The bar serves fortifying pints of Courage Best and Directors with a guest ale – often Wadworth 6X – plus a good range of wines and around 70 malt whiskies. Bar food includes soup with a sandwich; filled jacket potatoes; filled ciabatta; venison sausages and mash; salmon fillet with spinach and potato galette; and aubergine caviar and mushroom ragoût.

Skirrid Mountain Inn

Llanfihangel Crucorney, Gwent (01873 890258)

Hereford road, off A465, north of Abergavenny

The Skirrid is Wales's oldest inn and one of the most ancient in the whole of Britain. It has not only a long history but a bloody one as well. The origins of the inn can be traced back as far as 1100 when the ill-fated James Crowther was hanged from a beam in the bar for sheep stealing. Over the course of the ensuing centuries, more than 1,800 people have been hanged in the Skirrid, which doubled as the local court-house. Criminals were dispatched by hanging them from a beam above the stairs. The last hanging was in the late 17th century and, like the first, the crime was sheep stealing. The colourful inn has also been at the centre of such violent upheavals as Owain Glyndwr's revolt against the rule of Henry IV in the early 15th century, and the Monmouth Rebellion of the 17th century, when the Duke of Monmouth, the illegitimate son of Charles II, led a rebellion against James II in support of the duke's claim to the throne; he was captured and beheaded (but not in the Skirrid Inn). Not surprisingly, the Skirrid is haunted by many hapless souls who lost their lives there: the rope mark on the beam is clearly visible. Some visitors claim to have had the sensation of a noose around their neck and one woman had the burn marks to prove it. On top of all the violent events in the inn, there's an additional ghost of a soldier from Cromwell's time. The Skirrid has a studded wood door, stone walls and flagstones, a panelled dining room, pews, and a huge log fire. Beers come from Ushers of Trowbridge and include Best Bitter, Founders and a large range of seasonal ales. There's a good choice of wines, too. Food in the bar and restaurant, lunchtime and evening, includes home-made cawl (lamb stew); alehouse pie; local Dexter roast beef; and Crucorney trout. The Skirrid offers accommodation and is based in fine walking country that takes in the Black Mountains.

Grapes Hotel

Maentwrog, North-west Wales (01766 590208)
A496, just off A487

Perhaps it's not surprising that the Grapes is haunted, given its great age. It's a 17th-century former coaching inn and Grade-II listed building where Lloyd George and Lillie Langtry were both recorded as having taken tea here, but not together (though Lloyd George may have known her father). But the Grapes' main claim to fame is that it has two ghosts. One is an old lady in Victorian clothes who operates below stairs and a piano player who tinkles the ivories in a rather pallid way on the residents' landing. In spite of the ghouls, the Grapes is a remarkably cheerful place where you are guaranteed a warm welcome from locals, even though they may speak in Welsh. From the verandah and walled garden you can glimspe the Ffestiniog Steam Railway chuffing along. There are three bars inside with pews and settles rescued from a local chapel and welcome log fires in large fireplaces. The public bar, where cribbage and dominoes are played, has a large collection of brass blowlamps. This is an ale drinker's inn with a 30-strong list of cask beers mainly from Welsh independents that complement such regulars as Draught Bass, Morland Old Speckled Hen and Tomos Watkin Whoosh. Bar food and restaurant meals, lunchtime and evening, may include soup; sandwiches; lentil and wild mushroom medley; vegetable korma; cannelloni; lamb dopiaza; lamb chops with leek and Stilton sauce; tandoori chicken; and daily fresh fish. Desserts may include treacle sponge. Children are welcome in the restaurant. Accommodation is available: if you stay, don't forget to say, "Play it again, Sam" to the rather wan pianist on the landing.

Pubs near haunted buildings

BUCKINGHAMSHIRE ARMS

BLICKLING ROAD, BLICKLING, NORFOLK (01263 732133)

From Cromer follow A140 on to B1354 at Aylsham

A Jacobean coaching inn dating from 1693, the Buckinghamshire Arms was first built to house guests and servants for Blickling Hall: the pub is at the entrance to the hall and both are run by the National Trust. Blickling Hall is reputed to be haunted by Anne Boleyn (1507-36), the ill-fated second wife to Henry VIII and mother of Elizabeth I, who was executed on one of Fat Hal's trumped-up charges of adultery. The unspoilt pub has a small snug at the front and a larger bar with stripped wood tables, pews, an open fire in winter and old Spy cartoons on the walls. There's a spacious garden with tables: food is served from a building on the lawn in summer. Bar meals and evening restaurant meals may include home-made soup; open sandwiches or baguettes with a choice of fillings; grilled trout; rocket and Parmesan risotto; ploughman's; home-made steak and kidney pie; fried puy lentils with chorizo and salad; and traditional Norfolk treacle tart. There's a good choice of wine while hand-pumped beers include Adnams Best Bitter and Woodforde's Wherry from Woodbastwick, which also brews a house beer called Blickling. Children are not allowed inside the pub, where such traditional pub games as cribbage and shove-ha'penny are played. Accommodation is available. Blickling Hall (with a large collection of books and a famous downstairs kitchen) and gardens (herbaceous and mixed borders, great display of trees in autumn) are open Wednesday to Sunday.

Coach & Horses

Buckland Brewer, Devon (01237 451395)

Take A386 then A388 from Bideford; village signposted from main road

A thatched inn dating from the 15th century, the Coach & Horses was later used as a staging post and retreat by Royalists during the Civil War. The pub has been run by the Wolfe family for many years and they are dedicated to maintaining its ancient charm and tradition. It's a good watering hole for visits to Buckland Abbey, home to the famous sea dogs and scourge of the Spanish, Sir Francis Drake and Sir Richard Grenville. The abbey is reputed to be haunted by Drake and the fearsome Hounds of Hell. The pub has two bars, plus a small back room available for children. The bars have massive oak beams, an antique settle and two inglenooks. There's a strong emphasis on pub games, with a skittle alley, darts and cribbage. Hand-pumped ales include Flowers Original, Fuller's London Pride and Wadworth 6X. Bar food and restaurant meals may include home-made soup; sandwiches; ploughman's; fish pie; fresh fish; a choice of home-made curries; and liver and bacon. In good weather visitors can enjoy a drink and a meal on a front terrace or a side garden. Accommodation is available.

Ship

Mousehole, Cornwall (01736 731234)

Off A30; take coast road from Penzance; signposted from B3315

An old fishermen's inn with granite flagstones, low beams and panelled walls, the Ship is just a short drive from St Michael's Mount at Marazion. The fortified mount, set on a rocky island and reached by a causeway at low tide, is a scaled-down version of Mont St Michel in north-west France. The communities at both places were founded by monks but the buildings were used as prisons as a result of their remote positions. St Michael's Mount is said to be haunted by a seven-foot tall former prisoner. Back on the mainland, the Ship, set by the harbour and at the heart of an attractive village, offers a plethora of old photos, sailor's ropework and an open fire in the beamed and wood-panelled bar. There are tasty local ales from the St Austell Brewery, including Bosun's Bitter, Tinners Ale, Trelawny's Pride and HSD. Bar food and evening restaurant meals always include fresh fish and sea food caught at Newlyn, such as crab bisque; seafood platter and smoked mackerel with salad and brown bread; mussel;, plus pork and cider casserole and Thai turkey. On 23 December the pub produces Starry Gazy Pie to commemorate a brave attempt by local Tom Bawcock to rescue fishermen caught in a terrible storm out at sea; the day is known as Tom Bawcock's Eve. Children are welcome in areas away from the bar. Accommodation is available.

Sawley Arms

Sawley, North Yorkshire (01765 620642)
Off B6265 near Ripon; off A1

A stone-built pub with a magnificent array of hanging baskets and tubs, urns and pots by the porched entrance, the Sawley Arms is a good base for Fountains Abbey, a short walk away, which is reputed to be haunted by an entire choir of monks. When abbeys brewed before the dissolution (that man Henry VIII again), Fountains had a malthouse that was 60 square feet in size and it produced 60 barrels of strong ale every 10 days. Today you will have to make do with Theakston's Best and John Smith's Bitter in the Sawley Arms, which has been run for close on 30 years by June Hawes, who has imposed a powerful emphasis on home-cooked, no-nonsense English food. The pub has four small, comfortable rooms with log fires, armchairs, dining chairs and settees. Two rooms plus the restaurant are smoke-free. Bar meals and restaurant meals may include the likes of salmon mousse; sandwiches; leek and coconut soup; Stilton port and celery pâté; halibut steak and prawn and white wine sauce; sauté breast of chicken in mushroom and herb sauce; and plaice Mornay, plus bread and butter pudding and apple pie. There's a good choice of wines by the glass. Children over nine are welcome and accommodation is available. Fountains Abbey is floodlit on Friday and Saturday evenings in summer and a live choir – standing in for the ghostly choir of monks – performs on Saturday evenings.

Ship Inn

Low Newton by the Sea, Northumberland (01665 576262)
Off A1 and Northumberland Coast Road

Lindisfarne Castle on Lindisfarne or Holy Island is another haunt of disgruntled monks, where St Cuthbert and other brethren are said to appear from time to time. Like St Michael's Mount, Lindisfarne is joined to the mainland by a causeway at low tide; attempting to get back to the mainland in a car as the waters roll towards you is a frightening experience. If you make it back safely, a short and pleasant drive along the coast road brings you to the Ship at Low Newton, which stands by the beach in a small fishing village, packed with yachts in summer. The inn is a friendly, unspoilt fisherman's local that offers Ruddles Best Bitter and simple bar food lunchtime and evening such as crab sandwiches, toasted sandwiches and home-made apple pie. As Greene King acquired Ruddles in 1999, it's possible that the regular beer may change. On Lindisfarne itself, the Ship is highly recommended, with beams, wood panelling, seafood and vegetarian dishes and accommodation, but cask beers from the Border Brewery are only available in summer.

Snooty Fox

Main Street, Kirkby Lonsdale, Cumbria (01524 271308)
B6254, off M6

The Snooty Fox is a white-painted, listed Jacobean inn at the heart of an old Westmorland town. It's handy for visiting Sizergh Castle, which has wonderful gardens, with noted herbaceous borders, a great show of foliage in autumn and, just to keep it cuddly, a resident poltergeist given to throwing things around a bit. The Fox offers a number of small, comfortable bars, with wooden tables, pews, high-backed settles and armchairs, coloured engravings and old beer mugs hanging from the beamed ceilings, plus a lot of agricultural, horse-riding and (less pleasant) hunting memorabilia, including a stuffed fox. The bar counters are fashioned from English oak. There are tables outside on a terrace and in a garden with a children's play area. An excellent range of hand-pumped ales includes Hartley's XB, Tim Taylor's Landlord and Theakston Best, with a good choice of international wines, several by the glass. Bar meals and restaurant meals, lunchtime and evening, offer home-made soup, filled jacket potatoes; savoury vegetarian tagine with minted yoghurt; ragoût of monkfish and scallops with Noilly Prat and baby vegetables; Cumberland sausage; steak and kidney pudding; pork tenderloin; and crispy duck pancakes. Children are welcome in the dining room, which has a no-smoking area. Accommodation is available.

Note: *All the haunted buildings are owned by the National Trust. For information about opening hours and prices phone 020 8315 1111.*

Best of the Rest

Bottle House Inn

Smart's Hill, Penshurst, Kent (01892 870306)
Off B23188

Fordwich Arms

King Street, Fordwich, Kent (01227 710444)
Off A28, near Canterbury

Miners Arms

Water Lane, Eyam, Derbyshire (01433 630853)
Off B6521 near Bakewell

Swan

123 High Street, Brentwood, Essex (01277 2118480
Off A128

George

High Street, Dorchester-on-Thames, Oxfordshire
(01865 340404)
Off A4074

Stars of TV, film and radio

KINGS ARMS

ASKRIGG, NORTH YORKSHIRE (01969 650258)
Off A684 Sedbergh to Bedale road

The back bar of the inn is called the Drovers Bar in homage to the Drovers Arms in the television series *All Creatures Great and Small,* based on James Herriot's celebrated novels about his adventures as a vet in Wensleydale. The choice of the inn is fitting, for it was built in 1760 as stables for John Pratt's celebrated racehorses, and was converted into a public house and hotel in the early 19th century, when it was an important coaching inn on the Richmond to Lancaster route. The Kings Arms has many rooms, including the Club Room, which serves five-course meals, and the Silks Room, which specialises in steak and chops. A cosy front bar has wood panels, beams and an open fire. Bar food may include such local specialities as panhaggerty, which is pan-fried ham and spring onion potato cake, pork cutlet on sage and onion stuffing with prune and brandy sauce, feather fowlie, a soup of vegetables, pearl barley and chicken, peat bog, which is shepherd's pie with black pudding and oatmeal, and steak in Wensleydale sauce. Desserts may include hot chocolate pudding or bread and butter pudding. Children's meals are also available. Beers include Dents Bitter, Theakston's XB and John Smith's Bitter. There's a good wine list with several by the glass. The inn is handy for Aysgarth Falls and Castle Bolton, and offers accommodation.

WHITE HORSE INN

SCHOLES ROAD, JACKSON BRIDGE, WEST YORKSHIRE (01484 683940)
Off A616 near Holmfirth

Jackson Bridge is in the heart of *Last of the Summer Wine* country. This cheery and welcoming pub features in the long-running saga of Yorkshire ne'er-do-wells, and its walls are adorned with a vast array of stills and memorabilia from the series. But it's more than just a television prop: it's a real local, with open fires, a games room with darts and dominoes, and a large garden. Food is simple pub fare and Tetley Bitter is served by hand-pump. The pub is popular with walkers and hikers, and offers accommodation.

Salisbury

90 St Martin's Lane, London WC2 (020 7836 5863)
Underground: Leicester Square

This celebrated theatreland pub, which is packed with ornate glasswork and Art Nouveau bronze statuettes, appeared (renamed the Shaftesbury) in the 1960s film *Victim*, starring Dirk Bogarde. It was the first British film to deal sympathetically with homosexuality. Bogarde, who played a barrister, was blackmailed as a result of his double life. The Salisbury started life as a tavern called the Coach and Horses, and was renamed the Salisbury Stores in 1866: the term "stores" indicated that take-home beer sales of alcohol were available. In 1892, the building was pulled down and replaced with one of the last great Victorian gin palaces. It remains a brilliant example of the style, with its sumptuous etched glass, mirrors, bronze nymphs, and mahogany back bar. There are seats on the pavement in good weather. Bar snacks are available from noon until 7.30pm, and beers are from the Scottish Courage range, including John Smith's and Theakston's.

Magpie and Stump

18 Old Bailey, London EC4 (020 7248 5085)
Underground: St Paul's

This famous old London chop house was badly damaged in a bomb blast in the vicinity of the Old Bailey, and it took several years to restore it. The pub featured regularly in John Mortimer's long-running television saga about the irascible but lovable lawyer Rumpole. Sadly, the owners have modernised the upstairs rooms that help give the pub its grisly name. Before the Old Bailey was built, the area was the site of Newgate Prison, and, until public executions were abolished in 1868, the gentry used to pay £10 to view them from the first floor of the inn, enjoying the spectacle as crowds of up to 40,000 assembled below. The name of the inn was extended to include the word "stump" as a horrible pun on the hapless and headless victims of the executioner's axe. The two-roomed, wood-panelled inn still has high-back settles and leaded windows, and is a haunt of lawyers and their clients from the courts opposite. It serves such pub fare as bangers and mash, Cajun chicken, mozzarella and tomato salad, and burgers. Beers include Fuller's London Pride and the Czech lager Staropramen. The inn is closed at weekends.

Old Bull

Inkberrow, Worcestershire (01386 792428)
A422 Worcester to Alcester road

The bulging, half-timbered walls of this 16th-century inn seem to defy gravity, but the Old Bull is likely to last for a century or two more, or certainly for as long as *The Archers* runs on Radio 4, as it's the model for the Bull in Ambridge. As well as high-back settles, flagstones and oak beams, there are photographs of the actors in the radio soap and cart-loads of Archers' memorabilia. It's claimed that Shakespeare

once stayed here, but he plays second fiddle to the saga of the Grundys, the Gabriels and the rest of the bucolic grizzlers. The pub signs and an inscription on one beam promise Flower & Sons ales from Stratford-on-Avon, but the beers today come from Whitbread. They include Flowers IPA and Original, but they're brewed at the Boddingtons factory in Manchester: Whitbread despatched the Stratford brewery many moons ago. There are guest ales, such as Banks's Bitter and Marston's Pedigree but, sadly for Archers fans, no Shires Bitter. There's food lunchtime and evening, except Sunday evening, and includes soup, sandwiches, ploughman's, lasagne, and curries, with a Sunday roast lunch.

Best of the Rest

MALLYAN SPOUT HOTEL

GOATHLAND, NORTH YORKSHIRE
features in Heartbeat

JOLLY SAILOR

BURSLEDON, HAMPSHIRE (023 8040 5557)
featured in Howard's Way

Notes: *The Rovers Return in* Coronation Street *is not a real pub, but the three-sided building is open to visitors on the set of the Granada telvision studios complex in Manchester, complete with 'Newton & Ridley' beer.*

Inspector Morse's Favourite Pubs follows this section

Opposite: The White Horse, Jackson Bridge

Inspector Morse's Favourite Pubs

Kings Arms

40 Holywell Street, Oxford (01865 242369)

The Kings Arms had a special appeal for the sadly expired sleuth, as the Dons Bar thoughtfully provides a dictionary for the use of crossword addicts: Morse got annoyed if he failed to finish *The Times'* crossword in less than ten minutes. The spacious pub has a rambling warren of rooms, some of them with the feel of a gentlemen's club with their comfortable sofas and muted lighting. There's a large main bar, a smoke-free coffee room, and two tiny rooms at the back, while the Dons Bars has a tiled floor. The walls are decorated with ancient prints and photos of illustrious customers. In good weather there are tables on the pavement where on Sunday you can read the newspapers and take breakfast from 10.30am. Ales to suit the taste of the bibulous detective include Young's Bitter and Special plus the London brewery's seasonal beers, and a guest beer such as Wadworth 6X. There's an excellent choice of wines, with around 20 available by the glass, a good selection of malt whiskies (Morse enjoyed a Glenfiddich or two) while the bar food includes the likes of soup, sandwiches, filled jacket potatoes, beef and mushroom pie, curry, and spinach and mushroom lasagne. (Food in this section is mentioned for normal human beings: in pubs, Morse's watchword was "nae solids".)

Turf Tavern

4 Bath Place, off Holywell Street, Oxford (01865 243235)

The Turf is breathtakingly ancient, looking even older than its 17th-century origins. On winter evenings the three flagstoned or gravelled courtyards that form outside drinking areas are warmed by flaming braziers, adding to the antiquity of an ale house tucked away down an alley and surrounded by high stone walls and other venerable buildings, including part of Oxford's original city walls. Inside, the Turf has a series of small rooms with beams, low ceilings and head-crackingly low doors. The pub has scarcely changed a jot since Thomas Hardy drank there and used it in *Jude the Obscure*: Jude discovered that the barmaid, Arabella, was the wife who'd abandoned him years before. It's a melancholy note that would appeal to the morose Morse. With a splendid range of hand-pumped beers – Archers Golden, Flowers Original, Morland Old Speckled Hen, and five or six guests – it's not surprising that the Turf was the local Camra Pub of the Year for 1999. You'll also find some farm ciders and a good choice of Belgian beers. The bar food is simple and straightforward: sandwiches, ploughman's, filled jacket potatoes and steak in ale pie.

Perch

BINSEY LANE, BINSEY, OXFORD (01865 240386)

The Perch is on the outskirts of the city and is best reached by punt. By foot, visitors can walk across Port Meadow and cross a footbridge over the river. It was first recorded in the 15th century but it's much older and was popular with pilgrims on their way to the Church of St Mary in Binsey, which has a well with alleged magical healing powers. The ales in the Perch – Adnams Best, Marston's Pedigree and Old Speckled Hen plus a regular guest beer – have similar recuperative powers. You can sample them in this wonderful old inn with its thatched roof and porch, a bar with flagstones and beams, two log-burning stoves, a family room and a conservatory that leads to a spacious garden that stretches down to the river. Excellent food, lunchtime and evening, includes home-made soups; jacket potatoes and baguettes with a choice of fillings; steak and ale pie; vegetable platter; and daily specials that include a good range of vegetarian dishes – mushroom Stroganoff; vegetable Kiev; and veggie burgers – plus several fresh fish choices, chicken and mushroom pie, char-grilled salmon, and seafood pastry cases. As well as the ubiquitous Morse, the Perch was popular with Lewis Carroll, who read early drafts of *Alice's Adventures in Wonderland* to friends in the garden: we shall meet writer and sleuth again in the next inn...

Trout Inn

195 GODSTOW ROAD, LOWER WOLVERCOTE (01865 302071)

This inn featured so often in TV versions of *Morse* that it even has a bar named after him. It's also listed in the Thames Walk in this guide, but its second appearance gives the opportunity to expand on its fascinating location and history. To reach the Trout by road, drive north from Oxford along the A40, take the turning for Wolvercote and drive through the village to the Thamesside inn where you may be greeted by peacocks as you descend a stone terrace. Water cascades over a weir, fish leap from the water, and in the distance there's a tremendous view of the Oxford skyline. A rustic bridge leads to an island with a Victorian garden, arbours, stone statues and a sun dial. Inside the Trout there's a stone-flagged bar with lots of polished pewter and an ancient spit roaster driven by a clock mechanism above an enormous stone fireplace. There's a small parlour with oak seats, and an oak-beamed restaurant with a carved Jacobean bedstead behind the bar. The inn is knee-deep in history: Henry II's mistress, the Fair Rosamund, stayed in a nunnery close to the Trout. When the king was in residence in the inn, he would wave a lamp from his bedroom window and Rosamund would travel through a tunnel to spend the night with him: the tunnel comes up behind the bar in the modern restaurant.

The Turf Tavern, Oxford

The Queen, Eleanor of Aquitaine, discovered the king's infidelity, and, with the aid of a lamp, lured Rosamund to the inn. As she came out of the tunnel, she was seized by the queen's men-at-arms and taken upstairs to be killed. She was offered the choice of poison or the knife, and chose poison. Sad woman, even after she was buried, her body was dug up from its grave and thrown on the river bank. Her ring, now in the Ashmolean in Oxford, was found on the island in the river alongside the inn. Her headstone can be seen in a wall in Wolvercote. Rosamund's ghost is reputed to haunt the inn. She is said to walk the upper rooms and garden of the Trout. She has been seen in a bedroom but visible only from the knees up, for her ghost is walking the original floor, two feet below the present level. Centuries later, Lewis Carroll used to bring the real-life Alice to the Trout and take her punting on the river. The original inn was destroyed by Henry VIII while he was abolishing the monasteries but was soon rebuilt, using the stone from the ruined Godstow Abbey. Today, the ale Sergeant Lewis bought for Morse is Draught Bass while food may include the likes of breaded whole-tail scampi; lamb with white onion sauce; or roasted vegetable upside-down pie.

White Hart at Wytham

(01865 244372)

Signposted from A34 north of Botley

The White Hart takes its name from a badge awarded by Richard II to his troops following the Battle of Radcot Bridge in 1390. The attractive, creeper-clad pub (often featured in the TV *Morse*) is in a charming village with preserved thatched buildings owned by the university. The bar has flagstones, partly panelled walls, some high-back settles that run round most of the walls, two log fires (one with a hart in relief on the fireback) and a second no-smoking room. There are seats in a garden, where the old rural game of Aunt Sally is played. Beers include Adnams Best, Morland Old Speckled Hen and a regular guest ale. Bar food may include ploughman's; bread and pâté; jacket potatoes with a choice of fillings; vegetable Kiev; a good range of fish (trout, tuna and salmon); beef in ale pie; and grilled chicken.

Pubs with Dickens connections

Ye Olde King's Head

High Road, Chigwell, Essex (020 8500 2021)
A113; off M11

This ancient tavern has a 40-foot newel pole cut from forest pine that rises from ground floor to attic and inspired Charles Dickens to call the inn the Maypole in *Barnaby Rudge*. Dickens described it as an "old building with its huge zigzag chimneys and more gable-ends than a lazy man would care to count on a sunny day." The gable ends lean gently toward the wooden spire of the village church across the narrow road in a village in the Roding Valley that lies between the two ancient forests of Epping and Hainault. The coaching inn dates from the 17th century and records show it was serving good brown ale and haunches of forest venison to travellers in Tudor and Stuart times. But its origins are even earlier: old timbers in the inn show the adze marks of 15th-century craftsmanship. At the time of Elizabeth I and James I, the inn was used for the sittings of the Forty Days' Courts, which were held to settle disputes between the forest people and landowners. The great lattice-windowed upper room in which the courts were held is now the inn's dining room. Since Dickens wrote *Barnaby Rudge* in 1840, the dining room with its panelled walls has been known as the Chester Room, for the author used it for a scene in the book involving Sir John Chester. On the pavement outside the main entrance of the King's Head are great whitewashed stone balls. They are mounting blocks used by travellers to hoist themselves into their saddles or on to the roof seats of coaches. The inn also has Dick Turpin connections. The robber would often call in for a pot of ale to pick up news of impending coaches. It's claimed that some of his pistols lie within the walls of the inn, but they have never been found. The opening of a tunnel in the inn's cellar used to run under the road to the church and was used by Turpin to escape from his pursuers. A Dickens Suite to one side of the King's Head was built in 1901 by the then landlord to mark his daughter's 21st birthday. The inn is now owned by Scottish and Newcastle, the country's biggest brewing group. Food comes from a carvery that always has three joints on offer as well as vegetarian options. Hand-pumped beers are Courage Directors and Theakston's Best, plus an occasional guest ale.

Grapes

76 Narrow Street, London E14 (020 7987 4396)
DLR: Westferry; Underground: Shadwell

As well as Dickens, the Grapes has other artistic connections. Rex Whistler loved the old pub and came here regularly to paint the River Thames flowing past, while a splendid oil painting called "Saturday Night at the Grapes" by Alice M. West, which was exhibited at the Royal Academy in 1949, now hangs in the bar. There's been an ale house on the site since the 16th century but much of the area was destroyed by fire, and the present pub

Ye Olde King's Head, Chigwell, Essex

dates from 1720. It was used by Dickens for an inn called the Six Jolly Fellowship Porters in *Our Mutual Friend*, where he described it as having "not a straight floor and hardly a straight line, but it had outlasted and would yet outlast many a better-trimmed building, many a sprucer public house." In the novel, but not necessarily in real life, drink-sodden customers were rowed out to the middle of the river, drowned, and their corpses sold to anatomists for dissection. On a more cheerful note, the fictional version of the Grapes, almost certainly mirroring the real thing, sold hot purl, which was porter ale sweetened and spiced, heated in an iron funnel placed in the fire, and finally fortified with gin. Hot alcoholic drinks were common in Dickens' time, and

warmed workers, such as market porters and those who worked on the river. The tiny exterior of the Grapes, decked with hanging baskets, and with a frosted glass motif in the windows, leads into a small, half-panelled bar with cream-painted walls covered with paintings. There's a short bar counter with a small seating area, beyond which a couple of steps lead up to a terrace with large windows overlooking the Thames. The beers on offer are Adnams Best, Tetley Bitter and Ind Coope Burton Ale, with a regular guest beer. Bar food includes soup, sandwiches, bangers and mash, and fishcakes. Upstairs, there's a celebrated fish restaurant, where it's essential to book. When I wrote about the Grapes in a book called *Best Pubs in London* in 1989, I mentioned that Dr David Owen, founder of the Social Democratic Party, lived in a converted warehouse next door. The Grapes, I said, "is likely to outlast his splinter party". It's comforting to be right now and again.

Dirty Dick's

202 Bishopsgate, London EC2 (020 7283 5888)
Train and Underground: Liverpool Street

Dirty Dick's inspired Dickens to create the grotesque Miss Haversham in *Great Expectations*. She is based on a successful ironmonger and London dandy named Nathaniel Bentley, who lived at 46 Leadenhall Street. On the day he was due to marry, his wife-to-be fell ill and died. So grief-stricken was Bentley that he locked the room where the wedding breakfast was laid out and never went into it again. Bentley allowed his own appearance to fall apart. He stopped washing or changing his clothes, he didn't clean his shop, and neither did he bury his cats when they died. He had hoped to pine away and join his ill-fated fiancée, but life can be cruel, and, despite the filth, he lived to a ripe old age. Customers crowded his shop, expecting to find bargains among the grime. When Bentley finally died in 1819, the landlord of the Old Port Wine Shop in Bishopsgate bought the ironmongers and its contents, and moved them to his public house, which he renamed Dirty Dick's. Even when the pub was pulled down in 1870, the mummified cats, cobwebs and other grisly memorabilia were kept for its replacement. Fashions change and when Young's bought the pub it decided to clean away most of the grime, though the odd dead cat has remained: brewers are fond of cats as they catch mice and rats that would otherwise eat precious stores of barley. The dimly-lit ground floor bar has stripped wood, bar timbers and comfortable, intimate side alcoves, with the walls stripped back to their original brick. A barley twist staircase leads up to a wine bar and restaurant, while a separate entrance takes you down to another bar in the cellars. The ales are the impeccable Wandsworth brews of Bitter and Special and seasonal beers. There are good bar snacks and restaurant meals at lunchtime.

Olde Cheshire Cheese

Wine Office Court, off 145 Fleet Street, London EC4
(020 7353 6170/020 7353 4388)
Underground: Blackfriars

Fleet Street, the infamous "Street of Shame" when it housed the newspaper industry and such legendary figures as the real-life proprietors Lords Beaverbrook and Harmsworth, and the fictional Lord Copper of the Daily Beast, has long gone to greenfield sites and Docklands. But this remarkable old inn remains, almost lost up a tiny side alley that housed the Royal Excise until the Great Fire of 1666. The Cheshire Cheese, with its circular inn sign and sash windows, has a warren of small rooms, arranged higgledy-piggledy over the three storeys of a smoke-blackened building with sawdust on the floors, and blazing fires and ranges. The site is ancient, built in 1667 after the Great Fire on the site of the monastery of the White Friars. The cellars that survived the fire were excellent for storing casks of ale: the stone-vaulted cellar has a blocked tunnel that once led down to the Thames. In 1748 the esteemed lexicographer Dr Samuel Johnson moved virtually next door to 17 Gough Square. Curiously, there's no record of Johnson drinking there, but perhaps, as it was his local, the faithful Boswell didn't bother to mention it. Other literary luminaries who certainly did sup in the Cheshire Cheese include Congreve, Chesterton, Belloc, Pope, Voltaire, Thackeray, Conan Doyle, and Yeats as well as Dickens, who mentioned it in *A Tale of Two Cities*. They wouldn't notice many changes today, for fiercely traditional Yorkshire brewer Samuel Smith doesn't believe in mucking around with old buildings, and couldn't anyway make many changes as it's a listed and protected building. It has narrow, winding wooden staircases, crowded corridors, beer served through hatches, and three restaurants serving the likes of steak and kidney pie, roast beef, and nursery puddings. Downstairs there's an oak-beamed bar with an ancient flagstone floor and equally old wooden settles. The one hand-pumped ale is Sam Smith's Old Brewery Bitter.

Morritt Arms

Greta Bridge Co Durham. (01833 627232)
Off A66 near Scotch Corner

Arriving on a snow-bound night in 1838 on the London-Carlisle coach with Hablot K. Browne, better known as Phiz the illustrator, Dickens described the Morritt Arms as "the best inn I have ever put up at," and praised the gargantuan breakfast of "toast, cakes, a Yorkshire pie, a piece of beef about the size and much the shape of my portmanteau, tea, coffee, ham and eggs." Dickens and Browne were in the area to carry out research for *Nicholas Nickleby*, and the writer renamed it the George and New Inn in the novel. To commemorate his visit, the bar was named the Dickens Bar with, somewhat perversely, murals depicting characters from *Pickwick Papers*. They were painted in 1946 by the artist J.V. Gilroy, best known for his celebrated Guinness advertisements. A second bar is named the Walter Scott bar, for this famous writer also stayed here. The bars have open fires, oak settles and views of the extensive gardens. A good range of ales includes Black Sheep Best, Castle Eden Conciliation Ale, Tim Taylor Landlord and Tetley Bitter. Bar food, lunchtime and evening, includes such soups as broccoli and five cream cheese; sandwiches; prawns with spicy tomato mayonnaise; vegetable stir fry; and roast beef. There are also full meals in the upstairs Copperfield Restaurant, with a good range of New World wines. Children are welcome and accommodation is available.

Best of the Rest

Ship Hotel

Main Street, Allonby, Cumbria
Dickens stayed here with Wilkie Collins in 1857 while they collaborated on the Lazy Tour of Two Idle Apprentices.

Note: *See also the* **Spaniards Inn**, *London, NW3 (p.368), in the* Hampstead Pub Walk section. *In* Pickwick Papers, *Dickens used the inn for a scene in which Mrs Bardell was arrested as she took tea in the garden; she had failed to pay the costs of her breach-of-promise case with Mr Pickwick.*

Pubs with literary connections

WINDMILL

CLAPHAM COMMON SOUTH SIDE, LONDON SW4 (020 8673 4578)
Underground: Clapham South

I can't vouch with total certainty that the Pontefract Arms in Graham Greene's *The End of the Affair* was based on the Windmill. But the novel was set on Clapham Common during and just after World War Two, and the narrator, Bendrix (based on Greene himself) visits the Pontefract Arms on the Common several times, with his mistress Sarah, and her husband Henry, who was a leading civil servant. Given the decidedly upper middle class nature of the characters, it's likely they would have used a smart, upmarket hostelry rather than a basic boozer and the Windmill is the outstanding pub in the area. An inn has stood on the site since 1665 when the first alehouse keeper, Thomas Crenshaw, was also a miller with a windmill on the Common. The present inn is Victorian and is based on the site of the home of the founder of Young's Brewery in Wandsworth. The centre point is a spacious lounge with open fires, comfortable seating, a domed ceiling, wood-panelled walls and old prints, many with a windmill theme. The semi-circular bar serves the front section and a smaller area at the rear that includes a 19th-century painting showing the Prince Consort, the Duke of Wellington and Lord Palmerston celebrating in the original inn after a day at the races. At the time the Windmill stood on a coaching route that linked south London with Epsom Downs, where the Derby is held. There's a second large lounge where food is served lunchtime and evening and offers sandwiches; filled baguettes; burgers and salads; and steak and ale pie. The handpumped beers include Young's Bitter and Special plus seasonal brews. In good weather, drinkers spill out on the Common to eat and drink. Children are welcome in designated areas and first-class accommodation is available.

GEORGE INN

HUBBERHOLME, NORTH YORKSHIRE (01756 760223)
Village signposted from Buckden on B6160

The George was the favourite pub of that dour, pipe-smoking, ruminative and archetypal Yorkshireman, J.B. Priestley: his ashes were scattered in the churchyard on the other side of the bridge that crosses the river Wharf, which rises to the surface nearby. The hamlet of Hubberholme, named after the Viking King Hubba, stands at more than 1,900 feet on a road that links Fleet Moss and Hawes. The George has developed from buildings that were once a farm and a vicarage. It has two stone-flagged rooms with mullioned windows, heavy oak beams, bare stone walls and an open stove standing in a large fireplace. The ales include Theakston's Black Bull and XB, and Younger's Scotch, and there is a good range of malt whiskies and wines. Bar snacks and restaurant meals include soup and sandwiches; pasta with tomatoes, mushrooms and creamy cheese topping; mussels in garlic and cream; lamb and apricot pie; pan-fried breast of duck; moussaka; and peppered steak. There are tables outside with fine views of the moors and Wharfedale. The local church is famous for carvings by "Mouseman" Thompson. The George has seven bedrooms.

Butt & Oyster

Pin Mill, Suffolk (01473 780764)

Signposted from Chelmondiston on B1456, south-east of Ipswich

Arthur Ransome may be best known for his children's novels set in Lakeland but for my money *We Didn't Mean To Go To Sea* is the most dramatic and nail-biting of his books. It is set around Pin Mill and the River Orwell, and there are several references to the Butt & Oyster, the 17th-century whitewashed inn that is the centre of community life in this tiny hamlet. The pub is a genuine local for the folk who earn their living on the Orwell in their barges and wherries, and who rub shoulders at the bar with weekend yachting types. At low tide you can stroll down the causeway alongside the pub and stand between the large sailing vessels moored there. Inside the Butt & Oyster there is an enormous bowed window with views of the far wooded shore of the river which, at high tide, laps just below. The bar has flagstoned floors, high-backed settles, an open log fire and wood-panelled walls decorated by model sailing ships and old tobacco advertisements. From behind the long counter landlord Dick Mainwaring serves the full range of Tolly Cobbold ales from Ipswich. There are lunchtime sandwiches and ploughman's while a separate restaurant area beyond the main bar serves the likes of tuna and mushroom crumble; seafood Provençal; or Normandy pork. There is a weekend buffet, seats outside and a family room indoors.

Hill House

Happisburgh, Norfolk (01692 650004)
Off B1159

You approach the coastal village of Happisburgh (pronounced Hazeboro) down a pencil-straight road through poppy fields guarded by the tall tower of St Mary the Virgin and a red-and-white striped lighthouse like an outsize barber shop pole. The village is named after a dangerous sandbank off the coast. The Hill House, with an attractive whitewashed, dormered and red-tiled exterior, dates from the 16th century, when it was known as the Windmill, and became the Hill House in 1710. It was a favourite watering hole of Sir Arthur Conan Doyle, who wrote some of the Sherlock Holmes stories there: the inn still offers accommodation. It has heavy beams, an inglenook with a wood-burning stove and an open fire at opposite ends of the main bar, and a games area with bar billiards. There are good pub snacks and full meals in a dining area where children are welcome. Beers include Adnams and Shepherd Neame.

Sherlock Holmes

10 Northumberland Avenue, corner of Craven Passage, London WC2 (020 7930 2644)
Underground: Charing Cross, Embankment

After the Hill House for starters, this is the Full Monty for Holmesian memorabilia. Conan Doyle's face and name are engraved in the windows and there is a plethora of playbills and cinema and TV stills showing the many actors that have played Holmes and Watson, including the peerless Basil Rathbone as the great detective. Exhibits in cases include an awesome head of the Baskerville hound, Victorian police whistles, poison bottles, a magnifying glass, and a picture of the long-suffering landlady of Baker Street, Mrs Hudson. Her name is also enshrined above the food area, where hot dishes include macaroni cheese (a favourite dish of Dr Moriarty) and other standard pub fare. An upstairs restaurant is a brilliant recreation of Holmes's study, with booklined walls and a model of the detective. Beers include Boddingtons, Brakspear and Flowers. The pub was turned into a Holmes shrine for the 1951 Festival of Britain. If you wonder why it's near Charing Cross and not Baker Street then you're not a true Holmes' buff, for it was in the Northumberland Hotel opposite (now the War Office) that the detective first met Sir Henry Baskerville.

Tibbie Shiels Inn

St Mary's Loch, Borders, Scotland (01750 42231)
Off A708

Tibbie Shiels is an ancient inn in a breathtaking setting by the shores of St Mary's Loch and close to the Grey Mare's Tail waterfall and the Southern Upland Way footpath. It is named after Isabella (Tibbie) Shiels, the wife of a mole catcher who worked for the local landlord, Lord Napier, in the 18th century. Napier established Tibbie in the little cottage by the loch to run an inn for travellers. The pub was visited regularly by Sir Walter Scott and James Hogg, the shepherd poet of Ettrick, who befriended Tibbie. The Edinburgh *literati* regularly trekked to the isolated tavern. The back bar in the stone-built part of the inn is original. There are excellent bar snacks and full meals, including warming soups, stovies and cloutie dumpling pudding, Yarrow trout and a good selection of vegetarian dishes. Ales are from Belhaven and Broughton. Accommodation is available and the inn is popular with sailors, fishermen, walkers and bird watchers.

Tower Bank Arms

Near Sawrey, Cumbria (015394 36334)
B5285

The Tower Bank backs on to Beatrix Potter's home, Hill Top Farm (now owned by the National Trust) and also features in *The Tale of Jemima Puddle-Duck*: the wise old collie got the help of two foxhounds outside the pub and they went off to rescue the silly bird from the elegant gentleman with the sandy whiskers. The pub is a delight and wonderfully unspoilt: it has beams, a log fire in a cooking range, settles on a slate floor and a grandfather clock. Pub games, including darts, shove ha'penny, dominoes and shut-the-box, are played. Food comes in the form of lunchtime bar snacks (ploughman's, rolls, flan and home-made pie of the day) and evening restaurant meals: I'm not certain "local duckling" is in the best possible taste. Beers are from Theakston's, plus Belgian fruit beers and a good range of malt whiskies. The pub offers accommodation but be prepared to book some time in advance.

Opposite: Sherlock Holmes, London WC2

A Thamesside Pub walk:

Lechlade to Oxford

The entire walk takes around ten or eleven hours so you can pick out the stretches that interest you most or break up the walk by staying overnight in one of the pubs along the way. The starting point is the Trout Inn on the outskirts of Lechlade, a Cotswold market town on the Gloucestershire-Oxford border where both the **NEW INN** (01367 252296) and the **RED LION** (01367 252373) offer accommodation, or you could visit the quintessential Cotswold town of Burford close by where the **LAMB** (01993 823155) also has rooms at a price.

The **TROUT** is a popular pub name along the Thames. The first such hostelry is at St John's Bridge (A417; phone 01367 252313). It is the last pub on the navigable part of the Thames and is popular with those who use the river for pleasure or employment: there are moorings for boats by the water's edge. The Cotswold stone building, which may, as the name of the bridge suggests, have monastic origins, is alongside a weir and a lock with a statue of Old Father Thames, relocated from the river's source. The lock marks the point where the now disused Thames and Severn Canal once operated and made Lechlade, a mile away, an important inland port.

The pub, with its old beams, undulating stone floors and open fires, has a powerful trout theme. There is trout on the menu and stuffed in glass cases around the walls, though the fish doesn't feature in the saloon bar aquarium, home to carp, minnow, roach and whatever else is found in the Thames. Trout as food may come in the shape of trout in cream and cider sauce. Other meals and snacks, lunchtime and evening, include ploughman's, pizzas, Greek-style lamb, pork fillet in creamy bacon and Stilton sauce, and such vegetarian dishes as courgette and tomato bake. There is a no-smoking evening restaurant on Thursday, Friday and Saturday, where children are welcome; they are also welcome in other designated areas. Beers include Courage Directors and others from the Scottish Courage range. The Trout has a large garden where a marquee is raised for special functions, and Aunt Sally and boules are played. Tuesdays are jazz nights at the Trout, usually trad but sometimes featuring a modern group. The pub closes in the afternoon but is open all day Saturday in summer.

From the Trout continue along the river bank for five miles to Radcot Bridge. The river becomes a major waterway but the area is happily remote from towns and motorways. You pass several historic bridges and locks, while Second World War pill boxes, a defence against invasion, line the bank. The paths are rather overgrown in places.

The **SWAN** at Radcot Bridge (01367 810220) is one of several Morland's pubs along the route. As the manager pointed out, the Abingdon brewery has been taken over by Greene King, which plans to close it. The beer range (currently Morland Original, Old Speckled Hen and Ruddles County) is liable to change: he already has Greene King Abbot as a guest beer.

Radcot is a sleepy hamlet with a violent past. Over the centuries there have been many bloody clashes to control the ancient crossing of the river. The present bridge was built around 1154 and is the oldest on the river. In 1141 King Stephen defeated the forces of Matilda, Queen of Anjou, who had ambitions to the throne. The remains of the earthworks of her castle lie to the north of Radcot Bridge. The barons held out against King John here in 1387 and the spot saw several skirmishes during the Civil War. The Swan dates from 1873 and is situated on a small tree-lined island with facilities for mooring, camping and caravanning. The single bar has carpet in the lounge area and flagstones for the darts section. The walls are decorated with a large collection of stuffed fish. Food is served lunchtime and evening and includes jacket potatoes with a choice of fillings, cottage pie, pigeon pie, chicken Kiev, liver casserole, vegetable chilli, and steak and ale pie; there are daily specials. Children are welcome and accommodation (three rooms) is available.

A further five miles along the river bank brings you to a second pub called the **TROUT** (Bampton to Buckland road, near Faringdon; phone 01367 870382) at the delightfully named 18th-century Tadpole Bridge. The inn is a good resting point, for this is not the prettiest part of the Thames, with flat water meadows stretching away on either side.

The original bar is L-shaped and has a well-worn flagstone floor. There is a separate small dining room. The Trout is a splendid supporter of small craft breweries and offers Archers Village and Golden bitters from Swindon, along with such guest ales as Batemans XXXB, Fuller's London Pride and Greene King Abbot. Food includes home-made soups and sandwiches, ploughman's, baguettes with a choice of fillings, fish pie, pie of the day, mushroom roast, roasted goat's cheese and pickled walnuts on deep-fried celery, Cumberland sausage, pork fillet in Stilton and chive cream sauce, spicy meatballs in tomato sauce, crab and pepper cakes, and, of course, grilled trout with a herb crust. There's piped music but I forgot to ask whether this includes Schubert's Trout. Aunt Sally is played in the charming garden, there are moorings for boats, and the pub sells tickets for fishing along a nearby stretch of the river. Children are welcome in the eating area of the bar. Accommodation was planned for 2000: phone for up-to-date information.

A two-mile walk from Tadpole Bridge brings you to Ten Foot Bridge. Here you have a choice of walks: you can take the path across the bridge, go through fields to Duxford and rejoin the river at Shifford Lock. Alternatively and more interestingly, continue along the north bank, pass through gates at the end of Chimney Nature Reserve, and along the bank until you reach a wooden bridge. Cross the bridge and take a footpath to the left that takes you to Shifford Lock where you cross a wooden footbridge, join the south bank and continue to Newbridge.

The small village has two splendid pubs on either side of the river. The MAYBUSH (A415, south of the bridge; tel 01865 300624) is a single-storey cottage pub with an upper floor in the loft pinpointed by large dormer windows. The walls are made of rough stone with brick arched windows. Inside, the bar has a low ceiling, beams and some fine old oak furniture. The pub sits between the 13th century New Bridge and a narrow bridge over a subsidiary channel. Traffic congestion makes it easier to reach the pub by water, where there is ample mooring, than by road. The pub serves Morland Original and Greene King Abbot. Food is available lunchtime and evening, and offers steaks, cannelloni, steak and kidney pie, gammon and egg, scampi, filled jacket potatoes, filled baguettes and several vegetarian dishes including cauliflower and Stilton

Lechlade
NEW INN
& RED LION
St John's Bridge
TROUT INN
to Burford
THE LAMB
RIVER
to Faringdon
Radcot
to Bampton
THE SWAN
THAMES
Tadpole Bridge
THE TROUT
Nature Reserve
Ten Foot Bridge
Chimney
Duxford
Shifford
Shifford Lock
W
S
N
E
Newbridge
THE MAYBUSH
ROSE REVIVED
14 miles Oxford
THE FERRYMAN
Pinkhill Lock
Bablock Hythe
ferry
Swinford
Farmoor Reservoir
A34
to Oxford
TROUT INN
Wolvercote

bake. Children are welcome and there is a pleasant waterside garden.

Across the water stands the **ROSE REVIVED** (north of the bridge; tel. 01865 300221), an inn with a fascinating history. Although the pub is mainly 1930s in design, it dates from the 16th century and probably began life as a tollhouse for people crossing the bridge. According to local legend, Oliver Cromwell stayed at the inn during the Civil War to recuperate from his struggles against the Royalists. He accepted a challenge to test the revitalising qualities of the landlord's ale and placed the stem of a wilting rose in his foaming tankard. The rose was restored to full bloom and the pub's name was upgraded from the simple Rose to the Rose Revived. The inn has a waterside lawn that is lit at night and has a bouncy castle for children in summer. The building is constructed of Cotswold stone with a moss-covered slate roof and a large, semi-circular bay window overlooking the river. Inside, the inn's rooms have been knocked through but it retains a good pubby feel, aided by a large inglenook fireplace.

The Rose Revived is one of Morland's Artist's Fare eateries. Food is available all day from noon until 10pm and as well as a specials board with the likes of scampi, game pie, spinach and ricotto bake, and lasagne, the fixed menu offers soup, kiln-smoked trout, coated mushrooms, steaks, Cajun chicken, cannelloni Napolitano, tandoori vegetable masala, mushroom, red pepper and spinach parcel, beef Stroganoff, and Caribbean coconut chicken. There is a substantial wine list as well as Morland Original, Old Speckled Hen and Ruddles County (as explained earlier, the takeover of Morland by Greene King means the beer range may change). Food is served all day from noon until 10pm. There is first-class accommodation and renowned breakfasts.

The walk from Newbridge to the outskirts of Oxford is 14 miles. From Newbridge you pass the Ferryman Inn, where the route leaves the river for 2½ miles, or you can contact the landlord of the inn who runs an occasional ferry service across the river. The path on the other side runs by the river until it rejoins the official path at Pinkhill Lock. As you approach Oxford, traffic on the Thames becomes more frequent and the last pub has glimpses of the city's famous gleaming spires. The **TROUT** – yes, another one – lies off the main river by a

weir stream (Trout Inn, 195 Godstow Road, Lower Wolvercote, Oxford, off A40 at Wolvercote roundabout; tel. 01865 302071 – see also entry on p.249). The 17th-century inn has walls of Cotswold stone and a roof of local Stonefield slate, with original leaded casement windows and a tumbling ivy creeper over one gable end. Peacocks screech and strut on the lawns by the weir while a patio overlooks an island garden with grottos and statuary. The interior of the Trout has three well-furnished old bars and two restaurants, flagstone floors, fireplaces, and roof beams from which hang pewter beer tankards, old prints and weapons.

The present building dates from around 1646 when its predecessor on the site was destroyed by General Lord Fairfax during the Civil War. In more recent times the pub has been a haunt of Oxford academics and was a favourite watering hole of the bibulous sleuth, Chief Detective Inspector E. Morse: the beer Morse drinks and Lewis pays for is Draught Bass. The Trout is open all day and meals may include lamb with white onion sauce, roasted vegetables upside-down pie, or breaded whole-tail scampi. If you can take yourself away from this idyllic spot it is just a short walk along the main river bank into Oxford.

The Trout Inn, on the Gloucestershire-Oxfordshire border

Pubs with good gardens

Fox

WEST STREET, CORFE CASTLE, DORSET (01929 480449)
Off A351

The Fox not only stands in the shadows of the ruins of the gaunt castle but parts are built from the same stone: it's one of the boozers that Cromwell knocked about a bit. When the Sealed Knot re-enacts the Civil War battle of Corfe, you will find Roundheads and Cavaliers cheerfully supping pints of honest ale in the Fox when the sound of cannon fire has died away. The delightful garden, reached by a side entrance, has a plethora of attractive flower beds and a contorted apple tree. There are fine views over the valley dominated by the castle. Inside the pub there's an ancient, glass-covered well, fossils, a stone fireplace dating from the 14th century, and a striking picture of the castle. The small front bar is a bit of a squeeze on busy days and is packed with small tables and chairs. Food and beer are served from a back room. Meals include home-made soup, sandwiches, jacket potatoes and such hot dishes of the day as fish and chips, steak and kidney pie, and lamb rogan josh. Ales tapped straight from casks include Eldridge Pope Thomas Hardy's Bitter and Royal Oak, Greene King Abbot, Ind Coope Burton Ale and Wadworth 6X. In the same street you will find a replica of the castle before it was attacked by Cromwell's forces. The village is on the restored steam railway line from Swanage.

Three Chimneys

NEAR BIDDENDEN, KENT (01580 291472)
A262, one mile from village

The pub not only has its own attractive garden but is just down the road from Sissinghurst Castle with its own world-famous gardens restored by Vita Sackville-West and open to the public. The whitewashed and half-timbered 16th-century inn has a large verdant garden at the rear with a delightful pot-pourri of flowering shrubs and roses, curving borders that are a blaze of flowers in late spring and summer, and some nut trees at the far end. Diners can eat in the delightful garden room overlooking the grounds; children are welcome in this area. The pub is a warren of small rooms with low beams, wood-panelled walls and old settles on flagstoned floors. The small public bar, where locals gather, has a vast inglenook and a bar carved from solid timber. Food is served in the bar and garden room and includes such tasty dishes as home-made soup, stuffed green peppers, and salmon and dill filo tart. The wine list is highly regarded and beers straight from the cask include Adnams Bitter, Brakspear Bitter, Harveys Best and Morland Old Speckled Hen, plus local Biddenden cider: the beer range is likely to change and always features independent brewers. Despite the name, the pub has only two chimneys. During the Seven Years War in the 18th century French prisoners at Sissinghurst Castle were allowed to take a walk each day as far the junction of three roads – *les trois chemins* – where the pub stands (they weren't allowed inside the pub: this was before the Geneva Convention laid down strict rules for the humane treatment of prisoners-of-war). A corruption of the French nickname for the crossroads became the name of the pub.

Bells of Peover

The Cobbles, Lower Peover, Cheshire (01565 722269)
Off B5081

Although the pub overlooks the local church, the name has nothing to do with bell-ringing. It was once owned by a family called Bell, who ran it for several decades from the late 19th century. The setting is superb: you approach the pub by a cobbled lane, a porch leading into the pub is covered with foliage while the pub signs bears the arms of the Warren de Tabley family. By the side, an old coachyard leads to a large garden bordered by a stream and with many secluded spots among trees, trellises, chestnut trees and rose pergolas. A terrace at the front of the creeper-clad pub overlooks the half-timbered, whitewashed 14th-century church. Inside, the pub has a lounge with old settles, high-backed chairs, coal fires and a dresser. There's a collection of Toby jugs in the small bar. Food in the bar or restaurant offers soup, home-made steak and kidney pie, a good choice of vegetarian dishes, monkfish, and sea bass in tomato and basil sauce. Greenalls and Boddingtons beers are on hand-pump.

John Thompson Inn

Ingleby, near Melbourne, Derbyshire (01332 862469)
Signposted from A514 at Swarkestone

Unlike the late Bells of Peover, John Thompson is still alive and brewing. His splendid 15th-century converted farmhouse is an experience rather than just a pub. The setting is magnificent, with views of the Trent Valley from the lovely garden with its sweeping, manicured lawns and colourful flowerbeds. There are tables on the lawn and on an outside terrace. Inside, the inn has a spacious lounge with beams, old oak settles and tables, and old prints on the walls. Smaller side rooms offer pub games and an area set aside for children. Mr Thompson's home-brewed ales – with supplies of yeast brought every week from Burton-on-Trent – are rich and flavourful and include JTS and Summer Gold and other seasonal specials such as Porter in winter. Draught Bass is also available. Simple but generous and well-priced food includes filled rolls, home-made soup, roast beef and Yorkshire puddings and tasty desserts. Cold food only Sundays and Mondays.

Gate Hangs High

Banbury Road, near Hook Norton, Oxfordshire
(01608 737387)
A361, one mile from Hook Norton and Rollright crossroads

The pub name comes from a former toll gate that stood on the Banbury to Oxford road. You are welcomed by tubs and hanging baskets bursting with flowers while the wide lawn at the back has fine views, apple and holly trees and swings for children. The warm and friendly pub has a beamed ceiling and a copper hood over the hearth in the inglenook fireplace. Food in the bar and restaurant includes home-made soups such as lentil and celery, smoked haddock, ham and mushrooms in garlic sauce with tagliatelle, beef in red wine, and honey-baked ham with egg. The superb ales – Hook Norton Best, Old Hooky and seasonal specials – come from the nearby Hook Norton Brewery. Don't miss this imposing Victorian brewery that dominates the small village. You can also visit the Bronze Age Rollright Stones, a king and his army who were turned to stone by a witch, a legend that becomes curiously believable after a pint or two of Old Hooky.

Inn at Whitewell

Whitewell, Forest of Bowland, Lancashire (01200 448222)
Off B243

Good food and good wine clearly go together, for the Inn at Whitewell in the Forest of Bowland is another GPG Dining Pub of the Year and also gets a "bunch of grapes" symbol from the *Which?* guide. The inn, owned by the Duchy of Lancaster, is also an art gallery, wine merchant and (would you believe) a shirtmaker. The oldest parts of the inn date from the 14th century and were formerly the home of the "Keeper of the Foret", who looked after the royal hunting grounds. Beautifully set in the forest and on the banks of the River Hodder, it offers extensive facilities for anglers. Landlord Richard Bowman, a splendid name for the successor to the Keeper of the Foret, also runs Bowland Forest Vintners. The choice of claret is formidable, there's a wide range from the rest of France, while Australia features strongly among New World offerings. All the wines, numbering around 180, that are available at the inn can be bought to take away as well. The inn, with its log fires, ancient

Inn at Whitewell

settles, long-case clocks, and old sporting prints, offers a range of food that takes in soup, sandwiches, grilled Norfolk kippers, warm Roquefort cheese-cake, locally caught fish in the fish pie, sausage and mash, haddock, Welsh rarebit, and crispy belly of pork with a spinach salad and chilli dressing. Desserts include home-made ice cream. Children are welcome and accommodation, including some rooms in a converted coach house, is available.

Hundred House

Bridgnorth Road, Norton, Shropshire (01952 730353)
A442 six miles from Telford

The Phillips family who run the Hundred House don't just use their magnificent gardens as a showplace: they are working gardens and provide the inn's kitchen with herbs. Customers can also enjoy the roses, herbaceous plants and trees. The plants have crept inside too: from the creeper-clad, red-brick exterior you enter an interior decorated with hops and herbs hanging from the ceilings, and fresh and dried flowers, gourds and bouquets. There are Jacobean panelling and arches, stripped brickwork, open log fires, old quarry tiles and pews and settles. The food in the bar and restaurant, lunchtime and evening, is of the highest order and may include soups; focaccia bread with garlic, onions and rosemary; steak and kidney pie; local sausages and mash with onion gravy; hot potato cakes with aioli, onion rings and rocket; coriander-cured salmon with lime, peanuts and beansprouts; aubergine fritters with goat's cheese, tomato and red wine sauce; chicken stuffed with spinach, Brie and walnuts; venison with parsnip rosti, port and shallot jam; beef fajita with guacamole, salsa and tortillas; warm Thai salad of roast beef; and steaks. Desserts could include black cherry surpise or warm pecan pie. Hand-pumped beers include a house ale, Heritage Bitter, Woods Shropshire Lad, Everard's Tiger and Charles Wells' Eagle Bitter. The French-based wine list has around 20 by the glass and carafes of house wine. Children are welcome and accommodation is available.

Best of the Rest

Star

Old Heathfield, East Sussex (01435 863570)
Off B2203 and B2096

Pubs with real fires

Brocket Arms

Ayot St Lawrence, Hertfordshire (01438 820250)
B651, off A1

Almost lost down narrow country lanes yet just a few minutes from the A1, this unspoilt 14th-century inn used to be part of the nearby Brocket Hall estate, formerly owned by members of the Brocket family, who were the brewing Cains of Liverpool before their elevation to the aristocracy and, more recently, car insurance fraud. The pub has white walls, lattice windows, and a steeply pitched roof. The interior is even more striking, with two low-beamed bars, lanterns, wall settles, and a giant inglenook that dominates the main bar. The other bar has a wood-burning stove, so there's never any risk of feeling cold. Although popular with visitors (George Bernard Shaw's home is in the village at Shaw's Corner and is open to the public), the Brocket Arms is a genuine local where darts, dominoes and shove ha'penny are played. There are lunchtime snacks (soup, sandwiches, ploughman's, filled jacket potatoes, and macaroni cheese), an evening restaurant and cream teas in summer. Real ales include Adnams Broadside, Greene King IPA and Abbot, and Wadworth 6X on hand-pumps, with guest ales tapped straight from casks behind the bar. There's a good choice of wine, too. Children can eat in designated areas and there are large gardens at the rear. The pub claims to be haunted by the ghost of a Catholic priest who was tried and hanged from a beam during the Reformation. The village has the ruins of a church and its striking Palladian successor. Accommodation is available in the pub.

Prince of Wales

Woodham Road, Stow Maries, Essex (01621 828971)
B1012 near South Woodham Ferrers

The Prince of Wales's landlord, Rob Walster, was the founder of the Crouch Vale craft brewery in South Woodham Ferrers, but he has given up brewing to restore this delightful old weatherboarded pub in the Dengie Marshes. Heat in winter comes from a room that used to double as the village bakery, and the old oven not only warms customers but also makes bread and pizza. The pub is a ramble of small, interconnected rooms, including one for families. It was once the smallest pub in Essex but has since been extended. Excellent food is cooked by a Greek chef who will whip up a genuine moussaka along with mixed fish kebabs, Greek-style lamb chops, home-smoked haddock with tomatoes and poached egg, sandwiches, ploughman's, and baklava among the desserts. The real ales change constantly but you might find the likes of Harviestoun all the way from Dollar in Scotland, Otter from Devon, Bank Top from Bolton, and Young's from London. You'll also find Belgian ales, including fruit beers, on draught or in bottle, farm cider, and malt whiskies.

Wellington

Old Road, The Harbour, Boscastle, Cornwall (01840 250202)
B3263

The Wellington is a 16th-century, haunted coaching inn with a blazing log fire on cold days, and a long, low-beamed bar whose main feature is a range of church lamps donated to the inn by Thomas Hardy. Other guests have included Edward VII and Guy Gibson VC. The stained-glass windows date from 1846 while cats and dogs add to the homely feel in the bar. The Long Bar has such pub lunches as sandwiches, scampi and steaks while La Belle Alliance restaurant not surprisingly concentrates on English and French cuisine. Beers include Flowers IPA and St Austell Hicks Special, plus guest beers. Monday night is folk night. Accommodation is available and the inn is handy for the harbour and the witchcraft museum.

Old Dungeon Ghyll

Great Langdale, Cumbria (01539 437272)
B5343

The Old Dungeon's vast fire, blazing in an ancient black-leaded range, is an ideal place to dry your feet and revitalise yourself after walking on the nearby fells. This is a walkers' and climbers' pub, and you may well find socks and boots steaming in front of the fire. There's also a quieter bar and residents' lounge. From the windows hewn from the solid stone walls there are awesome views of the Langdale Pikes, including the Pike o' Blisco and Kettle Crag. Dungeon Ghyll waterfall is close by. Local Lakelands ales include Jennings Mild and Cumberland, and Yates Bitter, with Theakston's XB and Old Peculier from Yorkshire, guest ales, and farm ciders. Bar food includes sandwiches, filled jacket potatoes, Cumberland sausages, chilli con carne, and pizzas in the evening. Children have their own menu. It's essential to book for the no-smoking evening restaurant. Accommodation is available and breakfasts can be served to non-residents, useful if you're in the camp site opposite. Pub games are played, there are no juke boxes or other noisome machines, and spontaneous live music tends to break out at weekends.

Opposite: The Brocket Arms, Ayot St Lawrence, Hertfordshire

Sun Inn

High Street, Clun, Shropshire (01588 640559)
B4368

According to A.E. Housman, Clun is "the quietest place under the sun," but the fireplace in the flagstoned bar of this 15th-century inn makes up for any silence with its welcoming roar. The Sun has a "cruck" design in which curved timbers support the roof. There's a beamed lounge with high-backed settles, wall timbers, and an oak armchair. The inn offers accommodation, bar food and full restaurant meals, with a fine range of ales that includes Banks's Original and Bitter, Marston's Pedigree and the locally brewed Woods Special. Children are welcome in eating areas, and there's a terrace at the back of the pub. Clun has an 11th-century castle and is a good base for walking Offa's Dyke.

Crook Inn

Tweedsmuir, near Biggar, Borders (01899 880272)
A701

This amazing building is an ancient drovers' inn hidden inside a modern Art Deco hotel. There's been an inn or howf on the site since the 14th century; the present building dates from 1590 and is thought to be Scotland's oldest licensed premises. The inn was a clandestine meeting place for the outlawed 17th-century Presbyterian Covenanters, and takes its name from a landlady called Jeannie o' the Crook, who hid a fugitive in a haystack. Robbie Burns wrote his "Willie Wastle" poem while staying here. The centrepiece of the old bar of the inn is a superb stone fireplace that was built to the shape of a cartwheel: a wheel was set on fire and left a circular mark on the floor. The inn has airy lounges, a restaurant specialising in seafood, with such tempting dishes as honey lemon pickled kippers and lamb chops with gooseberry and mint sauce. Beers include Broughton Greenmantle from the nearby village of Broughton, birthplace of John Buchan: there's a small museum there in his honour. Accommodation is available and children are welcome.

Pubs with traditional games

Crown Inn

Debdale Hill, Old Dalby, Leicestershire (01664 823134)
Off A46

Francis Drake may spin in his hammock at the thought of Englishmen playing boules rather than bowls, but the French game, more properly called pétanque, has become hugely popular in Britain, and its focus is the Crown, a remote pub on the edge of the Vale of Belvoir (pronounced "beaver", none of your fancy Frenchifying, please), reached down a gated road. Regional and national competitions are played here in the half-acre landscaped garden, and unlike the more calm atmosphere of bowls, much heat and excitement is generated as the players attempt to get their boules closest to the small white ball known as a cochonnet or little pig. Visitors can try their hand at the game. The creeper-covered inn was once a farmhouse in the 17th century and shows its origins in the small, beamed rooms with open fires, prints on the walls, and fresh flowers in season. It's a real ale paradise, with the likes of Adnams, Black Sheep, Fullers, Greene King, Mansfield, Marston's, Morland and Tim Taylor's all tapped straight from casks in a ground-floor "cellar". Food, lunchtime and evening, is of the highest standard, and includes a remarkable ploughman's with Colston Basset Stilton, Melton Mowbray pork pie, home-cured ham, pickles, apple and a roll. Other dishes may include home-made soup, pigeon breast with bacon and red cabbage marmalade, potato cake filled with Stilton or Cheddar with mango chutney, oyster mushrooms with spinach and pumpkin risotto, roast red onion and grilled goats' cheese tartlets, roast chicken with sweet potatoes and basil sauce, and rib of beef in red wine and bay leaf sauce. Desserts may include Bakewell tart or chocolate and raspberry mousse. There's a well-chosen wine list and a good range of malt whiskies, Cognacs and liqueurs. If you drink outside in good weather, there's a pleasant terrace with tables and chairs as well as the garden where petanque is played. You can enjoy the fruit trees and roses here but watch out for small white piglets.

Lifeboat Inn

Ship Lane, Thornham, Norfolk (01485 512236)
Signposted from A149

This atmospheric, 16th-century smugglers' inn on the edge of the salt marshes offers shove ha'penny and dominoes, but its main claim to fame is the rare and ancient sport of penny-in-the-hole. The game is set into a high-backed wooden settle. The player has to throw 13 old coins against a lead backdrop, from where they have to pitch into a hole in the seat. Winners are rare: the publican "generously" offers a gallon of whisky to anyone who successfully lobs all 13 coins. The game was outlawed by George III (was there an outbreak of penny-in-the-hole hooliganism, or was the game ruined by the equivalent of the Arsenal off-side trap?) but is perfectly legal today. The Lifeboat is a splendidly rambling, white-washed inn, with no fewer than five open fires, old wooden settles, paraffin lamps, standing timbers, and heavy oak beams bestrewn with reed-cutters' tools, other farming equipment, and many guns. There are several small rooms off the main bar, a candlelit restaurant (booking essential), a pleasant convervatory with a vine, and a sunny back terrace. The pub concentrates on local ales, with the likes of Adnams Best, Greene King IPA and Abbot, and Woodforde's Wherry. There's a short and sensible wine list. Excellent food, lunchtime and evening, offers fresh fish and seafood daily, and may include Brancaster oysters, sea bass with Chardonnay and saffron sauce, monkfish, traditional fish and chips, and local mussels. Other dishes could include leek and cauliflower soup, filled baguettes, ploughman's, penne with mushrooms and cherry tomatoes in a creamy pesto sauce, and grilled tuna. Accommodation is available, there are good walks over the marshes, and the great sweep of Holkham Beach is nearby.

Rose and Crown

Perry Wood, near Selling, Kent (01227 752214)
Off A2 and A28

This small and remote 16th-century inn offers bat-and-trap, the game many believe to be the forerunner of cricket. It's an outdoor game where two teams of eight attempt to score runs, and bowl or catch out their opponents. The "trap" also acts as the wicket. A hard rubber ball is placed on top of the trap, the batsman taps a lever that sends the ball into the air, and he has to clout it down a 21-yard pitch (one yard less – wicket to wicket– of a cricket pitch) between two posts. If the ball

The Lifeboat Inn, Thornham, Norfolk

is not caught, he scores a run. A member of the fielding team then bowls the ball along the pitch at a wicket, painted on the trap. If the wicket goes down, the batsman, who cannot defend the wicket, is out. In spite of the mind-boggling complexity of bat-and-trap, it's enormously popular in Kent, and the players, like cricketers, love a few pints afterwards. The Rose and Crown quenches their thirsts with Adnams Best, Goacher's Dark and Harvey's Best, plus a regular guest beer. The old inn is decked out with flower tubs and hanging baskets in season, and inside there are standing timbers, heavy beams decorated with hop bines, two inglenooks with log fires, and a collection of corn dollies. Food in bar and restaurant, lunchtime and evening (not Sunday or Monday evenings) may include the likes of ploughman's; steak and kidney pie; fisherman's platter; Jamaican chicken; Thai green chicken curry; wild mushroom tagliatelle; and beef in red wine. Desserts may include pecan and maple pie and toffee apple tart. Cribbage, dominoes and shove-ha'penny are also played.

Bull

The Village, Stanford Dingley, Berkshire (0118 974 4409)
Off A4 and A340

The Bull naturally features the ancient game of Ring the Bull. It's one of the most frustrating games I've ever come across. It's a member of the "lobbing" group of pub games and is essentially an indoor version of quoits. A ring, replicating the ring in a bull's nose, hangs from a string and has to be lobbed, swung, spun or flipped on to a hook on the wall. You can get extremely bad-tempered playing this game, and the Bull fortunately offers soothing pints of Brakspear Bitter, and West Berkshire Skiff and Good Old Boy. The inn dates from the 15th century and has a half-timbered exterior, with beams and standing timbers inside, settles, and seats carved from old beer casks. Food in the bar, lunchtime and evening, may include soup; filled jacket potatoes; red peppers and sweet potatoes; vegetable lasagne; grilled goat's cheese; vegetable hot-pot; garlic bacon and mushrooms on toast; coquille St Jacques; chicken curry; fish pie; beef stew; and chicken breast with wild mushroom stuffing. There are seats at the front of the inn and a small garden at the rear.

Rhydspence Inn

Whitney-on-Wye, Herefordshire (01497 831262)
A438 one mile from Whitney

The Rhydspence (pronounced Rid-spence) is a breathtakingly ancient inn on the border between England and Wales: a stream running through the garden marks the actual dividing line between the two countries. The commanding black-and-white, half-timbered building lies back from the Hereford to Brecon road, standing sentinel-like over the border crossing and the great sweep of the Wye Valley beyond. The inn was built in the 16th century as a resting place for Welsh drovers taking their sheep to market. The carefully restored building has two comfortable beamed bars with standing timbers, cushioned wall seats, and log fires. Traditional pub games include dominoes, cribbage, and quoits, the last-named being the principal form of lobbing games, where horseshoes or rubber rings have to be thrown over pins in the floor. Players and watchers can refresh themselves with Draught Bass, Hook Norton Best and Robinson's Best, and Dunkerton's cider. Food in bar and restaurant (lunchtime and evening) makes good use of local produce as well as fish from Billingsgate Market in London. As well as fish you will find such dishes as organic Devon sausages and Welsh goat's cheese crêpes. There's excellent accommodation available in half-timbered bedrooms, one with a four-poster bed.

Note: *See also* **Star Inn**, *St Just, Cornwall (*Pubs for bird-watchers *section – p.208) with euchre, skittles and shut-the-box; and* **Birch Hall Inn**, *Beck Hole, North Yorkshire (*Quiet pubs *section – pp. 288–9) with quoits.*

Best of the Rest

Kings Head

Church Street, Wadenhoe, Northamptonshire
(01832 720024)
Off A605

Malt Shovel

Bradley Green, Somerset (01278 653432)
Off A39

Quiet pubs

Pot Kiln

Pot Kiln Lane, Frilsham, Berkshire (01635 201366)
Off B4009 and A34; one and a half miles south of Yattendon church

The Pot Kiln is an ancient ale house, 400 years old, built to refresh the thirsty workers who fired the kilns for a brick works that once stood alongside. Surrounded by meadows and beech woods, it's remote and peaceful: like all the pubs in this section it may have occasional live music (such as Irish bands on Sundays here) but its bars are free from piped music, jukeboxes and other electronic machines. Outside, the pub

The Pot Kiln

has the look of a large, brick-built country cottage. Inside there are three bars and a tap room, with bare boards, wooden benches and a log fire. The beer comes through a hatch in the entrance lobby and includes Brick Kiln Bitter brewed exclusively for the pub by the tiny West Berkshire craft brewery on the premises, which also brews Goldstar and other seasonal ales. Commercial beers include Arkells 3B and Morland Original. Cribbage, darts and dominoes are played in one bar. A candlelit back room is used for dining and is no-smoking. Bar food, lunchtime and evening, may include macaroni cheese or another pasta dish, tomato, bean and sage soup, parsnip and chestnut bake, ploughman's, chicken with tarragon cream sauce, salmon and broccoli fish cakes, and venison casserole, with home-made ice cream and sorbets. The pub is closed Tuesday lunchtime and there are only hot filled rolls on Sunday. Children are welcome in one room.

Drunken Duck

Barngates, Ambleside, Cumbria (01539 436347)

Off B5286 between Ambleside and Hawkshead, three miles south of Ambleside

There's no jukebox, television or electronic games in this isolated, 400-year-old Cumbrian ale house whose name comes from a story that's only believable after a pint or two of Barngates Cracker or Chesters brewed on the premises. Apparently, a landlady long ago kept ducks that one day supped from a leaking beer cask and fell into a drunken stupor. She thought they were dead and plucked them for the oven, whereupon (as they say in all the best fairy stories) they returned noisily to life. The landlady had to knit them little woolly pullies until their plumage grew again. You can read the legend in the long, narrow, beamed bar with log fires, and old prints and fishing artefacts decorating the walls. Food is served in the bar and two dining rooms. Chef Nick Foster has won high praise for the likes of Cumberland sausage with mash and wholegrain mustard grav;, leek, potato and Lancashire cheese bake; smoked salmon and bacon salad with herb mayonnaise; and, in the evenings, Roquefort and herb omelette with sautéed asparagus and roasted potato discs topped with mustard rarebit; potato tuille with caramelised red onion and mushroom mille feuille; curried chickpea fritters; duck breast served with butterbean cassoulet; and roast cod fillet with bouillabaisse. Desserts include sorbets and Westmorland dream cake. As well as the house beers, the inn also serves two other Lakeland ales, Jennings Bitter and Yates Bitter. The views, including a glimpse of Windermere, are superb. Children are welcome, and there is accommodation available.

DERING ARMS

STATION ROAD, PLUCKLEY, KENT (01233 840371)
Off B2077, two miles from village

The inn was built originally as a hunting lodge and is a riot of Dutch gables and mullioned, arched and leaded windows, some etched with the Dering family's coat of arms. It has thick stone walls, studded oak doors, stone floors and a blazing log fire. In the 17th century, a Cavalier Dering escaped from the Roundheads through one of the windows. Traditional pub games are played in the larger of the two bars, with beams garlanded with hop bines. While there is occasional live music, nothing taped or canned is allowed. Food starts with an all-day breakfast and saunters through an eclectic menu heavily focused on fish: landlord Jim Buss visits Hythe on the coast several times a week to buy fresh catches. You may find sea bass with sorrel sauce; halibut meunière; fillets of John Dory; or whole lemon sole. The centrepiece is a vast seafood platter of hot fish and cold shellfish, including crab, mussels, lobster and prawns. There are also pasta dishes, filled baguettes and vegetable soups. Many of the ingredients come from Jim's father's farm. The pub stages gourmet dinners in winter and summer barbecues in the garden. There's a 100-strong wine list while the Kent craft brewery, Goacher's, supplies its Dark and a house beer. There's no food Sunday evening or all day Monday. Children are welcome and accommodation is available.

BIRCH HALL INN

BECK HOLE, NORTH YORKSHIRE (01947 896245)
One mile north of Goathland

There's a timeless air to this lovely old inn in a peaceful village tucked away on the moors close to where Eller Beck and West

Beck meet to form the Esk. The pub was once two cottages and is the focal point of the village, acting also as the post office and sweet shop, as well as the meeting place for the local quoits team. The exterior has whitewashed, rough stone walls with an ancient painting of the nearby Thomason Fosse waterfall. Inside, there are two cheery rooms with flagstones and simple furnishings, both served by a hatch. Food includes celebrated hand-raised pies, sandwiches, and afternoon teas with beer cake. The hand-pumped ales are Black Sheep Bitter, Theakston's Best and a guest beer. It's a good spot for taking the North Yorkshire Steam Railway or walking along a separate disused railtrack to Goathland.

Cock

Lavenham Road, Brent Eleigh, Suffolk (01787 247371)
A1141

You reach the Cock on the fringes of Constable Country through gently rolling fields and village after village of ancient, half-timbered houses. The inn is also ancient, with a thatched roof and two tall, slightly wonky chimneys. It's known locally, and without a hint of irony, as "Sam Potter's Cock" in honour of a legendary past landlord. Inside, it's a simple old ale house with a tiny snug and a larger bar with a dartboard. Both rooms, served by a central bar, have open fires in winter. Food isn't served, but you can enjoy Adnams Best, Greene King IPA and Abbot, Nethergate's seasonal ales from Clare, and an occasional farm cider. The locals are friendly and will invite you to join them in darts or cards, but you might need to bone up on your "Suffick" dialect. It is, says the *Good Beer Guide*, "an absolute gem, thatched, unspoilt, and at peace with the world".

Cartwheel Inn

Whitsbury Road, Whitsbury, Hampshire (01725 518362)
Off A338 betwen Fordingbridge and Salisbury

This remote old village inn (OS 129138) is on the edge of the New Forest and close to Breamore Anglo-Saxon church. It's more than 200 years old and is Grade-II listed, the tile and slate-roofed building taking its name from its origins as a wheelwright;s shop. It has been a pub since the 1920s and is now the focal point of the isolated village, staging beer festivals in August and October. Conversation – an important tradition among forest folk – flourishes unhindered as there is no canned, taped or piped anti-intellectual effluent to interrupt it. The inn is an important outlet for Ringwood Brewery in the New Forest town of the same name, one of the earliest craft breweries that has now reached "small regional" status as a result of the ever-growing demand for its beers. You'll find Ringwood Best Bitter and 21 Not Out, the last-named introduced in 1999 to mark Ringwood's twenty-first anniversary. Other ales on sale include Adnams Broadside and Fuller's London Pride with regular guest beers. The inn, with its old beams, rafters and wall seats offers bar food lunchtime and evening (not Tuesday evenings in winter) and full restaurant service. Dishes may include sandwiches; ploughman's; filled jacket potatoes; chicken curry; bangers and mash in onion gravy; tuna steak; cashew nut paella; and local rainbow trout. The sheltered garden has a children's play area and stages barbecues in summer. Children are welcome in designated eating areas.

Malt Shovel

Brearton, North Yorkshire (01423 862929)

Off A61 and B6165

Dating from 1525, the Malt Shovel is the oldest building in Brearton and shows its noble age with its massive low beams, a wall made from a 16th-century oak partition, exposed stonework, open fires, a collection of tankards and an impressive oak bar that serves all the rooms. Nothing is allowed to interfere with the quiet hum of good conversation. There is a good choice of ale, including both Black Sheep and Theakston's from Masham along with Daleside Nightjar and guest beers. Country cider is served in summer. The inn is closed on Mondays but at other times, lunchtime and evening, food may include sandwiches; bean casserole; wild mushroom Stroganoff; nut roast with pesto; haggis, tatties and neeps; rabbit and mushroom pie; warm chicken salad with a lemon and caper dressing; seafood au gratin; and steaks. Desserts may include char-grilled banana with ice-cream and toffee sauce or apple and blackberry crumble. Pub games are played and children are welcome.

Griffin Inn

Coleshill Road, Church End, Shustoke, Warwickshire
(01675 481205)
B4116; off M6 junction 4

The Griffin has everything you could want from a rural local: good ale, good food, and pleasant, quiet surroundings. Not for nothing was it voted Camra local pub of the year in 1998. Next door stands Church End Brewery, in a 350-year-old stable workshop; as well as the Griffin, it supplies close to 100 other outlets with Cuthberts, Gravediggers, Wheat-a-Bix, What the Fox's Hat, Pooh Beer, Vicar's Ruin and Old Pal, plus a constant stream of seasonal brews. The bar of the inn has low beams with jugs attached, an old settle, and log fires in a fireplace and a big inglenook. As well as the home-brews, there is a tremendous choice of beers, including Highgate Dark, Marston's Pedigree and guests from all over the country, perhaps Tim Taylor's Landlord, Otter or Theakston's. Lunchtime bar food is simple but generous and may include fish and chips with mushy peas; steak pie and chips; and lasagne. There is a children's play area at the back of the pub and a large terrace.

Best of the Rest

Dukes Arms

83 High Street, Woodford, Northamptonshire
(01832 732224)
Off A1 and A510

Railway

Mill Lane, Heatley, Cheshire (01925 752742)
B5159

Scarlett Arms

Walliswood Green Road, Walliswood, Surrey (01306 627243)
Off A 281

Smoke-free pubs

Three Fishes

4 Fish Street, Shrewsbury, Shropshire (01743 344793)

John Sims, landlord of this Tudor inn, is the nicotine-free brain behind a small but growing network of pubs that offer customers the chance to enjoy good food, drink and conversation free from cigarette, pipe and cigar smoke. Mr Sims banned the weed from the Three Fishes because his pub has just one small, heavily-beamed and low-ceilinged bar where the fug sent the beer flat, ruined the food and caused customers to cough. The black-and-white timbered inn stands in a medieval part of Shrewsbury and is attractively decorated with old prints and bric-à-brac. You can appreciate the fine aromas and flavours of such ales as Adnams Bitter, Fuller's London Pride and Tim Taylor's Landlord. The Three Fishes concentrates on good home-made pub grub with real chips; soups; jacket potatoes; cod in beer batter; cauliflower and broccoli bake; quiche; sausage and mash; and steak and Guinness pie. Traditional desserts are of the spotted dick variety. There is a daily specials board. Food is served lunchtime and evening Tuesday to Friday, with lunch only on Saturday; no food Sunday or Monday. The pub encourages the art of conversation: there are no fruit machines or piped music. As there is just one bar, children are not admitted.

Old Crown

High Street, Skirmett, Buckinghamshire (01491 638435)

Off A4155 and B482

This delightful, 350-year-old Chilterns pub is owned by Brakspear of Henley and serves Bitter and Special Bitter straight from casks and delivered via a hatch. The Old Crown has three pleasant rooms – all smoke-free – with beamed ceilings from which beer mugs hang, two inglenooks and a vast collection of bric-à-brac made up of old agricultural tools, paintings and bottles. The pub was once three separate cottages, one of which was the village shop. The white-painted tap room with a quarry-tiled floor, trestle tables and an ancient settle is wonderfully unspoilt. The garden has picnic tables while a front terrace has old beer casks fashioned as seats and a bright display of flowers in tubs. Menus change regularly but you may find such dishes as home-made soup; ploughman's; smoked fish terrine; Stilton and walnut pâté; filled jacket potatoes; scallops in garlic, butter and basil; lasagne; and steak, kidney and mushroom pie. Food is served lunchtime and evening; no food Sunday evenings or Mondays except bank holidays. Children under ten are not admitted.

PLOUGH

CLIFTON HAMPDEN, OXFORDSHIRE (01865 407811)
A415

The Plough is not only non-smoking but also mercifully free from piped music. The bar has low beams, panelled walls, red and black floor tiles and ancient furniture, while there are a few tables and seats outside. The Courage-owned pub serves Courage Best, Directors and John Smith's on hand-pumps with a well-chosen wine list and a dozen or so malt whiskies. Bar food includes home-made soup; ploughman's; sandwiches; fusilli with sweet peppers and Parmesan; steak in ale pie; and smoked chicken salad. There is a two-course lunch on Sundays and a more extensive menu in the separate restaurant. Accommodation, including rooms with four-poster beds, is available in a building across a courtyard from the inn. The Plough is open all day and children are welcome.

NEW INN

NEW STREET, SALISBURY, WILTSHIRE (01722 327679)

New Inn is actually a very old name. Hundreds of New Inns sprang up in the time of Elizabeth I when she complained there were insufficient good hostelries for her to dine or stay at, and obsequious landlords rushed to provide her with better ale and tucker. Whether Sir Walter Raleigh smoked a pipe with her in a New Inn is not recorded but he wouldn't be able to do so today as Salisbury's pub of that ilk has firmly banned the weed. This is a marvellous old and heavily-beamed pub with half-timbered walls, an inglenook in one room, and a panelled dining room. The walled garden has striking views of the cathedral. Good ales come from Hall & Woodhouse (Badger Bitter and Tanglefoot) and Charles Wells Eagle Bitter from Bedford. Home-made food includes sandwiches; ploughman's; spinach and mushroom lasagne; broccoli and cauliflower bake; beef and mushroom pie; lamb and leek casserole; plaice stuffed with tomatoes; plus a good range of puddings. Children are welcome away from the main bar area and accommodation is available.

FREE PRESS

PROSPECT ROW, CAMBRIDGE (01223 368337)

The Free Press, named tongue-in-cheek after a temperance newspaper that failed after one issue, has been run by Chris Lloyd for 20 years. It has a tiny snug, regularly used by students as a stunt to see how many can crowd in and break the existing record, and a charming bar with a collection of oars and rowing prints: the pub is a registered boat club. Beers come from Greene King in the shape of XX Mild, IPA and Abbot Ale and Mr Lloyd offers a vast range of single malt whiskies. Home-made food runs to soup, with two vegetarian soups every day; Bombay vegetables; leek croustade or nut loaf as further vegetarian options; chilli; pork and cider casserole; beef in beer; and such delicious desserts as apple crumble, lemon torte and sticky toffee pudding. You can play cribbage or dominoes or soak up the sun in the paved back garden. "A gem", says *Camra's Good Beer Guide* and, as always, it is spot on.

Best of the Rest

(*smoke-free areas, not totally smokeless*)

OSBORNE VIEW

67 HILL HEAD ROAD, HILL HEAD, HAMPSHIRE (01329 664623)
Off M27

LOCO

31 CHURCH STREET, HAXEY, LINCOLNSHIRE (01427 752879)
Off A161

PHEASANT

ROCK LANE, HIGHER BURWARDSLEY, CHESHIRE (01829 770434)
Off A523

FERRY INN

KING STREET, CAWOOD, NORTH YORKSHIRE (01757 268515)
Off A19

The Free Press, Cambridge

Child-friendly pubs

Hawes Inn

Newhalls Road, South Queensferry, near Edinburgh (0131 331 1990)
Off M9 & A90. Train: Dalmeny

Nestling in the giant shadows of the Forth road and rail bridges, the inn has stupendous views of the river and the crossing points. The Hawes is a 350-year-old coaching inn, packed with local memorabilia. It was mentioned in *The Antiquary* by Sir Walter Scott (who called it "a very decent sort of place"), and more famously was used by Robert Louis Stevenson in *Kidnapped*: the abduction of David Balfour was planned here. The comfortable, rambling, wood-panelled rooms include one for use by families: children are not admitted after 8pm unless they are resident. There are two junior menus, one for small children, and one for teenagers. The young ones have a choice that includes dinosaur-shaped fish, and mini Kievs served with either spaghetti hoops, chips or mash, followed by ice cream. The teenagers' choice include cheese melt, spinach and ricotta pasta, and Chinese-style king ribs. Food for adults includes haggis, neaps and tatties, mussels, fresh fish, and steaks. There are outside tables while a back lawn has a children's safe area. Ales for adults include Deuchar's IPA, Arroll's 80 Shilling and Ind Coope Burton Ale. Edinburgh is just ten miles away.

Milbury's

Beauworth, Hampshire (01962 771248)
Off A272

Milbury's is named after the Millbarrow, a nearby Bronze Age cemetery. The inn was known as the Hare and Hounds in the 18th century, and the Fox and Hounds from the 1850s when the Millbarrow became briefly famous after a hoard of silver Norman coins was found there. Located in a remote position high on the Downs, the pub has flagstones, beams, open fires, wood panelling, and a 600-year-old well sunk 300 feet into the chalk, worked by a mighty 250-year-old treadmill. There's a room for families, who can also use the converted stables and skittles alley. A children's menu includes scampi and pizza, while adults can tuck into home-made soup, filled baguettes or jacket potatoes, mushrooms filled with cream cheese and spinach in puff pastry, steaks, and Thai green chicken curry. There's a tremendous choice of real ales, including Hampshire King Alfred's and Pride of Romsey, and Triple fff Moondance and Stairway to Heaven. The inn is in fine walking country, with the South Downs Way alongside and the Wayfarers Walk close by. Accommodation is available.

Rising Sun

Knapp, North Curry, near Taunton, Somerset (01823 490436)
Off A61 & A358; signposted North Curry

A visually stunning example of a 15th-century Somerset longhouse, the Rising Sun has exposed beams, carved wood panels, tilted walls with exposed stonework, an old bread oven, and fires in large inglenooks. The terraced garden has fine views over the Somerset Levels. The inn has a family room and a separate menu for children. It's renowned for its fish and seafood dishes and you may find salmon and seafood tart with dressed salad, smoked salmon and prawn double open sandwich, sea bass on fennel, lemon sole with Vermouth and lemon butter, skate wing with black butter, monkfish, half a lobster, trout fillets with dill mustard, John Dory with mussels and prawns, or moules marinières. There's a good range of vegetarian dishes, including a special nut roast with Provençal sauce. For meat eaters, there's roast duck with port and orange sauce or grilled steaks. There are such delicious desserts as treacle tart, or chocolate and hazelnut slice. Hand-pumped ales include Draught Bass, Boddingtons Bitter and Exmoor Ale, plus local ciders and a good wine list. Accommodation is available.

Marsham Arms

Holt Road, Hevingham, Norfolk (01603 754268)
B1149, four miles north of Norwich Airport

The eight-bedroom Marsham Arms is set in rolling countryside, yet it's a fine base for Norwich, the Broads and the coast. There's an outdoor play area with a slide, swings, see-saw and Wendy house, while the family room is in a carefully designed extension. The hotel has a good pubby atmosphere and is popular with customers of all ages. Even babies are thought of: there are cots in the bedrooms, and nappy-changing facilities. Food is served lunchtime and evening, and the children's menu includes vegetarian rissoles or smaller portions from the main menu. Adults get a choice of fresh seafood, vegetarian dishes, and salads. Hand-pumped beers include Adnams Best and Fuller's London Pride, and there's a good choice of wines as well.

BUCK INN

THORNTON WATLASS, NR RIPON, NORTH YORKSHIRE (01677 422461)
One mile off B6268 Masham to Bedale road

This is a pub for enthusiasts. You can play quoits here and the Buck has its own cricket team: it not only faces the village green but one wall acts as the boundary for the cricket ground. The rules are not approved by Lord's, but if a batsman hits the wall, it's four, while over the pub roof is six. It's a sort of cricket version of real tennis. The licensees can arrange fishing, golfing and horse-racing breaks. The garden not only houses the quoits pitch but there's a climbing frame, swing, slide, and bouncy motorbike for children. The bars have wood panelling, beams, fires, and wall settles, and a lot of cricketing memorabilia. Excellent food includes bread baked on the premises, ploughman's; turkey and coriander burgers; Thai green chicken curry; smoked haddock kedgeree; nut, wholemeal and celery croquettes with a sweet and sour sauce; and steak and kidney pie. There's a separate children's menu with dishes starting at around £1.50. The hand-pumped beers come from Yorkshire and include Black Sheep Best, Tim Taylor's Landlord, Theakston Black Bull and Old Peculier. Masham, home to both Black Sheep and Theakston, is nearby: there are tours of the Black Sheep Brewery available and good food in its own bistro.

ROYAL OAK INN

PONTROBERT, POWYS (01938 500243)
Off A458

Outside the Royal Oak there's an adventure playground; inside there are crayons and paper to amuse bored children. The kids' special lunch and dinner is good value and includes pizzas and sausages. There's a good range of real ales for parents, including Draught Bass, Marston's Pedigree, Morland Old Speckled Hen, Worthington Best and Tetley. The pub has three bedrooms, cots and a baby-listening service. Pontrobert is a good base for touring West Wales.

Pubs with religious roots

New Inn

Coleford, Devon (01363 84242)

Off A377 Exter to Barnstaple road; four miles west of Crediton

There is a sprinkling of pubs called the New Inn that tend, actually, to be very old. The New Inn in Coleford dates from the 13th century and is one of the oldest ale houses in England. Several theories surround the name: some say it's a corruption of Our Lady's Inn, others say it was given to licensed premises built alongside a monastery and supplied with ale brewed by the monks, while yet more historians argue that it marked the site of an even older building replaced by a new inn, especially where monks had ceased to brew and handed over the rights to an inn keeper. Later, in the time of Elizabeth I, New Inns were built throughout the country when the monach complained about the poor inns she visited on her trips. Whichever way you slice it, the name has powerful religious roots. This New Inn is Grade-II listed, with a white-painted, cob and thatched exterior, and beams, a log fire, settles, stone wall seats, paraffin lamps and lots of china and ancient prints. Bar food and restaurant meals are based on locally-sourced ingredients, such as Devon cheeses for the ploughman's. Other dishes may include mussels in cider and cream; vegetable crumble; roasted vegetables on couscous; Dartmouth smoked trout with apple and mint jelly; and several fish dishes made from the latest catch at Brixham. Real ales include Badger Best, Otter Ale (from a Devon craft brewery) and Wadworth 6X. Accommodation is available.

Six Bells

Chiddingly, East Sussex (01825 872227)

Off A22 Uckfield to Eastbourne road

The Six Bells is a pub in the heart of the village, next door to the church and church hall. As with many old inns with the word "bell" in the name, it's a reference to the number of bells in the church steeple. The Six Bells has old beams, low ceilings, brick floors, fires in winter, wooden pews, old posters, and enamel advertisements. Bar food, lunchtime and evening, may include French onion soup; ploughman's; cheesy vegetable bake; shepherd's pie; and Stilton and walnut pie, with such desserts as chocolate nut sundae, banana split or raspberry pie. Ales include Harvey's Best from Lewes and Courage Best and Directors, all tapped straight from the cask. The garden has a goldfish pond and a boules pitch while the church has an interesting monument.

BULL

COTTERED, HERTFORDSHIRE (017763 281243)
A507

While pubs called the Bull often show the animal on inn signs, the origins of the name are religious and stem from bulla or la boule, the sign of a monastic order. The Bull in Cottered, near Baldock, opposite thatched cottages and surrounded by trees, has low beams in the lounge, a wooden floor, an open fire and masses of horsebrasses. Traditional pub games – cribbage, dominoes and shove-ha'penny – are played in the locals' bar. There's a small dining room, too. Bar meals (not Tuesday evening) may include filled jacket potatoes, home-made soup, ploughman's, stir-fried chicken or mushroom and sweet pepper Stroganoff, with such desserts as bread and brandy pudding or chocolate cheese cake. The evening menu has additional dishes including such specials as fried squid, feta salad, or Stilton and Guinness pie. There's a good wine list. Handpumped ales are from Greene King and include IPA, Abbot and seasonal beers.

LAMB

SHEEP STREET, BURFORD, OXFORDSHIRE (01993 823155)
A40

The Lamb at Burford is a magnificent 15th-century inn built of mellow Cotswold stone; the name is a reference to Christ, the Lamb of God. The elegant building has stone-mullioned windows, high-winged settles, antique wooden armchairs, flagstones and polished wood floors and a log fire in winter topped by a superb mantelpiece. Lunchtime bar food may include cream of celery, walnut and Roquefort soup; steak and mushroom pie; lamb with roast aubergines; salmon and lemon grass fish cakes; ploughman's; and filled baguettes. The no-smoking restaurant is open in the evenings or for Sunday lunch. There's an excellent wine list while the handpumped ales include Adnams Bitter, Hook Norton Best and Wadworth 6X – look out for the ancient beer engine in a glass cubicle. There's a back terrace that leads down to a pleasant lawn with flowers and shrubs. Accommodation is available.

Pubs with pets

WHITE HART

CONGRESBURY, SOMERSET (01934 833303)
Wrington Road, one mile east of A370

The White Hart is an attractive pub in large grounds, opposite a working farm and next to a riding centre, with an aviary in its huge rear garden. The birds include cockateels, canaries and finches. It's a family pub where children are welcome not only in the garden (which also has climbing frames and swings) but in a large conservatory stocked with books and toys. There's a special children's menu or kids can choose smaller portions from the adults' menu, which includes some vegetarian options. The main bar has beams and open fires and there are weekend barbecues in good weather. Beers come from Hall & Woodhouse and include Dorset Bitter, IPA and Tanglefoot.

RED LION

HINXTON, CAMBRIDGESHIRE (01799 530601)
Two miles from M11 junction 9; off A1301

When the children have had their fill of Duxford Aircraft Museum, you can refuel at this delightful 16th-century inn bursting with beams and timbers, horsebrasses and grandfather and grandmother clocks, with stuffed animals and a live, talkative parrot called George. Outside in the picnic garden there's a paddock with a goat and a pony. The inn offers both bar meals and full meals in a separate restaurant with a no-smoking area; children are welcome in the eating area of the bar and the restaurant. You can choose from soup; ploughman's lunch; steak and ale pie; tandoori chicken; Scotch salmon steak; and such desserts as lemon meringue pie and toffee crunch. Ales from East Anglian brewers include Adnams, Greene King and Nethergate.

Prince Albert

62 Silver Street, Ely, Cambridgeshire (01353 663494)
Off A10

When your neck is in knots from gazing up at the many splendours of Ely Cathedral and the kids are bored with brass rubbing, hurry off to this splendid old-fashioned boozer, described by the *Good Beer Guide* as a "classic town local". It is charmingly small and old-fashioned inside, with open fires, but there is a fine garden where, unusually, the managers don't mind if you eat your own food as long as you buy drinks. Pub food (lunchtime only) runs to such simple but welcome fare as sandwiches and ploughman's. The high spot of the garden is the collection of birds, including budgies, cockateels, canaries and finches. There is also play equipment for children. Adults can sup Greene King XX Mild, IPA, Abbot Ale and the brewery's range of seasonal ales.

Crown Inn

Colchester Road, Wormingford, Essex (01787 227405)
B1508, at north-west end of village between Colchester and Sudbury

The Crown is a 17th-century inn in a Stour Valley village where members of John Constable's family are buried in the churchyard; the church features in some of his paintings. The inn has a wealth of beams and open fires in two bars: one is a genuine and now rare public bar, while the lounge has wood-panelled walls. A room between the lounge and the restaurant can be used by families while the large garden has a collection of bantam hens, geese and ornamental pheasants in a safe play area for children. Food, served lunchtime and evening, includes a daily hot lunchtime special, several vegetarian dishes, fresh fish and ploughman's. Ales are Greene King IPA and Abbot.

Wight Mouse Inn

Chale, Isle of Wight (01983 730431)
B3399, off A3055

The Wight Mouse, attached to the Clarendon Hotel, is one of the most child-friendly pubs in Britain with no fewer than three family rooms and a large garden with climbing frames, swings, slides, an adventure challenge, a special area set aside for toddlers, a pets corner with dogs, rabbits, lambs and kittens, and rides on two Shetland ponies called Arthur and Sid. There are occasional Punch and Judy shows and live music every evening. The old stone pub, opposite Blackgang Chine, has a pleasant bar with an open fire and a games room with pews and oak tables where dominoes and pinball are played. Food comes in the form of both bar snacks and full restaurant meals. You can choose from sandwiches, soup, ploughman's, vegetarian pasta bake, fisherman's platter and several daily specials. Children's portions are available. As well as more than 300 whiskies and 50 wines, the pub offers beers from Gales, Marstons and Wadworth.

SWAN

MILLWOOD END, LONG HANBOROUGH, OXFORDSHIRE
(01993 881347)
Off A4095

The Swan, a charming and unspoilt one-bar village local, has a large enclosed garden with just about every attraction for children, including guinea pigs and rabbits as well as an adventure course and such pub games as Aunty Sally and skittles. When the weather is poor, families can retreat to an outhouse with a pool table. Bar snacks are available lunchtime and evening. Beers come from Morrells and include Bitter and Varsity (the Oxford brewery no longer exists and the beers are brewed under licence by Thomas Hardy of Dorchester). The Swan is a good base for Blenheim Palace, the Roman remains near Coombe, and Wychwood Forest.

THREE CUPS

NEAR PUNNETTS TOWN, EAST SUSSEX (01435 830252)
B2096, two miles from Heathfield towards Battle

This ancient inn has low beams, wood panelling, large bay windows and an inglenook with an open fire and a black mantelbeam that dates the place from 1696. Chickens and ducks roam in the large rear garden while friendly pub pets include two dogs, Lettie and Monty, and a ginger cat called Hattie. A dining room, where children are welcome (there's a no-smoking area), leads on to a terrace overlooking the garden. Home-made bar food includes soup, sandwiches, ploughman's, cauliflower cheese, meat or vegetarian lasagne, fish and chips, and steak in ale pie. Beards and Harveys ales are joined by regular guest beers. It is good walking country as the pub is in the Sussex Weald.

THREE CROWNS

WISBOROUGH GREEN, WEST SUSSEX (01403 700207)
A272 Petworth to Billingshurst road

The Three Crowns dates from the 15th century and stands in a delightful village. It has a patio and garden where children (accompanied by adults) can play with rabbits and guinea pigs. The pub also has a dog called Louis and a cat called Leo. There are swings and other amusements in the garden while a family room has games for children to play. Good pub food, lunchtime and evening, includes chicken nuggets, fish fingers and other children's standard fare, plus soup, lasagne, steaks, vegetable cannelloni, potato, cheese and spinach pie, and whole Dover sole. Beers are from Greene King and local craft brewer Ballards.

STRINES INN

BRADFIELD DALE, SOUTH YORKSHIRE (0114 2851247)
Signposted from A616, also from junction of A57 and A6013 at Ladybower Reservoir

The Strines is home to several rescued animals. In the garden you will find Gideon, an old donkey, as well as pigs, goats, geese, sheep and a rabbit called Budweiser: I trust he's named after the Czech beer, not the American version. The stone-built inn is ancient, dating from the 13th century. The main bar has a welcoming coal fire as well as black beams decorated with copper kettles, and wall benches and chairs. There are two smaller rooms, one of them non-smoking. Children are welcome to eat away from the main bar. Home-made bar food includes sandwiches, soup, jacket potatoes, ploughman's, vegetable bake, giant Yorkshire puddings with a choice of fillings, grilled trout and daily specials. The ever-changing range of real ales could include Boddingtons, Marstons and Morland. The inn is set in the High Peak National Park and has stunning views. Accommodation is available.

Note: *Please monitor children carefully in pub gardens as they have been known to allow pets to escape.*

Boars Head

Aust, Gloucestershire (01454 632278)
Just off M4 junction 21

The Boars Head has an aviary and rabbits in the delightful setting of a sheltered garden that also has a medieval stone well. Children are welcome inside the old pub, too, with its big smoke-blackened beams, stripped stone walls, tables made from old beer casks and high-backed winged settles. There are two log fires and a pleasant dining room with tables set with candles and fresh flowers. The ales are Courage Best and Directors with Eldridge Pope Royal Oak backed by a good choice of single malt whiskies. Food, lunchtime and evening, could include soup; sandwiches; salad bar; smoked salmon and scrambled eggs; haunch of venison; fresh plaice; and Sunday roasts, with such desserts as fruit crumble.

Waggon and Horses

Doulting Beacon, Doulting, Somerset (01749 880302)
Off A37 and A367

The big attraction for families in this splendid 18th-century inn is a large walled garden with flowering shrubs, a wildlife pond, a climbing frame for children, a paddock with horses, a goat, wildfowl and pens with a range of rare birds. Not surprisingly, eggs are for sale. The inn is astonishing, with a raftered upper storey reached by a flight of stone steps, and a bar with antique furnishings and paintings for sale by local artists. Two further rooms are non-smoking. This palatial hostelry is owned by Ushers of Trowbridge and sells the brewery's Best Bitter, Founder's Ale and seasonal brews. The food is eclectic and of the highest quality, ranging from Austrian to Chinese dishes. As well as soup and sandwiches, you may find Thai prawns in filo pastry with garlic dip; spicy bean casserole; omelettes with free-range eggs supplied by the generous birds in the garden; lasagne; chicken breast topped with ham, cheese and tomato; and steaks. Desserts may include steamed ginger and lemon pudding or treacle tart. There is a good choice of wines. By way of enterainment, the inn offers a skittles alley and regular classical and jazz concerts in the gallery, which also stages art exhibitions. This is a quite remarkable place where children are welcome but must be on their best behaviour.

Pub Walk in the Chilterns and Chess Valley

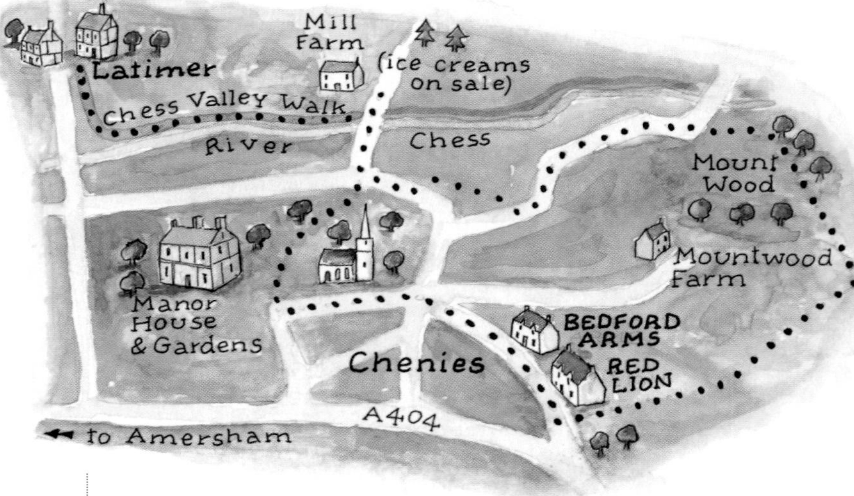

This easy-going walk starts at the **RED LION** in Chenies, Buckinghamshire, just off the A404 Amersham road. The white-painted building has burgundy-coloured window frames and window boxes. The front bar has a large bowed window, old photos of the area and a model of Stephenson's Rocket. There's a dining room and a small snug at the back, and you can eat and drink outside on benches in front of a small cottage that adjoins the pub.

The pub has a good reputation for food (lunchtime and evening), which includes soup, filled baguettes, jacket potatoes with a choice of fillings, grilled Mediterranean tomatoes with melted cheese and black olives, kiln-smoked trout, pasta with bacon, olive oil, parsley and shaved Parmesan, venison burgers, minced beef koftas, lamb curry, orange roughy on a bed of leeks and fennel with a Pernod sauce, ploughman's, and such home-made pies as chicken, spinach and egg, fish, peas and chips in a cheese sauce, and pork, apple and redcurrant. Vegetarian dishes include cauliflower cheese, five-bean chilli, and Stilton and vegetable parcels. Daily specials may include carrot and coriander soup, chick peas with chard, baked halibut, or venison stew.

Hand-pumped real ales include the local Vale Brewery's Notley Bitter and Lion Pride, which is a house beer brewed by Rebellion of Marlow, along with Benskins Best and Wadworth 6X. Service is friendly and attentive, down to bringing, unasked, a bowl of water for my dog.

The Red Lion, Chenies, Bucks

The walk starts alongside the pub, with a sign indicating a public footpath. You go down a narrow passageway between the pub and the next-door garden and through a metal gate into a meadow with the low, wooded Chiltern hills in the distance. On the other side of the meadow you pass through a wooden gate, cross a track and go over a stile on to a path with a farm on the left and a tall hedge to the right.

The path takes you into another meadow with a beaten grass track that leads towards a hedge. You go through a gap in the hedge, over a path and stile, and into a field of tall grass that drops down steeply and gives fine views of other fields rising ahead of you, with a wood to the left. A stile takes you into the wood, rich in bird song, and – the only jarring note on the walk – a Thames Water Sewage Treatment Works to the right. You now reach a road, which you have to walk along for a short distance until steps on the left take you up into the woods and on to a path above the road.

A short walk along the path brings you to steps that take you down to the road again. You now have a choice: just a few yards along the road, an entrance to the left takes you back into the woods and you can continue the walk back to Chenies. However, if you cross the road another road leads off that takes you over a humpbacked bridge over the River Chess to Mill Farm where excellent ice creams such as Loseley are on sale. From the farm you can follow the Chess Valley Walk for about a mile to the village of Latimer with many half-timbered houses and cottages. If you decide to do this stage of the walk, stout shoes or boots are advisable as the path can get soggy in places. After visiting Latimer you have to retrace your steps back along the riverside to Mill Farm, over the main road and back into the woods.

Signs offer footpaths to left and right. Bear right and follow the broad path that climbs quite steeply through the woods. The path is overhung by branches and on a Saturday afternoon a church bell was tolling nearby, possibly for a wedding. The ground to either side of the path is thickly carpeted with leaf mould and my dog suddenly went snuffling after a pigmy shrew, a rare breed, that scuttled across the path.

You reach a T-junction at the top of the path. Turn left and a short distance ahead you will see a stile. There is a path on the other side

with another stile. Clamber over both stiles and continue along a track between the trees and then over yet another stile. You are now on a road that runs alongside Chenies Manor, an Elizabethan house with magnificent gardens open to the public*.

Turn left at a sign for Chenies. The manor grounds are to the left: watch out for a hollowed-out tree struck by lightning at some time in its history. You reach the main road by Chenies School. Bear right as the road forks and walk past some attractive brick cottages until you reach the BEDFORD ARMS hotel on the left. If you need a small libation, it offers Courage Best, Directors and Theakston's Best. Bar food includes soup, deep-fried mushrooms, tomato and mozzarella salad, duck liver pâté, trio of sausages, Bedford burger, fried plaice goujons, poached salmon salad, and battered cod with chips and peas. If you continue past the Bedford Arms (which also has a restaurant and accommodation) you find yourself back at the Red Lion (which closes in the afternoon). The walk will take between 45 minutes and an hour; allow two hours if you add on the Chess Valley Walk.

Chenies Manor is open to the public on Wednesdays and Thursdays, 2pm to 5pm, from Easter until the end of October. Entry to house and gardens is £4.50; half price for gardens only. The grounds include a physic garden, kitchen garden, white garden, sunken garden, and a yew tree maze. Further information 01494 762888.

Veterans of the *Good Beer Guide*

Queen's Head, Newton, Cambridgeshire

QUEEN'S HEAD

FOWLMERE ROAD, NEWTON, CAMBRIDGESHIRE (01223 870436)
B1368, off M11 and A10

In common with the other pubs in this section, the Queen's Head has appeared in every one of the first 25 editions of the *Camra Good Beer Guide*, and pubs have to offer consistently good beer and other facilities to win the support of Camra members. A former coaching inn close to Cambridge, the Queen's Head stands at the junction of five roads. The dark brick building, dominated by a tall chimney, started life as a farm in the 17th century. The farmer gained a reputation for his home-brewed beer, so he turned the building into an ale house. It has hardly changed since then. The main bar has bowed windows, a cross-beamed ceiling, a curved high-back settle, scrubbed benches, a yellow tiled floor, a large fireplace, and a loudly ticking clock. A corridor leads to a small room where you can play such traditional old pub games as Devil Among the Tailors (a version of table skittles), and Nine Men's Morris, an Elizabethan board game. The inn has been in the same hands for as long as it's been in the *Good Beer Guide*, and David and Juliet Short have built a fine reputation for the quality of the Adnams' ales they tap straight from casks: Best Bitter, Broadside and Extra, with Regatta in summer, Old Ale in winter and Tally Ho at Christmas. There are country wines, too, and usually a couple of farm ciders. Simple, tasty meals include home-made soup made from vegetables and flavoured with home-grown herbs; sandwiches made from bread from a local bakery; Aga-baked jacket potatoes filled with cheese and butter; or toast and dripping. In the evening there's soup again, with plates of cold meat or cheese. The head of the queen on the inn sign is that of Anne of Cleves, though she has no known connections with the area. Before the First World War, George V and Kaiser Wilhelm used to pop in for a pint, and the Shah of Persia, before he lost the Peacock Throne, and his wife once had lunch here. A goose called Belinda, who used to patrol the car park and hiss in a terrifying manner at drivers, was stuffed after her death and now has pride of place in a glass case.

Rose & Crown

89 High Street, Ridgmont, Bedfordshire (01525 280245)
A418; off M1 junction 13

Landlord Neil McGregor has a love affair with Rupert Bear, the little ursine star, who talks in rhyming couplets, of a newspaper strip cartoon and spin-off annuals for around 80 years. Rupert Bear annual covers and other memorabilia decorate this 17th-century, attractive brick building that was once part of the Duke of Bedford's estate. Spot the sign for Nutwood Ales: they're not on sale but as Rupert anoraks will tell you, Nutwood is the home of the bear and his "chums". There's also a collection of English sheepdog china and the bar has brasses and a brick fireplace with an open fire. The inn belongs to Charles Wells of Bedford and sells the brewery's Eagle Bitter and Bombardier along with seasonal brews. There's a good selection of whiskies as well. A games area offers darts, dominoes, cribbage and shove-ha'penny, plus that Transatlantic intrusion, pool. Bar food, lunchtime and evening, may include sandwiches; macaroni cheese; steak and ale pie; lasagne; Cumberland sausage; vegetable tikka; and avocado bake. In summer the pub is a riot of tubs and hanging baskets and there's a large tree-lined garden with picnic tables. The grounds also offer facilities for camping and caravanning. Children are welcome in a family room.

Cock

23 High Street, Broom, Bedfordshire (01767 314411)
Off A1 and B658; from A1 follow signs for Old Warden and aerodrome and watch for sign for Broom

Step back in time before the advent of the bar and hand-pumps in this listed building. The Cock stands in a row of ancient cottages opposite the village green. It's a 17th-century ale house, with Greene King beers (IPA, Triumph, Abbot and seasonal brews) tapped straight from casks. There are four small, quarry-tiled rooms with latched doors, wood-panelled walls, rustic furnishings, log fires and table skittles. The rooms are connected by a central corridor that leads to the kitchen and the cellar. The rear garden, with a safe play area, has a camp site attached. For all its rustic simplicity, the Cock offers some excellent food: tenants Gerry and Jean Lant provide home-made soups such as broccoli and cauliflower; home-made nut roast en croute; breaded mushrooms; chicken balti; gammon and chips; steak and mushrooms braised in red wine; peppered pork; and liver and bacon casserole. Children's helpings are available. Desserts include apple pie, chocolate pudding, and treacle pudding and custard. Sunday roasts use home-grown vegetables. Children are welcome in designated eating areas.

Farriers Arms

35 Lower Dagnall Street, St Albans, Hertfordshire (01727 851025)
Off A5183, A1, M1 and M25

The Farriers is a vibrant, unspoilt, classic backstreet boozer with a tiny, cramped front bar with a few wall benches, and, up a couple of steps, a spacious back lounge with comfortable seating. The walls are wood-panelled, the ceiling is a deep nicotine colour, and the toilets are in the backyard. The Farriers is home to cricket and football teams, while enthusiastic darts players perform to the right of the front bar. Although Draught Bass is on offer, this is first and foremost a McMullen's pub and the Hertford brewery's AK, Country and Gladstone are served in impeccable condition. According to a plaque on the outside wall, the Farriers was the base for the first branch of the Campaign for Real Ale in the early 1970s. This is not strictly accurate as there was a short-lived branch in the Midlands before the South Herts branch was formed. But at a time when the Farriers was one of only a handful of St Albans' 66 pubs to serve cask beer, it was used almost daily by the founding fathers of the campaign, who set up office in the city (the campaign is still based in St Albans, in Hatfield Road). The pub hasn't changed a bit since then, down to such simple lunchtime fare as sausage, egg and chips, or ham, egg and chips.

Star Tavern

6 Belgrave Mews West, London SW1 (020 7235 3019)
Underground: Hyde Park Corner

An elegant Georgian building in a cobbled mews off Belgrave Square, the Star has a veritable cornucopia of hanging baskets and flowering tubs outside in spring and summer. It stands, in its three-storeyed glory, next to an arched entrance to the mews. The ground floor is a mix of coffee house and gentlemen's club, with artefacts from the tea and coffee trade on the dark green walls, heavy curtains, deep leather armchairs and sofas, and slowly revolving ceiling fans; all it lacks is a punkah wallah. There's a large upstairs room that's used for functions and has staged at least two press receptions for the launch of the *Good Beer Guide*. Downstairs, the small bar at the front also acts as the food servery. Simple dishes, lunchtime and evening, include sausage, chips and beans, steaks, and sandwiches. The Star is owned by Fuller's and serves the brewery's Chiswick Bitter, London Pride, ESB and seasonal beers in splendid nick.

Fisherman's Tavern

10-12 Fort Street, Broughty Ferry, Tayside, Scotland
(01382 775941)
Off A92

This is the only Scottish pub that has appeared in every edition of the *Good Beer Guide*, a remarkable achievement that speaks volumes for the quality of the beer served here, currently Belhaven Eighty Shilling and St Andrew's Ale, Boddingtons Bitter, Maclay Eighty Shilling and guest ales. You can reach the pub by sea, tying up at a jetty. There are four drinking areas inside, but the centrepiece is the original bar with its ship's lights and tables; there's a quieter lounge, while a cosy back room has a genuine Victorian, coal-fuelled fire. As well as the excellent beers, there is a good choice of whiskies and country wines. Bar food, lunchtime and evening, offers soup; filled rolls or jacket potatoes; pasta dish of the day; breaded Norwegian scampi; chicken balti; steak and ale pie; and tortilla with spicy chicken and chilli filling. There's folk music on Thursday evenings, children are welcome in eating areas, the breakfast room is no-smoking, and accommodation is available. (Eighty Shilling in the name of a Scottish beer refers to a 19th-century system of invoicing, based on strength. The weakest beer, similar to an English mild, is Sixty Shilling, Seventy Shilling is roughly equivalent to Bitter, Eighty Shilling to Best Bitter, and Ninety Shilling to a strong ale.)

Note: *Other pubs that appeared in the first 25 editions of the* Good Beer Guide *are: Fleur de Lis, Bedford; Butt & Oyster, Pin Mill, Suffolk (p.260); Sow & Pigs, Toddington, Bedfordshire; Rising Sun, Tarporley, Cheshire; Blue Anchor, Helston, Cornwall (p. 64); New Inn, Kilmington, Devon; Ship Inn, Axmouth, Devon; Square & Compass, Worth Matravers, Dorset (p. 225); Jolly Drayman, Gravesend, Kent; Empress Hotel, Blackpool; Crown & Tuns, Deddington, Oxfordshire; All Nations, Madeley, Shropshire (p. 171); Cherry Tree, Tintern, Gwent, Wales; Buckingham Arms, London SW1; Fox & Hounds, London SW1; Roscoe Head, Liverpool; Star, Netherton, Northumberland. There were no Scottish pubs in the first edition of the guide, but the Fisherman's Tavern, Broughty Ferry, Tayside (p. 314), appeared in the first 25 editions that included Scotland.*

Red Lion pubs

OLD RED LION

418 ST JOHN'S STREET, LONDON EC1 (020 7837 7816)
Underground: Angel

This fine Victorian local is one of 600 British pubs that bear the name of the Red Lion. This one includes the word "old" in the title to distinguish it from another Red Lion, now defunct, in the vicinity. It was the tradition centuries ago for inns to salute a monarch or powerful baron, and Red Lions take their name from the coat of arms of John of Gaunt (1340-99). During part of Edward III's reign and, later, Richard II's rule, Gaunt (a corruption of Ghent, where he was born) acted as virtual dictator of England and was hugely disliked: Wat Tyler's peasant revolt in 1381 singled out Gaunt's palace for destruction. Inexplicably, Red Lion is still the most popular pub name in the country. This particular one is an impressive, four-storey redbrick building a few yards from the Angel road junction, named after another celebrated inn. Although the Old Red Lion dates from the 18th century, it was rebuilt in Victorian times, and had to retain a right-of-way through the pub to Goswell Road. The resulting passage is cut off from the front bar by a fine wood and engraved glass screen. Both the front bar, with a wooden settle, and the spacious, pillared back room are served by a long counter where Draught Bass and Fuller's London Pride are dispensed. According to a local legend, which is inscribed on a text on the wall, the Norfolk radical Tom Paine wrote his celebrated call-to-arms, *The Rights of Man*, in the pub. In fact, he wrote it in the American colonies, but he may well have been a visitor to the pub, as Clerkenwell and Finsbury were for long a haunt of radicals. Lunchtime food in the Old Red Lion is excellent and is based on fresh ingredients supplied every day by local markets. There are always two or three hot dishes, including a vegetarian option. The Friday fish dish, such as fisherman's pie, or cod in a pastry envelope, should not be missed. The pub has another claim to fame: it has a celebrated small upstairs theatre, where several young playwrights and actors have launched their careers. According to the landlord, one of the most celebrated members of the acting fraternity, the late Trevor Howard, was once in the bar "as pissed as a rat". The pub is closed on Sundays.

Red Lion

1 Waverton Street, London W1 (020 7499 1307)
Underground: Green Park

This couldn't be more different from the rumble and bustle of the Angel, a Red Lion set in one of the most attractive and tranquil areas of Mayfair. Seated inside on winged settles on bare floor boards, you could be forgiven for thinking you were tucked away in a rural ale house. Only the scenes of London that decorate the walls, and the daily copy of the *Financial Times* in the gents', give a clue to the pub's true position. Unusually for this part of London, landlord Greg Peck serves food lunchtime and evening. You may find sandwiches; Cumberland sausage; ribs with barbecue sauce; fish and chips; and daily specials. The hand-pumped ales are Courage Best and Directors, Greene King IPA and Theakston's Best. Mr Peck also serves a legendary Bloody Mary if you're feeling a touch hungover.

Red Lion

24 Long Street, Cerne Abbas, Dorset (01300 341441)
Off A352

This cottage-style pub is mainly Victorian in style, but there are some far older touches, including an imposing, 16th-century fireplace in a bar dominated by a fine wooden counter. Beer buffs will be impressed by the Groves Brewery windows, a *memento mori* of one of England's many lost breweries. There's a striking wooden serving counter and a large collection of china. In true West Country fashion, the pub has a skittle alley, and cribbage, darts and shove ha'penny are also played. The hand-pumped ale is Wadworth 6X and there are regular guest beers, too, along with a decent wine list. Food, lunchtime and evening, in bar and restaurant, uses vegetables from allotments in the vicinity. Dishes may include soup; filled jacket potatoes; cannelloni filled with spinach and ricotta; several other vegetarian pasta dishes; and chicken breast and chips, with such desserts as apple cake and crème brûlée. Cerne Abbas has a ruined Benedictine abbey and is best known for the Romano-British giant cut from the chalk hills that overlook the delightful village (*see* Royal Oak, *page 17*).

Red Lion

Snargate, Kent (01797 344648)
B2080, two miles from Brenzett

This is a true rural ale house: no frills, no thatch, no roses round the door. It stands on the lonely road between Tenterden and New Romney, a white, 450-year-old building that was last modernised in 1890. It has been run by members of the Jemison family since 1911, and Doris Jemison has no intention of letting it go, a fact emphasised by her position in front of the bar, where she knits ferociously like a tricoteuse at the guillotine. She's helped by her daughter, a further sign of family content and determination. There are two simple rooms with bare boards, tongue-and-groove panelling, and a few ancient beams. One room has a bar billiards table, while the main room has a marble-topped counter with pewter and brass hand-pumps. The pumps are ornaments, for the ales – Goachers Light from Maidstone, Adnams, Batemans, Oakham or Swale – are tapped straight from casks. There's also a local cider called (you've been warned) Double Vision. The pub is a veritable museum of traditional pub games: you can try your hand at bat and trap (*see* Rose & Crown, *pp283–4*), skittles, shove-ha'penny and toad-in-the-hole, a variation on penny-in-the-hole, where small, coin-shaped weights are thrown into a hole in a pub seat. Apart from crisps, the Red Lion doesn't sell food. Snargate, on the edge of the Romney Marsh, is a remote little community that came into existence in the 13th century, when a sluicegate or snaregate was opened on the Appledore to Romney waterway in 1254.

Red Lion

Stiffkey, Norfolk (01328 830552)
A149

This Red Lion, in a village of delightful flint-faced cottages close to the sea, has a special place in beer lovers' hearts. Norfolk in the 1960s and 70s was ravaged by the now defunct London brewer Watney Mann. Not content with foisting the awful Red Barrel keg beer on the populace at large, Watneys bought and eventually closed all three of Norwich's once proudly independent brewers, Bullards, Morgan, and Steward & Patteson. It also went on the rampage in the countryside, closing scores of rural pubs. Stiffkey lost all three of its pubs and was virtually wrecked as a community, with nowhere for the cricket, football and darts teams to meet. Great was the rejoicing in the village when the Red Lion reopened in the early 1990s. This 18th-century brick and flint building has been sensitively renovated, and its old beams and wooden floors have been retained. Stairs connect the three spacious bars and there are open fires, oil lamps, pews, wall seats and settles. There's a separate games room with darts, cribbage and dominoes. Food is available lunchtime and evening, and includes local fish and seafood, such as Stiffkey (pronounced "Stookey") mussels, Cromer crabs, and Blakeney whitebait. Look out for Stiffkey fish pie, whole plaice, lemon sole, pheasant breast and samphire, and steak and kidney pie, followed by such tempting desserts as apple and cinnamon ice cream. There's a tremendous offering of East Anglian ales from Adnams, Elgood's, Greene King, and Woodforde's. Wines, including several by the glass, come from Adnams, too. Accommodation is available.

RED LION

BURNSALL, NORTH YORKSHIRE (01756 720204)
B6160 Ilkley road

You don't expect to find too many pubs in God's Own County named in honour of the Duke of Lancaster, but this is an exceptional, 16th-century, creeper-clad ferryman's inn lit by gas lamps, heated by a solid-fuel stove, and dominated by a vast, copper-topped counter. The panelled walls of the bar have paintings and photos of local fell-racing scenes, while the no-smoking lounge has beer served through a hatch. There are gas lamps on a back terrace, with fine views of the River Wharfe. Hand-pumped ales include Theakston's Best, Black Bull and Old Peculier from Masham, plus Morland Old Speckled Hen, and a good choice of wines, with several by the glass. Imaginative food, lunchtime and evening in bar and restaurant, may include sandwiches; Red Lion Yorkshire ploughman's; fresh pasta; venison; ratatouille and blue Wensleydale cheese; steak and kidney in ale pie; smoked haddock topped with Welsh rarebit; and tuna steak salad. Desserts may include chocolate sponge, and bananas with rum ice cream. Burnsall is in the Yorkshire Dales, fine walking territory, and the Red Lion offers accommodation.

Opposite: Old Red Lion, St. John's Street, London EC1

RED LION
PUNCH TAVERN
THEATRE

Pubs with unusual names

FLITCH OF BACON

THE STREET, LITTLE DUNMOW, ESSEX (01371 820323)
Off A120

This small 15th-century country inn takes its name from the Whit Monday custom of awarding a side or "flitch" of bacon to any married couple in the village who can prove they have lived for the past year without a quarrel. The small timbered bar has pews for seats and such traditional pub games as cribbage and dominoes. There's folk music one evening a week and Morris Men perform outside in the summer. The regular beer is Greene King IPA with such guests as Fuller's London Pride, Crouch Vale Bitter and Nethergate Umbel Magna. Bar food may include the likes of soup, ploughman's, local ham and eggs, sausage hot-pot, smoked salmon and scrambled eggs, pork and apple, and steak and kidney pie. There's a Sunday buffet. The inn stands opposite a large and pleasant green. Children are welcome in the restaurant until 7.30pm and accommodation is available.

TOWN OF RAMSGATE

62 WAPPING HIGH STREET, LONDON E1 (020 7264 0001)
Underground: Wapping

This 17th-century ale house was first called the Red Cow, and changed its name in honour of the Kentish fishermen from Ramsgate who used to land their catch on Wapping Old Stairs by the pub. Inside the pub there's a magnificent etched mirror depicting Ramsgate harbour when it was a major fishing port. As well as an unusual name, the pub is also rare (possibly unique) in having its own gallows. It was used at Execution Dock in 1701 to hang Captain Kidd. Kidd has gone down in history as a pirate. In fact, he was a commissioned privateer who fought the French but made the fatal mistake of swindling some of his aristocratic patrons, who then had him tried by parliament. The cellars of the pub doubled as cells for press-ganged men waiting to be put on ships, and for alleged criminals awaiting transportation to the Americas or Australia. In more companionable times, the pub today is decked with hanging baskets outside, while inside there's a wooden platform at the back that offers fine views of the Thames. Bar food lunchtime and evening may include an all-day breakfast; sandwiches; hot filled baguettes; vegetable tikka; steak and ale pie; fish and chips; and tagliatelle carbonara. Hand-pumped beers include Draught Bass and Fuller's London Pride, plus a regular guest such as Young's Special.

Bishop Out of Residence

2 Bishops Hall, Kingston-on-Thames, Greater London (020 8546 4965)

This is a 20-year-old pub on the site of an old tannery overlooking the Thames by Kingston Bridge. The name was chosen in a competition run by Young's Brewery of Wandsworth. Youngs had planned to call this new outlet the Kingston Ram (the ram being the brewery mascot and symbol) but there was already a Ram pub in Kingston, so Young's turned to its customers for ideas. The pub is close to the official residence of William of Wykeham (1324-1404), who was Lord Chancellor, Bishop of Winchester, and founder of Winchester College. With so many demands on his time, he was not often in residence at Kingston, a theme taken up by the pub sign that shows a mitred bishop fishing in the Thames. You can enter the pub from the road, with its bowed frontage, or from the river walk, where there are some tables for eating, drinking, and viewing in good weather. Inside, there's a spacious bar overlooking the river, with a second room on the first floor. Landlord Roger Woodall serves only home-made food that includes steak and kidney pie, and ten vegetarian dishes every day. The Young's ales include Bitter, Special and seasonal brews such as the renowned Winter Warmer.

Dirty Habit

Hollingbourne, Kent (01622 880880)
B2163, off A20

The habit in question refers not to customers but to the fact that the inn was originally part of a monastery. Monks were prodigious brewers and quaffers of ale until our friend Henry VIII closed them down. In Kent the monks had the ability to choose the pick of the hop crop for their bibulous endeavours and it's not surprising that an inn dating from the early 15th century should have hop bines tumbling over the beams in the bar. In fact,

Bishop Out of Residence, Kingston-on-Thames

the date of the inn coincides neatly with the arrival of the hop plant in England: it was brought to Kent by Flemish settlers, who preferred the hopped bières of the Low Country to the heavy and malty unhopped ales they found across the Channel. A battle over ale and beer went on for centuries in Britain and Henry VIII banned his court brewer from using the climbing plant. The Dirty Habit's beams are extremely low, it has ancient settles, deep and comfortable armchairs, open fires, panelled walls, and a candle-lit dining area. The ales on hand-pump include Draught Bass, Fuller's

London Pride, and Wadworth's 6X and Farmer's Glory. Home-made fruit wines are also served. Bar food is served lunchtime and evening and may include home-made soup; filled baguettes; beef in ale pie; Scotch salmon wrapped in filo pastry; steaks; pasta dishes, chicken satay; and Chinese roast pork. Children are welcome and the inn is ideal for keen walkers, being based on the North Downs Way.

PETER TAVY INN

PETER TAVY, DEVON (01822 810348)

Off A386, three miles from Tavistock

Peter Tavy must not be confused with Peter Davy, one of Uncle Tom Cobley's companions on the famously ill-fated trip to Widdecombe Fair. Village and pub take their name from the church of St Peter that stands on the banks of the River Tavy. The small, whitewashed and stone-built moorland inn, reached down a narrow lane, dates from the 15th century. It was originally a smithy and a miners' cottage, and was refashioned as an ale house for masons working on the church. There are hanging baskets and flower tubs around the porched entrance. Inside there are beams, settles set in the deep mullioned windows, more settles on the slate floor, standing timbers, and a dominating stone fireplace. Tables are invitingly candlelit at night. The dining room is no-smoking. Daily menus are chalked on two blackboards, one for starters and main courses, a second for desserts. Starters could be tomato or leek and Stilton soup; baked avocado with prawns; spinach pancake with savoury mushrooms; or port and Stilton pâté; followed by chicken tikka; cannelloni ricotta; monkfish in a creamy garlic sauce; seafood lasagne; duck with fresh mango sauce; baked cod with cheese and tomato; cashew nut paella; or vegetable cottage pie. Desserts may include toffee pear crumble, treacle tart or apple charlotte. There are also simpler bar snacks such as filled ploughman's and baguettes. Beers include Cotleigh Tawny, Princetown Jail Ale and Best, and Summerskills Tamar Best from the West Country, with Draught Bass and Badger Best. Luscombe organic cider is also served. Children are welcome in the restaurant and accommodation is available.

Mortal Man

Upper Road, near High Green, Troutbeck, Cumbria
(01539 433193)
Pick up Troutbeck sign at junction of A591 and A592

This marvellous 300-year-old inn stands in a lovely village at the foot of the fells and with breathtaking views over to Windermere. Its unique name stems from the legend of a giant buried in the inn's foundations. The original inn sign was painted by an impecunious artist named Ibbetson who, in order to settle his bill with the landlord, Tommy Burkett, painted a sickly wretch on one side and a hale and hearty fellow on the other who, with his glowing nose, closely resembled Bardolph in Shakespeare's *Henry V*. The sign was accompanied by a couplet:

Thou mortal man, that liv'st by bread
What is it makes thy nose so red?
Thou silly elf with nose so pale
It is with drinking Burkett's ale.

You can enhance the colour of your nose today with the likes of Marston's Pedigree, Theakston's Best or a guest ale. The panelled and beamed main bar has settles and a blazing log fire in winter. A smaller second room is set aside for dining. Food, lunchtime and evening, may include home-made soup; sandwiches; filled baguettes and jacket potatoes; Thai chicken curry; fresh vegetable stir fry; gammon and egg; steak and kidney pudding; and grilled swordfish steak. There's a thoughtful separate menu for children. Accommodation is available. Folk and blues are performed on Sunday evenings. It's marvellous walking terrain but please leave your muddy boots outside.

Pubs saved for their communities

Three Tuns

Salop Street, Bishop's Castle, Shropshire (01588 638797)
Off B4385

Bishop's Castle, which has neither a bishop nor a castle, is border country: the dividing line between England and Wales is close by, along with Offa's Dyke. The Three Tuns is an ancient inn, built in 1642, and brewing has always taken place on the site. The current small, 12-barrel brewery was added in Victorian times and was run by the Roberts family until 1976. It's a classic four-storey "tower brewery", now a Grade I listed building, with malt store and "liquor" (water) tanks at the top, feeding the brewing vessels and fermenters below. Everything works by gravity, a utilitarian Victorian method employed in such bigger breweries as Harvey's of Lewes and Hook Norton in Oxfordshire: the system avoids the use of pumps, that have a habit of breaking down. If you are brave enough, you can stand on the platform for the malt hoist at the top of the brewery and look out over gently undulating border countryside. A group of friends used to meet in the pub on Boxing Day but when they turned up in 1996 they found it was closed. The group included locals Jan and Robin Cross, solicitor Robert Anthony and his wife Margaret, and from Islington in London leading barrister Sir Louis Blom-Cooper and his wife Jane, who have a holiday home over the border in Montgomeryshire. Determined not to lose their favourite hostelry, they raised the money to buy the pub and brewery. Robert Anthony carried out the conveyancing work and Margaret Anthony is now the licensee. The Three Tuns reopened in July 1997 and lovers of the old inn and its ales came from all over the country to celebrate. A professional brewer, Steve Dunn, and local restaurateur Elaine Fraser were recruited to supply ale and victuals. The pub remains quite unspoilt, with two bars, flagged floors, heavy beams, wooden settles, a Jacobean staircase, a kitchen range and, in the small locals' bar, an impressive wall clock built by the Anglo-Swiss Watch Company. The draught beers are Sexton's Bitter, XXX Bitter and Offa's Ale with regular seasonal ales such as Old Scrooge at Christmas. Old Scrooge also comes in a bottle-fermented version, along with Bellringer and Cleric's Cure. Visitors can buy their own home-brew kits, cases of bottles or small casks of beer to take away (for availability, phone 01588 638023). Imaginative food includes potato and fennel soup; beef in Three Tuns ale; ratatouille with mozzarella and salad; chilli con carne with wild rice; and a strong emphasis on fresh fish and seafood in the shape of fish soup, fish pie, seafood salad and cod. Desserts include rhubarb crumble, apricot and brandy butter pudding, and lemon tart. Accommodation is available in a converted stable block.

Note: *Shropshire is a county strong on community: the* Six Bells, *Church Street, also in Bishop's Castle, is owned by a trust formed to save the pub from re-development. It also has a small brewery behind the pub that brews Big Nev's, Cloud Nine and Old Recumbent. In Clunton, a town with strong Housman connections, the* Crown Inn *was saved from closure in 1994 when locals raised £150,000 to buy it.*

HARROW

LITTLE BEDWYN, WILTSHIRE (01672 870871)
Off A4, south-west of Hungerford

The Harrow is a brick-built Victorian inn, near the Kennet and Avon Canal, that was saved from closure by the villagers in 1991. They formed a co-operative to raise finance: the biggest shareholder put in £5,000, the smallest £100. After eight years of running the pub, the co-op found the strain too much and at the end 1998 it was sold to Roger and Sue Jones, who re-opened on December 18, just in time for the busy Christmas period. The delightful inn has three inter-connected rooms, the middle one of which has been retained as a snug where locals can sup their ale. The rooms have polished board floors, country chairs and wooden tables and a large wood-burning stove. The emphasis is on top-quality food and the Joneses offer bar snacks such as baguettes, pasta, and salads with such main dishes as lamb cassoulet, chicken and Stilton pie, liver and bacon, roast fillet of cod in chilli sauce, char-grilled steak, confit of duck with apple chutney, char-grilled sweet peppers, vegetable risotto, lobster and prawn risotto and such desserts as lime brûlée, bread and butter pudding and pineapple with rum and raisin sauce. The 35-strong wine list offers champagne, New World wines, and dessert wines by the half bottle. There's a good range of malt whiskies, Cognacs and Armagnacs while the "wine of the country" – real ale – comes in the shape of Butts, a small craft brewery near Hungerford, Hook Norton and Ringwood. Accommodation is available.

Red Lion

Preston, Hertfordshire (01462 459585)

Off A505 and B656, south of Hitchin

In the late 1980s Whitbread announced it planned to turn this early 19th-century ale house into a Beefeater. The villagers rose up in arms, discovered the Red Lion was a listed building and thwarted the giant brewery. Whitbread said it would sell the pub to the villagers on the undertaking that they all put in the same amount of cash – a rare example of capitalist egalitarianism. The villagers came up trumps, raised £150,000 and became the proud owners of the pub. In the mid-1990s, they leased the Red Lion to Phil and Sue Cross, who have sensitively restored the interior. "People who haven't been in for years and some who have been abroad for decades come back and say the pub is how they remembered it," Phil says. The Red Lion has one bar, a roaring log fire, beams and rustic prints on the walls. The food is all prepared on the premises by Sue and ranges from sandwiches and ploughman's to cottage pie, steaks and three vegetarian options. The ales include Bateman's XXXB and Greene King IPA plus regular guest beers.

The Plough, Horbling, Lincolnshire

Plough

4 Spring Lane, Horbling, Lincolnshire (01529 240263)
Off A15 and A52

The Plough dates from the 1750s and looks the part: untouched and unspoilt, it is a ramble of small rooms with beams, wooden floors and open fires. When the pub was in danger of closing, the parish council took it over as a local amenity. It is now leased to Ruth and Terry Light who revel in the history and antiquity of the place. "The middle bar is called the Swaton Room," Terry explains. "It's named after a nearby village. When Swaton lost its pub, the regulars came to the Plough but, in the manner of rural Lincolnshire, they weren't allowed to mix with the locals and had their own separate bar." Home-cooked food includes beef Stroganoff; duck à l'orange; mushroom thermidor; broccoli and cheese bake; and steak Diane. Beers include Bateman's XB and other local independents.

Royal Oak

Meavy, Devon (01822 852944)
Off A386 and B3212 near Yelverton

The Royal Oak is ancient but it's a mere stripling compared to the oak tree outside that gives the pub its name: the tree is 1,000 years old and is thought to be the oldest in the country. The 15th-century thatched pub was originally owned by the local church, which sold it to the parish council in 1894 on condition that the profits were ploughed back into the local community. The Royal Oak is on the edge of Dartmoor and has pews from the church next door, slate floors, a vast fireplace in one bar with a bread oven, and old rural prints on the walls. Locals play euchre, a card game that originated in North America but is now considered a West Country speciality. Food, lunchtime and evening, includes soup and sandwiches, ploughman's, filled jacket potatoes, cheese and vegetable bake, chilli, vegetarian spaghetti bolognaise, mussels and cockles, shepherd's pie, Cumberland sausage, meat or vegetarian lasagne, and such old-fashioned desserts as spotted dick and custard, and apple crumble. Beers include the local Meavy Valley Bitter, Draught Bass and Courage Best. Several farm ciders are also available. Children aren't allowed inside the pub but there are picnic tables and benches on the green opposite and at the front of the building.

Note: *See also* **Old Crown** *(pp. 202–3,* Pubs for Cyclists *section): the pub's brewery has been bought by the local community.*

Pub walk in Hertfordshire

The walk starts and ends in the attractive village of Ashwell, with many ancient half-timbered buildings and the tallest church steeple in the county. The village is off the A505 Baldock to Royston road. You can also get to Ashwell by train from Kings Cross (Ashwell & Morden station is about two miles from the village). The base for the walk is the **BUSHEL & STRIKE** (Mill Street, 01462 742394), which offers bar and no-smoking restaurant meals, good local ale, and accommodation. The hand-pumped ales include Charles Wells Eagle Bitter and Bombardier from Bedford with such guest beers as Adnams Broadside or Badger Tanglefoot.

The main bar of the pub has a blazing fire in winter, with comfortable leather Chesterfields on the polished wooden floor. A passage leads to a conservatory restaurant fashioned from the village's old school hall: get ready for the stunning *trompe l'oeil* depictions of hills, horses and plants. You can eat here or in the front bar with tables laid with fresh flowers, salads and desserts in cabinets, and old coaching prints and local photographs on the walls.

Food, lunchtime and evening, may include home-made soup, grilled goat's cheese with gooseberry conserve, steak, kidney, mushroom and ale pie, ratatouille and Brie lasagne, lamb kleftiko, loin of pork with braised pears and prunes marinated in Armagnac, or chicken breast stuffed with pâté, plus a wide range of salads. Children are welcome in designated eating areas.

When you leave the pub, pause to look at the church with its Graffiti Scratchings on the interior of the tower wall, including a drawing of the original St Paul's Cathedral in London before it was destroyed by the Great Fire of 1666, and inscriptions referring to the plague of 1349 and the great storm of 1362. Now head for the High Street where the 14th-century Bear House has a rare architectural feature – seven quatrefoils in its north-east corner that acted as ventilators for its food store. The High Street becomes West End. When it meets Hinxworth Road, leave West End and join the road for a short distance. As it curves right, leave it for a chalky track. After a short

Bushel and Strike, Ashwell, Hertfordshire

walk between the backs of gardens you will be in open countryside, with a hedge to one side, with spectacular views over three counties, Cambridgeshire, Bedfordshire and Hertfordshire.

Follow the track and the hedge to a T-junction. Turn right and follow another hedge downhill with a water tower in the distance. Ignore a path going left and continue ahead, with Hinxworth church now coming into view. Keep straight on along a series of field edges and you eventually pass between a barn and a garden, followed quickly by a metal gate on the right. You can pause on the walk to visit Hinxworth Place, a 15th-century stone manor house built from locally quarried stone. After Hinxworth Place, pass through the metal gate and follow a hedge for a few yards to a post at a hedge corner. Turn half left and walk across a large open field, watching for the tiled roof of a barn straight ahead. Keep straight on, past another post in a hedge corner, follow a hedge interspersed with trees into the field's far left-hand corner and then on to a road.

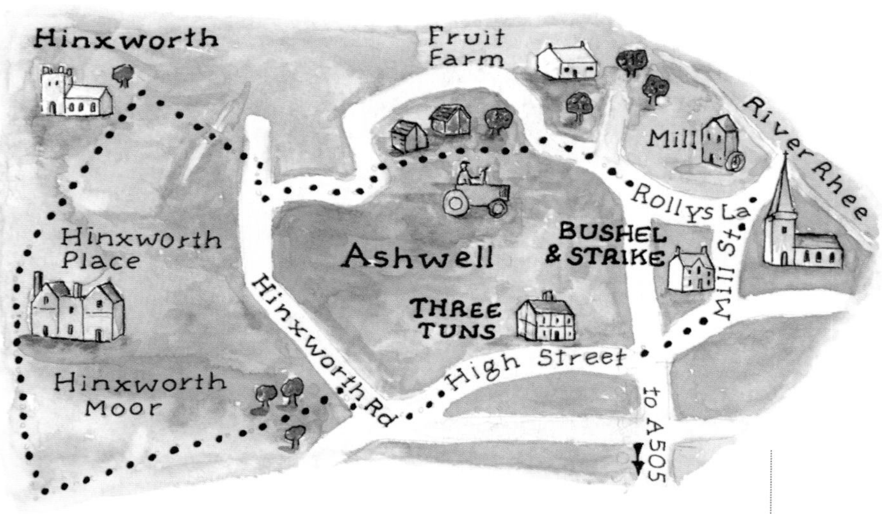

Cross the road to a bridleway, which is the drive to Arbtree Farm. Walk along here for a quarter-mile to a concreted area close to some barns. Turn right and enter a field and aim for two grey barns ahead. A footbridge on the far side of the field takes you on to a path into a smaller field. This leads to a gap in the hedge and a second footbridge. Go through the gap and into a field and immediately turn left, following the hedge to a lane at the corner of the field.

Turn right into the lane and then left at a T-junction near the grey barns. As you pass a bungalow and farm, keep on the lane to its second left bend and then on to a footpath sign on the right. Climb over a stile and head across the field. The path curves to the right as it crosses the field and you head towards more barns and then join a lane from a stile. Ashwell parish church is now in sight. Turn right into the lane and keep on past a fruit farm. Keep going forward at a road junction and continue into Rollys Lane, with a view of Ashwell Bury to the left. At the end of the lane turn right into Mill Street, pausing to look at the mill and the river, and then you are back at the Bushel & Strike.

The pub is open all day on Saturdays and Sundays but closes weekday afternoons. The **THREE TUNS** in the High Street is open all day, every day, has Greene King IPA, Triumph and Abbot Ale, bar meals and restaurant meals, and accommodation (01462 742107). Children are welcome in eating areas of the bar.

Glasgow pubs

Babbity Bowster

16-18 Blackfriars Street (0141 552 5055)

Babbity Bowster is a brilliant interpretation of an 18th-century coffee house-cum-pub by owner Fraser Laurie, based in a tall town house in the stylish Merchant City area and across the road from the Old Fruit Market. It's named after a Scottish dance and the theme is stressed in drawings of musicians on the walls along with fetching scenes of Glasgow. The ground-floor bar is spacious and well-lit from large windows, with plenty of standing room as well as seats at wooden tables on stripped wood floors. Warmth comes from an open peat fire. Breakfasts (including kippers and Arbroath smokies) are served from 8am and there is a strong emphasis on food all day long until 11pm. Bar meals include home-made soups, stovies, and both meat and vegetarian versions of haggis, tatties and neaps. There's a large first-floor restaurant and accommodation is available. Babbity Bowster always serves Maclay's 70 and 80 Shilling ales from Alloa plus a wide range of guest beers. There are excellent wines and, of course, a good range of malt whiskies. Live traditional music is played at weekends and in good weather you can play boules on a terrace.

Blackfriars

35 Bell Street (0141 552 5924)

Pub meets café bar in the Merchant City with a long bar, a small standing area and plenty of wood tables in the main section and on a raised area by large bowed windows. The cafe atmosphere is heightened by candles in wine bottles on the table and the walls are decorated with beer and theatre posters. The main wall opposite the bar is dominated by a Pre-Raphaelite gilt-framed, mock-medieval mirror that could have come from its London namesake, Fleet Street's Black Friar. The pub side is stressed by a splendid range of beers, with such familiars as Tetley joined by craft ales from Belhaven, Caledonian and Houston. There are usually a couple of Belgian draught beers as well as wines and whiskies. Excellent food lunchtime and evening includes home-made soup; crêpes; haggis and neaps; lamb hot pot; chargrilled burgers (friends from Chicago were impressed);

Babbity Bowster, Blackfriars Street

jacket potatoes; quiches; and vegetarian versions of tikka massala and chilli. There are pizzas and tapas in the evening. Live bands play several times a week in a downstairs lounge.

Mitre Bar

12-16 Brunswick Street, off Trongate (0141 552 3764)

The Merchant City is a jewel, cleaned up and generally made user-friendly, but the Mitre remains as an old-fashioned (in the best sense of the term) Glasgow "drinking shop" from a previous era. It's small, cramped, marvellously welcoming and dominated by a horseshoe bar, topped by snob screens, that serves Belhaven 60 Shilling Ale (the Scottish equivalent of an English dark mild) and "Mitre Merchant Ale", a house version of Belhaven's St Andrew's Ale, plus the delectable Belgian Hoegaarden white beer served from a giant "Big Bertha" porcelain fount. Both ends of the bar have small and surprisingly intimate seating areas: if you're feeling brave and are not too obviously English, ask them to turn the piped music down. Food is "Scottish pub basic": such as ale and onion pie. Ignore the Mitre and you'll miss a small piece of Scottish pub history.

Horseshoe Bar

17 Drury Street (0141 248 4467)
Underground: Central

The Horseshoe is a classic *belle epoque* bar with an imposing exterior with four large lamps and stained glass windows, including those brought by the original owner, John Y. White, from his Union Bar on nearby Union Street. Inside there's a huge banjo-shaped mahogany bar and gantry with old spirit levels inset into it. Everywhere there are horseshoe motifs. There are two horseshoe-shaped fireplaces surmounted by horseshoe-shaped mirrors, tiled murals, a mosaic floor, ornate ceiling and heavily carved woodwork around the walls. Brass bell plates ring the walls, recalling the time when such plush establishments had waiter service, and a portrait of Queen Victoria that is not exactly flattering: no doubt the artist thought it unlikely Her Mjesty would drop in for a jar and see it. Mottoes above the bar include one attritubuted to Queen Victoria herself that suggests she enjoyed the occasional dram: "Total abstinence is an impossibility; and it will not do to insist on it as a general practice." Another, from T.L. Peacock, says: "Not drunk is he who from the floor can rise alone and still drink more, drunk is he who prostrate lies without the power to drink or rise," while G.S. Calverley adds some doggerel with "He that would shine and petrify his tutor should drink Draught Tennents in its Native Pewter." There's no Draught Tennents anymore but the bar offers Draught Bass, Greenmantle and Caledonian 80 Shilling. Children are allowed in an upstairs restaurant while bar food is both amazingly generous and cheap.

Three Judges

141 Dumbarton Road (0141 337 3055)
Underground: Kelvinhall

This must be close to Mecca. Away from the trendy city centre, this is a magnificent and unspoilt Glasgow tenement pub across the road from Kelvinhall Underground station. Landlord Charlie Rennie kept the real ale flag flying when Glasgow was a keg beer desert: he has served, incredibly, 1,400 cask-conditioned ales in five years and planned to hit 2,000 by the turn of the century. His walls are decorated by framed awards by the Glasgow branch of the Campaign for Real Ale. His dedication to good beer is emphasised by the vast number of beer mats that are stuck to walls and ceiling. The Three Judges has a long bar with a brass rail and a foot rest, and there's plenty of standing room plus comfortable leatherette wall seats. The Three Judges always features ales from Maclay's of Alloa and on my most recent visit also offered Abbey Bellringer, Archer's Golden Bitter, Durham Magus and Royal Clarence Pitchfork. You go there to drink: food comes in the shape of pork pies.

Best of the Rest

Bon Accord

153 North Street (0141 248 4427)
Underground: Charing Cross

Old Printworks

36 North Frederick Street, off George Square
(0141 552 8160)
Underground: Buchanan Street

Edinburgh pubs

Café Royal

17 West Register Street (0131 556 1884)
Train: Waverley

Nothing can quite prepare you for this: the marble floor, the leather bench seats, the ornate moulded ceiling, the tiled fireplace, the chandeliers, and the vast central bar with a magnificent mahogany gantry. Is it a pub, a bar, an inn? Certainly not that utilitarian Scots term, "a drinking shop". It's an *establishment*, a homage to the pomp and pride of Victorian Britain, a pride underscored by the most famous feature of all, the six tiled murals depicting inventors and innovators: Benjamin Franklin, William Caxton, James Watt, George Stephenson, Robert Peel, and Michael Faraday. If you wonder why Peel is included, the answer is that he introduced calico printing as well as establishing the first organised police force, nicknamed "Peelers". Nice of the establishment to include an American revolutionary, but the Scots have always been less insular than the English. Etched glass doors lead to the Oyster Bar that serves fish and seafood in surroundings every bit as elegant as the bar: there is wood panelling, more tiled murals, and a series of stained glass windows illustrating such gentlemanly pursuits as archery, tennis, rugby and cricket. If the inclusion of cricket surprises you in Scotland, remember that two Scots have captained England: Mike Denness, and the patrician Douglas Jardine, he of the unseemly practice of "bodyline" bowling against the Australians in the early 1930s. Back in the bar, there are all-day snacks, such as the ubiquitous Scots mince pie. The ales include the succulent Deuchar's IPA, brewed a short distance away at the Caledonian Brewery in Slateford Road. If, for any reason, you shouldn't like one of the finest beers brewed in the entire island, there's also Courage Directors, McEwan's 80 Shilling and Theakston's Best.

Guildford Arms

1 West Register Street (0131 556 4312)
Train: Waverley

As the address suggests, the Guildford is just round the corner from the Café Royal, and it vies with it as the most sumptuous drinking place in

Edinburgh. There's another riot of Victoriana, approached through heavy velvet curtains at the door and windows that make you wonder for a moment just what sort of place you are entering. The main bar has mahogany panelling, impressive old advertising mirrors, painted ceilings and plasterwork, and several intimate snugs and alcoves. The small restaurant in a first-floor gallery is reached via stairs with another fine mirror decorated with tigers. The Guildford always has a tremendous choice of ales and often stages a beer festival during the Edinburgh Festival. You'll usually find Belhaven 60 Shilling, Deuchar's IPA, Orkney Dark Island and other Scottish craft brewers' guest beers, such as Harviestoun's 70 Shilling and Ptarmigan. Lunchtime bar snacks include filled rolls, steak pie, and haddock and chips. Children are not admitted.

Bannerman's Bar

212 Cowgate (0131 556 3254)

Behind and beneath a plain exterior, Bannerman's is an astonishing and rumbustious ale house based in a series of vaulted cellars in a crypt beneath the Royal Mile. It was built in 1770s as a port cellar and oyster bar, and was frequented by Robert Louis Stevenson. Before being restored as licensed premises in 1980, the site had been a dwelling house and a bleach workshop. It has flagstoned floors, stone walls, stone fireplaces, an impressive mahogany gantry, tables fashioned from wooden casks and, through an archway, a back room with some oak hogsheads against a wall, casks that hold 54 gallons of beer. In the evenings, Bannerman's is very much a young drinkers' haunt, with DJs and discos, and is best avoided unless you happen to be young. At quieter times of the day customers can revel in the unique atmosphere of the place and enjoy Caledonian 80 Shilling and Deuchar's IPA, with regular guests from other Scottish independents, such as Maclays or Heather Ale. There's a good range of malt whiskies, lunchtime bar snacks, and breakfast on Sunday.

Bow Bar

80 West Row, (0131 226 7667)

between George IV Bridge and the Grassmarket. Train: Waverley

This is a wonderfully cheery drinking shop where the staff have a fine sense of humour: spot the deliberately aged photo of them in

Cafe Royal, West Register Street

19th-century clothes and moustaches. The other great feature of the Bow Bar (handily placed for the castle) are tall founts for dispensing draught beer. Many Scottish bars have gone over to the English hand-pump and beer engine, but tall founts, primed by air pressure in the cellar, are the traditional method of serving beer, meeting a legal requirement that the glass should be filled above the bar in view of the customer. The founts here are genuine antiques, made by such once-famous manufacturers as Aitkens and McGlashan, who used to export their dispense systems to North America. The regular beers on offer are Caledonian Deuchar's IPA and 80 Shilling, and Tim Taylor's Landlord, with such guests as Inveralmond and Backdykes. The Bow has wall seats and a fascinating collection of memorabilia, including enamel cigarette advertising, advertising mirrors, a 1930s wireless, and a gas fire. The imposing mahogany gantry holds close to 150 malt whiskies, vodkas, rums, and gins. The bar snacks are simple but adequate, and there's no canned music to spoil the conversation. A marvellous place.

Starbank Inn

64 Laverockbank Road, foreshore (0131 552 4141)
between Leith and Granton

The Starbank is a splendid old ale house on the banks of the Firth of Forth. It has a telescope for customers to watch the river from the L-shaped bar, where the "L" forms an almost separate public bar. The main lounge has an open fire, a huge mirror (obligatory in Edinburgh bars), and picture windows overlooking the river. The entire bar is decorated by a plethora of water jugs, trays, mirrors, and old advertisements for brewers and distillers. The regular beers include Belhaven Sandy Hunter's Ale, IPA, 80 Shilling and St Andrew's Ale, and Tim Taylor's Landlord, with such guests as Broughton, Harviestoun, and Marston's. There's a good choice of wines, all served by the glass, and malt whiskies. Bar food and restaurant dishes, lunchtime and evening, include good soups such as lentil, Scotch broth or cream of vegetable, ploughman's, marinated herrings, mixed seafood salad, poached salmon, haddock mornay in cream and cheese sauce, chilli con carne, mince with potatoes, mushroom Stroganoff and pasta dishes suitable for vegetarians, and roast leg of lamb. The restaurant is in a pleasant conservatory, and there's also a back terrace.

Newcastle pubs

CROWN POSADA

31 THE SIDE, OFF DEAN STREET (0191 232 1269)

This is not just a magnificent Newcastle pub but is a classic, one of the finest unspoilt ale houses in the country. It's a glowing architectural jewel, a shrine to Pre-Raphaelite design – and it has a good choice in beer. There's an imposing stone façade topped by a gold crown, and fine stained-glass windows. There's more stained glass inside in screens by the bar, and awesome candelabra, gilt mirrors with mounted lamps, Victorian embossed wallpaper, and a superb moulded ceiling. It's a small pub, the main room so long and narrow that it's more like a corridor than a bar. There's a tiny snug at the front that is commandeered by regulars and where newspapers are provided. Mercifully, there are no jukeboxes or television. The beers on offer are Castle Eden Conciliation Ale, Jennings Bitter and regular guets beers. Food is just sandwiches: go to marvel, not eat.

BIERREX

2A HANCOCK STREET, BEHIND CIVIC CENTRE (0191 281 5653)

If you want proper sit-down food as well as beer, then head for this newish (1994) Continental-style bar. The ground floor, with its deep leather seats, is a like a gentlemen's club, while the first floor has a sunny, summery green-house feel. BieRRex is dedicated to quality Belgian, Czech, Dutch and Swedish beers, with some of those on draught served from porcelain "Big Bertha" founts. The Belgian beers include the Trappist-brewed Chimay, the strong golden ale Duvel, Leffe abbey beer, the powerful Kwak, and an ale called Student, which appeals to customers from the nearby universities. From the Czech Republic there's the divine Budweiser Budvar and Black Regent dark lager, Schneider Weisse wheat beer from Germany, and from Sweden Spendrups Old Gold, one of the finest and underestimated pale lagers in the world. Sangria is mixed on the premises and there's a British-brewed beer called Green Leaf Hemp Lager: drink it but don't inhale. Food, served from noon to 10pm, with brunch on Sundays, includes *croque monsieur* and *croque madame*, frites with mayonnaise (to make any passing Belgians feel at home), crêpes, a choice of salads, and Belgian-style waffles.

Bodega

125 Westgate Road (0191 221 1552)

Another sumptuous Newcastle pub, this one is of Edwardian origin. The Bodega, next to the Tyne Theatre, was named Regional Pub of the Year by Camra in 1997. It lives up to its name with lavish decor, the highlights of which are two majestic stained-glass ceiling domes. The pub is divided into several sections, including some intimate booths. The lunchtime food is excellent, with good vegetarian options, and the beers include brews from two local craft breweries, Big Lamp Prince Bishop and Mordue Workie Ticket, plus Theakston's Best and guest beers. Mordue also supplies its Geordie Pride, sold here as No. 9; if you don't know this is the number on Alan Shearer's shirt, then don't go in on match days, when the Toon Army comes in to refuel. If, like the High Court judge who once asked. "Who is Mick Jagger?", you don't know who Alan Shearer is, you'd best stay away from Newcastle.

Bridge Hotel

Castle Garth (0191 232 6400)

By the High Level Bridge and facing the castle keep, this fine old inn has a flagstoned seating area outside where you can look over the Tyne and the city walls. Among the many rooms inside this Grade II listed building is a Victorian lounge with high ceilings, large mirrors, an enormous mahogany carved fireplace, snob screens, and leather seats; the public bar has some impressive stained glass. The Bridge serves good lunchtime food, with some vegetarian dishes. The ales include Draught Bass, Black Sheep Best Bitter, Boddingtons Bitter, Mordue Five Bridge Bitter, and guest beers. There's good lunchtime food and there are regular folk nights in an upstairs lounge: the folk club claims to be the oldest in the country. I once made a speech in the folk club, while the folk singer Alex Glasgow entertained. Shortly afterwards, he emigrated to Australia. It wasn't that bad a speech...

Fighting Cocks

127 Albion Row, Byker (0191 276 1503)

It's worth making the hike out to this suburb not only for the pub but for the tremendous views of the Tyne, the city skyline and the bridges, as well as an amazing school across the road that has Chinese pagodas on the roof. The pub is the brewery tap for the nearby Four Rivers craft brewery and dates from 1896 or before, making it one of the oldest pubs in the city. A grisly mural of a cock fight was discovered when the pub was being renovated. The floors are bare boards, and a raised area by the big plate-glass front windows contains smart chairs, tables and sofas. The Fighting Cocks is establishing itself as a community pub, with poets and storytellers on Sundays, quiz nights during the week, and evenings for live acoustic music. The jukebox is free (it was donated by Mike Wallbank, one of the owners of Four Rivers) and features classic rock. The pub also boasts one of the last remaining space invaders machines in the country. At present, food runs only to toasties but a kitchen was being added. The Four Rivers hand-pumped ales are Moondance (hoppy and chocolatey from dark malt), Legion (pale bronze with a massive citric fruit character from the hops), and Centurion (exceptionally pale with a fine balance of juicy malt and spicy hops). You'll also find ales from the Castle Eden Brewery from County Durham.

Magnesia Bank

1 Camden Street, North Shields (0191 257 4831)

A tremendous Victorian community pub (close to the Metro station), it's another Camra award-winner, with stupendous views of the great sweep of the Tyne as it turns towards Newcastle. The bar is spacious and divided into several sections, with a raised area set aside for diners offering the best views. The excellent food, with a children's menu that includes pizzas, comes in large portions, and features several vegetarian options, such as pasta dishes (food is not available on Sunday evenings). There's live music on Thursdays and Sundays. This is the nearest outlet for Mordue beers (its Workie Ticket won the Camra Champion Beer of Britain award in 1997) and sells both the champion ale and Geordie Pride plus several other ales from craft breweries, including Black Sheep and Durham.

Best of the Rest

Bacchus

High Bridge (0191 232 6451)
Train: Central; Metro: Monument

Duke of Wellington

High Bridge (0191 261 8852)
Train: Central; Metro: Monument

Head of Steam

2 Nevill Street (0191 232 4379)
Train/Metro: Central

Hotspur

103 Percy Street (0191 232 4352)
Metro: Haymarket

New Bridge

2 Argyle Street (0191 232 1020
Metro: Manors

Dublin pubs

Porter House

16–18 Parliament Street (00 353 679 8847)

We'll start with the one Dublin pub that doesn't sell Guinness. The Porter House is a brilliant 1990s creation by Oliver Hughes and Liam LaHart, who have fashioned pub, restaurant and micro-brewery from a former bar known as Rumpole's, a haunt of lawyers in the Temple Bar district. The elegant ground-floor bar has marble floors, lots of stripped wood and a back room with tables, bench seats, and fascinating old Irish beer and whiskey posters. A vast collection of beer bottles in cabinets dominates all three floors: you can have bar meals on the ground floor and full restaurant meals in the Oyster and Stout Cafe. On each floor you can see the house brewery, from the copper mashing and boiling vessels at the top to the fermenters below. The beer includes a creamy, bitter-sweet Plain Porter (Plain is an old Dublin expression for Porter, immortalised in Flann O'Brien's famous poem "A Pint of Plain is Your Only Man"), Oyster Stout (made with real Dublin Bay oysters, tangy and bitter with a seaweedy, iodine finish), and a roasty, fruity and massively hoppy Wrasslers XXXX Stout. The stout is based on the recipe of a beer from Deasey's, a long-defunct brewery, and was the favourite bevvy of Michael Collins, founder of the Irish Free State. The pub also brews Porter House Red, one of the few real ales in the republic, and a strong beer called An Brain Blasta. You can buy a sampler tray of all the house beers. Food includes generous filled baps and such daily lunchtime specials as potato and celery soup, vegetable casserole and rice, and peppered lamb. The bar opens at 12.30pm and has late nights until 1.30am Thursday and Friday, and midnight on Saturday. There's frequent live music, with jazz on Sunday afternoon and traditional Irish on Saturday evening. The Porter House has quickly become a Dublin institution. Not to be missed.

Palace Bar

21 Fleet Street, off Westmoreland Street (00 353 677 9290)

As the name of the street suggests, this is the centre of Dublin newspaper life, with the offices of the *Irish Times* nearby. In more bibulous times, reporters were given their assignments in a corner of the bar known as "the

Intensive Care Unit". The bar has been frequented by more serious literary figures, as sketches on the walls of Samuel Beckett, James Joyce, W.B. Yeats and Seamus Heaney testify. The wood-panelled front bar is long and narrow, served by a long counter with a bank of redundant hand-pumps (unpressurised stout disappeared from Ireland in the 1960s) and a wood back bar that holds glasses, wine and whiskey bottles, and is topped by old casks, copper serving jugs, and a wind-up gramophone. Look out for the striking engraved mirrors advertising Power's "pure pot still whiskey". At the rear, the bar opens out into a large and comfortable area with tables and seats, and where the sun streams in through a skylight. Beers include Guinness, Murphy and Kilkenny.

Davy Byrne's

21 Duke Street, off Grafton Street (00 353 677 5217)

Leopold Bloom had a glass of wine and a Gorgonzola sandwich with a dab of mustard in Davy Byrne's in a scene from *Ulysses*, while James Joyce himself described the bar in the dead centre of Dublin as "a moral place". It has changed a tad since Joyce's day: the ochre and blue-pillared entrance leads into a riot of Art Deco that dates from a thorough redesign in the 1940s. The many murals include three stunning ones called Morning, Noon and Evening by Cecil ffrench Salkeld, a poet and artist who was the father-in-law of Brendan Behan (Behan had a notorious fight outside the bar in 1954). There is also a cartoon called "The Passing of the Holy Hour", commemorating the ending of afternoon closing. There are three spacious bars and food includes lobster bisque, roast rib of beef, Irish stew, cottage pie and smoked cod. As well as Beamish, Guinness and Smithwick's beers, you can sample the bar's famous cocktails, wines and whiskeys. There are many legends built around the bar. In the 1920s, during protracted negotiations in London over Irish independence, Michael Collins sent a telegram to Davy Byrne: "Send over a bottle of brandy and a soda syphon to settle the Irish question". Byrne was not renowned for his generosity but he did give Arthur Griffiths a free bottle of wine on the day independence was achieved.

Opposite page: Davy Byrne's

21
21
21 Davy Byrnes

John Mulligan's

8 Poolbeg Street (00 353 677 5582)

Mulligan's claims to be the oldest bar in the city, first licensed in 1782. Poolbeg means Little Pool and the street was once under water until the River Liffey was walled in. When the Theatre Royal stood nearby, Mulligan's was a haunt of actors and theatre-goers. The bar at one time had a market licence, which meant it could serve drinks to market workers at odd hours: this suited the likes of Brendan Behan, who also needed the odd drink at unsocial hours. Mulligan's is popular with journalists and the young John Fitzgerald Kennedy drank there in the 1940s when he worked for Hearst newspapers in Ireland. His brother Teddy and Bing Crosby also headed for Mulligan's when they were in Dublin. The exterior has lettering on the windows advising that the bar trades in wine, spirits and as a whiskey bonder. Stout used to be bottled on the premises when it left the Guinness brewery. Mulligan's, bursting with good cheer, has three bars and an upstairs lounge. The walls are decorated with old Theatre Royal posters and the bar was once the headquarters of the Society for the Preservation of the Dublin Accent.

Kavanagh's

1 Prospect Square, Glasnevin (no phone number listed)

There are several bars in Dublin named Kavanagh. This one is distinguished by being nicknamed The Gravediggers. It backs on to Glasnevin Cemetery and has a hatch in the back wall through which muddy gravediggers pass a shovel, which is returned loaded with glasses of Guinness. This is one of the finest traditional Dublin bars, often used as a film set but unspoilt despite its fame. It has swing doors, a wooden snug and a long main bar divided into cubicles. It is a good stop for a last pint on the way to the airport but find time to visit the cemetery, the final resting place of those fierce antagonists, Michael Collins and Eamon de Valera, along with Charles Stewart Parnell, who was a Protestant but was given the singular honour of being buried in a Catholic cemetery. There is a monument to Daniel O'Connell, the first Irishman to sit in the British parliament. The cemetery is also the last resting place of Brendan Behan: trust him to be buried by the back door of a pub.

J Walsh

6 Stoneybatter (00 353 679 9693)

Here's another wonderfully unspoilt old Dublin boozer, a Republican haunt in the 1920s, off the tourist track and not featured in any guide books. It's a simple, small drinking shop with a long wooden counter linking the two main bars. There's a tiny snug that will accommodate about three or four slim people: if it's locked ask the barman (the "curator" in these parts) to let you have a peek. Walsh's has some stained glass windows and old beer and cigarette adverts on the walls. I bumped into Brendan Dobbin there, a master brewer who has built small breweries in most parts of Ireland and Britain. He was building a new pub-brewery for Hughes and LaHart of the Porter House. Brendan comes from the North of Ireland. "Who has the most unpopular accent in here?" I asked him. "My English or your Ulster one?" "Mine," he replied, but very, very quietly.

Note: *There's a feast of tales involving Brendan Behan and Dublin pubs. He told the story against himself of going into the* Blue Lion *in Parnell Street one day "and the owner said to me 'You owe me ten shillings, you broke a glass the last time you were in here'. 'God bless and save us,' I said, 'it must have been a very dear glass if it cost 10 shillings. Tell us, was it a Waterford glass or something?' I discovered in double-quick time that it wasn't a glass that you'd drink out of he meant – it was a pane of glass and I'd stuck somebody's head through it."*

Les 3 Brasseurs

Lille bars

Les 3 Brasseurs

22 Place de la Gare (00 33 320.06.44.25)

This is the perfect start to a boozy stagger round Lille. From Lille Europe, the Eurostar station, walk down the Avenue Le Corbusier to the older and far more impressive main railway station, Lille Flandres, where the Place de la Gare is packed with bars. Les 3 Brasseurs is to the left of the station. There are now four Les 3 Brasseurs in France but the one in Lille was the first. It was the brainchild of Patrick Bonduel and was the first brew pub in France when it opened in 1986. The management has a tendency to live off past glories and service can be rudimentary and brusque when the bar is busy, but it's worth a visit to sample the atmosphere and the beer. The cramped front bar houses a Lilliputian (Lille-putian?) brewery reached by a short flight of stairs to the cellar. At the rear and to the left, the bar opens out in to a larger area set aside for eating. There are also tables on the pavement. The whole enterprise is a celebration of beer and the revival of brewing in Northern France and Flanders in particular. The bar usually has four beers on offer at any one time and you can sample them all by ordering *une palette*, which brings you small sample glasses of the house beers in a wooden shoe. The beers are all warm-fermented ales in the regional style and include a pale, perfumy Blonde, a nutty Ambrée, a dark and roasty Scotch, and – the stand-out brew – a wheat beer called Blanche de Lille, aromatic and wonderfully refreshing. Service is fast and furious and food is based around the local Flemish speciality, flammekueches, a cross between a tarte and a pizza, with such toppings as onions, tomatoes and goats' cheese, or mushrooms and bacon. Salads all have dressings made from the house beer while another popular dish, "le Welsh", is our old friend Welsh rarebit, with Cheddar cheese cooked in the amber beer. The menu for beer and food comes in the shape of a newspaper, *La Gazette*, which also explains the brewing process.

Café Jenlain

43 place Rihour (00 33 320.15.14.55)

The bar is five minutes' walk from place de la Gare or one stop (Rihour) on the small métro system that was the brainchild of former prime minister and mayor of Lille, Pierre Mauroy. Jenlain is owned by the Duyck brewery in the village of Jenlain near Valenciennes, which did much to revive the fortunes of brewing in Northern France with its amber-coloured *bière de garde* (keeping beer) in a bottle with a Champagne-style wire-cradled cork. The pale brick exterior of the bar has been beautifully restored, with gargoyles above the main entrance and the names of the brewery's beers picked out in pastel colours. The interior is plain, functional but comfortable, with plate-glass windows giving a good view of the small square. Jenlain's main beers, Jenlain and the pale Sebourg, are on draught, with an unfiltered version of Sebourg called *bière fraîche*. The bar also offers beers from other

French craft breweries, including Bailleux, Bavaisienne and Trois Monts. Food includes such specialities as carbonade of beef cooked in Jenlain and mussels cooked in Sebourg. There is an evening piano bar upstairs.

TAVERNE DE L'ÉCU

9 RUE ESQUERMOISE (00 33 320 57.55.66)

From Place Rihour walk a few metres into the splendour of the main square, the Place Général de Gaulle, with its magnificent buildings and statue to the soldier-cum-statesman who was born in Lille. The rue Esquermoise runs out of the square where the Taverne de l'Écu is reached down a corridor. The vast bar has a rumbustious past as concert hall, German-style beer garden, cinema and finally porn movie house before being rescued and turned into a brew pub in 1997. The burnished copper brewing vessels can be seen from the bar. The main beer is *bière blanche*, a refreshing, fruity wheat beer: plus, in the style of Les 3 Brasseurs, pale, amber and brown beers. Other draught beers include Pelforth Brune from the local commercial brewery owned by Heineken, Wickse Witte, a wheat beer from another Heineken subsidiary in Maastricht, and the powerful Belgian Kwak which comes in a glass held in a wooden shoe in case your fingers lose all sense of feeling after drinking it. There's a vast range of bottled beers, including "Guiness": I have yet to encounter a single French bar when Guinness is spelt correctly. Beyond the bar area there's a brasserie and a balcony, both set aside for eating. Food includes *écuflettes*, the house interpretation of flammekueches, tavernettes, which are flammekueches with a potato cake base, pancakes, carbonade flamande and chicken in beer.

LA TAVERNE FLAMANDE

15 PLACE DE LA GARE (00 33 320 55.11.26)

You can't miss this large bar with its garish neon sign: it's the first port of call for many visitors for its wide range of quality beers served either on the terrace or in the spacious and comfortable interior. Draught beers include Rodenbach, the magnificent "sour red" ale from Belgian Flanders, and Jenlain. The large range of bottled beers includes La Choulette and Trois Monts. Look out, too, for L'Angelus from the Brasserie d'Annoeullin, a Northern France classic made from wheat as well as barley: with a remarkable orange-citrus aroma and flavour, it's the Grand Marnier of the beer world. Food includes genuine pizzas and the ubiquitous flammekueches.

Au Bureau

36-39 place de la Gare (00 33 320 21.00.01)

The name is an elaborate joke: the founder, Serge de Decker, told his wife he was just popping to the office when in fact he was opening a series of bars called Le Bureau. There are 60 of them throughout France. They are modelled on Decker's idea of a British pub and, of course, are nothing like any British pub you've ever been in. But Au Bureau is comfortable, with plush seats, etched glass screen, highly polished wood and brass fittings. The beer list offers an eclectic European range with many large commercial brewers' beers you wouldn't leave home let alone pop to the office to drink, but you will spot such French specialities as L'Angelus, Trois Monts, Jenlain and Ch'ti. Ch'ti comes from the Castelain brewery near Lens, in the heart of the old coal fields. The name derives from Picardy dialect and means *"c'est toi"* – it suits you. The blonde is wonderfully spicy and aromatic while the amber and the brown versions have deep malty and hoppy characteristics. The brewery makes a point of stressing that its beers are not pasteurised, yet another subtle joke, as it's based in the rue Pasteur. There's a long food menu in Au Bureau, including "le Welsh".

Note: Vinothèque Rohat, *66 rue Faidherbe (00 33 320 06.29.92) is in a short street that links place de la Gare and the main square. It's a "wine merchant's" that stocks nearly all the beers from Northern France with badged glasses. Closed all day Sunday and Monday morning. All the bars are child-friendly and, unlike in British pubs, food is usually served all day. As well as the métro, there is a brilliant tram system that will take you into the suburbs and as far as Douai and Cambrai.*

U Fleku

Prague bars

U Fleku

11 Kremencova, Nové Mesto (New Town), Prague 1
(00 420 2 29.32.46)
Metro B to Karlovo námesti; trams 3, 9, 14 and 24, tram stop Lazarská.
Open 8.30am-11pm every day.

U Fleku claims, with some justification, to be the world's oldest brewpub: brewing has been going on here since at least 1499. The tavern and brewhouse were bought in 1762 by Jakub Flekovsky and became known first as U Flekovskych and eventually just U Fleku: U, like the French "chez", means "at the place of". The tiny brewhouse produces 6,000 hectolitres a year of just one beer, a 4.5 per cent alcohol dark beer, or 13 degrees in the Czech system of measurement. Though it looks like stout, it's actually a dark lager; the taste is sublime, with chocolate, coffee, liquorice and creamy malt flavours underpinned by bitter hops. U Fleku's wall bears a portrait of the present brewer and the inscription "God bless the mother who gave birth to a brewer", a statement of such profound good sense that it survived the Communist period. The beer is served in six interconnecting rooms with wood panelling, tables and benches. The menu features dishes of pork and dumpling, carp and dumplings, and dumplings with extra dumplings. If you like dark beer and dumplings, this is paradise.

On some evenings, a three-piece oompah band moves from room to room. In their early 20th-century military uniforms, they recall the heady days of the young Czech republic. There's a burlesque show in an upstairs room that will set you back around £2. Don't let the waiters palm you off with glasses of a tonsil-stripping, sticky herb liqueur called Becherovka (dubbed "Buggeroffka" by a group of visiting British beer writers). Stick to the beer.

U Kalicha (The Chalice)

12 Na bojisti, Nové Mesto, Prague 2 (00 420 2 29.19.45)
Metro C to I P Pavlova; trams 4, 6, 11, 16 and 22 to I P Pavlova.
Open 11am-3pm; 5pm-11pm every day.

This is the tavern that inspired Jaroslav Hasek to write his comic masterpiece "The Good Soldier Schweik" ("Svejk" in Czech), the greatest malingerer of all enlisted men and a boozer and womaniser of Falstaffian proportions. Hasek based Svejk on a character of the same name who was the porter at the inn when it offered accommodation. In 1911 Hasek sat in U Kalicha and listened to the stories of soldiers who had survived the war in Bosnia-Herzogovina, and the novel about the good soldier slowly developed. The modern pub-cum-restaurant is a tourist trap (there's a rather naff *fin-de-siècle* sentry box in the entrance hall where you can be photographed masquerading as Svejk) but it should not be missed for the documents relating to Hasek's life and work; the Lada hall is a celebration of the work of Josef Lada, who memorably illustrated the "Good Soldier". The main room of the restaurant, set out with formal, white-clothed tables, has service from waiters in Habsburg period uniforms and drooping moustaches. The walls are covered in quotations from the book, including the occasion when Svejk had his collar felt by the secret policeman Bretschneider and said to the barman, "I've had five beers, a couple of Frankfurters and a roll. Now give me one more slivovice and I must go, because I'm under arrest." By Prague standards, the food is rather good and offers more than the staple pork and dumplings. The beer? Well, according to Svejk it was Velké Popovice, while his friend Sapper Vodicka thought it was Staropramen. Today it's the ubiquitous Pilsner Urquell, but the brand of beer was relatively unimportant to Hasek's heroes. "They've got girls there, too," cried Svejk. "So, see you there at six after the war," Vodicka shouted down to him.

U Zlatého Tygra (The Golden Tiger)

11 Husova, Staré Mesto (Old Town), Prague 1
(00 420 2 26.52.19)
Metro A to Staromestská. Open 3pm-11pm (closed Sunday)

On my first visit to Prague in the mid-1980s, I found a queue of men patiently waiting in the snow and bitter January cold outside the Golden Tiger. This famous bar doesn't open until the afternoon but dedicated beer lovers go there in droves, for it has the reputation of serving the best glasses of Pilsner Urquell (Plzensky Prazdroj in Czech) in the city, drawn from casks in the cellar. The name of the beer means "original source of Pilsner" and was the first-ever golden lager, brewed in Pilsen in the early 1840s. The spacious tavern, with an arched ceiling, a few seats and wall benches, has a radical and Bohemian reputation that stretches back to the days of the Austro-Hungarian empire, when Czechs would meet here to talk in their banned language (the nearby National Opera House was built by public subscription to enable operas in Czech to be performed).Vaclav Havel was a regular here, watched by the secret police, who would periodically cart him back to jail; more recently, President Havel entertained President Bill Clinton at the Golden Tiger on a visit to Prague. Hot and cold meals are served but the Golden Tiger is best known for its beer cheese. On my first visit, it was the only food on offer; it consists of blending together soft cheese, raw onion and a sprinkling of beer, the tasty dish eaten with copious amounts of bread.

Na Vlachovce

217 Zenklova, Lieben, Prague 8 (00 420 2 84.05.76)

Trams 5, 12, 14, 24 to Ke Stírce. Open 8am to 10pm every day.

You enter this bar through a door built from a giant beer barrel, so you know they mean business. Na Vlachovce takes its name from the family that once owned the surrounding estate in the Prague suburbs. It stood for years on Red Army Street but the name was changed after the Velvet Revolution of 1989. The importance of the bar to beer lovers is that it's one of the rare outlets in the capital for Budweiser Budvar from Ceské Budejovice in South Bohemia, a town better known by its old German name of Budweis. (You won't find American Budweiser in the Czech Republic: the locals don't seem to like it, for some unaccountable reason.) After a genuine Bud or two in the spacious, comfortable, German-style beer hall, venture into the beer garden at the rear, where you will find 30 old wooden lagering tanks from the brewery that have been turned into holiday chalets, with two bunks in each (not recommended accommodation in winter). Under the old regime, the tanks cost around £1 night; the price has shot up since 1989 but they remain a cheap form of accommodation in a city now busy with tourists and the inflation they bring in their wake. Roast pork, surprise, surprise, is the house speciality of the bar, which often features live music. It also sells Black Regent dark lager from the Trebon brewery.

U Cerného Vola (The Black Ox)

1 Loretanské namesti, Prague 1 (00 420 2 53.86.37)

Tram 22 to Pohorelec. Open 9.30am to 9pm every day.

This splendid, homely tavern is close to the castle (Hradcany) and the Loretto church, which houses a magnificent collection of jewellery. The tavern dates from only 1962 but has the air of an ancient hostelry with its leaded windows, tiled stove, candles, beamed ceiling and wooden benches. The back room is called the Knights' Hall and its entrance is marked by the royal coat of arms of George of Podebrady, while the walls are decorated with the arms of Bohemian families. Astonishingly, this piece of brilliant kitsch was built under the old regime, but the party bosses wanted Western hard currency and the pub proved a major attraction for tourists. In the summer of 1989 I spoke quietly in the Black Ox to a man named Vaclav who said Czechoslovakia was a prison that would never open. Six months later, his namesake was heralding freedom from a balcony in Wenceslas Square. The Black Ox is now owned by a co-operative that donates some of the profits to charity. Beers are the brilliant and under-rated pale and dark Kozel lagers from the Velké Popovice brewery: kozel means billy goat, an ancient brewer's symbol for strength and virility. Food is our old friend beer cheese, or sausages. There are good restaurants around the Loretto over the road.

U Pinkasu

15 Jungmannovo náměstí, Nové Mesto, Prague 1
(00 420 2 26.18.04)

Metro A and B to Mustek. Open 9am to midnight every day.

Turn left at the bottom of Wenceslas Square to find one of Prague's best and most central taverns, named after Jakob Pinkas, a tailor who brought the first supplies of Pilsner Urquell to the city in the 1840s when a medieval ban on beers brewed one mile outside the city walls was lifted. The tavern is close to the memorial to Josef Jungmann (1773-1874), the Czech linguist and poet, who became the leading figure in the Czech National Revival and who was responsible for the development of the modern Czech language. More than a million glasses of Pilsner beer are consumed in the tavern every year. Thirty employees are kept busy in the cellars looking after the beer stored in seven ten-hectolitre casks. The oldest room, to the right, serves only beer and is a basic but cheery pub, while the more modern room to the left serves beer with food. There is more seating on the first floor. U Pinkasu is famous for its white-coated waiters who are not allowed to use trays and have to juggle vast numbers of foaming glasses with their hands. Food is reasonably priced and is served from early morning to late at night. In his book "Magical Prague", Bohumil Hrabal wrote: "Every gourmand hankers after ordinary food once in a while. I recommend going without breakfast and nipping off in the morning to U Pinkasu, behind Wenceslas Square at the bottom, and having a glass of Pilsner. The speciality here is the Pinkas goulash which, if desired, is served in a little pot and it is eaten with a spoon and a roll. Then you can have another glass of Pilsner beer." In the mid-1980s, when I asked for a vegetarian dish, I was offered a plate of lentils with a fried egg in the centre. They do better now.

U Medvídku (The Little Bears)

7 Na Perstyné. (00 420 2 26.61.14)
Metro B to Národní trída; trams 6, 9, 18, 21, 22.
Open 11am to 11pm (closed Sunday)

The Little Bears, a welcome outlet for Budweiser Budvar in central Prague, has been a brewery, a music hall, a haunt of leading city officials, and a scene in a detective story written by Jirí Marek: under the old regime, the police HQ was a few yards from the tavern and the detectives would go there for breakfast. Vaclav Havel commented wryly on the proximity of the tavern to the police station when he hosted a party there in 1975 after an amateur company had performed one of his plays. The building dates from the 14th century, with Renaissance portals from the 16th. The small entrance to the tavern belies the size of the main room, entered through a wooden door. There's a smaller, more intimate room at the back, and there's a beer garden in a courtyard in the summer. The menu is extensive by Czech bar standards and the rich, warming soups are recommended. There are modern photos and advertisements for Budweiser Budvar on the walls, which is served, along with Black Regent, from an enormous beer tap in front of the kitchen. An old beer wagon stands in the centre of the main room. In the late 1990s I made an impassioned speech in English in defence of the freedom of the Budweiser Budvar brewery, then threatened with possible takeover by its bigger American namesake. The speech was rapturously received by diners, no doubt on the grounds that they didn't understand a single word I said.

Brussels bars

À La Morte Subite

7 rue Montagne aux Herbes Potagères (00 32 2 513.13.18)

The name means Sudden Death but don't panic: it comes from a dice game played here with a "sudden death" finish. Opposite the Galeries Royales St Hubert arcade near the Grand' Place, this Brussels institution is full of faded Belle Epoque finery, with sumptuous mirrors on which prices are displayed, and patched leather seats and tables disappearing into infinity. Service is brisk if grumpy (some people go there to enjoy the insults) from waiters and waitresses dressed in severe black and white uniforms. The house beers are labelled Morte Subite and offer various interpretations of the singular style known as lambic, which is confined to Brussels and its suburbs. Lambic is made by spontaneous fermentation, using wild yeasts in the atmosphere. Gueuze is a spritzy, blended version of young and old lambics, while kriek and frambozen have cherries and raspberries added. Morte Subite are not especially good examples of the style but will gently break you into these stark, uncompromising, sour but wonderfully quenching beers. Watch out also for Trappist ales from the Chimay and Rochefort abbeys. Bruxellois snacks include *tête pressée* (brawn) and *fromage blanc.* Open every day from 10am (12 noon Sundays) to 1am.

Le Bier Circus

89 rue de l'Enseignement (00 32 2 218.00.34)
Métro: Parc

If I lived in Brussels, this simple, homely bar would be my local. It stands next to the Cirque Royale theatre and the front bar has wooden tables and seats on a tiled floor, the walls decorated with old beer posters. Excellent jazz is played quietly over speakers. There's a tiny middle room beyond the serving counter and a large back room decorated with paintings of such famous cartoon characters as Tin-Tin and Asterix. The vast beer list includes classy gueuze from Cantillon and Frank Boon, the classic Duvel and De Koninck Belgian ales, sour red beer from Rodenbach, and the full Trappist range from Chimay, Orval, Rochefort, Westmalle and Westvleteren. There are wheat beers, organic beers and many ales from Belgian micro-breweries.

Food includes soup, sandwiches and spaghetti. I bumped into an Arsenal supporter there, but no bar is perfect. Opens 12 noon to 2.30pm and 5pm to midnight, later at weekends; all day Saturday. Closed Sundays unless there is a concert next door.

FALSTAFF

19 RUE HENRI MAUS (00 32 2 511.87.89)

A stunning combination of Art-Nouveau, Art-Deco and Rococo, this elegant bar is alongside the Bourse and has superb mirrors and stained glass. This is the sort of European bar Brits find astonishing: it opens every day from 7am to 5am and hot meals (including *cuisine à la bière*) are served from noon until closing time, with snacks at all hours. There's an ornate main bar, often busy with diners, and an extension used mainly by customers who want to sample a beer range that includes Chimay Blue, Duvel and Witkap Tripel. Watch out for Gordon's Scotch, brewed by our chums at Scottish Courage back home, and wonder why this rich, malty and fruity ale is deemed suitable only for Belgians.

IN 'T SPINNEKOPKE

12 PLACE DU JARDIN AUX FLEURS (00 32 2 511.86.95)

The Little Spider is a genuine Brussels estaminet, a tavern that specialises in good food as well as beer. This is a veritable shrine to beer cuisine: Spanish-born owner Juan Rodriguez has written the seminal work on the subject, *Cuisine facile à la bière*. The tavern sells the full range from the finest of the lambic breweries, Cantillon: lambic and a sweetened version called faro on draught plus bottled gueuze, kriek and frambozen. There are some 70 other beers, including the rarely sighted Westvleteren Trappist ales. Daily lunchtime specials include the classic Low Countries dish carbonnade flamande, plus pot au feu, rabbit in lambic, and chicken waterzooi: the helpful staff will prepare a vegetarian dish if you ask. There's a tiny terrace area at the front in good weather. Opens 11am to midnight daily (closed Saturday lunch and all day Sunday); hot food 12 noon to 3pm and 6pm to 11pm, booking essential. The tavern is about five to 10 minutes' walk from Grand' Place: pick up rue Van Artevelde, and then rue des Six Jetons will take you to the Little Spider.

Poechenellekelder
RUE DE CHÊNE (00 32 2 511.92.62)

This is the ideal tourist café, opposite the famous Mannekin Pis statue on rue d'Étuve: a puppet theatre on the first floor performs the story of the leaky Mannekin. The split-level bar offers around 40 beers including Blanche de Bruxelles wheat beer, Cantillon gueuze, raspberry beer from Vanderlinden, four Trappists, and two with the forbidding names of Delirium Tremens and La Guillotine. There are bar snacks including *tête pressée* and *Bruxellois tartines*, a collection of puppets and a game similar to bar billiards. Opens 10am to midnight (2am weekends).

De Ultieme Hallucinatie
316 RUE ROYALE (217.06.14)

The name does not require translation. You will find this glittering example of Art-Nouveau, popular with young Bruxellois and Brit ex-pats, at the far end of the rue Royale, beyond the Botanical Gardens. There's an expensive *haute cuisine* restaurant at the front: keep on going for the bar area, with a walled terrace at the back. The beers number around 30 and include the Cantillon range of lambic/gueuze plus the brilliant De Koninck ale from Antwerp on draught, along with spicy Dikkenek and hoppy/fruity Sezoens. You can indulge in another Belgian classic dish of mussels. Opens 11am to 3am weekdays, 4pm to 4.30am weekends. From the city centre, take trams 92, 93 or 94 down the rue Royale to Ste. Marie Church and walk back to the bar.

À La Morte Subite

Hampstead pub walk

Both Hampstead and nearby Highgate have pubs called the Flask, recalling the times in earlier centuries when Londoners would clamber up to the two villages and fill leather flasks with pure spring water rather than drink the infected liquors of London proper that caused repeated outbreaks of cholera. Today's visitors to the excellent hostelries in Hampstead and alongside the surrounding heath will find an abundance of good beers made from fine spring waters with the added pleasure of the smack of malt and hops.

Our first watering hole is the FREEMASONS ARMS, 32 Downshire Hill, NW3 (020 7433 6811) in a spectacularly lovely part of Hampstead, with fine mansions and cottages in Downshire Hill itself and along South End Road that leads down to Hampstead Heath railway station. If you come by car there is a large car park opposite Downshire Hill on the heath. Keats Grove, with John Keats's house, is a turning off South End Road.

The Freemasons is a spacious pub with a striking white-washed exterior set back from the road behind a terrace. Hanging baskets provide splashes of colour in season. To the rear there is a large, rambling garden that is often packed at weekends. The original pub, like many of the surrounding houses, was built in the early 19th century. It was declared unsafe in the 1930s and had to be demolished. So the bowed windows, high-back settles, glass partitions and wood panelling may look Queen Anne in style but the present pub is only some 60 years old. The clever design of the interior is based on one large room but it has many nooks, crannies and alcoves that give an air of intimacy.

The pub is a Bass Vintage Inn: as well as Draught Bass and Worthington Bitter on hand-pumps there is a good wine list. Food is served lunchtime and evening and may include the likes of French onion soup with a hefty wedge of bread, Caesar salad, mushroom and mascarpone bake, spicy beans with caramelised onion rice, beef and Bass ale pie, steaks, chicken, and swordfish steak. The Freemasons is one of only a handful of pubs left in London with a skittle alley, a pleasant plebeian touch in haughty Hampers.

From the Freemasons, turn left into South End Road and walk for about five minutes. The road becomes East Heath Road, with elegant brownstone apartment blocks and houses on either side. Turn left into Well Walk, a tree-lined street with a raised pavement on the right-hand side. Well Walk marks the importance of clean water to the village. On the left you will find a red-brick building called Wellside, on the site of the Old Hampstead Pumproom. Almost opposite there is a chalybeate well donated by the Gainsboroughs to "the poor of Hampstead". You soon pass the WELLS TAVERN (which you may enter if you are desperate for a Whitbread beer) or carry on to the top of Well Walk and into Flask Walk, with another watery artefact on the right, The Wells & Camden Baths and Wash House: the Victorian dwellers in Hampstead village were clearly *corpore sano* inside and out.

Flask Walk rises steeply until, as you round a slight bend, you see the pleasing sight of the FLASK TAVERN at Number 14 (020 7435 4580). The Flask is a down-to-earth, no-nonsense Young's boozer, a reminder that long before authors, artists, luvvies, and the rich moved in, Hampstead was a working-class village of humble cottages. The Flask even has a public bar, as rare as rocking-horse droppings in London these days.

When I was a Flask regular some years ago, the public was the haunt of members of the London Symphony Orchestra, known in those days as "Andy Previn's Band": how they managed to play a note after quaffing deeply of Young's Bitter remains a mystery. There are a few tables on the pavement at the front and a tiny yard at the back. The public bar is plain and cheery, and darts and cribbage are played there. It's divided from the saloon by a Victorian screen that, on the lounge side, has some colourful *fin de siècle* Parisian paintings. The front of the saloon opens into a spacious area that leads in turn into a newish restaurant area at the back. There are a few tables in a small yard at the back and there are also tables and chairs, with bright Young's Brewery brollies, on the pavement at the front. The uncompromisingly hoppy Young's regulars – Bitter and Special – are joined by the Wandsworth brewery's seasonal brews. There's a decent wine list and good coffee ground to order. Home-cooked food is available lunchtime and evening (not Sunday or Monday evenings) and may include imaginative soups such as pumpkin, sandwiches, seafood and asparagus lasagne, curries, chicken and mushroom in mustard sauce,

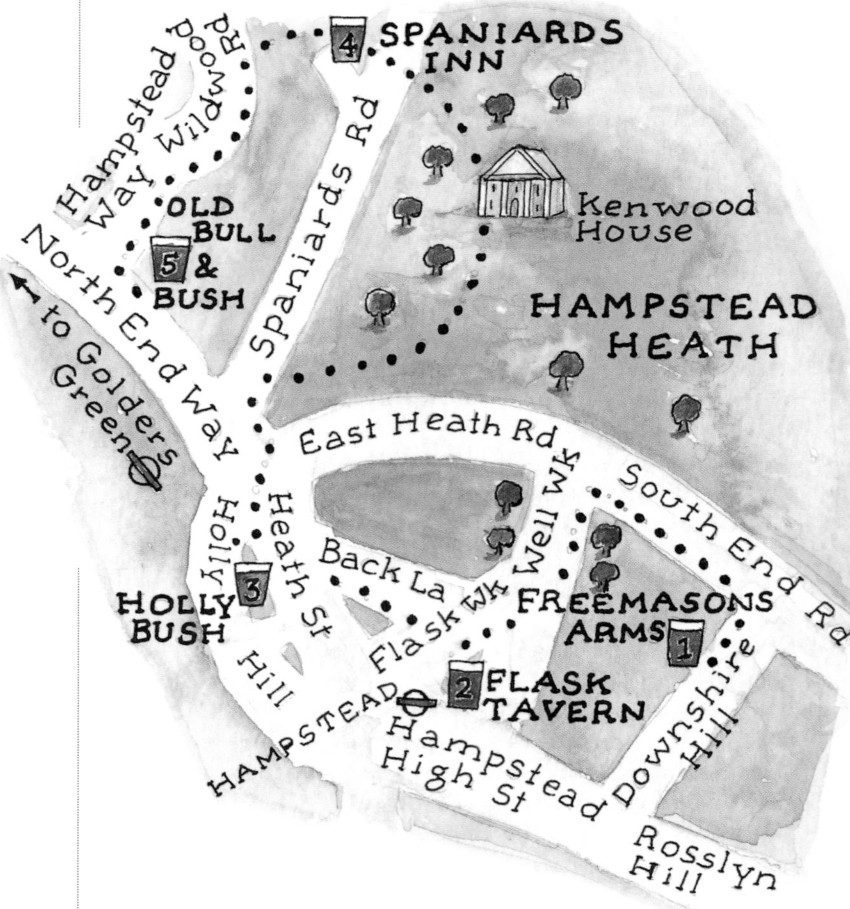

and such vegetarian offerings as pasta with artichoke hearts and creamy pesto sauce.

From the Flask, walk a few yards up Back Lane into Heath Street. Opposite, the glass-fronted All Bar One has replaced the Nag's Head, owned and run in the 1970s by the Campaign for Real Ale as an example to the rest of the world of what a good ale house should be. To the left a flight of steps bears a sign for Holly Mount. Clamber up and round the twisting steps and lane until, panting, you reach the top and step back in time.

Round the bend and ahead is one of London's finest ale houses. A faint, illusory mist seems to hang around the lamp-lit exterior of the HOLLY BUSH (020 7435 2892), once a favourite haunt of Dr Johnson, the faithful Boswell, and Charles Lamb. When the pub's former owners, Allied Domecq, threatened a dreaded "refurb" a couple of years ago, the Hampstead *literati* rose up and told the upstart sherry retailers where to get off. Now English Heritage has its fingers on the pub's pulse.

The small pub, decked out with hanging baskets and gas lamps outside, has a long history, though not always as an ale house. It was once the home of the artist George Romney and his stables now form the back bar. When Romney died in faraway Kendal the building was sold to Hampstead Constitutional Club who in turn sold it to a local licensed victualler. It eventually became a rare London outlet for the Watford brewer, Benskins.

The Holly Bush has a genuine prole-and-plush air to it, from the unspoilt front bar with high-back wooden settles, a sagging ceiling, gas lamps and boarded floors, to the George Romney Room at the back with etched-glass alcoves, ochre-painted brick walls, and wood panelling. There are snacks and a few hot dishes lunchtime while the ales include Tetley Bitter, Theakston XB and Greene King IPA, though food policy and ales are likely to change under new ownership: the Holly Bush was one of thousands of pubs bought in the summer of 1999 by Punch Taverns from Allied Domecq.

Another flight of steps close to the pub takes you back down to Heath Street. Climb to the top of the street, with its smart restaurants and art galleries, until you reach Whitestone Pond. Cross the road to

North End Way, walk along for just a few yards and turn right into Spaniards Road. Almost immediately you can turn, at last, on to Hampstead Heath itself. A broad, well-trodden path runs in front of you. To the right, through the trees, there is a superb view of the London skyline in the distance, including the Docklands high-risers and the Millennium Dome.

Keep left when the path divides, with more flickering glimpses of London and even St Paul's through the trees. The path drops steeply into a dell, then rises again below hanging trees, including some splendidly ancient oaks. Stay on the path as it crosses open heath and then narrows, with trees and thickets on either side. You will quickly reach Farm Cottage on your left, then the path bends round and leads into the car park of Kenwood House.

Leave the car park through large gates and you are back on Spaniards Road. The **SPANIARDS INN** (020 8455 3276) is some 200 yards on the left, on the other side of the road. The inn (with a listed outbuilding – a former tollhouse – across the road) is rich in history, though which bit of the history you care to believe depends on your gullibility and the number of pints you consume. Some say it is called the Spaniards as it was built as a residence for the Spanish ambassador to the court of James I. Others say, more prosaically, that it was turned into an inn by two Spaniards in the 18th century, who fought a duel over a woman who then spurned them both. During the anti-Catholic Gordon Riots of 1780, the landlord of the Spaniards, Giles Thomas, saved Kenwood House and its collection of paintings from being torched by the mob: Thomas poured copious amounts of ale down their throats and, when they were incapable of movement let alone affray, called the cavalry to feel their collars.

The pub also claims to be the birthplace of Dick Turpin, who was certainly busy in the area in the early 18th century and even had a secret tunnel built connecting two Highgate pubs so he could escape his pursuers and still get a pint down his neck. He is said to have stabled his horse, Black Bess, in the tollhouse across the road. And, a charming grace note, John Keats heard a nightingale singing in the inn's back garden, which inspired him to pen his "Ode to a

Nightingale". In Keatsian mood, you might settle for a "draught of vintage" or a "beaker full of the warm South" in the pub.

Some of the history might be arguable and even tacky (there is, of course, a Dick Turpin Bar) but you cannot deny the period feel of the place, with alcoves, snugs, a porch room by the main entrance, bare boards, oak panels and nicotine-stained ceilings. The large, trellised back garden, lamplit at night, is a delight. Food, served noon to 9pm weekdays and noon to 5pm on Sunday, includes fish and chips, vegetable Wellington, feta cheese salad, steak and kidney pudding, sausage and mash, and hot chicken Caesar salad. The hand-pumped ales are Draught Bass and Fuller's London Pride.

We have one more pub to visit. From the Spaniards, turn right and round a hair-raising corner by the pub – the pavement peters out for a few yards – and walk along for about 100 yards until you find Spaniards End. This is a private road but almost immediately you can turn on to the heath. The main path bears to the right through trees and thickets and drops down steeply, with steps helpfully carved in the ground. You pass a modern house on the right with an incongruous palm tree in the garden, and then the heath falls into Wildwood Road. Follow it round to the left or, if you prefer softer going, go back on to the heath where you can walk, horses permitting, along a riding track. Both road and track bring you quickly to Hampstead Way. Follow this to the left, marvel at the kind of houses where you half expect to see Philip Marlowe calling on General Sternwood, and then turn left into North End Way.

The **HARE & HOUNDS** pub confronts you, but keep straight on for just a few yards and you will find one of London's most celebrated pubs, the **OLD BULL & BUSH** (unlisted phone number). The pub was made eternally famous by Australian-born musical hall star Florrie Ford in 1903 with her song "Come, come, come and make eyes at me, down at the Old Bull & Bush". But it predates the music hall by several centuries. It began life as a farm in 1645 and became an inn in 1721. Hogarth lived on the spot and laid out the garden. Later it was frequented by Gainsborough, Reynolds, Garrick, Wilkie Collins, George du Maurier and, inevitably, that great toper Dickens. The arrival of the

Underground brought a more plebeian class of clientele who appreciated the art of Florrie Ford. The present version of the pub, with a brown brick exterior with tall chimneys, a large gable, and hanging baskets, dates from 1924. Inside there are many alcoves, high-back settles, log fires, masses of old photos of faded musical hall entertainers, and wooden beer casks on a gantry. Food, available noon until 10pm every day, includes spring vegetables and pasta soup, iced summer fruits with raspberry coulis, mushroom dipper, fish and chips, Cajun chicken, Caribbean chilli, sausage and mash, beef stew and dumplings, seafood medley and, vegetable heaven, a blend of fresh vegetables in creamy cheese sauce. There's a separate children's menu. The ales are Tetley Bitter, Old Speckled Hen and Marston's Pedigree. The Pedigree was in splendid nick but at £2.15 a pint you may need to extend your overdraft before visiting the pub. As with the Holly Bush, this is an ex-Allied Domecq pub and the beers may change.

You can now walk down North End Road to Golders Green and the Underground or continue up the road, back towards Hampstead.

The Spaniards Inn

Chester pubs

ALBION

ALBION STREET (01244 340345)

In a city bursting with history – Roman remains, striking half-timbered buildings, and medieval walls – it's not surprising that a pub should choose a theme from the past, though the First World War comes as a bit of a surprise. But the Albion is dedicated to what the managers prefer to call the Great War, with memorabilia by the bucket-load: old recruiting posters, "Your Country Needs You", pictures of wounded soldiers, the whole wrapped around by Edwardian fireplaces, flock wallpaper, leather sofas and lamps. Two of the breweries whose ales are on offer, Cains and Greenalls, were around when the lads were off fighting for King and Country. They are joined by regular guests, such Tim Taylor's Landlord. The food, lunchtime and evening (no bar food Monday evening; restaurant evening only) is called Trench Rations and comes in generous portions unknown in the mud of Ypres. The dishes include corned-beef hash with pickled red cabbage; Staffordshire oatcakes with Stilton, mushroom and gammon (there's a meatless version available); pork and herb sausages with caramelized onions, creamed potatoes and fresh vegetables; haggis and tatties; chicken Madras; roast turkey and savoury stuffing served with cranberry and apple sauce; fresh pasta with blue cheese and black olive sauce; cottage pie; sandwiches; and daily desserts chalked on a blackboard. Not just a pub: an experience. We don't want to lose you, but we think you ought to go…

OLD HARKERS ARMS

1 RUSSELL STREET (01244 344525)

The meals come in equally generous portions in this cleverly converted Victorian canalside warehouse, with tables outside in good weather where you can watch the boats go by. Inside, there are large airy windows, solid wooden furniture, bare boards underfoot, a gallery of decorative prints, lamps, a library at one end, and a bar built from salvaged doors. There's a rotating policy of hand-pumped beers, though you will usually find Boddingtons Bitter, along with such guests as Cottage Champflower from

Somerset, Cheriton Diggers Gold from Hampshire, Hook Norton Best from Oxfordshire, and, nearer to home, Thwaites Bitter from Blackburn or Tim Taylor's Landlord from Keighley. Food, in bar and restaurant, may include soup; sandwiches; filled ciabatta; cod and chips; Guinness and mushroom pie; chicken tikka; Chinese pork with spicy sauce and noodles; and such desserts as lemon tart with raspberry sauce or sticky fig and ginger pudding. There's a roast lunch on Sundays and children are welcome until 7pm.

MILL HOTEL

MILTON STREET (01244 350035)

There's more canalside pleasure at the Mill, a converted 18th-century corn mill standing alongside the Shropshire Union, built to link Ellesmere in Shropshire with Ellesmere Port on the Mersey. The building has kept its original brick walls, pitch-pine beams, and old cannon barrel stanchions that hold up the floors. While the Mill is a busy, 76-roomed hotel, it has a spacious bar with a genuine pubby feel to it, and, most important, it's a continuous beer festival with a tremendous range of handpumped beers. There is a house beer brewed by Coach House of Warrington and on my visit it was joined by the likes of Bateman's, Roosters and Weetwood, plus big brewers offerings from Theakston's. The Bateman's beer was Dark Mild: there's always one dark mild available in a bid to help preserve the endangered style. Bar food, lunchtime and evening, offers a good range of dishes including soup, filled baguettes; steak and ale pie; and mushroom and Quorn Stroganoff. The evening Canaletto restaurant includes goat's cheese; lobster bisque; steaks; chicken breast with Stilton; oven-baked duck breast; lemon sole; monkfish; stir fry vegetables; nut and pasta bake; vegetable risotto; stuffed peppers; and a range of salads. There's a good range of wines, including Old and New World. The hotel has a glass-sided canal boat moored alongside where meals are served, and is also available for canal trips. Children are welcome and the accommodation is comfortable and reasonably priced.

Falcon

Lower Bridge Street (01244 314555)

This is an inn that breathes antiquity. It is heavily timbered, dating mainly from around 1600, though the giant stone blocks on which it stands and the deep cellars are even older, probably from the 13th or 14th century. The inn stands at the heart of old, renovated Chester, and is just across the road from the Rows, the medieval, two-storeyed, timber-framed shopping area. There are wonderful views from the front lounge, reached up a short flight of steps. There's good, simple bar food, such as soup, sandwiches, steaks, fish and a vegetarian option. The chief delight is the Sam Smith's Old Brewery Bitter, priced at around £1.50, remarkable value for such a tourist trap as Chester. The Yorkshire brewery also has a draught Bavarian-style wheat beer and its lagers are made according to the German Purity Law, with yeast flown in from Bavaria on a regular basis. Look out Sam Smith's tremendous range of bottled beers, such as Taddy Porter and Imperial Stout. Pint in hand, tour the ramble of small rooms, squeezing between the standing timbers and minding your head on the massive beams. Tours of the cellars are available and there is live jazz on Saturday lunchtimes.

Union Vaults

Egerton Street (01244 322170)

The Union is only 100 yards from the Mill Hotel but this is chalk and cheese, a smashing, old-fashioned, no frills, street-corner boozer, often boisterous with the banter of locals. The plain, but spacious front bar has bare boards and a small serving counter, with a bar billiards table against the window. It seems at first like a one-bar pub, but it's a Tardis – bigger inside than the exterior suggests – with two additional rooms reached through archways offering comfortable leather chairs and sofas. It's an ale house good and proper (there are pies if you're peckish) with Greenalls Bitter on the pumps and, most importantly, the succulent, juicy/hoppy bitter brewed by the Plassey craft brewery across the border in Wrexham. This is a true pub, the kind we can't afford to lose.

And finally...

the pub where I'd like to hang my jug

Olde Gate Inn

Well Street, Brassington, Derbyshire. (01433 620578)

From Ashbourne (A52) take the B3035 Wirksworth road and watch for faded sign for Brassington near Carsington Water

In the Olde Gate the fires were alight in leaded ranges in both bars, even though it was early September. "It was a bit nippy first thing," landlord Paul Burlinson said. The Olde Gate won the Homefire Real Pub Fire of the Year award in 1999 and the pub must have warmed the cockles of the judges' hearts when they stepped through the low porch entrance to find welcoming fires to left and right. It is an ancient ale house, dating from 1616, in a Peak District hill village of mellow stone buildings, close to the church and opposite a house that used to be a toll gate.

Brassington is remote, a fair haul from the nearest town of Ashbourne in the centre of Dovedale, yet the village was once on a major turnpike from London to Manchester. One small frame in a window in the main bar of the inn opens on a latch: "They used to send a glass of ale through there on a long pole to the coach driver," Paul said.

The Olde Gate doesn't have to shout history at you. It's built into the weft and the warp of the building, massively covered in creeper outside. Beyond the main bar there's a third room used as an overspill on busy days. It is wood panelled, with a small log fire and a stag's head on the wall, and was used as an emergency hospital for troops injured in the English Civil War. Paul said it couldn't be proved but it's thought that Bonnie Prince Charlie's troops may also have used the inn during their attempt to get a Stuart back on the throne. It's possible because Charles Stuart certainly got as far as Derby before accepting he was outgunned by the Redcoats.

It comes as no surprise to learn that the inn is haunted. It has been the subject of a paranormal investigation and a previous landlady had the place exorcised. "Both my daughter and I have heard the sound of a child crying upstairs," Paul said, the kind of information that raises the hair on the neck of even an arch sceptic.

The area around Brassington is ideal for walkers, climbers and ramblers. The hills are dotted with the shafts of now disused lead mines, the entrances blocked to stop animals falling into them. The mines were started by the Romans and the last one closed at the turn of the century. The lead from the area was prized. The low black beams in the Olde Gate are ships' timbers rescued from the wrecks of the Spanish armada, and they were given to the pub in exchange for supplies of lead.

As you enter the Olde Gate, stooping through the low porch, you are met by a hatch in the central island servery, with hand-pumps offering Marston's Pedigree. Turn right and you are in the main bar, spacious, comfortable, with scrubbed wooden tables and benches on the flagstone floor and tankards hanging from the beams. The room is dominated by the enormous range that has copper jugs, scuttles, tongs and warming pans in every nook and cranny. The centrepiece is the fire, installed in Victorian times, and creating so much heat that a small brass tap built into the range can provide boiling water.

To the left of the entrance is a smaller back bar, with more wooden furniture and another, scale-downed range. "That was put in about 30 years ago," Paul Burlinson said. "The room used to be the kitchen and living room of the owners before it became a bar. The inn was originally two or three cottages that were knocked into one."

Paul and his American wife Evie have run the pub for 12 years. Paul has been in the pub trade since he was 19 years old. The Olde Gate has been a Marston's tenancy for around 30 years. "It was probably privately owned before that," Paul said. "It was in the same family for 45 years." He produced an ancient print of the inn with the owner, William Pounder, and his family standing outside. "He had a wooden leg," Paul laughed. "That must have given him some extra capacity."

Paul and Evie don't bother to open in the afternoons as there isn't the demand, even in the summer, with Chatsworth, the Blue John Mine and Carsington Water close by. It's closed Monday lunchtimes and there's no food at all on Mondays. Paul, ever helpful, says there's another Marston's house in the village if the Olde Gate is closed. The grub is excellent, prepared by Paul and with a transatlantic touch from Evie. The chalk board offered roast beef and Yorkshire pudding, Cumberland sausage with mash, vegetables and gravy, Norwegian prawn open sandwich, honey roast ham salad, ploughman's, ciabatta bread with such fillings as smoked salmon and cream cheese, salami and Swiss cheese, and Stilton and mango chutney, as well as baguettes with a choice of fillings, including turkey, Swiss cheese and pepperoni, and Cheddar cheese and tomato.

And then there's the Pedigree. Paul takes guest ales from Marston's and Banks's range, but the Olde Gate is a Pedigree pub. Paul gets through three barrels a week. He allows each cask to stand in the cellar for three days before tapping and spiling to allow the Burton beer to enjoy the full fruits of its volcanic second fermentation.

And what a joy to drink! As sulphury as a freshly struck Swan Vesta, with a delicious blend of malt, hops and tangy fruit on the palate. Lord Byron once observed, "There are things in Derbyshire as noble as in Greece or Switzerland." How sad that he couldn't include the pleasures of Pedigree. Izaak Walton, the famously Compleat Angler, was advised by a friend, Charles Cotton, "I am for the country liquor, Derbyshire Ale if you please, for a man should not, methinks, come up from London to drink wine in the Peak." Wise words. And why bother to go back to London? Paul Burlinson said that occasionally in winter Brassington gets cut off by the snow. I can think of nothing better than hanging my jug on the beam in the Olde Gate, supping some Pedigree, toasting myself by the fire, and waiting for the Manchester coach to get through. No rush.

Pub Index by Name

Pub Index by County/Region

Proposal for new Entry

This book is deliberately limited to just 500 of the best pubs in Britain (plus a couple of dozen bars from four European towns and cities famous for their bar culture) and the author has explained his criteria for selecting them in the Introduction (pp. 6–7). The total represents a tiny percentage of the number of pubs in Great Britain, less than one percent, so there will obviously be some omissions.

An update of this book may well include suggestions from readers with their choices of Britain's best pubs. If you would like to nominate your local, please do so on the form below. Give your name and address, as well as that of the pub you wish to nominate, and the category into which it belongs. Also give a brief (100 words maximum) explanation why it deserves to be included.

Send this form to the publisher:

Britain's 500 Best Pubs, Editorial Department, Carlton Books Ltd
20 Mortimer Street, London W1N 7RD

Name: . . . .

Address: . . . .

Tel:/Fax:/email: . . . .

I wish to nominate:. . . . .

Address: . . . .

Telephone No: . . . .

Road/closest station:. . . . .

. . . .

Category:. . . . .

Reason for inclusion: . . . .

. . . .

. . . .

. . . .

. . . .

. . . .

. . . .

. . . .

. . . .

. . . .

. . . .

. . . .

. . . .